TEMPLES FOR TOMORROW

TEMPLES FOR TOMORROW: LOOKING BACK AT THE HARLEM RENAISSANCE

Edited by
Geneviève Fabre and Michel Feith

INDIANA UNIVERSITY PRESS
Bloomington and Indianapolis

This book is a publication of

Indiana University Press
601 North Morton Street
Bloomington, IN 47404-3797 USA

http://www.indiana.edu/~iupress

Telephone orders   800-842-6796
Fax orders   812-855-7931
Orders by e-mail   iuporder@indiana.edu

© 2001 by Indiana University Press

The paper used in this publication meets the minimum requirements of American National Standard for Information Sciences—Permanence of Paper for Printed Library Materials, ANSI Z39.48–1984.

Manufactured in the United States of America

Library of Congress Cataloging-in-Publication Data

Temples for tomorrow : looking back at the Harlem Renaissance / edited by Geneviève Fabre and Michel Feith.
    p. cm.
    Includes bibliographical references and index.
    ISBN 0-253-32886-1 (alk. paper) —
ISBN 0-253-21425-4 (pa : alk. paper)
    1. American literature—Afro-American authors—History and criticism. 2. American literature—New York (State)—New York—History and criticism. 3. Afro-Americans—New York (State)—New York—Intellectual life. 4. American literature—20th century—History and criticism. 5. Afro-American arts—New York (State)—New York. 6. Afro-Americans in literature. 7. Harlem Renaissance. I. Fabre, Geneviève. II. Feith, Michel, date.

PS153.N5 T45 2001
810.9'89607471—dc21

                     00-063426

1 2 3 4 5   06 05 04 03 02 01

CONTENTS

Part III. The Negro Mind Reaches Out: The Renaissance in International Perspective

Foreword

"It was the best of times; it was the worst of times": the incipit of Charles Dickens's *Tale of Two Cities* may be an apt description of the contradictory visions held by actors and critics of the Harlem Renaissance. It was an idea and a project; a moment and an era; a state of mind and a battleground. This collection of essays is not intended to be a comprehensive study of a rich and complex movement; instead, it focuses on certain figures and issues, strains and trends that reflect the contributors' fields of interest.

Several considerations guided us in the selection and organization of the topics discussed. Taking 1925 as a landmark, we moved backward and forward to examine some artistic works, texts, events, or figures that were significant in the genesis, development, or aftermath of such a movement. Sudden and dramatic as was the famous Civic Club dinner that brought the Renaissance into being, it was announced, prepared, and followed by other major occurrences; and if Alain Locke's anthology is a key document, it was important to compare it with other texts in which the New Negro idea found, earlier or later, similar or divergent formulations.

The time span of the Renaissance has been often discussed by scholars; it is usually seen as being framed by two eventful years, 1919 and 1929, yet we found that historians often disagree and that even its main actors offer different dates and interpretations for its beginnings and its end. Thus, in this volume, we looked into earlier years and also felt justified in extending our scrutiny beyond 1929. Even though the economic crisis of the Depression brought drastic changes in American society and in the modes of artistic or literary production, the impetus black creation had received during the Renaissance still endured among artists and writers; some started reminiscing and bringing new perspectives on the era. The implications and ramifications of the Renaissance were numerous, and in that respect, they do justice to the ambitions of its mentors, who dreamed of carrying it beyond the boundaries of the locus and time that were for some years its main stage. It is part of the African-American odyssey, the history of a people insistently struggling to assert their presence and identity.

Like its time frame, the preeminence of Harlem during this renaissance has also been contested. We have been attentive to the fact that it was both a historical and symbolic center. Renaissances that did occur in other cities, like Washington, Philadelphia, or Chicago—and the writings of New Negroes attest that they were aware of their existence—are not studied in this volume; but the constant movement that drew people toward and away from Harlem to other centers of activity receives particular scrutiny. It is not the least perplexing feature of this renaissance that the hub where all converged was also a point of departure toward different horizons, and that some aspects of the local scene were deliberately neglected. Rather than taking issue with the elitist stances that led to such silences, we have brought into the picture neglected art forms and figures such as Ethel Waters and Oscar Micheaux; we have given due attention to those who, like Langston Hughes or Zora Neale Hurston, were bolder in their introduction of the blues and folk idiom in their poetics and more attentive to what happened outside the circle of the "niggerati."

Some essays come from scholars who have done new research and bring in new data, notably in music, and the visual arts. Others examine more familiar issues (race, modernism) and texts (by W. E. B. DuBois, Nella Larsen, James Weldon Johnson), but offer new perspectives or interpretations. Still others place the Renaissance in a more international context in relation to other movements and address two major issues: the translation and the reception of its ideas abroad and among peoples of African descent. We approach the Renaissance as part of American as well as diasporic cultural history. Most essays deal with main currents in the intellectual thought and artistic life of the United States, often in relation to what was happening in the larger world; they examine certain ideas and concepts of art and culture or experiments with expressive forms. All attest to the diversity of activities that led to the construction of a new poetics, which actually became more inclusive than what was originally planned.

Acknowledgments

This book would never have been published without the persons and institutions that helped us organize an international Conference on the Harlem Renaissance in Paris in January 1998; without all the participants who contributed with significant essays that could not, unfortunately, be included in this collection; or without the editors of Indiana University Press whose time, expertise, and devotion were invaluable.

Our gratitude goes to the University Paris 7 Denis Diderot; to staff, colleagues, and graduate students from our research laboratory, and from many other French, European, and American universities; to the Centre d'études africaines américaines (CEAA); to the Florence Gould Foundation; to the Cultural Services of the American Embassy, the Rectorat of the University of Paris, the Africana studies program of New York University, and the Commission franco-américaine, which gave Michel Feith a Fulbright scholarship.

Reference librarians of the National Humanities Center provided Geneviève Fabre with documents at the initial stage of this project; we wish to express our thanks for the crucial contributions of librarians, archivists, and directors of collections who have given individual assistance to each contributor. A huge debt is due to Arnold Rampersad for his suggestions and sustained support and to Manthia Diawara for his help in turning this project into a book.

We particularly appreciated the patience and diligence of the contributors, their willingness to accept constraints of formatting and editing, and the careful attention they gave to our queries and remarks. It is only natural to recognize the efforts of many people who contributed to the project and gave us practical help: Jeanine Lecourt for her careful handling of multiform administrative tasks regarding the Center for African American Research; Benedicte Alliot for her helpful hints and support; Fatiha El Ghorri for her efficient use of Web sites; Michel Fabre, Helene Chabaille, and Giani Candusso for their contribution in typing the bibliography or formatting the text; Randall Cherry for typing the chronology; and the staff of the Institute Charles V for the final printed version of the essays.

It is impossible to name here the many scholars and friends who have aided us. We hope that this volume, which is also theirs, will be a fitting tribute.

TEMPLES FOR TOMORROW

"Temples for Tomorrow": Introductory Essay

Geneviève Fabre and Michel Feith

> Negro things may reasonably be a fad for others, for us they must be a religion.[1]

> We build our temples for tomorrow, strong as we know how, and we stand on top of the mountain, free within ourselves.[2]

The Harlem Renaissance is one of the most controversial moments in African-American literary and cultural history, yet it is considered a crucial era, a landmark, a site of memory for all those—scholars, historians, art or literary critics, writers and artists—who want to bear witness to its achievements. The terms that define it, "Harlem" and "renaissance," may have been questioned (was Harlem so central? was there a real renaissance?), its premises, objectives, and agenda criticized, and still the name has been kept, the event has been celebrated, gauged in all its dimensions. New archives are created, anthologies keep appearing, and a stream of scholarly work is being published, each work revealing a greater diversity of voices, innovative viewpoints, and modes of expression.

The selection of papers presented in this volume emanates from a conference held in Paris in January 1998. We did not try to be exhaustive and deal with all aspects of such a complex era. Following the lead of recent scholarship, we view it as both a very unique and specific moment—one centered around Harlem and the New Negro impetus publicized in Alain Locke's 1925 anthology—and as part of a more general American and world context encompassing the problems of modernity, colonialism, and Pan-Africanism, of national identity and transnational, transcultural solidarities and networks.

Historically, we have been attentive to the first signs of the Renaissance, even if we saw the mid-twenties as its center of gravity. Considering earlier expression of the ideas that were to prevail then, events that had deep resonance on—or were influential in the emergence or decline of—the movement, led us to span a period that starts in the 1910s and extends well into the late 1920s and early 1930s. The Harlem Renaissance was a moment of hope and confidence, a proclamation of independence, and the celebration of a new spirit exemplified in the New Negro. Against the grain of enduring stereotypes, in defiance of disparagement or subservience, this rebirth and awakening seemed to herald a new age, calling for heightened race consciousness and pride, for resourcefulness and creativity. Such confidence came from an awareness of changing times, of better opportunities created by the Great War and the Great Migration that set African-Americans flowing through the United States and between continents.

There was also the sense that the New Negro was definitely entering—and creating—American history and, at the same time, that a new scene and occasion were being offered for an unprecedented encounter with other New World blacks from the British and French Caribbeans as well as with Africans who were also "coming of age." There was the exhilarating feeling that all could share in a great promise and dream of worldwide unity, in which emancipation could no longer be denied; that new configurations of racial attitudes would change images of the Negro. Finally, there was the naive hope that whites would participate in this "revolution" and be themselves transformed in the process.

PRIDE OF PLACE

The choice of place to carry on this project was deliberate and was to become highly symbolic. New York was the center of the arts and of the American publishing world; Harlem was the Negro mecca where many migrants "kept coming." Charles S. Johnson and Locke tried to attract artists to the growing black metropolis with the hope of creating a cultural capital that would become a nexus of attention for both the black and the white worlds. Even though most of the Negro renaissance artists had only an indirect and fleeting contact with Harlem—because many came from elsewhere and moved on to other places—their names and work were to be associated with the movement, whether or not they were willing to acknowledge the affiliation. Whether "home to Harlem" or "a long way from home," to borrow the expression from Claude McKay, one of the Renaissance's wayward children, the bond to Harlem was real, secret, and sacred, and we have in fictional or autobiographical writings memorable and moving accounts of their first encounter with what Randolph Fisher called the "city of refuge." Harlem, the locus of the Renaissance, became emblematic of many experiences and experiments, a site of action and of memory, celebrated through diverse writings, from James Weldon Johnson's *Black Manhattan* (1930) to Langston Hughes's *The Big Sea* (1940).[3] Nancy Cunard drew attention to the diversity of its population, foreign or close to the American Negro, West Indian but also Latin American in that section that became Spanish Harlem; she also noted the competing national spirits among these groups at a time when the Garvey movement (the Universal Negro Improvement Association, or UNIA, advocating the return to Africa) was gaining momentum. Harlem was the place where blacks and whites, and all the intermediate shades of color—dark-skinned, mulatto or near-white—met and interacted. It was a place of great religious fervor expressed in many revival meetings, of unrestrained pleasure and entertainment, of high and low life in the exclusive social clubs or elegant arteries, in "Strivers's Row" or in the cafés, jooks (juke joints), cabarets, drag balls, and rent parties.

As an international magnet, Harlem had both centripetal and centrifugal dimensions. To the first aspect corresponds the creation of a new ethos, as rather optimistically expressed by Locke:

> Within this area, race sympathy and unity have determined a further fusing of sentiment and experience. So what began in terms of segregation becomes more and more, as its elements mix and react, the laboratory of a great race-welding.[4]

Harlem appears here as an antidote to black diasporic dispersion: people of African descent, who had been kept separate by a history beyond their control, were now able to unite again into a new entity, one bearing a striking but ironic resemblance to the American "melting pot" extolled by Israel Zangwill in 1908 in his famous play by that name. Locke even waxes messianic when he makes Harlem "the home of the Negro's 'Zionism'": Pan-Africanism (NN 14). One can easily track the shift from fact to symbol, from demographic and cultural prominence to (secular) myth. Every nationalism, including incipient black nationalism, needs a capital. Whatever Harlem's actual importance as a center of African-American culture and society, its elevation to the status of "black mecca" and metropolis confirms it and initiates an ideological dynamic of its own.

But Harlem owes its vitality to the very diaspora it recenters. As Brent Edwards shows in chapter 16, it was also one in a string of international capitals and played a role similar to that of Paris, London, or Marseilles in the articulation of a transnational consciousness. Geographically speaking, the focus of the essays in this volume is Harlem. Yet, just as the eyes and minds of Renaissance actors went in all directions, we will follow them in their adventures and explorations—toward the South, an often neglected pole; toward other metropolises; or toward Africa and the Caribbean—moving back and forth, trying to "map" the Renaissance among all these points.

CONSTRUCTING/DECONSTRUCTING "RACE"

It seems to us that, from a historical as well as a geographical point of view, the Harlem Renaissance was an era when, paradoxically, boundaries were constantly set up and erased, and heeded or ignored. This paradox was most blatant in the sphere of race or racial definitions. Nowhere have frontiers been so rigid, as DuBois rightly saw when he wrote "The problem of the twentieth century is the problem of the color line" (NN 385). No other era has known such a resurgence of racial theory justifying existing practices and encouraging further discrimination, segregation, and violence to chastise any transgression. Yet it was also the time when the American dream of constructing a democratic order, a republic founded on a pluralistic ethos, found new expansion and support.

References to color, a euphemism for race, became more frequent. America was defined all in black and white, thus jeopardizing the dream of a truly egalitarian democracy. Actually, the cultural pluralism of the time pertained primarily to the new immigrant groups from Europe and seldom included Negroes or blacks. Yet, between the two races existed another group that became more visible and active, at exactly the moment when the word and category used to define it disappeared from the census: mulatto. Accordingly, or so it seems, the literature became full of stories of "passing," that term being the title of a novel by Nella Larsen (1929) and a short story by Langston Hughes ("Passing," written in 1933). Jean Toomer himself, after his encounter with Harlem and Georgia (see Boelhower and Rampersad, chapters 1 and 10, respectively), passed into the white world; his life and career were plagued with the double bind of trying to transcend these "hypnotic divisions" while remaining imprisoned in them. As Alessandro Portelli argues in his article on James Weldon Johnson's *The Autobiography of an Ex-Colored Man* (1912), stories about passing deny the validity of mutually exclusive racial categories, yet still attest to their enforced strength. The frontier was nevertheless so porous that Walter White, one of the leaders of the National Association for the Advancement of Colored People (NAACP), could be drawn into the confidence of white lynchers in the South, while he was investigating their crimes.[5]

A much more complete study than this could analyze the history of the words "color" and "race" throughout the Renaissance and could reflect upon the fortune of the term "Negro" (which became the rallying designation of the times) as it was used in Garvey's *Negro World*, by the NAACP, in the New

Negro (anthology and movement), and in Nancy Cunard's *Negro* (1934). No wonder that the authors of the essays in this volume have been so attentive to racial issues, to the contradictions involved, to the constant pressure to define people only in terms of black and white, and to the resistance of those who wanted to be considered as both, or neither.

The same type of contradictions was to be found in the ideological definition of the New Negro, a definition central to any understanding of the Renaissance, which was often referred to as the "New Negro movement." It was important to grasp some of its implications in order to probe deeper into the coexistence of two different simultaneous postulations: an emphasis on racial pride, consciousness, history, and heritage and on a desire for integration into American society. The whole ambiguity of the movement is encased in these words by Locke:

> The Negro mind reaches out as yet to nothing but American wants, American ideas. But this forced attempt to build his Americanism on race values is a unique social experiment, and its ultimate success is impossible except through the fullest sharing of American culture and institutions. (NN 11–12)

The quote hovers between hardly reconcilable opposites: Americanism and "race values" or constructionist and essentialist assumptions. Segregation and social inequality are the factors that justify an immersion in ethnic distinctiveness, both as solidarity in action and as a politics of cultural pride—culture under pressure. But if full equality were achieved, such compensatory formations would run the risk of disappearing. We are then confronted with a paradox: ethnic exclusiveness depends on repression; the conditions for its unfettered expression are also those that threaten it most.

In his recent discussion of black leadership, Manning Marable extends the concept of DuBoisian "double-consciousness" and makes it a constituent trait of the ideological field of black intellectual life. The author of *Souls of Black Folk* is credited with attempting to reconcile the two opposite sides of the nineteenth-century debate: integration and black nationalism. His efforts were geared toward "construct[ing] a synthesis based on his cultural understanding of black identity."[6] This collusion of politics and culture finds its clearest expression in the 1926 "Criteria of Negro Art" and its famous advocacy of art as propaganda. "The struggle against racism was at its core a two-sided cultural conflict, an attempt to undermine racist stereotypes and beliefs among whites and to restore a sense of identity and pride among nonwhites" (Marable 46).

On the one hand, a democratic, egalitarian drive aimed at dismantling racial differences, to the point of denying their epistemological validity; on the other, the need to foster ethnic pride allowed for a more exclusivist outlook. The first aspect was illustrated by DuBois's conviction that "African-Americans were profoundly American and had the democratic right to perform music drawn from the European experience" (47), which amounted to the refusal of the creation of a ghetto, cultural or otherwise. The second vision is exemplified by DuBois's support to the writers and artists of the Harlem Renaissance, through publication in *The Crisis* and the bestowal of prizes and rewards, and in his tireless activity on behalf of a Negro theatre, from the creation of the Krigwa Players in Harlem to the pageant *The Star of Ethiopia* (1911), with the aim of making such spectacles "a means of uplift and education and the beginning of a folk drama" (50).

If, as Marable argues, DuBois failed to articulate a coherent dialectic between these universalistic and particularistic projects (57), we can see how crucial their antagonism was to the aesthetics and cultural politics of the Harlem Renaissance by contrasting figures like Langston Hughes and Zora Neale Hurston with Countée Cullen or George Schuyler and, more specifically, by examining the delicate balancing act performed by its mentor, Alain Locke. His special blend of "double-consciousness" seems to echo his dual persona as Howard academic and publicist of the Renaissance. Locke the philosopher had a view of the questions of race and culture that was ahead of its time, but which remained largely confined to the lecture room; his more conventional approach is the one that constitutes most of the published work of the twenties.

One year before the *New Negro,* an article titled "The Concept of Race as Applied to Social Culture" denied the fixed relations between physical race and cultural output, stating that "race . . . is regarded as itself a culture-product"[7] and not the contrary. Cultures are composite; races may change their cultural makeup under certain circumstances—in the *New Negro,* Locke states that the deportation from Africa to America transformed the black temperament from a hieratic to an emotional one (NN 255). Still, he does not advocate the replacement of the concept of race by that of culture-group:

> Race accounts for a great many of the specific elements of the cultural heredity, and the sense of race may itself be regarded as one of the operative factors in culture since it determines the stressed values which become the conscious symbols and tradition of the culture. Such stressed values are themselves factors in the process of culture making, and account primarily for the persistence and resistance of culture-traits. (Harris 1989, 194)

Race is therefore a fiction, but an operative one, which might enhance group esteem and power, and this justifies retaining the concept in its modified form. But the article does not echo an earlier statement that the mythic constructions of race "were rooted in a race practice of discriminatory treatment that had existed since ancient times."[8] In spite of his uncompromising indictment of racism—visible in his advocating the principles of "cultural equivalence" and "cultural reciprocity" (73)—Locke held back from following the philosopher's path of debunking all mythical constructions, however useful. There is a possibility that the decision not to do away with a word as charged with biological, deterministic connotations as the concept of "race" may explain his occasional, yet troubling, tendency to slip back into the more common acceptation of the term.

> African sculpture has been for contemporary European painting and sculpture just such a mine of fresh *motifs*, just such a lesson in simplicity and originality of expression, and surely, once known and appreciated, this art can scarcely have less influence upon the blood descendants, bound to it by a sense of direct cultural kinship, than upon those who inherit by tradition only, and through the channels of an exotic curiosity and interest. (NN 256)

The emphasis on the connection between blood and culture is interpreted by Jeffrey Stewart as an adaptation to the demands of the popular, intended audience of *The New Negro,* as well as to more opportunistic motivations such as a desire for wider recognition in "cosmopolitan literary circles," or "increasing dependence in the late 1920s on the financial support of Charlotte Mason," the one-time patron of Zora Neale Hurston and Hughes (*Race Contacts* xlvi). One might suggest that this residual "racial idealism" (xlvi) fit both Locke's aesthetic agenda of cultural assertion by blacks against widespread racism and the practice of most Harlem Renaissance artists.

> No matter how much one wanted to claim that discrimination against Negroes was arbitrary and that the society ought to be color-blind, since there were no differences among people, still one felt the need to hold on to some claim of distinctive Negro character. . . . Without distinct Negro character, there could be no Negro genius.[9]

Thus, a social and cultural demand for things Negro and the internal dynamics of the African-American community sponsored a soul-searching operation aimed at determining the "Characteristics of Negro Expression" (the title of a 1934 essay by Zora Neale Hurston), a search often based on scant knowledge of the realities of African culture and a too obvious desire for positive propaganda. The warping of history in DuBois's pageant *Star of Ethiopia* might, in retrospect, exemplify the great lengths to which the enterprise sometimes went (Lorini, chapter 8).

The topic which divided the actors of the Renaissance—that of the relations between race, culture, and art—remains as complex as ever. Responses other than Locke's and DuBois's were given by various artists and intellectuals, and it is perhaps in this diversity that the explosion of creativity in the era found its most compelling expression.

COLLABORATION AND PATRONAGE

The preceding pages have pointed at one of the most contested issues of the Renaissance, an issue which plagued it and still affects any present evaluation: that of black-white interactions. Across a wide spectrum ranging from "racial co-operation" (George Hutchinson) to co-optation by the whites (Nathan Huggins, David L. Lewis), opinions differ and controversies flare. To assess the complexity of the question, we might draw help from McKay's reminiscences in his autobiography *A Long Way from Home,* published in 1937.[10] McKay had a singular itinerary that took him first from Jamaica to British intellectual circles in London. He arrived "home" to Harlem in 1912. As a poet and radical, he was both included in and on the margins of the New Negro movement; his viewpoint, therefore, is at the same time unique and more comprehensive than most.

McKay's first insight into the backdrop of the Renaissance, that of the radical magazines and the people contributing to them, seems to confirm George Hutchinson's contention that the movement was a product of intercourse and interaction rather than an unequal exchange. Max Eastman, capitalizing on McKay's experience with the London magazine *Dreadnought,* asked him to become associate editor of *The Liberator* (McKay 1970: 97). There McKay met men like William Groper and Michael Gold and also became acquainted with Carl Van Doren of *The Nation.* He even served as mediator between black and white progressives by arranging a meeting between Robert Minor, editor in chief of *The Liberator* and such "black Reds" as "[Hubert Harrison], Harlem street-corner lecturer and agitator . . . Grace Campbell, one of the pioneer Negro members of the Socialist Party; Richard Moore and W. A. Domingo, who edited *The Emancipator,* a radical Harlem weekly; Cyril Briggs, the founder of the African Blood Brotherhood and editor of the monthly magazine, *The Crusader. . . .*" (108–109). The aim of the meeting was to infuse more class-consciousness into Marcus Garvey's Universal Negro Improvement Association (UNIA).

McKay also met some of those he calls "the more conservative Negro leaders" (109): DuBois—whose *Souls of Black Folk* had shaken McKay "like an earthquake," as did "Returning Soldiers" (an editorial in the spring 1919 issue of *The Crisis*)—Walter White, James Weldon Johnson, Jessie Fauset, and the white "godmother of the NAACP," Mary White Ovington (110–13).

These encounters are more than facts and dates; they denote a cross-class, cross-ethnic cooperation because radical and less radical groups were mixed or collaborating across the color line. What is more, the black community was itself pluri-ethnic, as shown by the importance of West Indians like Domingo or Moore and, of course, McKay himself. This common activism bears out Locke's assertion that

> The Negro mind reaches out as yet to nothing but American wants, American ideas. . . . So the choice is not between one way for the Negro and another way for the rest, but between American institutions frustrated on the one hand and American ideals progressively fulfilled and realized on the other." (NN 12)

But the shared project of fully applying the ideals of democracy and equality should not hide the deep rifts within and between the various individuals and organizations present. McKay insisted on the class bias of many leaders of the NAACP, which Hubert Harrison had dubbed the "National Association for the Advancement of Certain People" and defined as "the progeny of black snobbery and white pride" (McKay 1970: 114). It is true that a certain mutual ignorance prevailed in the relation of black radicals with the Harlem Renaissance; McKay himself was introduced, through his *Liberator* connections, to Greenwich Village tearooms and parties, but he was never invited to the nice houses of the Negro elite in Harlem. His description of Jessie Fauset is particularly to the point: "She belonged to that closed decorous circle of Negro society, which consists of persons who live proudly like the better class of conventional whites, except that they do so on much less money. . . . Could there be a more commendable prescription for the souls of colored Americans than the bitter black imitation of white life?" (112).

The great absent in many discussions of the Harlem Renaissance is the UNIA of Marcus Garvey, a movement whose program, in advocating race separatism as opposed to inter-ethnic cooperation, flew in the face of both socialists and moderates. If we bear in mind that between 1916 and 1927, the dates of Garvey's arrival in the United States and of his expulsion, the UNIA was the most important African-American organization in terms of numbers and influence, the following statement questions any narrow definition of both the Harlem Renaissance and its project:

> The masses of Negroes in America, the West Indies, South and Central America are in sympathetic accord with the aspirations of the native Africans. We desire to help them build up Africa as a Negro Empire, where every black man, whether he was born in Africa or in the Western world, will have the opportunity to develop on his own lines under the protection of the most favorable democratic institutions. . . . Africa will develop an aristocracy of its own, but it shall be based upon service and loyalty to race. . . . [O]ur program [is] the only solution to the great race problem. There is no other way to avoid the threatening war of the races that is bound to engulf all mankind, which has been prophesied by the world's greatest thinkers; there is no better method than by apportioning every race to its own habitat.[11]

Although antagonisms flared between such leaders as DuBois, Locke, and Garvey, it would be impossible to deny Garvey's influence on the movement. His mass appeal, opposed to New Negro elitism, his back-to-Africa activism, and his love for parades all placed him on the troublesome and despised fringe of the Renaissance. The most telling sign of his influence was the 1920 Madison Square Garden Convention, which drew 25,000 delegates from all over the United States and abroad, in support of the populist leader's own brand of Pan-Africanism. Garvey's Pan-Africanism was in competition with DuBois's vision, which was embodied in several Pan-African congresses from 1900 and in his many articles on the subject in *The Crisis*. *The New Negro* featured this perspective through DuBois's article "The Negro Mind Reaches Out," which also illustrated editor Locke's interest in the subject, which he had demonstrated earlier in his 1924 *Opportunity* essay titled "Apropos of Africa." The UNIA also had a cultural program in many ways comparable to that of Renaissance mentors, in that it sponsored musical performances and art exhibitions, and its press organ, *The Negro World*, published a number of pieces by prominent New Negro writers, including McKay. Garvey's insistence on race pride and assertiveness tied in with DuBois's notion of art as propaganda,[12] and even with Locke's aesthetic project of race rehabilitation through artistic achievement.

Just as a double, simultaneous postulation could be detected in Harlem Renaissance definitions of race, a pull toward inter-ethnic cooperation and a contrary impulse for racial exclusivism polarized the field of cultural production. Locke's perfect phrasing of this ambivalence—"this forced attempt to build his Americanism on race values" (NN, 12)—confirms that it is the very denial of participation in mainstream life that defines black difference, a difference whose ultimate aim seems to be self-erasure through integration or *métissage*. In the intermediate stage of the New Negro movement, Americanism and (Pan-)Africanism constantly rebounded on each other, in both the political and aesthetic fields. In other words, what Locke described could be interpreted as the rise of a pressure group, one working within American society on the terms of that society, but whose ethos needed justification in terms of race consciousness, a consciousness which in turn opens it to transnational solidarities: that is the role he assigns to intellectuals and artists.

The other bone of contention about black and white relationships at the time of the New Negro movement was the influence of white patrons on African-American artists and writers. On the positive side, there was much interaction, which made for the bestowing of attention, recognition, and support. On the negative side, many assumptions persisted, even on the part of such friends as Robert Minor who, according to McKay, "said he could not visualize [him] as a real Negro. He thought of a Negro as of a rugged tree in the forest (McKay 1970: 143)." Such positive stereotyping ties in with the primitivism and exoticism that most whites who went to Harlem were seeking. This imitation and appropriation of black art, the commercial profits taken by whites, were nowhere more obvious than in the performance world, where white persons often led or directed black performers artistically or otherwise.

> Many white people see Negroes from a white point of view and imagine that they can express it even better than themselves. When I saw the white man's *Blackbirds* in Paris and remembered *Shuffle Along,* I was very sad. The *Blackbirds* flashed like a whip from beginning to end, rushing the actors through their parts like frightened animals. (143)

What could have been a theatrical tribute was changed into the epitome of exploitation. Still, there were some memorable events of cross-ethnic celebration, like the international dance organized by *The Liberator,* whose spirit "magnetized a motley throng . . . all shades of radicals responded, pink blood and red . . . Mayflower American and hyphenated American," and unfortunately was brought to an end by the Metropolitan police "aghast at the spectacle of colored persons mixed with white in a free fraternal revel" (149).

It therefore seems that if the Negro was in vogue in the 1920s, there was a double vogue: on the one hand, the rather exploitative passion for the primitive and exotic seen in cabarets and revues, and even in the influence some white patrons tried to exert on their African-American *protégés;* on the other hand, a more genuine interest among white modernists, an interest which was not necessarily devoid of misunderstandings. Mentors of Negro art—like the powerful Mrs. Mason, who was "godmother" to Hughes, Hurston, and Locke;[13] or the French collector of "primitive" arts Paul Guillaume—could fall into the first category. More problematic, to varying degrees, would be the "negrophilia" of playwrights Eugene O'Neill and DuBose Heyward and of writers Fanny Hurst, Julia Peterkin, William Faulkner, or Sherwood Anderson, as well as the interest in black music on the part of European composers Darius Milhaud and George Antheil, or its quite imitative incorporation in the idiom of a George Gershwin. The complex relation of Carl Van Vechten (author of *Nigger Heaven,* 1926) to the Harlem Renaissance is still a matter of passionate debate among today's specialists. The question of primitivism and modernity, much discussed by Locke in relation with the New Negro, was picked up again by prominent art critics such as Robert Goldwater, who insisted on the centrality of "art nègre" in modernist thinking. It became a central issue in an international debate and was further examined in 1931 in the *Revue du monde noir.*

According to McKay, the circle within which collaboration between black and white took place remained marginal:

> I don't think that it ever occurred to [the "Talented Tenth"] that perhaps such white individuals were searching for a social and artistic significance in Negro art which they could not find in their own society, and that the radical nature and subject of their interest operated against the possibility of their introducing Negroes further than their own particular homes in coveted white society. (McKay 1970: 322)

It is this "Uncle Tom attitude" (322) that McKay stigmatizes and blames for the failure of the New Negro movement to reach the status of a real renaissance, instead contenting itself with being "an uplift organization and a vehicle to accelerate the pace and progress of smart Negro society" (321). Still, his definition of a renaissance as "one of talented persons of an ethnic or national group working individually or collectively in a common purpose and creating things that would be typical of their group" (321) does fit the project and achievement of many black artists and intellectuals in the 1920s.

One must add that their endeavors did not depend only on white monies. African-American patrons did exist, among whom were A'Lelia Walker, the beauty salon millionaire, and gangster Casper Holstein; black colleges did their part by stimulating debate and creating a reading public and by giving prominent intellectuals teaching positions; grants and prizes were handed out by the NAACP, the Urban League, and the UNIA—often through their magazines like *The Crisis, Opportunity,* or *The Negro World.* Patrons also gave writers and artists some measure of financial support by commissioning and publishing poems, stories, essays, and illustrations and by providing them with a genuinely African-American audience. *The Crisis* went as far as to sponsor DuBois's venture into children's literature, *Brownies' Book,* a monthly publication which lasted only two years, from January 1920 to December 1921, and foreshadowed some of the New Negro's objectives: it invalidated stereotypes by presenting children with black heroes and eminent contributors to American culture and society, intending to arm them better for their relations with white people. Given this plurality of patronage, a—relative—measure of independence was available to the African-American creators of the time; thus, the problem of the social representativeness of the elite must then be perceived as the same for the Harlem brand of renaissance as it was for its European or American predecessors and contemporaries.

ANATOMY OF A (RE)BIRTH

In this volume, the Renaissance is approached mainly as a project, one whose most concise expression might well be that of Locke: "rehabilitating the race in world esteem" (NN 14). Emanating from a few Harlemites, this impetus was taken over and developed by many more and spread in unforeseen ways. It was also questioned and criticized, with humor, irony, or violence. More positive viewpoints were contributed by those who tried to reorient, reformulate, and complete the initial plan. Central to the project were ideas and ideals put in remarkable formulas that became mottoes and incentives for action and change: self-consciousness, self-respect, advancement, elevation, or uplift. Awakening, or rebirth, was the key metaphor, evoking a people's "Dusk of Dawn," convincing them that a new era was at hand, one that was opening new horizons, possibilities, and—to use a word that recurs so often—opportunity, which was the title of one of the influential magazines of the time.

This project was framed at a period of great expectations, in an era when there were many sympathetic ears, as well as many liabilities. The qualities of character and spirit of "the darker races" were celebrated by whites who saw them not only as more romantic and exotic for having been spared the discontents of civilization, but also as "saved." Another form of recognition came from Europe through different channels: through the black soldiers' contributions to the war, through the appreciation of jazz by European composers and audiences, through the discovery of African art by prominent artists—Picasso, Matisse or Braque—and by the general public. Yet the period was also that of the 1919 race riots, of the revival of the Ku Klux Klan under the influence of Griffith's *Birth of a Nation* (1915), of overall racial radicalization. As Arnold Rampersad states in his essay (chapter 1), the time of the Renaissance was also a moment of "racial doubt and racial shame," enforced feelings of inferiority, which the project of the movement actually set about to counteract, although with mixed results.

The project rested on a philosophy, but also on a collective effort to develop artistic expression among people of African descent, with the aim of ending decades of invisibility, challenging assumptions and prejudices, and stimulating the imagination. If the goals were to achieve social justice and racial equality, the arts were seen as a propitious field for advancement as well as for self-realization. The reference to a "New Negro" was itself as old as 1900: it dated to N. B. Wood's book *A New Negro for the New Century*, and was prefigured in Booker T. Washington's 1895 Atlanta Exposition speech. With the emergence of writers like Paul Laurence Dunbar and Charles Chesnutt; Will Marion Cook's "Clorindy" (1896), a pioneer attempt at serious syncopated music; Samuel Coleridge-Taylor's *Hiawatha* trilogy; and the recognition in Paris of painter Henry O. Tanner, the 1890s had actually been a sort of trial run for later developments.[14]

The movement of the twenties was called a "renaissance" from its inception. The cultural polysemy of the term, used to the full, makes it another symbolic correlative of the movement itself,[15] a coming out of the Dark Ages: "By shedding the old chrysalis of the Negro problem we are achieving something like a spiritual emancipation" (NN 4). This "second Emancipation" sets out to transcend the days of slavery and the failures of the Reconstruction era; instead of being bestowed, like the first one, it was actively pursued through self-expression and the will for self-determination.[16] Such a parallel between artistic creation and a political agenda evokes other renaissances: the American renaissance of the nineteenth century, which was an artistic declaration of independence, and European movements like the Irish Renaissance of Yeats and Synge. "Without pretense to their political significance, Harlem has the same role to play for the New Negro as Dublin has had for the New Ireland or Prague for the New Czechoslovakia" (NN 7). While the American connection can serve as a model and a justification, the second association harks back to romantic definitions of national identity and culture and establishes political solidarities with the awakening of oppressed peoples in Europe, Africa, and Asia.

The most obvious reference is, of course, to the European Renaissance of the fifteenth and sixteenth centuries, a rediscovery of classical civilization after the supposedly oblivious interregnum of the Middle Ages. Africa, too, had its classic forms of art, the most prominent being sculpture. The severing of the link with the past, together with the scorn piled by white people on "primitive" expression, had amounted to an eclipse, one that was ended with Picasso and the Cubists' use of African art in their avant-garde experiments. This revaluation amounted to a reconnection to cultural origins and a revival of ethnic pride and led Locke to hope for a new vitality of African-American culture in a manner similar to the innovative impetus that characterized the Italian *rinascimento*.

As did its classical predecessor, the movement imposed an image of the "Renaissance Man," whose epitome, uniting accomplishment with his period's characteristic eclecticism, was Paul Robeson. An individual who could equally experiment and gain recognition in sports, academic pursuits, the theatre and film industry, or the concert hall—his interpretations of Negro spirituals were famous—he was an indefatigable thinker, militant, and traveler. DuBois, founder of the NAACP, social scientist, writer of fiction and countless essays, editor of *The Crisis*, and Pan-Africanist *emeritus*, represented, together with James Weldon Johnson and Alain Locke, this ideal as embodied in the earlier generation. Oscar Micheaux, writer and filmmaker, is another, though somewhat marginal, example. But the Renaissance was not a men-only venture: in spite of often adverse circumstances—including sexism from within their own ranks—prominent women came to the fore in the twenties and thirties and shouldered "the task of Negro womanhood," as the title of Elise Johnson McDougald's *New Negro* article had it. The famous example of anthropologist, playwright, and novelist Zora Neale Hurston should not deflect attention from DuBois's assistant editor for *The Crisis,* journalist and writer Jessie Fauset; novelist Nella Larsen; poet and illustrator Gwendolyn Bennett; artist Lois Mailou Jones; and pioneer sculptor Meta Warrick Fuller. Numerous other women, fighting for intellectual and creative emancipation within the movement, made a difference in the Renaissance.

While the mentors of the Renaissance were insisting on the use of native sources and the exploration of history or of racial and cultural heritage ("Not all our young writers are deep enough in the subsoil of the native materials"[17]), they had an ambivalent attitude toward aspects of this heritage. The first decades of the century witnessed a remarkable increase and interest in social-sciences research on black life. The recovery of historical memory initiated by Arthur Schomburg and Carter G. Woodson, founder of the Association for the Study of Negro Life and History and the *Journal of Negro History* and originator, in 1926, of the Negro History Week; the sociology of DuBois and Charles S. Johnson; Locke's largely unpublicized philosophical probings into the logics of racial differentiation and exclusion; the anthropological and folkloric research of Melville Herskovits, Zora Neale Hurston, Arthur H. Fauset, and James Weldon Johnson all provided the grounds for a more realistic treatment of the traditional folk culture and its metamorphoses on the urban scene. Yet, while Locke advocated a return to the classic roots of African art ("The Legacy of Ancestral Arts," NN 254–67) and extolled the harmonic beauty of the spirituals, he was socially and aesthetically uncomfortable with the success of jazz and the blues.

The most ambitious part of the mentors' advice to the African-American artist was perhaps not so much pride in legacy ("the American Negro is not a cultural foundling without his own inheritance"—Locke, NN 256) as liberation from "the overburdening sense of cultural indebtedness." This declaration of independence was to be the stamp of the movement's own brand of modernism. The New Negro had to innovate. Locke looked at African art that inspired so many modern artists for "the lesson of a classic background, the lesson of discipline, of style, of technical control pushed to the limits of technical mastery" (NN 256), and praised it for its complex patterns and substances, for its sophistication and power, for offering a wealth of symbolic and decorative material. If African idioms had been a ferment in modern art, they likewise had to be an inspiration for the culturally awakened Negro.

Africa was thus legitimately chosen as the matrix of the new culture; the rediscovery of this continent confronted the New Negro with puzzling interrogations regarding primitivism, exoticism, and the issue of modernity that were also considered in many debates over visual art, music, or dance. It also raised the issue of identity. What was the place given to African ancestry and to Africanness in the New Negro concept? Africa for Locke was more an idea, an inspiration, than an essential component; the New Negro was an American Negro, conceived of within the New World and a significant segment of the American nation.

"[T]his slumbering gift of folk temperament . . . needs reachievement and re-expression" (NN 267). In their concern for "native" material and idioms the framers of the Renaissance could not ignore the folk: "Here in the very heart of the folk spirit are the essential forces and folk interpretation is truly vital, representative only in terms of these" wrote Locke in his preface to *The New Negro* (xxv). Yet they remained half-hearted in their praise; neither were they all immune to certain prejudices or stereotypes regarding the "temper of the American Negro," its naive exuberance, sentimentalism, and lack of control and sophistication. They seemed to despise or ignore the black man or woman "further down," were condescending in their approach, and encouraged stylization in which they saw the foundation of the modernism they called for. If folk material was taken into account, it still had to be elevated into high art. "[R]ace expression does not need to be deliberate to be vital. . . . This was the case with our instinctive and quite matchless folk-art, and begins to be the same again as we approach cultural maturity in a phase of art that promises now to be fully representative" (NN 47–48). In the contrast he establishes between folk instinct and artistic maturity, Locke follows the intellectual matrix of European romanticism, which describes the evolution of national culture: from the folk idiom created anonymously in close relation with the soil, through the laws and customs of the state, to the delicate efflorescence of "high," elite art—the only form which can claim excellence.

The conservation of this conceptual pattern is striking at a time when certain practices of modernism were throwing doubt upon the validity of the rift between high and low cultures—one might think of the constant recourse to the "minor," decorative arts by Matisse; the incorporation of popular tunes and fanfares in Ives's music; or such New Negro experiments in the folk voice as Zora Neale Hurston's short stories, Langston Hughes's poems, or James Weldon Johnson's poetic sermons. The fact of inscribing African-American artistic strivings in the structural framework of European culture must have been one manner of "rehabilitating the race in world esteem," but it was ironically phrased at a time when a general questioning of the very notions of culture and civilization provided black art forms the straightest path to recognition.

RENAISSANCE AS PERFORMANCE

"The Negro's universal mimicry is not so much a thing in itself as an evidence of something that permeates his entire self. And that thing is drama." The first words of Zora Neale Hurston's 1934 "Characteristics of Negro Expression" hint at the specifically performative dimension of African-American identity. This can be understood on several levels, from a use of language favoring action words and metaphor (*Norton Anthology* 1,019), to a certain theatricality pervading every situation of communication and communal intercourse. More generally, race itself can be seen as a masquerade whose stakes, in a prejudiced society, are often the very possibility of survival. The eloquent title of Paul Laurence Dunbar's poem "We Wear the Mask" (1896) points to the need to conform to those mainstream definitions which informed minstrelsy and the primitivist school of thought alike. Yet the exceptional gifts of African-Americans in the lively arts of entertainment were also means to fight or displace stereotypes, to gain acceptance or recognition. Music and stage performance were key elements in the New Negro vogue of the twenties. Black music, from the spirituals to jazz and the blues, unleashed onto American popular culture a virtuosity that seemed to emerge spontaneously from an oral mode of creation and transmission, a virtuosity pervaded with the African-derived characteristics of call-and-response and syncopation together with a physicality intensely connected with the rhythms of the dance. The insistence of Harlem Renaissance intellectuals and critics on the need for black drama was determined by several factors: the popularity of drama and the existence of outstanding black talent; the imperative to counteract the stereotypes conveyed by the minstrel tradition and its subsistence in vaudeville; and, finally, the powerful counter-propagandistic evidence of stage presence as an assertion of the physical and symbolic right of residence on the national scene of the African-American community.

Most essays in this book address expressive forms and the artistic exertions an idea or thought called for. Literature and the arts were often analyzed in close association, and it seemed essential to probe into the interaction between them. It is important to note the role that journals and *The New Negro* itself performed, in that respect, by promoting creativity in writing and soliciting visual artists; the unprecedented development of illustrations encouraged these associations between literature and the visual arts. Simultaneously, music was sensed as a major idiom that became a central reference for all, including writers like Toomer or Hughes and visual artists like Aaron Douglas.

Although literature, painting, and sculpture knew an unprecedented explosion during the Renaissance, one must not fail to also recognize the crucial dimension of music in the definitions given of the movement. In a way, music could metonymically stand for the other arts of the period. The twenties were actually called the "Jazz Age," and the Renaissance was marked by a heightened consciousness of music. This was evidenced by the works of Rosamond and James Weldon Johnson, by the writing of DuBois in *Souls of Black Folk* and his editorials in *The Crisis,* or by Locke's *New Negro* statements and his 1936 essay "The Negro and his Music." There was constant interaction among writers, artists, and musicians as well as a wealth of experimentation with music in literature and the visual arts. Creators were attracted to different aspects of the music: Langston Hughes favored the blues, Jean Toomer concentrated on the spirituals and jazz. Zora Neale Hurston was critical of the neo-spirituals. James Weldon Johnson elicited a pioneering interest in the black sermon in verse (*God's Trombones*—1927) and in the tunes, styles, and texture of folk music in his *Book of American Negro Poetry* (1921), an interest which found a creative outlet in his own poems. One could argue that music provided the pattern, the pace, the mood of the Renaissance as a new poetics, with its major trope, syncopation (Feith, chapter 2).

As was true for most cultural production of the period, one can isolate two different poles and sites. Nowhere, perhaps, as in the realm of music is the division between high and low forms so sharply drawn or the debate on folk expression so acute with all its contradictions. Although the intellectual elite's preference went to higher genres—recitals in concert halls, operas, and symphonies—they asserted the historical and inspirational importance of folk music and acknowledged it as the most distinctive Negro art form. This position was not without ambivalence: the music of the folk, especially the blues and jazz, was associated with the stereotypes they crusaded against and was seen as the primitive expression of an uncivilized people; it was also viewed as the symbol of a freedom from restraint that many longed to achieve. Ironically, international recognition of the music forced them to consider it as an important component of Renaissance art and to advocate the integration of black tunes and rhythms into Euro-American genres. Whenever composers or musicians received praise from Locke, it was always on the grounds that they had managed to create higher forms out of "a broken musically illiterate dialect" (NN).

Although Langston Hughes, in his enthusiastic response to *Shuffle Along,* exclaimed, "Let the blare of Negro jazz bands . . . penetrate the closed ears of colored intellectuals,"[18] Locke and his peers were reluctant to applaud the popularity of such shows; yet they were driven to extol pre-Renaissance musicians—like W. Marion Cook or James Reese Europe—for having brought Negro music and rhythm to the American stage. The popular musical developments that took place during the Harlem Renaissance definitely were not those they had anticipated. Show, entertainment, cabaret music; hit songs and steps; ragtime, new jazz piano style; and tap dancing or rent party music were in vogue. The blossoming of musical shows in the twenties and thirties (extending to the forties and later) was remote from the New Negro agenda; so was the importance of the black artist in urban night life. The appearance of Roland Hayes in New York Town Hall in December 1923, or the development of choral and orchestral music—exemplified by the production of James P. Johnson's *Yamekraw* at Carnegie Hall in 1929 and the works of Florence Price, Margaret Bonds, Nathaniel Dett, and William Grant Still, or the creation of the Harlem Symphony Orchestra—was considered far more significant than was the popular success of musicals with such titles as *Chocolate Dandies* (1924) featuring Josephine Baker, *Blackbirds* (1928), or *Hot Chocolate* (1929). Bessie Smith, Louis Armstrong, and Duke Ellington were hardly mentioned in Locke's anthology.

The New Negroes seem to have been more attentive to the transition from low to high music than to the interaction between the two. The many musical worlds that throve during the era seem separated by an invisible frontier—as were their audiences, which only rarely came together: Sugar Hill, the Dark Tower, and the Rhythm Club for the "higher" tastes; legions of smaller clubs and places for the "lower" tastes.

The Renaissance was, as we saw, a time of intense theatricality, when performances stormed the stage: on Broadway, but also on back stages, in cabarets, and in music halls. The Renaissance itself was born in a sort of dramatic effervescence—with its grand gatherings, dinners, soirées, and clubs, its literary contests and prize-giving ceremonies. It occurred at a time of spectacular street performances and entry into the public sphere: silent protest marchers, war regiments celebrating their return with visual and musical military display, or Garveyites parading with great pomp and ceremony. Although on the surface they seem to have addressed different audiences and to have ignored one another, it would be interesting to study the relations among all these happenings. Ironically, if Harlem became the stage of dense theatrical activities, these took place on the fringes of the circles created by the literati and were looked upon with a mixture of contempt and fascination.

Some essays in this volume touch upon that question: what went on in the margin? How did it reflect upon the Renaissance itself? Were not some artists or shows that seem to have been neglected very much part of the movement? The more insurgent group of New Negroes claimed this popular dramatic and musical tradition as their own and tried to establish a new folk theater on its base. The official framers of the Renaissance wavered between blame and praise: they continued to promote more sophisticated, enlightened art forms, but paid genuine attention to the inspirational function of this vernacular idiom. Locke admitted that the folk spirit could be at the core of the new aesthetics. James Weldon Johnson—who, with his brother Rosamond, had immersed himself in the theatrical world and had first worked with Bob Cole, famous for his "coonshows"—became a dedicated collector, anthologist, and adapter; he combined scholarly research with relentless artistic creativity and pointed to the rich connection between poetry and religious or secular songs, between music and performance.

One more irony in an era so concerned with the emergence of a Negro theater was that it opened in 1917 with the success of a trilogy written by a white dramatist, Ridgely Torrence (*Three Negro Plays*—1917), thus promoting a theater where the duality "white dramatist, Negro theme" was prominent. DuBose Heyward, whose *Porgy* (1925) was later transformed into the jazz-inspired opera *Porgy and Bess* by George Gershwin, and Eugene O'Neill (*The Emperor Jones*—1920) wrote of black characters, whereas black authors still found it difficult to produce their plays—Jean Toomer's *Balo* was staged only once, and his "Kabnis" was rejected by O'Neill's assistant. This led to the appearance of outstanding black comedians forced into roles that still pandered to white imagination and expectations: *The Emperor Jones,* when it was taken from Broadway to Harlem, was rejected by uptown African-American audiences. The serious Negro theater that was after the heart of the literati had to compete with popular commercial shows and with white-authored drama; it nevertheless led to the production of plays, to the publication of anthologies, and to the formation of new theater companies (among them, DuBois's Krigwa Players, the Lafayette players, and Chicago's Ethiopian Theater). The new repertory never reached the vitality of the musical extravaganzas and revues that were stirring large audiences and revealing so many talents, new voices, and ways of dancing: Williams and Walker or Florence Mills, Robeson and Josephine Baker, or composers like William Marion Cook; steps like the Cakewalk and the Charleston, the Black Bottom and the Lindy Hop. It is that distinctive tradition that contributed to a large extent to the vogue of the Negro, set everyone "runnin' wild" breaking the "walls of Jericho"; if it did not fully accomplish the liberation from minstrelsy that the New Negro had dreamed of realizing, it is at least to be credited for much of the popularity of the Roaring Twenties. More importantly, it brought West Indians and American blacks together in a deeper understanding of the binding force of artistic expression in the African diaspora.

Richard Long, noting in his *Grown Deep: Essays on the Harlem Renaissance*[19] the contemporaneousness of the Harlem Renaissance and the emergence of modern dance as an American concert-theatrical genre, draws attention to three dimensions of this exchange:

> [T]he core dance activity of trans-urban African-Americans in the dancehalls and on stage; peripheries of that activity in the ballrooms and on the stages of white America, as well as in emerging modern dance; the sense of mission and the trajectory of African-American pioneers in modern concert-theatrical dance. (81)

The first two domains are concerned with the general reversal of sublimation in the post-war years, a period in which a desire for the full enjoyment of life brought about the first sexual revolution of the century. Ballroom dancing was then under the sway of jazz and the different steps originating from it; the vaudeville stage and the cinema choreographed this mood, often along primitivistic lines, as with the triumphant reception of Josephine Baker in Paris's *Revue nègre* shows. Yet, just as in the visual arts the rediscovery of African sculpture paved the way for a modernism based on "ancestral" classicism, a new field was opened by the conjunction between performance and research on varieties of Afro-American and Afro-Caribbean dances. Such was the mission of the innovative synthesis reached by the most famous of these pioneers, Katherine Dunham, who extended to the whole world the impact of "black dance in its exalting and spirit-enhancing role in African life and in its utilitarian but also redemptive role in the folk life of the diaspora" (Long 93).

The original impetus for the development of a specifically African-American network of film production, distribution, and audiences was the 1915 release of the technically innovative *Birth of a Nation,* by D. W. Griffith, which was an apology for the Ku Klux Klan and conveyed the worst minstrel-type caricatures of black people. The outrage in response to this film gave rise to picket lines at theaters and attempts to create an independent industry that could counter the stereotypes rampant in American popular culture. During the twenties, in the margin of the Renaissance, directors and companies such as Oscar Micheaux, the Lincoln Company, and the Colored Players established a fragile, underfunded, ill-distributed motion picture art, which featured all-black Westerns, gangster movies, comedies, and melodramas. This parallel industry would survive until the fifties (Wright 36).

Just as every major stage show soon had its cinematic version, it is also to that tradition of performance, music, and dance that the visual artists of the Renaissance were to pay tribute, integrating it into their new poetics. Artists like Archibald Motley, Aaron Douglas, or Miguel Covarrubias ("Rhapsody in Blue" 1927, "Lindy Hop" and "Rumba" 1936) highlighted the interaction among the arts, combined the aural and visual, the movement and the sound, as well as rhythms, forms, and colors. They captured in complex pictorial compositions the idea and the experience, the spirit, emotions, and sensuality of performance—musicians, dancers, and their audiences in action, so that painting itself became a composite—visual, musical, and choreographic—performance.

This conjugation of several artistic expressions contributed to create new criteria for Negro art beyond the prescriptions of the mentors, opened a wider range of possibilities, and revealed a new interpretation of "the souls of black folk" placed more emphatically at the core of the aesthetics. Although the various performance arts of the twenties and thirties were heavily influenced by the ideological framing of African-American presence in the United States, they at least allowed a peep from behind the masks of race. The Renaissance as an idea and project was carried along with black successes in the "lively arts." But there might still be another way in which the culture of performance framed the movement. A word like "renaissance" is in itself performative: by providing a common ethos and mission to a variegated production, it actually directs it, and induces new expression. While black literary and artistic output definitely showed some signs of increase and change by the time Locke published his anthology-manifesto, the latter polarized the field in a way that provoked a quantum leap, New Negro output thereafter occurring mainly in reaction to it. In this sense, a self-proclaimed renaissance can be a fiction invested with a form of what Claude Lévi-Strauss called "symbolic efficacy."

MANIFESTOES AND CRITICAL DEBATES

Nothing would be more delusive than to assume that the Renaissance was a unified movement. Many were those who attacked, as McKay did, the "convention ridden and head ossified Negro intelligentsia," or the "blue vein societies" among the African-American elite, and by contrast praised the extravagant paraphernalia to be found along Seventh and Lenox Avenues, in Marcus Garvey's halls, in churches and cabarets.[20] In another pique at this intelligentsia, Langston Hughes wrote in his own manifesto, "The Negro Artist and the Racial Mountain" (*The Nation* 1926), "We younger Negro artists now intend to express our dark skinned selves without fear or shame" (*Norton Anthology* 1,271). As irritation increased against the prescriptions and guidelines set on artistic expression, and against the New Negro credo, the dissidents became more defiant and iconoclastic. McKay's objections tended to center on issues of class, whereas Hurston's and Hughes's revolved more on faithfulness to, and recognition of, folk culture. This oppositional ferment gave birth to the short-lived but highly symbolic magazine *Fire!!* (1926), whose very title encapsulated the radicalization of the younger "Harlemites."

In many respects, *Fire!!*—on the board of which Wallace Thurman, Zora Neale Hurston, Aaron Douglas, Langston Hughes, Gwendolyn Bennett, and Bruce Nugent all served—can be considered as another declaration of independence, expressing anger and irreverence, only two years after the *Survey Graphic* issue on Harlem had first popularized the idea of a cultural awakening. The younger generation was eager to be more autonomous in their artistic choices and designs and to create a shift toward other aspirations and goals, to stage, as it were, a renaissance within the Renaissance.

One is struck again by certain contradictions: as these insurgents voiced their impatience at their elders, they also implicitly acknowledged a continuity and a debt of sorts, as well as some agreement on the basic tenets of the Renaissance, on racial issues, and on the need to create a racial art. In his 1926 essay, Hughes added two new metaphors for the movement: that of the mountain, and that of the temple. The former alludes to all the obstacles encountered, in the view of enduring or growing racism, on the way to self-expression. It also evokes a movement upward, a determination to proceed, to conquer the world, and to build in the very face of adversity. The image is a more collective, more voluntarist variation on the uplift philosophy of DuBois and Locke and is a biblical echo which was later to be developed by Martin Luther King in his famous speech, "To the Mountain Top." The mountain and the "temples for tomorrow" belong to the same register of the sacred, of the assertion of communal spirit; they exemplify the project of the Renaissance as a relatively optimistic vision forward, toward the future. Hughes thus reiterated, more emphatically and with a new twist, what Locke and his followers stated in their own calls—but Hughes took it one step further, in the same way artist Aaron Douglas contributed to create a visual imagery translating those ideals (Kirschke, chapter 3).

In this insurgency against their mentors, there was thus perhaps less antagonism toward the ends than there was impatience at the pace the Renaissance moved, at the moderation of certain stands, at the compromises accepted. The younger artists were either more directly confronted with, or more sensitive to, certain issues: patronage, "Negro" material and idiom, audience. They were irritated that the prerequisites for black art should still be set by prominent whites, such as the awe-inspiring and powerful Mrs. Mason.

Paradoxically, the younger, more rebellious minds of the Harlem Renaissance were those who were most subjected to constraints and limitations apparently more easily accepted by their elders. *Fire!!* exploded at white patrons—or matrons—who tried to keep the New Negro from damaging their own exotic and primitivistic image of the old Negro as well as at black intellectuals who had accepted orientations for racial art implicitly dictated by white tutelage or by the expectations of white editors and readers. Was the misunderstanding concerning concrete responses to the many obstacles plaguing New Negro expression between intellectuals and artists—the latter having to cope daily with the act of creation, which eludes definitions and prescriptions—or did it more truly arise between two diverging concepts of what black art should be about: a clearer *artistic* engagement toward the folk being contrasted to the privileging of "higher" forms of creation? One would be tempted to observe another split within the younger generation, one between those who moved toward these higher forms and those who opted for the "folk" or the vernacular.

Actually, issues of race and art could intersect every which way. The desire to control the image of African-Americans and a widespread uplift ideology drew critical attention to the responsibilities of the writer. "What white publishers won't print" (1950) was, in the words of Zora Neale Hurston, all that escaped the stereotypes of primitivism and argued, on the basis of ethnographic realism, for the common humanity and Americanness of both races. Within this context, the sheer number of manifestoes and blueprints published during the Renaissance points at the diversity of writing practices as much as at a need for defining "Criteria of Negro Art," as exemplified in the title of DuBois's 1926 essay. Comparing the latter with Locke's 1925 *New Negro* contributions and Hughes's "The Negro Artist and the Racial Mountain" can help one understand how choices of form and subject were closely interwoven in a network of contradictory ideological premises, which both stressed the necessity of representativeness and chafed at its rigidity.

Being closest to the genteel tradition, DuBois recoiled with disgust from the sensationalism and anti-bourgeois attitude of younger writers like McKay: if, after reading McKay's *Home to Harlem,* he felt "like taking a bath," it was because he sensed that the portrayal of ethnic and sexual promiscuity provided "that which a certain decadent section of the white American world, centered particularly in New York, longs for with fierce and unrestrained passion, [and] wants to see written out in black on white, and saddled on black Harlem."[21] But the morality whose tenets DuBois advocates is that of the white Protestant bourgeoisie, which the Sugar Hill black elite tried to emulate. It does not correspond to the mores of the majority of working-class Harlemites: color becomes a smoke screen for class, and the defense of a respectable image for the black community is actually a proof of Americanization on other than racial lines.[22] Thus, the *Fire!!* group did not protest only against "whitewashed" visions of life and art, to use Jean Toomer's phrase, but also against the restrictions to artistic freedom that the theoretical disciples of DuBois embodied. To

DuBois's idea of art as propaganda they opposed Locke's "beauty rather than propaganda," thereby arousing fears of a "decadence" among more conservatively minded thinkers.[23]

Hughes advocated identification with the vitality of the urban working classes—his interest in the common, low-down Negro soon became part of an international, more militant movement which, under the influence of communism, was eager to forge new images: the "folk" was celebrated with respect and also fascination for the primordial forces it embodied, and black artists tried to assess its racial and cultural distinctiveness. Both Hughes and DuBois accused their opponents of playing the game of the whites. Locke was more liberal in his assertion of the freedom of the artist to choose even color-blind subjects. Yet for him, the most obvious and desirable option for a black author was to draw his inspiration from the folk temperament and from African-inspired modernism. In spite of crucial differences, Locke's system actually comes quite close to Hughes's definition of artistic freedom. When external impositions, by blacks and whites alike, are condemned, creation necessarily turns inward, where it finds a deep ethnic core, the basis of black art.

As we establish these distinctions and emphasize tensions and divergences, we are also aware of the predicament all artists found themselves in, of the ambivalence of their responses, of their constant wavering and meandering, and of the contradictions in which most of them were caught. Composer Florence Price seems to have made the clear choice to "uplift" vernacular forms by integrating them into the classical idiom, thereby giving them an artistic dignity recognizable by white people. After all, was that not exactly what the German romantics had done to their own popular tunes, and what Dvořák had been commissioned to perform for American musical identity? On the other hand, popular performers Duke Ellington, Louis Armstrong, or Ethel Waters had a more sinuous trajectory between contradictory audience expectations and were accordingly subjected to criticism.[24]

UNACCOMPLISHED OR THWARTED DESIRES?

Given the importance of white patronage and influence and given the double-edged indebtedness to primitivism, it is easy to dismiss the achievements of the Harlem Renaissance as imitative and derivative (Huggins 1971: 306). Too easy, perhaps, in the sense that the full appreciation of a work of art depends on a sympathetic approach even of its contradictions. Actually, the essentialist fallacy at work in the theories of the New Negro was often one of the problematic issues with which artists were confronted in their creative praxis. Most members of the movement, most notably the *Fire!!* group, were renegades to some degree at one time or another. But we do believe that the common project of most of the artists grouped in the Harlem Renaissance was to control the image of black people in an assertion of pride in the face of political oppression and stereotyping.

It is often stated, to condemn the superficiality of the movement, that the Renaissance depended exclusively on a period of prosperity and ended with the beginning of the Great Depression. Yet, such clear-cut classification of period may be misleading. True, the economic hardship affecting blacks and whites meant reduced activity for Harlem's cabarets, a decrease in private patronage, and an impoverished readership. The economic basis for the Renaissance, which its proponents were often reluctant to recognize for what it was, seemed to disappear. The Depression years were marked by the emergence of protest literature and theatre. Yet the Negro Unit of the WPA (Work Projects Administration) gave a new impetus to writers and artists. Some continued to create in the renaissance idiom. Aaron Douglas and Zora Neale Hurston are cases in point: the former's murals and the latter's novels are often presented as some of the most characteristic expressions of the movement, in spite of the fact that they date from well into the thirties. Further attesting to the survival of the New Negro ethos is the vehement debate between Hurston and Wright on the subject and style of black writing. Although Zora had often stated her defiance toward broad generalizations, her fictional treatment of rural folk life and southern vernacular performance, in a subversive blend of primitivism and modernism, favors the cultural emphasis of the Renaissance much more than the social protest usually associated with the thirties.

The emphatic swing of the critical pendulum, in the 1980s and 1990s, from the protest dimension of black writing to a revaluation of the Renaissance—a swing that reached its apex with the recent elevation to icon status of writers like Jean Toomer or Zora Neale Hurston—encourages us to look for a possible explanation in a common denominator between the twenties and our times. George Marcus and Michael Fisher allude to such a connection in their discussion of the contemporary "crisis of representation in the human sciences":

> The current period, like the 1920s and 1930s before it, is thus one of acute awareness of the limits of our conceptual systems as systems. . . .
> Older dominant frameworks are not so much denied—there being nothing so grand to replace them—as suspended. The ideas they embody remain intellectual resources to be used in novel and eclectic ways. The closest such previous period was the 1920s and 1930s when evolutionary paradigms, laissez-faire liberalism, and revolutionary socialism and Marxism all came under energetic critiques. . . . The atmosphere was one of uncertainty about the nature of major trends of change and the ability of existing social theories to grasp it holistically.[25]

The Harlem Renaissance as cultural critique from the margins seems to confirm this analysis. The shifting positions of the social sciences and the arts in the fight against racial stereotypes and for the affirmation of an African-American presence in the United States, the central position given to the aesthetic field in race rehabilitation, the simultaneous creation and subversion of a black cultural nationalism all seem to hint at a period of epistemological doubt such as our own, when the simple truths of an academic culture of protest no longer hold. The modernism of the Renaissance, like our much-vaunted postmodernism, now seems to express radical doubt on the possibility of any "realistic" mode of representing history, or identity. Willy-nilly caught in a world of fictions, New Negro writers, intellectuals, and artists might just have tried to create usable, provisional ones—images and narratives "to feed the soul."

Even if a contemporary approach to the premises of the movement might reveal a possibly self-defeating contradiction at its heart, we should perhaps pay heed to King Lear's advice to, in the presence of extreme situations, "reason not the need." Looking back on the New Negro era from the remoteness of the fifties, Locke tried to set his action in a dialectical context, hinting that the times demanded a sort of artistic affirmative action, a temporary surrender of more general principles: "The generation to which I belong had to do more than its normal share of defensive, promotive propaganda for the Negro, but it is my greatest pride that I have never edited a book on a chauvinistically racialist basis" ("Frontiers of Culture" [1950], *Philosophy* 233–34). Yet, when he goes further and states that the Harlem Renaissance movement "made culture a market-place commodity," was tainted with "exhibitionism and racial chauvinism," and was "plagued with profiteering parasites almost to the point of losing decent public presentability" (232–33), one cannot help wondering if the same ductility of judgment which made him shift his approval to racialism in the 1920s and proletarian art in the 1930s does not make these pages an expression of the *Zeitgeist* more than an objective evaluation.

A more generous assessment can be inferred from Frantz Fanon's comments on *négritude,* which might have been inspired by the Renaissance and shared in its hope of restoring black pride and rehabilitating the race in the eyes of the world (Michel Fabre, chapter 17). In a text titled "Black Experience as Lived,"[26] Fanon ironically depicts the trajectory of a symbolic black man trying to defuse the hostile gaze of a racist society. The man's first attempt is to out-reason hatred by proving the equality of all men. To no avail. Appeals to African history are also ineffectual in countering an image of present backwardness. "I had rationalized the world, and the world had rejected me in the name of color prejudice. Since, on the plane of reason, no agreement was possible, I threw myself headlong towards irrationality. Let the white man be more irrational than I am" (Fanon 98). This new attitude, a compound of instinctual, artistic, and spiritual strivings, amounts to a revaluation of black potential: it is *négritude*, a healing but incomplete existential position. Fanon then presents Jean-Paul Sartre's response to it in *Black Orpheus:* "As the negative moment in a dialectical progression from white supremacy to the bringing about of a race-less society, *négritude* is meant to self-destruct, it is a passage not an achievement, a means and not an absolute end" (Fanon 108). But the lack of sympathy of such purely conceptual analysis might have destructive consequences on the existential plane. In a situation of alienation, lucidity could become an amputation; what was needed was oblivion of historical determination, not added emphasis on it. "In terms of consciousness, black consciousness is self-immanent. I am not potentiality something, I am fully what I am. I do not need to strive for universality. . . . My Negro consciousness does not present itself as a lack. It is. It adheres to itself" (109). Coming as it does at the wrong moment, the loss of this illusion is experienced as an impediment to creation and action, and leaves only a feeling of frustration and emptiness. If the Harlem Renaissance project of affirmation took the form of a similar delusion, it was quite possibly a necessary and fruitful delusion, not one to be looked down upon. At least it provided the rationale and impetus for an unprecedented and fascinating collective assertion of African-American cultural stamina and paved the way for further developments throughout the century.

NOTES

1. This is a reference to a quote by Alain Locke in a volume edited by Nathan Huggins called *Voices from the Harlem Renaissance*. Note that the 1992 edition of the *New Negro* has an almost identical subtitle. To avoid confusion, we are referring to Nathan Huggins's as *Voices* (1995).
2. Langston Hughes, "The Negro Artist and the Racial Mountain," *The Norton Anthology of African-American Literature*. H.L. Gates and N. McKay, eds. (New York: Norton, 1997), 1271.
3. The importance of Harlem as a site of memory and discovery is dealt with in William Boelhower's and Dorothea Löbbermann's articles in this volume.
   In the rest of this introductory essay, references to the articles in this book will be indicated in parentheses by the name of the contributor.
4. Alain Locke, ed. *The New Negro: Voices of the Harlem Renaissance* (New York: Atheneum, [1925] 1992), 6–7. (This work is subsequently referred to as NN.)
5. Walter White, "The Paradox of Color," NN, 365.
   Similar stories of temporary "passing" by White are mentioned in Claude McKay's *A Long Way From Home* ([Lee Furman, 1937] New York: Harcourt, Brace and World, 1970), 110–11.
6. Manning Marable, *Black Leadership: Four Great American Leaders and the Struggle for Civil Rights* ([Columbia University Press, 1998] New York: Penguin, 1999), 43.

7. Leonard Harris, ed., *The Philosophy of Alain Locke: Harlem Renaissance and Beyond* (Philadelphia: Temple University Press, 1989), 193.

8. Jeffrey C. Stewart, "Introduction" to Alain Locke's *Race Contacts and Interracial Relations: Lectures on the Theory and Practice of Race* (Washington, D.C.: Howard University Press, 1992), xxv–xxvi.

9. Nathan Huggins, *Harlem Renaissance* (New York: Oxford University Press, 1971), 151.

10. Claude McKay, *A Long Way From Home* ([Lee Furman, 1937] New York: Harcourt, Brace and World, 1970).

11. Marcus Garvey, "Africa for the Africans," *Norton Anthology* 976–77.

12. A discussion of the pageant form as pride propaganda might unearth some striking similarities between DuBois's *Star of Ethiopia* show and UNIA uniformed processions, in spite of the deep personal and political hostility between the two leaders. See A. Lorini's analysis of *Star* in chapter 8 of this volume.

13. See Huggins's depiction of the relations between Charlotte Mason Osgood and Langston Hughes or Zora Neale Hurston (1971: 129–36).

14. John S. Wright, "A Scintillating Send-Off for Falling Stars: The Black Renaissance Reconsidered," in Tracy E. Smith, *A Stronger Soul Within a Finer Frame: Portraying African-Americans in the Black Renaissance* (Minneapolis: University of Minnesota, 1991), 14.

15. It is almost impossible to give a comprehensive definition of a "renaissance." According to André Chastel, who writes about the European Renaissance and its three main aspects of scientific discovery, artistic explosion, and return to classical forms of thought and representation, the frame of mind which best corresponds to renaissance is that of optimism and confidence. "[F]or the first time there is a documented feeling of the complete solidarity of all aspects of human life, and the idea that they can be modified simultaneously. Better still, one can recognize 'the spirit of the Renaissance' from a certain *self-awareness,* or *self-consciousness,* which is quickly turned into exaltation and includes the certainty that the order of things is taking, has already taken, a new course. . . . Perhaps one should simply characterize the 'myth of the renaissance' as an irrepressible confidence in the possibility of solving all difficulties, of overcoming all obstacles and contradictions, once due awareness is achieved in each domain and for each situation" (André Chastel, *Mythe et crise de la Renaissance* (Paris: Skira, 1989), 8–10 (translated by M. Feith).

Arnold Rampersad, in chapter 1 of this volume, nuances this optimistic outlook by noting that most recent "renaissances" actually try to counterbalance or transcend feelings of inferiority. Both visions seem relevant to an analysis of the Harlem brand of "rebirth."

16. Arnold Rampersad, "Introduction" to NN, xiv.

17. Locke in Huggins, *Voices,* 1995: 312–13.

18. "The Big Sea," in Huggins, *Voices,* 1995: 370.

19. Richard Long, *Grown Deep: Essays on the Harlem Renaissance* (Winter Park, Fla.: FOUR-G, 1998).

20. "A Negro Extravaganza," in Huggins, *Voices,* 1995: 133.

21. DuBois, "Two Novels," *Norton Anthology,* 759–60.

22. Melville J. Herskovits, "The Negro's Americanism," NN 355–56.

23. David Levering Lewis, *When Harlem Was in Vogue* (New York: Oxford University Press, 1979), 196.

24. See, in the present collection, the articles by Rae Linda Brown on Florence B. Price (chapter 4) and Randall Cherry on Ethel Waters (chapter 5).

25. George M. Marcus and Michael M. J. Fischer, *Anthropology as Cultural Critique: An Experimental Moment in the Human Sciences* (Chicago: University of Chicago Press, 1986), 10–12.

26. Frantz Fanon, "L'expérience vécue du noir," *Peau noire, masques blancs* (Paris: Seuil [1952], 1995), 88–114.

1. Racial Doubt and Racial Shame in the Harlem Renaissance

Arnold Rampersad

It is an honor to be invited to contribute to this volume, as it was an honor to take part in the conference that inspired it. That conference was presided over, in a real sense, by Michel and Geneviève Fabre, whose contributions over the years to our understanding of the African-American subject have been so considerable. Also welcome was the conference's special focus on the writer Jean Toomer, whose book *Cane* now has an official place in the French higher educational system. Further, I was impressed by the critical work of the large number of younger scholars, including graduate students, who took part in the proceedings. Certainly they helped me to understand somewhat better the slippery subject that I was determined to address at that conference on the Harlem Renaissance.

If I, myself, doubt my ability to understand fully the origins and structure of a cultural renaissance such as that which occurred in New York in the 1920s, it may be useful to remember that doubts have been expressed about the very existence of the Harlem Renaissance. Some have questioned whether it ever happened or whether it was not always already happening in the historic Africanist cultural response first to slavery and then to Jim Crow, so that no particular section of time or place may deserve to be privileged and called "renaissance." Furthermore, many people certainly would object to associating terms such as guilt and shame with the Harlem Renaissance, or with any other cultural renaissance for that matter. Nevertheless, a modern renaissance (English, Irish, American, what-have-you) seems to me to depend in a fundamental way on the presence of strong feelings of inferiority, cultural and otherwise, at the very moment—paradoxically—of the repudiation or transcendence of those feelings of inferiority in the name of progress, emancipation, and independence.

An even more old-fashioned way to put this matter would employ terms such as "hope" and "memory"; but I prefer the psychological structure that includes and names feelings of inferiority side by side with the emerging ability to overcome those feelings in the process of creating a body of art worthy of being called renaissance. A renaissance, I would say, involves a negotiation of the often vexed tension between the native and the foreign, the past and the present (and the future!), the canonical and the disruptively new. It demands both a sense of vulnerability and the optimistic strength to envision and pursue a project of immense cultural rehabilitation and renovation. It demands a collective sense of equipoise on the part of those artists who would participate prominently in it and thus lead a people (English, Irish, American, African-American, what-have-you) into what is imagined to be a transformed future.

What do I mean by racial guilt and racial shame in the Harlem Renaissance? A colleague in attendance at the conference asked me whether I really meant to say white racial guilt and black racial shame. I didn't. My main concern is with something quite elementary and yet, I think, much neglected: the individual psychological impact on black artists and writers of the staggering weight of racism aimed at them during this period. I am referring here to the various permutations of the black response to racism, but in particular to the racism that bred—and breeds—what we call low self-esteem and even self-hatred; of the resulting divisions within the "black" community along color lines as well as class lines; of issues not only of literal racial "passing" and flight, but also metaphorical versions of passing and flight; and the ways, admittedly impossible to map, in which the black mind reconstituted and reconstitutes itself in the face of the repeated woundings inflicted by racism. These are, of course, far too weighty as questions to be addressed definitively in a brief essay; but I think that it is important to raise them in any serious discussion of the Harlem Renaissance—and certainly in a discussion that prominently features the life and work of Jean Toomer.

In general, the term Harlem Renaissance conjures up images of anything but guilt and shame. If there is a paragraph of prose most often taken to represent the spirit of the age, it is probably the ringing conclusion of Langston Hughes's essay manifesto "The Negro Artist and the Racial Mountain," published in the *Nation* in 1926:

> We younger Negro artists who create now intend to express our individual dark-skinned selves without fear or shame. If white people are pleased, we are glad. If they are not, it doesn't matter. We know we are beautiful. And

ugly too. The tom-tom cries and the tom-tom laughs. If colored people are pleased, we are glad. If they are not, their displeasure doesn't matter either. We build our temples for tomorrow, strong as we know how, and we stand on top of the mountain, free within ourselves.[1]

The younger artists—men and women such as Hughes, Countée Cullen, Wallace Thurman, Zora Neale Hurston, Rudolph Fisher, and Nella Larsen— seemed to possess the mixture of courage and confidence that Hughes's essay identifies as the proper spirit of the age.

And if there is a single poem that appears to have inaugurated the movement, it has frequently been identified as Claude McKay's stirring sonnet of 1919, "If We Must Die."[2] Although devoid of specific references to race, this poem appears to defy the enemies of the people called "we" and "us" by McKay in his poem and identified by blacks in that riot-torn year as unquestionably themselves (although, inexplicably, McKay later denied any intended reference in the poem to blacks). The most memorable among other defining poems of the age certainly include several by Hughes himself about the beauty and dignity of blacks. I am thinking of poems such as "The Negro Speaks of Rivers" ("I bathed in the Euphrates when dawns were young. / I built my hut near the Congo and it lulled me to sleep. / I looked upon the Nile and raised the Pyramids above it"); or "My People" ("Beautiful, too, are the souls of my people"); and "Dream Variations" ("Night coming tenderly / Black like me").[3] Such poems are the opposite of any expression of racial shame and sing instead of a healthy, invigorating self-love.

Yet, as I have said, it might be important to see the Harlem Renaissance not as the triumph of an aggressive racial confidence, but as a necessary mixture of confidence and insecurity out of which came the most important literature of the age. We may wish to recollect and not gloss over the opening of that same triumphant essay by Hughes, "The Negro Artist and the Racial Mountain." There, Hughes tells of a young black poet, a friend, who seeks to disassociate himself from racial identification as a writer. "'I want to be a poet, not a Negro poet,'" Hughes's friend confides, "meaning, I believe," Hughes adds, "'I want to write like a white poet'; meaning subconsciously, 'I would like to be a white poet'; meaning behind that, 'I would like to be white'." (*Nation* 692). And along with McKay's ringing "If We Must Die," we might remember the same poet's sonnet on Africa that ends "Thou art the harlot, now thy time is done / Of all the mighty nations of the sun."[4] Or McKay's casual remark in a letter of 1928 to Hughes himself: "The only way of creating self-respect among Negroes as a group is by showing that they have none."[5]

To turn from emphasizing racial confidence toward emphasizing racial confusion might be necessary, as I am arguing, but certainly it is also unpopular. The degree of unpopularity might be gauged from the tone of responses not long ago to Gerald Early in his position as editor of a collection of essays.[6] The basis of this collection was responses by certain black writers today to the theory of inherent African-American double-consciousness enunciated by W. E. B. DuBois in his epochal book *The Souls of Black Folk* (1903). Apparently, few African-American artists among those approached by Professor Early would concede the idea that cultural ambivalence, along with a complex of related ambivalences, was or could be a necessary aspect of the African-American condition. Most respondents seemed determined to deny any personal ambivalence on their part on this crucial matter—when, in fact, it might be argued that such ambivalence is not only perfectly natural to being a black American, but is a source of some of the deepest cultural distinctions, for better and for worse, between blacks and the rest of Americans.

In any event, the Harlem Renaissance is framed chronologically on either side by two documents that look, in the first case, prospectively toward it and, in the second, retrospectively at it. Together, they may underscore the wisdom of the vision of the era as deeply marked by confusion among black Americans about their identity and about the role of their artists in exploring, developing, and illuminating that identity. I am thinking first of DuBois's book of essays and miscellaneous other writings called *Darkwater: Voices from Within the Veil* (1920), which he obviously saw as a kind of sequel to *The Souls of Black Folk;* and, second, of Richard Wright's scathing indictment of the achievement of black writers, including those of the recently faded Harlem Renaissance, in his essay "Blueprint for Negro Writing" (1937). "Generally speaking," Wright judged there, "Negro writing in the past has been confined to humble novels, poems, and plays, prim and decorous ambassadors who went a-begging to white America . . . dressed in the knee pants of servility [and] were received as though they were French poodles who do clever tricks."[7] (One must go to the philosopher George Santayana, I think, to find as scathing an indictment of what others call a renaissance, as when Santayana dismissed the literary American outpouring of the mid-nineteenth century as "a late Indian summer of the mind" that led, ultimately, only to "a harvest of leaves."[8]) In his writing that followed, Wright dramatized his indictment of black culture with his book of novellas *Uncle Tom's Children* (1938), his novel *Native Son* (1940), and, above all, his autobiography, *Black Boy* (1945). Indeed, *Black Boy* may offer the most bitter denunciation of typical black American life ever offered by an African-American writer: Wright mused on "the strange absence of real kindness in Negroes, how unstable was our tenderness, how lacking in genuine passion we were, how void of great hope, how timid our joy, how bare our traditions, how hollow our memories, how lacking we were in those intangible sentiments that bind man to man, and how shallow was even our despair."[9]

Earlier, in 1920, DuBois's *Darkwater* had cast a harsh light on American race relations. In *The Crisis,* the magazine he edited for the National Association for the Advancement of Colored People (NAACP), DuBois had been calling for some years for a black renaissance, then had announced its imminent arrival with almost uncanny precision about the time his *Darkwater* appeared. But to read *Darkwater,* with its sardonic and embittered tones, its styles at times lyrical but more memorably vituperative, dogmatic, and propagandistic ("All art is propaganda," DuBois would declare in *The Crisis* in 1926), is surely to be visited by grave doubts about whether the creative spirit central to that text, or any text as tortured as *Darkwater,* can ever participate effectively in a cultural flowering that accurately can be called a renaissance.[10] And indeed it might be said that DuBois, despite his stimulating role as an editor and publications such as his novel *Dark Princess* (1928), was not really of the Harlem Renaissance, that it was largely an affair of youth from which he was to a large extent barred by his age (he turned sixty in 1928). However, his difficulties in this regard may have had less to do with age in itself than with the crisis of racial self-confidence that *The Souls of Black Folk,* ironically, had probed so astutely a generation earlier. Perhaps we may see in DuBois's infamous exchanges early in the 1920s with the most charismatic of the black leaders of the age, Marcus Garvey, some telling aspects of this problem. But this is a topic to which I will return.

It should be no surprise to anyone that the writers of the Harlem Renaissance, on the whole, doubted themselves. They attempted to operate as thinkers and artists in the face of a deep-seated intellectual and scholarly antagonism to their very beings. If their own renaissance began in 1917, according to one judge, with the staging of the white writer Ridgely Torrence's sympathetic *Three Plays for a Negro Theatre* ("the most important single event in the entire history of the Negro in the American Theatre," according to James Weldon Johnson), it might also be said that at about the same time, white racism had its own sort of triumphant rebirth with the premiere in 1915 of D.W. Griffith's motion picture *Birth of a Nation,* based on Thomas Dixon's immensely successful antiblack novel *The Clansman* (1905).[11] The movie, as we know, helped to make possible the renaissance of the Ku Klux Klan, when an Atlanta preacher, Joseph Simmons, revived the organization not simply as a weapon against blacks but to "maintain Anglo Saxon civilization on the American continent from submergence due to the encroachment and invasion of alien people of whatever clime and color."[12]

Supporting this rebirth around 1915 was the preponderant weight of contemporary scientific opinion on race. That weight rested in some part on the publication in the United States of two major texts: in 1911, a translation of

Houston Stewart Chamberlain's two-volume *Foundations of the Nineteenth Century* (written originally in German by the English-born son-in-law of the composer Richard Wagner and first published in 1899); and then, in 1912, a translated, abbreviated version of Count Arthur de Gobineau's *Essay on the Inequality of Human Races* (1853–55). Chamberlain's racism was nationalistic and exclusionary, with firm beliefs in the supremacy of "Aryan blood" and in Teutonic culture. To Gobineau, however, miscegenation was not only inevitable but actually necessary to racial progress; nevertheless, he claimed, blacks were marked by a characteristic gluttony, sensuality, and low intelligence for which, in compensation, they possessed a certain artistic capacity based in superior sensory equipment. This fundamental difference between Chamberlain and Gobineau needs to be borne in mind; at the very least, it testifies to the variety and thus the special resilience of pseudo-scientific racism. Together, the two men's works mightily stimulated American racial thought; but they were hardly alone.

The intellectual climate of the 1920s, during the main years of the Harlem Renaissance by any reasonable reckoning, as it applied to the subject of race may be judged by some of the pronouncements in this era by liberal scholars. William MacDougall of Harvard, for example, in his *Introduction to Social Psychology* (1908) and, more importantly, his Lowell Lectures that became *Is America Safe for Democracy?* (1921), warned of the grave perils of race intermingling. A similar warning came from Charles B. Davenport, who, harping on ambitiousness combined with intellectual incompetence, noted how "one often sees in mulattos an ambition and push combined with intellectual inadequacy which makes the unhappy hybrid dissatisfied with his lot and a nuisance to others" (Gossett 379). No less an authority than the president of the American Sociological Society, Henry Pratt Fairchild, a professor of sociology at New York University, declared, "The principle has been propounded and urged by certain broadminded and sympathetic persons that there should be no racial discrimination in any American legislation. Nothing could be more unsound, unscientific, and dangerous. Racial discrimination is inherent in biological fact and in human nature. It is unsafe and fallacious to deny in legislation forces which exist in fact" (387).

And there was Dr. Lothrop Stoddard, author of more than twenty books, including *The Revolt Against Civilization: The Menace of the Under Man* (1922), which warned white America about the danger of race-mixing. The white races, especially the Nordic, who formed the key human factor in civilization, were in danger of being overrun by inferior, darker races with higher birthrates. Stoddard is, of course, an interesting footnote to F. Scott Fitzgerald's 1925 classic *The Great Gatsby*, where Tom Buchanan "broke out violently" at one point that "Civilization's going to pieces. . . . Have you read *The Rise of the Colored Empires* by this man Goddard? . . . Well, it's a fine book, and every-body ought to read it. The idea is if we don't look out the white race will be utterly submerged. It's all scientific stuff; it's been proved."[13] Other characters make fun of Buchanan, as does Fitzgerald himself; but one wonders how many black people in the 1920s in New York, and anywhere else for that matter, could find a joke in his ignorant rumblings.

We could look, too, at such books as Clinton Stoddard Burr's *America's Race Heritage* (1922), which warned about the power and influence of racial groups given by predisposition to radicalism, communism, and anarchy; and Kenneth L. Roberts's *Why Europe Leaves Home* (1922), which argued that while America was a product of Nordic genius, the influx of Alpine, Mediter-ranean, and Semitic races would lead to a mongrel people lacking in character and ability. Charles Conant Josey's *Race and National Solidarity* (1923) railed against the menace of colored races at home in the United States and abroad. Charles W. Gould's *America a Family Matter* (1923) posited that Egypt, Greece, and Rome all fell because of the infusion of degenerate blood into their noble stock.

Against the grain of this scientific and pseudo-scientific racism was a com-paratively weak set of responses—weak, that is, until the rise of Nazi Germany dealt a near-death blow (but not a deathblow) to scientific racism. The leading figure was clearly Franz Boas, the German-born and educated "father" of Amer-ican anthropology, who laid the twin foundations of modern anthropological philosophy and methods: cultural relativism and the field study. Against the twin pillars of Gobineau and Chamberlain, Boas set his own influential text *The Mind of Primitive Man* (1911). Speaking out against racial pseudo-scientists, Boas had a significant intellectual and personal influence on DuBois in partic-ular among black intellectuals in the first decade of the century; in the second, he had an even more personal and professional impact on Zora Neale Hurston. Boas is surely an essential figure in the long intellectual foreground of her nov-elistic masterpiece *Their Eyes Were Watching God* (1937), the delayed but also perhaps the single most acclaimed achievement of the Harlem Renaissance.

The argument against black inferiority was a hard one to carry, given what was arrayed against it virtually everywhere. The most lively voice for blacks was probably that of Garvey, with his Back-to-Africa movement. "When we come to consider the history of man," Garvey insisted, "was not the Negro a power, was he not great once? Yes . . . When Europe was inhabited by a race of cannibals, a race of savages, naked men, heathens and pagans, Africa was peopled with a race of cultured black men, who were masters in art, science, and literature; men who were cultured and refined; men who, it was said, were like the gods."[14] Garvey pointed to a rosy future for blacks. "I have a vision of the future, and I see before me a picture of a redeemed Africa, with her dotted cities, with her beautiful civilization, with her millions of happy children, going to and fro" (Garvey 77–78).

These were fine words; but in some ways, their essential hollowness, and the hollowness of some of DuBois's own pronouncements, may be intuited from the acrimonious nature of the exchanges between the two men even as the renaissance, with its emphasis on race pride, began to take hold. To DuBois in 1923, Garvey's life exemplified the power of white racism and mulatto snobbery to cripple the black soul. Garvey, a "little, fat black man, ugly but with intelligent eyes and big head," was little more than "a demagogue, a blatant boaster, who with monkeyshines was deluding the people"; Garveyism was "mere rodomontade and fatuous propaganda."[15] To Garvey, DuBois, in spite of his many books on black culture and history, was "trying to be everything else but a Negro. Sometimes we hear he is a Frenchman and another time he is Dutch and when it is convenient he is a Negro. Anyone you hear always talking about the kind of blood he has in him other than the blood you see, he is dissatisfied with something, and . . . if there is a man who is most dissatisfied with himself, it is Dr. DuBois."[16]

There is at least an element of truth in Garvey's charge, no matter how cavalierly he expressed it; it may stand here for a condition that was an essential part of the Harlem Renaissance, if not of black culture in general. DuBois often spoke of the superiority of blacks to whites; paradoxically, he also sometimes challenged the core ideas of racial science common at the time. But he also seemed capable at times of imagining what was almost, in effect, the natural inferiority of blacks, even if more often he denied it. DuBois indeed seemed to harp, as Garvey said, on his mixed ancestry and sometimes appeared less than sanguine about the intellectual potential of blacks other than himself, as perhaps in his reckless words, quoted previously, concerning Garvey.

So indeed did many of the other writers and artists of the Harlem Renaissance swing between polarities of confidence and the vacuum of confidence that white America worked hard to create and maintain in them; so did they swing between—on the one hand—an acceptance of the "laws" of racial science that relegated them, as often as not, to the bottom of the social scale, and, on the other, some more positive sense of the African past and the black American potential.

Often, when black artists vigorously asserted pride in their "race" and cultural heritage, they came to such a position at the very least by a tortuous route. Even Langston Hughes, who made himself the standard-bearer for race pride among the writers, is hardly exempt from scrutiny on this score. Hughes's confidence in and commitment to black folk was perhaps the most prominent feature of his art; but how did he come to achieve that confidence in the face of strong factors (such as his father's evident disdain for his fellow blacks, as well as class and color differences between the poet and the masses of the people) that might easily have led Hughes in the opposite direction? Elsewhere I have written about Hughes's neglect by his parents and his probably compensatory determination quite early in his life to fill this void of affection by the creation of poems, in particular, that would bind him to the masses of black folk, to whom he became, in a sense (or so I have argued) psychologically mortgaged. In this general connection, one might also raise questions about Hughes's sexual identity, and about the cynicism about the human condition, largely concealed in his art, that was a feature of his last years. In short, the smiling confidence of the poet in his prime obviously conceals tensions that probably originated in his experience of the inherent African-American crisis of self-esteem I am trying to illuminate here.

Countée Cullen, Hughes's main rival among the younger poets of the movement, invites scrutiny on this score more obviously than does Hughes. Perhaps more than any other writer of the movement, Cullen wore his heart on his sleeve, and his heart was defined, not to say ravaged, by his conflicted feelings of self-worth that had everything to do with being black when he yearned for "racelessness," and, perhaps, with being bisexual or gay when he placed a premium on respectability. Cullen not only saw an essential tension between the color of his skin and the act of literary creation but made a morbid poetry of this tension. One of his best known poems acknowledges the mystery of God's many earthly wonders but ends by citing what the poet considers the most perplexing mystery of all: "Yet do I marvel at this curious thing: / To make a poet black and bid him sing."[17] Cullen's vicariously autobiographical poems are often pitiable cries of pain and shame: "Some are teethed on a silver spoon, / With the stars strung for a rattle," he wrote in "Saturday's Child"; "I cut my teeth as the black raccoon / For implements of battle" (Cullen 18).

In "The Shroud of Color" (an image that so offended Hughes that he wrote a poem quietly but firmly repudiating it), Cullen extended his sense of a conflict between blackness and beauty to include a conflict between blackness and spirituality itself:

"Lord, being dark," I said, "I cannot bear
The further touch of earth, the scented air;
Lord, being dark, forewilled to that despair
My color shrouds me in, I am as dirt
Beneath my brother's heel . . ." (Cullen 26)

And in "Heritage," perhaps Cullen's most frequently cited poem, the speaker of the poem accepts almost without reservation the imputation of inherent black barbarism dear to white racists: "Not yet has my heart or head / In the least way realized / They and I are civilized" (Cullen 41).

And yet, as pathological as such imagery appears to be, in some ways Jean Toomer is an even more fascinating case than Cullen where race, self-esteem, and the production of art are concerned. It was perhaps for this reason, so little noted generally, in addition to the more obvious reason of its literary power, that Toomer's *Cane* absolutely dazzled the small but ambitious black American writing community, including both Hughes and Cullen, on its appearance in 1923. (Several of Hughes's poems around 1923 and 1924 seem to echo verbal effects to be found in *Cane*.) Certainly, few books have ever offered more alluring and yet disturbing images of black-American life. At the heart of its appeal is the opening succession of fragmentary sketches of black women that combine bravura lyricism with an almost indefinable quality of mystery, set against the backdrop of a sensuous yet menacing South. The setting then moves to what is in effect the black urban North. Here, lyricism gives way, by and large, to oddly compacted images and situations that verge on the surreal. The last major section, loosely in the form of a drama, sends a confused northern black intellectual into the South under the threat of death at the hands of whites.

For all its praise of black beauty, *Cane* nevertheless reverberates with an ominous sense of the coming extinction of the entire black-American race at the hands of both the violent white South and the sordid social conditions forced on blacks in the urban North. For Toomer, this was no idle conceit; more provocatively, his idea of the coming death of black culture was linked to his sense of his own apotheosis, or the apotheosis of people like himself. After all, even before the appearance of *Cane*, he had begun to wrestle with a theory of his own racelessness and, relatedly, of the absurdity of race as a category. He would come to see the appearance of *Cane*, and its achievement of a *succès d'estime* in certain circles, as further encouragement for him to quit the race to which he belonged according to racist American convention and to move toward a personal renaissance that would presage the coming of a new world order.

Both the melancholy mood of *Cane* and Toomer's related desire for racial transcendence were encouraged around 1922, as is well known, by his first major exposure to Eastern philosophy, when he began to read relevant texts and to try exercises ("presumably yoga or Zen," according to his principal biographers), write haiku, and experience "something of the nonmaterial beyond the tangible realm."[18] Then came his discovery, just as *Cane* appeared, of the teachings of the sage Gurdjieff, whose own complex theories and techniques for the development of higher human consciousness had no place, apparently, for the banality of race. After a stint at Fontainebleau-Avon, where Gurdjieff had his seat, Toomer returned to America. He first tried out his new wisdom briefly on a bemused Harlem, then sought a wider, whiter audience. His stay at Fontainebleau and his devotion to Gurdjieff's teaching eventually made him one of the two or three leading exponents of the cult in the United States.

Once Toomer's writing became detached from the subject of race, however, it began to suffer. The emphasis in *Cane* on lyricism, mystery, and the Gothic horror of American race relations gave way to didacticism. His theory of race-lessness—or of the new American race, as he liked to call it—turned out to mean the bleaching out from his writings of almost any mention of blacks and race friction. Positive claims have been made for two of his works, the 800-line poem "Blue Meridian" and the play "The Sacred Factory," but by the time he died in 1967, he had good reason to regard himself as a complete failure. Ironically, the rise of black studies and black consciousness in the 1960s, movements antithetical to everything Toomer had come to stand for in his mature years, brought about the reprinting of *Cane* in the very year he died and led to the revival of his reputation. The book has never been out of print since and possibly will never be.

It is important, I think, to explore this curious tension between the perception of Toomer as a black writer and his own wishes on the subject. Let me emphasize that it is not my intention at all to question the wisdom of those persons who have succeeded in having *Cane* accepted as a significant literary text for examination purposes here in France. Indeed, I see this acceptance as a great thing for all concerned, a substantial token of our changed world. But as much as I admire *Cane,* inevitably I find myself listening to discussions of Toomer's art, and especially of Toomer's ideas, and find myself thinking that the man probably does not need an analysis of his theories as urgently as he needed a psychiatrist during his lifetime, especially one (such as Franz Fanon) equipped to deal with the interplay between race and identity. In Toomer's case, one might specify more: the tragedy of his family's fallen grandeur (a grandfather had been an eminent figure during Reconstruction); his skin color, which was light enough to allow Toomer to pass for white; a determination (evidently) never again to be poor; and the possibility of a personal unscrupu-lousness matched by an intellect both nimble and flighty—and yet, and at the same time, literary artistry of genuine power.

It is important to concede—no, to recognize aggressively—the high qual-ity of Toomer's artistry because, in my opinion, his ideas on race, his theory of a new coming race and the new man, and all that simply do not stand up to a close examination. At the conference that inspired this volume, Diane Wil-liams delivered a provocative paper, "Jean Toomer and Eugenics." Either in the discussion that followed or in a response to Matthew Guterl's also excellent paper on Toomer, Madison Grant, DuBois, and Daniel F. Cohalon, someone in attendance suggested that Toomer had been progressive in asserting the beauty of the mixing of races and the eventual emergence of a new, superior "man."

However, it might be important to recognize that if in this instance Toomer was decidedly not echoing one of the two great foreign intellectual influences on American racial thought in the 1920s, he was almost certainly echoing the other and was not necessarily the wiser for having done so. In other words, if he was denying in his race-thinking the influence of Chamberlain's *Foundations of the Nineteenth Century*, he was surely influenced by Gobineau's *Inequality of Human Races* or by ideas deriving from Gobineau. As we have seen, Gobineau indeed believed in the necessity to progress of miscegenation, although it was probably not miscegenation of the sort we would envisage as progressive. In any event, Gobineau's theory of miscegenation got nowhere with most white American intellectuals or quasi-intellectuals interested in race; for them as Americans, miscegenation always raised the specter of black-white sexual relations and was therefore always potentially a horror. However, it is not surprising that Gobineau's ideas on this score should find, directly or indirectly, a sympathetic listener in someone like Toomer, who could build enthusiastically and ingeniously on them mainly because he was equipped by his skin color and class position to effect the kind of miscegenation that America (at least in certain parts of the North) was prepared to tolerate—if barely. The South was not so prepared, as Faulkner, for one, made clear in such fictions as *Light in August* (1932) and *Absalom, Absalom!* (1936).

Gobineau, incidentally, should probably be given a prominent place (as he is not now) on the long list of French intellectuals who have helped Americans learn how to think. This list (so often a feature of scholarly and critical papers today) would go back through Gobineau to Tocqueville and beyond. I am sure that French intellectuals in our own time have had a more salutary effect on African-American studies than Gobineau exerted, but one cannot expect or demand consistency of quality in such a volatile aspect of our lives. Besides, Toomer is responsible ultimately for the integrity of the ideas he chose to advertise, including both the alluring ones he offered in *Cane* and the specious, hurtful ones that came later and worked in effect mainly to taunt and humiliate millions of blacks who did not have his options of ethnic dissimulation and flight.

Acknowledging that it is truly difficult to get at the heart of these matters in the lives of the writers of the Harlem Renaissance, I would suggest that perhaps the most effective way of addressing this issue is through the admittedly limited but indispensable form of the biography. This is not the occasion for me to delve into the limitations of biography, including the limitations of my own work in the form. In fact, I should want to congratulate us on how far we have come in the African-American version of biography, led by Professor Michel Fabre, whose study of Richard Wright's life, appearing in 1973, set the standard for all future biographies of African-American writers. But I need to point out how much is still lacking in the field. Only a few of the authors who deserve full biographic treatment have been the subjects of full-scale biographies. Several deserving writers (McKay, Toomer, DuBois, Walter White, James Weldon Johnson, for example) have had their life stories told by historians and not by literary biographers. And the greatest number, of course, have been neglected, more or less: Jessie Fauset, Cullen, Wallace Thurman, Arna Bontemps, Rudolph Fisher, and Georgia Douglas Johnson, to name but a few.

Many reasons explain the dearth of biographic studies, and perhaps most of these reasons are professional in nature. However, I have also always sensed inhibitions peculiar to the political and cultural situation in which black-Americans find and have found themselves and which in some ways is not so different now from the world of the 1920s. There is still an abiding suspicion of biography as, in some ways, the ultimate act of violation, especially of our dead heroes; and there is also an entrenched unwillingness to appear to be lending aid and comfort to the enemy by conceding the depth of the psychological wounds inflicted by racism.

This is all understandable, surely, but I think it is our duty as scholars and students of African-American literature and culture to press on, respectfully but firmly, with the essential task we have set ourselves, which is to render as accurately as we can the genuine features of African-American history and culture, explaining those features to the best of our ability. The conference that inspired this volume, so ably and so generously conceived and staged, was an inspiring example of what we can accomplish together toward achieving our common goals.

NOTES

1. Langston Hughes, "The Negro Artist and the Racial Mountain," *Nation* 122 (June 23, 1926), 694.

2. Claude McKay, "If We Must Die," *Liberator* 2 (July 1919), 21.

3. Langston Hughes, "The Negro Speaks of Rivers," *The Collected Poems of Langston Hughes*, Arnold Rampersad, ed. (New York: Vintage, 1995), 23; "My People," 36; "Dream Variations," 40.

4. Claude McKay, "Africa," *Liberator* 4 (August 1921), 10.

5. Arnold Rampersad, *The Life of Langston Hughes Vol. 1: 1902–1941: I Too Sing America* (New York: Oxford University Press, 1986), 171.

6. Gerald Early, ed., *Lure and Loathing: Essays on Race, Identity, and the Ambivalence of Assimilation* (New York: Viking Penguin, 1993).

7. Richard Wright, "Blueprint for Negro Writing," *Richard Wright Reader,* Ellen Wright and Michel Fabre, eds. (New York: Harper and Row, 1978), 37.

8. Douglas L. Wilson, ed., *The Genteel Tradition: Nine Essays by George Santayana* (Cambridge: Harvard University Press, 1967), 78.

9. Richard Wright, *Black Boy* (New York: Harper, 1945), 33.

10. W.E.B. DuBois, "Criteria of Negro Art," *The Crisis* 32 (October 1926), 297.

11. James Weldon Johnson, *Black Manhattan* (New York: Atheneum, 1972), 175.

12. Thomas Gossett, *Race: The History of an Idea in America* (Dallas: Southern Methodist University Press, 1963), 340.

13. F. Scott Fitzgerald, *The Great Gatsby* (New York: Scribners, 1995), 17–18.

14. Marcus Garvey, *Philosophy and Opinions of Marcus Garvey* (New York: Atheneum, 1969), 77.

15. W.E.B. DuBois, "Back to Africa," *Century* 105 (February 1923), 539.

16. *Negro World,* January 8, 1921.

17. Countée Cullen, "Yet Do I Marvel," *Color* (New York: Harper, 1925), 3.

18. Cynthia Earl Kerman and Richard Eldridge, *The Lives of Jean Toomer: A Hunger for Wholeness* (Baton Rouge: Louisiana State University Press, 1987), 120.

PART I.
CRITERIA OF RENAISSANCE ART

New York in the 1920s was probably the first place and time in African-American history in which a critical mass of intellectuals and artists could create a genuine movement and group dynamic. As a magnet attracting young black culture-makers from all over the country and beyond, Harlem created the conditions for a unique cross-fertilization between talented individuals and diverse artistic fields; it also served as a forum for discussion and the elaboration of a cultural ethos. If the 1921 production of *Shuffle Along* actually marks, as Langston Hughes argued, the beginning of the Harlem Renaissance, it was an auspicious start because a musical is, by definition, a form of "total art," uniting literature, music, dance, drama, and the visual arts. Similarly, the literary production of the period was deeply infused with a sense of the interdependence of all artistic media.

The vogue of Negro themes and subjects stemmed primarily from the realm of the "lively arts." The cabarets of the "Jazz Age"; Broadway and the successive avatars of minstrelsy, the vaudeville and the musical; the slums—these were the focuses of mainstream attention, as was an interest in "quaint," vernacular musical styles such as spirituals, jazz, or the blues.

These "mongrel" forms of popular culture bore the imprint of white audiences' tastes, yet they did not completely escape African-American creative control nor alienate black audiences. The existence of two state-of-the-art "race" industries, that of the record business and that of the cinema, point at the growth in numbers and purchasing power of a public whose tastes were to be taken into account. The careers of moviemaker Oscar Micheaux (Taylor, chapter 6) and performer Ethel Waters (Cherry, chapter 5) are exemplary: both were borderline cases, carrying their innovations on traditional expression into new, crossover genres. The Harlem Renaissance often distrusted the new popular culture and its media, preferring creations that lifted presumably nobler folk forms like the spirituals into the realm of "high art." Classical composers Samuel Coleridge-Taylor, William Grant Still, Nathaniel Dett, and Florence B. Price made such attempts (Brown, chapter 4) in parallel with the infusion of African-American musical idioms and themes into European music—as in Claude Debussy's "Golliwog's Cakewalk" (1906–1908), Igor Stravinsky's "Ragtime" (1918), or George Antheil's *Jazz Symphony* (1925).

The other major influence on the development of Harlem Renaissance arts was the rediscovery of African sculpture through the European avant-garde. In his book *Modernist Art and Popular Entertainment in Jazz Age Paris 1900–1930*, Jody Blake studies the simultaneous crazes, in France's capital, for African-American music and dance and for so-called primitive arts. Cubism and surrealism are the two most famous movements embodying this critical conflation of Western and non-Western civilizations and epistemologies. Yet, modernist primitivism was also a means to reach a new aesthetic syncretism as an antidote to the fragmented perception of life proceeding from increasing mechanization, moral relativism, and scientific doubt. Correspondences between the arts—such as a relation between tonality in music and color in painting ("painted sounds") or between dance rhythms and sculptural forms—could recreate a feeling of completeness and were inspired from a late-romantic view of African civilizations as holistic.

Although this raises disturbing questions about the aesthetic co-optation of African and African-American arts by European and American modernism, it also provides a clue to the foundation of Alain Locke's call for a "school of Negro art" that would give direction to the works of many artists (NN 264) and of W. E. B. DuBois's cultural nationalism. Locke's and DuBois's stances could be seen as an attempt by the so-called "primitives" to reappropriate their depiction in international modernism. In this politics of image, the relationship with primitivism was bound to be ambiguous, the latter being both a weapon for cultural recognition and acceptance and an array of mainstream-defined stereotypes (Feith, chapter 2).

To stimulate recognition and creation, various foundations and exhibitions were set up to show both classical African art and the works of black American artists. The most famous supporter, Alfred Barnes, opened his collections of African sculpture to artists like Aaron Douglas or to the janitor-turned-painter Palmer Hayden. The 135th Street branch of the New York Public Library organized a large visual arts exhibition in the twenties and was later decorated with Douglas's famous series of murals, *Aspects of Negro Life* (1934). Further encouragement and economic support was given by magazines such as *The Crisis, Opportunity,* or the Garveyite *Negro World* and by the publishing industry, in the form of a boom of illustration orders that might have protected New Negro artists from the fate of a Henry O. Tanner in the preceding generation: exile and a shift away from black themes. Yet many artists did travel and broaden their creative horizons in Europe—Aaron Douglas, Meta Warrick Fuller, William H. Johnson, Hale Woodruff, Archibald Motley—and became full participants in the international modernist movement.

One might detect a metonymy of this growing assertiveness and control of the African-American image in the partial devolution, between the time of the

Survey Graphic edition on Harlem and that of the *New Negro* anthology, of the illustrations from German-born artist Winold Reiss to Aaron Douglas. Yet there was no consensus on the extent and meaning of this new control and on the ways to achieve it: some intellectuals of the time, like George Schuyler, asserted that the very idea of the existence of black characteristics was an imposition and that the real way to fight racist stereotypes was to renounce such clichéd fiction ("The Negro-Art Hokum," 1926). Of course, the reason for the possibility of studying the art of the Harlem Renaissance today is that most artists did not follow Schuyler's advice.

2. The Syncopated African: Constructions of Origins in the Harlem Renaissance (Literature, Music, Visual Arts)

Michel Feith

The unity of the Harlem Renaissance as a historical moment and aesthetic movement has sometimes been questioned. Bundling together, under a single name tag, the extraordinary variety of the production of the time—which bridges at least two generations of African-American intellectuals and artists and several means of expression—might seem at best a convenient simplification. But trying to envisage the New Negro movement as a project rather than as a specific achievement could be a way to find a common purpose behind the widely different outlooks on the meaning of the Renaissance, as well as of African-American identity and culture. This chapter attempts to find such a unifying factor in a desire to control the image of black Americans by themselves, as opposed to the hitherto prevalent other-definition of stereotypes. The postwar era, characterized by the increased urbanization of African-Americans, seems to have been the first period in history when a project of this type had any chance of success. Even the precedent of the 1890s, which now appears as a rehearsal of the Harlem Renaissance, did not reach the same proportions and fame. It is also clear that by adopting the broad viewpoint of the image of the "race," one can encompass different artistic media, such as literature, music, and the visual arts.

We will still need a good deal of modesty before proceeding: systematic views are always flawed. What is more, because the material is so diverse and abundant, our study will have only a restricted basis. Owing to its double nature as an overview of achievement and as a manifesto, we will take as our starting point the seminal *New Negro* anthology of 1925.[1] One could hardly wish for a better introduction to the politics of image.

In the first part of this chapter, I will attempt to examine a few definitions of identity, in the context of American cultural nationalism, following some of George Hutchinson's analyses. A crucial aspect of any artistic construction of African-American identity is the representation of Africa emerging from the aesthetic production: this representation will form the subject of the second part of this essay. We will finally try to ascertain the passage from black image to black vision, from African-America as subject matter to the voluntarist elaboration of an aesthetic mode of perception originating in a cross between Modernism and a specific folk culture. The lingering question in this chapter will therefore be that of heritage: what claims to authenticity can a definition of identity have when it is based on an invention of origins?

DEFINITIONS OF IDENTITY

In his *The Harlem Renaissance in Black and White*,[2] George Hutchinson contends that the Harlem Renaissance was the product of what he calls "inter-racial cooperation"—which could be better defined as "inter-ethnic" coopera-tion, given that "race," in spite of its overdetermined social currency, is an in-valid concept in anthropology. More surprisingly, Hutchinson argues that for many intellectuals of the twenties, who were looking for a "usable past" as a support for American cultural nationalism, the only truly American culture was African-American. Writers and critics such as Van Wyck Brooks and Waldo Frank, in their rejection of the materialism of the United States, found few native traditions on which to build a real culture:

> The America [Brooks] saw lacked the peasantry and folk traditions of European cultures, from which great cultures are supposed ordinarily to de-velop. . . . Black writers, on the other hand, would point out that the United States *did* have a native folk culture, born of suffering and intimate contact with the soil, emotionally expressive, and above all rich in spirit as only the culture of an oppressed people could be.[3]

This passage reminds the reader of some of the developments in DuBois's *The Souls of Black Folk* (1903), both coming quite close to a literal rephrasing of European romantic nationalism, as first exposed by Herder. According to this concept, a national culture evolves from the contact between a specific soil and a specific folk, giving birth to a language and folklore, which in turn pro-duce a particular type of high art and social institutions. The national *Kultur* is an emanation of the *Volksgeist* (spirit of the people), which it reflects at a "higher" level. This concept, which originated in Germany, soon became the dominant ideology in the Western world; it was the leading spiritual force be-hind the movements of German and Italian unification at the end of the 19th century and also provided a rationale for such cultural emancipation attempts as the Irish Renaissance, which Locke refers to as a model of the New Negro movement (NN 50).

George Hutchinson states that both Locke and DuBois developed a philosophy of cultural pluralism, according to which culture is a social product rather than a racial output. It may be so; but at the same time, the phraseology of a certain romantic nationalism cannot be made light of. One more example will suffice at this stage. It is another pronouncement by Locke on spirituals, in which the conjunction between a "race genius" and a "soil" is unmistakably put forward:

> The spirituals are really the most characteristic product of the race genius as yet in America. But the very elements which make them uniquely expressive of the Negro make them at the same time deeply representative of the soil that produced them. (NN 199)

If "the Negro was in vogue," according to Langston Hughes's formula, it may well be because the African-American idiom participated in this attempt at defining a "usable" folk culture in the United States. Between the extremes of excessive closeness to the European anti-model (the genteel culture of the Northeast or the pioneer world of the West) and excessive difference (Native American civilizations), African-American culture, because of its mixed nature, could provide a workable example of a purely American folk tradition. We might therefore venture the hypothesis that those intellectuals, black and white, who saw black culture as the true folk culture of the United States, as well as an image of its future evolution, did so not because they perceived it as a separate entity, but as a consequence of its plural heritage.

Yet, in a romantic cultural nationalist view, black culture had a double folk identification, which stemmed from the two "soils" of its origins: the American South and Africa. "The Dixie Pike has grown from a goat path in Africa," Jean Toomer states in *Cane*.[4] But, in silencing the trauma of the "middle passage" and the deculturation of slavery, the poetic phrase begs the question of how to articulate, in an identity-building process, the dialectics of cultural continuity and disjunction, a process which is crucial to any consideration of the politics of image. The artistic treatment of African origins during the Harlem Renaissance might shed some light on these heterogeneous "soils of black folks."

LOOKING BACK: THE IMAGE OF AFRICA IN THE WORKS OF HARLEM RENAISSANCE ARTISTS

The central project of the Harlem Renaissance can be defined as that of controlling the image of black people, of refusing categorizations imposed from the outside. This is at least what can be inferred from Locke's statement in his preface to the *New Negro* anthology: he bestowed on African-American art the aim of "rehabilitating the race in world esteem . . . a revaluation by white and black alike of the Negro in terms of his artistic endowments and cultural contributions, past and prospective" (NN 14–15). This declaration can help us assess the importance of a politics of image: because stereotypes both reflect and reinforce oppression, the act of counteracting them has symbolic efficacy. What emerges from this manifesto is the project of creating an artistic identity for African-Americans as worthy objects and as gifted subjects of art. This is very close to DuBois's notion of art as propaganda[5] or, in Nathan Huggins's ironic formulation, "The vogue of the New Negro, then, had all the character of a public relations promotion."[6]

Africa is a particularly sensitive bone of contention in this respect: the stereotype of the African as a savage has been used to justify oppression, racial inferiority having as its logical counterpart social inferiority. Hence the elaboration by several Renaissance artists of a "counter-stereotype," which is necessarily also a type, a synthetic figure, symbolizing heritage. This hypothesis seems to contradict Hutchinson's theory of the strong influence on New Negro intellectuals of Josiah Royce's philosophy of "wholesome provincialism" and cultural pluralism, according to which regional or ethnic identities are based on consent rather than descent, on identification rather than birth (Hutchinson 79).

Such a process of identification might nevertheless have recourse to a few role-models, which are little more than idealized abstractions. This reminds us of Werner Sollors's criticism of Royce, the latter apparently proposing a falsely pluralistic model, because the province is presented in terms as monolithic as the national entity it is supposed to contradict. Furthermore, in Royce's acceptation, the province and its individual denizen can be seen as mutual metaphors, which leads to the slippery notion of representativeness and, in aesthetic terms, to the type.[7] After all, the collective singulars "the Negro" and "the New Negro" are just such allegories.[8] It goes without saying that the representations of African-American life by Renaissance writers and artists were varied and complex and far exceeded any synthetic type or types. Yet, in the absence of direct knowledge of Africa, the images of the inhabitants of that continent were bound to be more symbolic than actual and therefore subject to revealing simplifications.

A Pan-African Image

The first characteristic of the type is its Pan-African nature. Two main visions are proposed and very often fused: the Egyptian and the West African.

The Egyptian theme is omnipresent in the visual arts of the time, one of

Figure 2.1. Meta Warrick Fuller: *The Awakening of Ethiopia*. ca. 1914, bronze cast, 67 × 16 × 20″. Schomburg Center for Research in Black Culture, Arts & Artifacts Division, The New York Public Library, Astor, Lenox and Tilden Foundations.

the early examples being Meta Vaux Warrick Fuller's *The Awakening of Ethiopia* (1914) (fig. 2.1). The sculpture represents an erect woman in Egyptian garb, wrapped in mummy-like funeral bands, yet waking up from death or slumber. This signifies the awakening of black people to a new consciousness after the sleep of oppression or historical forgetfulness. It might, of course, also embody the hope for emancipation of African-American women—the artist included—at the beginning of the century.

Lois Mailou Jones's *Ascent of Ethiopia* (1932) features the same representative figure, but within a wider narrative context. The picture is actually a rendering of African-American history, which follows the displacement of African figures from the old continent who are following a star to the modern United States, where they find symbols of the cultural activities of black Americans: art, drama, music. The painting seems to answer Locke's and DuBois's programs perfectly: it gives an account of history and tradition in a euphemized way—the middle passage being toned down to a providential call and ascent. This painting serves as a tribute to the achievements of the race in artistic matters; it can therefore be deemed a work of propaganda in support of African-American pride. The influence of DuBois's *Star of Ethiopia* seems probable. The huge pharaoh-like figure on the right-hand side represents the transhistorical spirit of the "race," a tutelary soul pointing at heritage and permanence. This face, a profile in the ancient Egyptian style, is truly Pan-African because it unites a black skin with pharaonic regalia.

The same type of quasi-transcendent figure is to be found in the sphinx-like profile dominating Aaron Douglas's *Building More Stately Mansions* (1944). Its origin is signified by a pyramid next to it and a silhouette with an Egyptian hairdo in the opposite, lower-right corner. The painting seems to equate the architectural feats of ancient Egypt with the task of anonymous black workers building skyscrapers and bridges in modern cities. The epic dimension is enhanced by the technique of representation, the most celebrated influence on Douglas, borrowed from pharaonic funerary murals and in which the human body is represented facing the viewer, while the head is turned sideways. A burning house in the lower-left corner might allude to the war, or to racial tension, the dark past which a voluntary action of reconstruction and improvement might help overcome.

The poetry of the Harlem Renaissance also featured Egyptian references prominently: for example, in Gwendolyn Bennett's "Heritage" (1923—*Norton Anthology* 1,227), or Sterling Brown's striking superposition of Egyptian history and American geography in "Memphis Blues" (1931—*Norton Anthology* 1,217).

In "The Negro Speaks of Rivers" (1921, NN 141) Langston Hughes also includes Egypt in the black man's streams of heritage: "I looked upon the Nile and raised the pyramids above it." Once again the collective, allegorical "I" signifies pride, the enduring, transhistorical strength of the community's spirit, comparable to a river, whose eternal form is composed of myriad individual droplets of water: "My soul has grown deep like the rivers." It is of no little interest to notice that in Hughes's poem and in Douglas's painting, the conception of origins is hardly limitative. *More Stately Mansions* features more than African and Egyptian architecture; there are also a Buddhist pagoda and a Roman portico; the rivers mentioned by Hughes comprise the Nile, the Congo, and the Mississippi, but also the Euphrates. Besides reappropriating Egyptian references into a Pan-African concept of beginnings, these two artists enlarge their vision to the common patrimony of mankind.

Such a claim of ancient Egypt as part of the heritage of African-Americans is especially interesting. The origins of the Egyptian people and their civilization have been the subject of fierce debate. The population and language are usually referred to as Hamito-Semitic, indicating a mixture of Mediterranean and African influences, and the form of government seems to have been derived from the first city-states of Mesopotamia. Relationships with the interior of the continent are attested by the complex rivalries between the Egyptian empire and the kingdoms of Nubia or the Sudan. In spite of the short period of Meroe's domination, which DuBois makes much of ("The Negro Mind Reaches Out," NN 406), the direction of cultural influences is difficult to assess.

Whatever the case might be, Egypt and Ethiopia both belong to East Africa, whereas the overwhelming majority of the slaves imported to the United States came from West Africa.[9] The reappropriation of these two empires by the Harlem Renaissance appears therefore as a product of contemporary Pan-Africanism; a common colonial situation offsets the large geographical and cultural differences between black and white, as well as between the eastern and western parts of the continent. Another important motivation for this abrogation of distances lies in the impetus toward a politics of pride. At a time when very little was known about such West African empires as that of Mali, Egypt and Ethiopia were the only two African civilizations comparable to that of the United States, as far as power, influence, and architectural grandeur are concerned. Their annexation to a composite image of African heritage was therefore a key component in the fashioning of ethnic pride.

But, as Sterling Brown's "Memphis Blues" can remind us, Egypt had long had another meaning in African-American culture. The Negro spirituals allegorically identified black folks with the Hebrew slaves of *Exodus* and identified the subjects of "Ole Pharaoh" with the white planters and their overseers. There is therefore an ambivalent image of Egypt in the works of the Harlem Renaissance; one being a support for positive identification and race pride, the other picturing the white oppressors in Egyptian garb. The use of this reference can therefore be defined as syncretic, unifying two parallel traditions, a cultured one and a popular one. In the spirituals and the biblical tradition, God punished the Egyptians for their mistreatment of the slaves. Historically, on the contrary, the Hebrew slaves were at the origin of the religion of the white masters; an identification with the pharaoh's subjects might have meant symbolic dominance over the white world.

Whatever the psychological complications of this use of the past, the image of Egyptian heritage at work in the Harlem Renaissance—and later—is clearly a fabrication; it participates in the creation of a New Negro ethos. Like a myth, this complex and ambivalent icon is able to unite symbolically unsolvable oppositions and contradictory identifications.

West Africa: The Double-Edged Sword of Primitivism

The elements that represent Africa in Renaissance art and literature can be reduced to a limited number. Because, at the time, New Negro creators had very few opportunities to visit the continent, they selected emblematic symbols, in a quasi-metonymic way. These symbols were first the signifiers of the African landscape: the jungle, with its exuberant vegetation characteristic of a tropical climate, and a few animals such as the lion and elephant. This luscious nature connotes the maternal image of "Mother Africa," a picture of origins. Music and dancing, tom-toms and rhythm are associated with the people, whose body is depicted as a locus of power and sensuous beauty. Uniting the physical and the spiritual stand the masks and statues of African art.

All these ingredients can be found in the dancing figure of Richmond Barthé's *Feral Benga* (1937) or in the *Copper Masks* series (1935) by Sargent Claude Johnson, but even more in the celebrated mural by Aaron Douglas titled *The Negro in an African Setting* (1934), a panel in the historical series *Aspects of Negro Life* (fig. 2.2). The subject matter is a war dance, in which two figures perform in front of a fetish and a choruslike audience wearing Egyptian-inspired headdresses. The setting and subject are unified in the picture plane, suggesting the deep communion between man and nature, soil and folk in Africa. The striking organization of the planes of light is a complex interaction of circles and lines. Such an interplay between concentric, angular, and undulating shapes stresses the (poly)rhythmic unity of the picture, drawing its inspiration from African music.

The elements we have spelled out are also present in the poetry about Africa. They are used by Countée Cullen in his "Heritage" of 1925 to dramatize the conflict between the restraints of American life, which are seen as consequences of the Christian religion's denial of the senses, and the call of the blood, the rhythmic and instinctual truth that is the core of African heritage.

> What is Africa to me:
> Copper sun or scarlet sea,
> Jungle star or jungle track,
> Strong bronzed men, or regal black
> Women from whose loins I sprang
> When the birds of Eden sang?
> (*Norton Anthology* 1,314)

True, Africa is here seen through clichés, not through experience. The idealized quality of the picture becomes obvious when expressed in terms of the Christian myth of Eden. Still, it is more than "a book one thumbs / Listlessly, till slumber comes" (lines 31–32); even though the intellectual filiation is scant and artificial, the body has kept a sense of rhythm, either as a racial characteris-

Figure 2.2. Aaron Douglas: *Aspects of Negro Life: The Negro in an African Setting*. 1934, oil on canvas, 6 × 6'. Schomburg Center for Research in Black Culture, Arts & Artifacts Division, The New York Public Library, Astor, Lenox and Tilden Foundations.

tic or as a means of cultural survival. The inheritance of suffering is also a support for identity, which leads to a questioning of white civilization: "Lord, I fashion dark gods, too. . . . Not yet has my heart or head / In the least way realized / They and I are civilized" (lines 126–28).

The same themes are to be found in Claude McKay's early poems such as "Outcast" (1922—*Norton Anthology* 987), and again in Gwendolyn Bennett's "Heritage" (*Norton Anthology* 1,227). Some of Langston Hughes's early poems, such as "Afro-American Fragment" or "Danse Africaine," can be added to our list, as can the short story "Sahdji," by Bruce Nugent (NN 113–14).

Whatever the more or less implicit criticism of stereotypes visible in the works we have mentioned, they still seem dangerously close to these stereotypes, in their depiction of a synthetic, idealized Africa. A tropical nature; sensuous, physical natives bent on dancing and playing music; a hint or more of savagery—all these ingredients of primitivism might explain the success enjoyed by Harlem Renaissance artists as a sort of co-optation by white people. This is the interpretation of the movement given by Nathan Huggins and David Levering Lewis.[10] It may nevertheless be possible to give a less dismissive interpretation of these primitivistic traits; they might be seen as an integral part of the New Negro project without questioning the integrity of this project.

Primitivism is first of all a vitalism. As such, it partakes of the general questioning, taking place at the end of the 19th and the beginning of the 20th centuries, of the respective positions of "life" and "civilization." Life became identified with the spontaneous, instinctual, sexual parts of human existence; whereas civilization and culture were increasingly seen as restraints and frustrations. This revaluation of the body and the instincts over intellect and social conformity found expression in the works of such writers and thinkers as Friedrich Nietzsche, D. H. Lawrence, Virginia Woolf, and, of course, Sigmund Freud and the psychoanalytic school.

As a consequence, the qualities often negatively associated with Africans and African-Americans—such as spontaneity, emotionalism, and sensuality—were suddenly endowed with positivity. From the point of view of the American cultural nationalism we mentioned earlier, a position of vantage was thus created for blacks in the modernist *épistème;* no wonder that some artists and writers were eager to fill it, thereby converting shame into ethnic pride. The primitivism of the New Negro movement appears to have obeyed a logic of *overdetermination*—a process of sharing a common intellectual field with the mainstream, but at the same time having specific motivations and strategies within this common *Weltanshauung.* This does not mean that it was innocuous or that it was not co-opted, at an early or later stage, by the dominant culture. But at least it does not deserve to be dismissed or demonized, as has sometimes been the case.

Like its Egyptian counterpart, the West African heritage of black Americans is not the rediscovery of some atavistic identity; rather, it is the creation of an identity and of a few types adapted to the needs of the times. Paradoxically this claiming or reclaiming of origins is a proof of integration in American and in global intellectual trends.

Except for DuBois, few African-American intellectuals and artists of the twenties had had the opportunity to visit Africa; their rediscovery of African arts was by way of white anthropologists and European modernists. Heritage, then, must not be seen as a given, but as a creation, a look backward which shapes its object in the process. This delving into the African past (added to, but not exclusive of, a consideration of African-American history or the complexities of the present) may have been the choice of those artists who were most influenced by late romantic definitions of nationalism and culture, by the notion of *Volksgeist;* in a word those who were closest to the ideas of the European and American mainstreams of the time. It is actually the paradox of nationalism to have been the most internationally widespread idea at the turn of the century, and possibly even today.[11]

SYNCOPATED VISION: A DEFINITION OF BLACK FORM

To fully restate the presence of African-Americans in the arts, their treatment as subject matter should be complemented by the evolution of formal qualities defining a black vision, a whole array of strategies of representation articulating a difference in perception from the mainstream. In the words of Locke, this shift in emphasis is defined as an "increasing tendency to evolve from the racial substance something technically distinctive, something that as an idiom of style may become a contribution to the general resources of art" (NN 51); or, in other terms, "Our poets have now stopped speaking for the Negro—they speak as Negroes" (NN 48). As readers and critics of the end of the 20th century, we do not believe in "racial substances," or in artistic forms organically evolved from them, whatever the expression might mean. This terminology we have analyzed as a scion of romantic nationalism and its essentialist assumptions. However invalid its epistemological phrasing, the project did exist and was one of the important impetuses behind some of the most innovative work of the Harlem Renaissance. We shall examine it, not as sprouting from a defined collective self, but as a construction of this collective self in the specific field of artistic production, through the privileging of certain *overdetermined* formal qualities of the work. Once again, we shall find syncretism in operation, between the African-American folk tradition, on the one hand, and the experiments of European modernism, on the other, especially in its interest in African art and sculpture. The latter brings an emphasis on abstract, hieratic formal qualities; the folk tradition contributes its participatory, lyrical aspect (NN 254).

Imitation with a Vengeance

In painting, the most obvious of these strategies of formal appropriation is working "in the style of" Matisse or other European modernists. Palmer Hayden's *Fétiche et Fleurs* (1933) or Malvin Gray Johnson's *Self-Portrait* (1934)

CRITERIA OF RENAISSANCE ART

(fig. 2.3) are cases in point. The latter, for example, is a portrait of the artist with African masks. It seems to justify Romare Bearden's criticism that the Renaissance was purely imitative of white masters. But this is imitation with a vengeance, a form of signifyin(g) on influence. Whereas for the French avant-garde, African masks were meant as a shock to the viewer, a declaration of savagery, a questioning of "civilization," for the African-American painter they might bear associations with such notions as heritage, origins, pride. Instead of radical otherness, there is a feeling of continuity, of tradition. This informing presence of the past might be represented in Johnson's painting by the fact that one of the masks gives the shape and the other the color of the artist's face. Here, the visual evidence of juxtaposition begs the question of the rediscovery of African art through Europe and of the ambiguities of heritage. It amounts to a deeply ideological displacement of the accent of modernism, for the purposes of identity-definition.

From Folk Art to "High Art"

Many of the most widely hailed experiments of the Harlem Renaissance are those that take as their basis various types of folk expression and that convey their formal structure into better-recognized art forms, such as concert music, poetry, or the novel. Whether or not the artists themselves shared Locke's elitist philosophy, they did follow the pattern of romantic cultural nationalism advocated by the editor of *The New Negro*. In this trajectory from soil to folk to high culture, music seems to have had a preponderant role during the Renaissance as the model and origin of most attempts at defining specific "Characteristics of Negro Expression" in the arts.[12]

Because of its centrality in the culture, music was the most likely candidate to serve as a model and inspiration for other African-American arts. One of the striking characteristics of black cultures in protestant America is the prevalence of "motor memory" over "image memory" because the iconoclastic nature of Protestantism did not permit the kind of syncretism, which developed in Catholic colonies, between African deities and rites and the worship of the saints. Therefore, music and rhythm became the main vectors/supports of African cultural survival in the United States.[13] On the other hand, African-American music was the most widely recognized form of folk culture, popular among both blacks and whites, and therefore the clearest marker of identity and belonging. No wonder then that jazz, the blues, or the spirituals influenced many authors who wanted to signify their debt to the folk. Musicality was also one of the main traits of several modes of oral performance such as ballads or sermons, which helped bridge the gaps between music and literature.

Let us now examine the three main characteristics of African and African-

Figure 2.3. Malvin Gray Johnson: *Self-Portrait.* 1934, oil on canvas. National Museum of American Art, Smithsonian Institution, Gift of the Harmon Foundation.

American music to determine how they influenced other forms of expression. First and foremost, African music and its various offspring favor rhythm over melody and harmony; this predominance often goes as far as a polyrhythmic interweaving of *tempi*. This leads us to the second characteristic: syncopation, which can be defined briefly as a displacement of accents in a given rhythmic structure, such as the carrying-on of a note of the melody onto a weak beat or the stressing of weak beats. Call-and-response, or antiphony, is the third important aspect, pointing at the communal nature of African and African-American performance, be it music-playing or storytelling. Audience participation implies a dialogue between the soloist and the community, making for both individual expression and general solidarity and interdependence. If we add the vestigial presence of the African pentatonic scale in the famous "blue notes," we now have a number of traits, not necessarily peculiar to black folk music but concentrated in it, which might serve as an approximative alphabet of style for Harlem Renaissance experiments in defining an African-American artistic identity.[14]

Many critics have already shown how folk poetry was integrated into Renaissance poetry. *God's Trombones* (1920) by James Weldon Johnson is a variation on the spiritual sermon; Langston Hughes's use of the blues has become famous; African-American ballads, such as that of John Henry, inspired poets and even a series of paintings by Palmer Hayden. Sterling Brown and Hughes added work songs to that variegated repertoire. These poets tried to convey the mood of the folk forms they recycled and to pay tribute to the genius for striking metaphor and word coinage that they exemplified, and which Zora Neale Hurston called the "will to adorn."[15]

> And God stepped out on space,
> And he looked around and said:
> I'm lonely—
> I'll make me a world.
> (*Norton Anthology* 775)

These opening lines from James Weldon Johnson's "The Creation," a poem from *God's Trombones,* render the qualities of humor and metaphysical concreteness of the folk sermon, which appealed to one Harlem Renaissance intellectual. What really anchors the poem in the black tradition, and distinguishes it from an attempt at rendering local color from outside, is the musical quality of the verse, carried over from the spiritual sermon itself. The variable length of the lines echoes the rhythm of the performance, in which a regular beat, corresponding to the orator's pauses for breath, encompasses a different number of syllables, pronounced at an elastic tempo, according to the amount of information or the emphasis which is conveyed. This variation within a single beat is called the syncopation of lines. In this sense, we can say there is a clear connection, in Renaissance poetry, between the African-American tradition and modernist experimentations in free verse, leading to an idiom which is at the same time identifiable as avant-garde and folk expression.

The call-and-response pattern, which is another of the characteristics African-American music shares with other types of oral performance, was often inscribed in poetry in the repetition of lines, whole or in part. It reminded the reader of the antiphonal dialogue between soloist and audience in the spirituals and work songs or of the performer's answering himself, as it were, in the blues. The blues pattern is to be found in "Tin Roof Blues" (1931) by Sterling Brown, one of the Harlem Renaissance poets who incorporated the widest spectrum of folk forms in his work:

I'm got the tin roof blues, got dese sidewalks on my mind,
De tin roof blues, dese lonesome sidewalks on my mind,
I'm goin' where de shingles covers people mo' my kind.
(*Norton Anthology* 1,220)

In prose narratives, call-and-response was dissociated from a purely musical context through the rendition of oral storytelling situations, which also involve give-and-take between the narrator and a group of narratees present in the story, thereby signifying (on) the reading public. This is what Henry Louis Gates, in reference to Hurston, calls "the speakerly text."[16] It is exemplified in *The New Negro* by this author's short story "Spunk," in which the chorus of loungers in the village store not only witness and comment on the events, but actually make them happen by influencing the protagonists. In Hurston's *Their Eyes Were Watching God* (1937), the neutral narrative voice gets caught in the heroine's act of recounting her life to her friend, while the presence of a curious porch audience looms large in the background. Thus the story becomes a "play of voices," answering one of Hurston's own "characteristics of Negro expression": drama (*Norton Anthology* 1,020).

A Syncopated Renaissance?

Rhythm and antiphony appear as crucial formal qualities belonging to the African-American tradition and as traits which were widely used at the time of the Harlem Renaissance to define a specific black aesthetic within the context of American modernism. But the concept of syncopation could be a more encompassing notion, which might give a fuller account of the common project of both formal innovation and ethnic appropriation.[17] Syncopation might be seen as a shared trope unifying the creative impetus behind the music, the visual arts, and the literature of the renaissance, and intimately connected with the will to control the image of African-Americans. It could be paralleled with

Henry Gates's master trope of black expression, signifyin(g), or "repetition with a difference."

Gates defines signifyin(g) as an awareness that language never means only one thing at a time, as a subversion of the language of the masters and its pretense at being univocal. Such an awareness is seen as a necessity for African-American survival in an oppressive society; such a subversion is a space of freedom when freedom is denied. This dialectic between imitation and invention is also what constitutes an African-American literary tradition, one that signifies not only on white influence, but on itself as well.[18] Our suggestion to use syncopation as a defining trope of the Harlem Renaissance is aimed at supplementing Gates's analysis with a recognition that music was the wedge through which black culture gained recognition and evolved its most innovative attempts at defining an artistic identity.

Our understanding of the term syncopation will encompass its formal and metaphoric meanings. Syncopation was the main trope for the Africanization of Euro-American music. It gave birth to the spirituals and jazz, among other musical genres. It consists in a displacement of accent, in a sort of "creative distortion" of rhythm. By stressing weak beats, it can be said to reveal and valorize the "shadow" or "background" of the dominant beat. It can therefore represent an apt metaphor for the situation of a minority, especially as it tries to assert pride and identity through artistic means—one may be reminded of the title of Ralph Ellison's collection of essays, *Shadow and Act* (1964).

Syncopation can also be paralleled to the project of the most innovative avant-garde movement of the time, namely cubism. As a matter of fact, cubist aesthetics was based on a fragmentation of the representation of the object, which was reconstructed rhythmically on the picture plane. Such rhythmic distortion can be easily compared to syncopation; in the same way, the juxtaposition of multiple perspectives and points of view on the object can remind us of antiphony, as for example in *Cane,* whose construction oscillates between modernist collage, cubist perspectivism, and the tradition of call-and-response. After all, the last corresponds to a sort of harmonized, auditory collage of different subjective contributions to a central theme.

Cubism itself is indissolubly connected to African art. For Picasso and Braque, African sculpture was a means of questioning the Western visual canon based on the centrality of human proportions. "What Picasso cared about was the formal vitality of African art, which was for him inseparably involved with its apparent freedom to distort."[19] The modernist era was marked by a de-centering of the subject through the exploration of the unconscious; a de-centering of Western values through an interest in other cultures, a cultural relativism paradoxically fostered by the extension of imperialism through colonialism; and, in the arts, the abolition of the centrality of the human figure and Cartesian perception. Cubism was one of the most radical of these questionings, one that is often deemed as metonymic of the whole; its attempt at fractioning the object and reconstructing it in a rhythmic composition integrating time and multiple points of view even reflects the scientific revolution of the time: Einstein's theory of relativity.

It is in this coherent use of "creative distortion" and defamiliarization that we can find a real collusion between the modernist project and that of the African-American group. In this de-centering of the center—representational and ethnic—the relevance of the syncopating or syncopated African acquires its full significance. The Harlem Renaissance could claim as its own special locus a meeting point between modernist experimentation and a minority culture or situation; this amounted to a questioning of the Western tradition from a (rediscovered) African diasporic standpoint.

No wonder then, given this common ground, that many African-Americans participated in the avant-garde movements of the twenties. Still, their integration in the general cultural renewal of their time should not hide the fact that it was an avant-garde with an added dimension; even if it could not be limited to it, it had a largely ethnic character. In its attempts at defining a specific identity against a larger civilizational entity, it duplicated the situation of the American cultural nationalism of the beginning of the century, which tried to detach itself from European influence. This, of course, should help us relativize the accusations of provincialism sometimes leveled at the Harlem Renaissance (Huggins 308); there is a chance such accusations do not apply to black artists of the movement more than to their white contemporaries.

We could even qualify the Harlem Renaissance of "syncopated modernism," in the sense that it does displace the accent of modernism from a questioning of Western values and modes of representation to a celebration of African-derived cultures, in the name of the very tenets of the new Western avant-gardes: innovation and creative distortion. This would be a formal counterpart to the overdetermined uses of primitivism in the depiction of African heritage.

A pictorial example might clarify our analysis. Aaron Douglas's *Song of the Towers* (1934) (fig. 2.4) is another part of the *Aspects of Negro Life* series at the Schomburg Center of the New York Public Library. In the central presence of music and some of its structural features, it echoes the already mentioned *The Negro in an African Setting*. The scene is transported to the United States, making of the painting a comment on contemporary America rather than on the past, the link with the former picture showing the persistence of tradition. Formally speaking, the work stages the confluence of synthetic cubism and the African heritage in the angularity and rhythmic interaction of the color planes. Mu-

Figure 2.4. Aaron Douglas: *Aspects of Negro Life: Song of the Towers*. 1934, oil on canvas, 9 × 9′. Schomburg Center for Research in Black Culture, Arts & Artifacts Division, The New York Public Library, Astor, Lenox and Tilden Foundations.

sic itself is figured through the saxophone at the center—the position of the fetish in the earlier painting—which embodies the African-American spirit and a form of freedom. From the point of view of contents, we therefore have a "song under towers." It is the distortion of the perspective of the towers and smokestacks which gives the work its full title, by exemplifying the "music of the towers," possibly to show how the quintessential African-American artistic expression can transform a potentially oppressive and alienating environment.

Music, and more specifically jazz, is therefore both a thematic component and the organizing principle of the picture. The syncopated quality is to be found in the rhythmic displacement of accent occurring in the interaction between the diagonal and concentric lines—or between towers and sound waves—and especially visible in the shifts in hues resulting from the super-position of the different color planes they delimit. Background and foreground, weak and strong elements, are blurred and contaminate each other. The paint-ing can then be termed a spiritual equivalent of the African-American ethos embodied in music.

Douglas's consistent use of black silhouettes can also strike a chord in this syncopated concert. Their poses, harking back to Egyptian funeral art, become symbols of heritage and dignity. The fact that only the contours are visible can be interpreted as an ingenious solution to the problems of surface and depth inherent in cubism and after. The very flatness of a silhouette on the picture plane participates in an exploration of the painterly nature of representation and amounts to a Matisse-like rejection of classical perspective. But they are also shadows, general and unidentified; signifyin(g) on the "invisible" status of minorities in the United States, they also paradoxically represent everyman in an African garb. It seems the perfect visual equivalent to our concept of syncopation: a rhythmic, musical stress on the weak beat, which comes to proud prominence against a background of suppression.

This epic project, which Douglas shared with many other artists of the period, might explain the fact that Harlem Renaissance painters and sculptors hardly ever ventured beyond the figurative dimension of their art. Their pro-duction was, as a rule, less iconoclastic than some cubist portraits, in which the human figure is so distorted as to become unrecognizable. If the New Negro project really *was* control of image and identity-building, figuration was of the essence. How to use image as a support for pride and self-assertion in the face of mainstream stereotypes, while radically questioning the very nature and validity of all representation? The special brand of modernism, which we have called syncopated, of the Harlem Renaissance was at the same time central and specific, bold and innovative, but within self-imposed limits; it laid the groundwork for other, later experiments that could transcend these restrictions.

In the general, cross-genre artistic project of control of image, embodied in an aesthetic philosophy inspired by a cultural nationalist *épistème*, the repre-sentation of the syncopated African as a type, or collection of types, is one crucial thematic element in a reappropriation of heritage. It is at the same time a way of integrating—and often signifyin(g) on—the modernist uses of Africa. The same overdetermination of traits can be witnessed, on the formal plane, in the general trope of syncopation, or creative, rhythmic distortion. The innovations of modernism are here rephrased as characteristics of African-derived cultures, and especially as African-American, whereas, paradoxically, the rediscovery of these traits, or their uses in "elevated" art, were initiated by the evolution in mainstream aesthetics.

But if syncopation, sometimes also called "stop-time" due to its rhythmic variations, can be compared to cubist experiments in variations of points of view, one can ultimately connect the project of the Harlem Renaissance to a syncopated picture. One can easily feel the common impetus, the intention of making a portrait of African America, past and present and possibly future; but this portrait remains elusive because of the multiplicity of sometimes contradictory perspectives adopted by the actors themselves. The heated debate between George Schuyler's "The Negro-Art Hokum" and Langston Hughes's "The Negro Artist and the Racial Mountain" (both 1926) is relevant here: both try to inscribe black culture and artistic expression within the general context of America and modernism; but they are at variance about the respective emphasis to be given the two terms. Whether race is incidental (Schuyler) or a social-spiritual unit (Hughes), the problem is the tension between integration and specificity in the new image to be presented to the world.

The New Negro, which as an anthology reflects these various trends, can possibly be read as an apt snapshot of the Harlem Renaissance: it renders its vitality, its character of collaborative work between black and white, older and younger generations, cultural nationalists and integrationists, as well as different artistic fields. In a word, once again, the unity of the project is felt, but it is impossible to reduce it to a single formula, a unified figure or type. We might then again see syncopation as a unifying trope of the project and achievement of the movement, with the twist that our critical evaluation, like any other, is subjected to the perspectivist relativism which reveals the influence of the observer on the object; we might then never be able to go beyond the vision of a "syncopated Renaissance."

NOTES

1. Alain Locke, ed., *The New Negro: Voices of the Harlem Renaissance* (New York: Atheneum, [1925] 1992). Abbreviated as NN.

2. George Hutchinson, *The Harlem Renaissance in Black and White* (Cambridge, Mass.: Harvard University Press, 1995).

3. Hutchinson 101–102. According to the latter, all white intellectuals did not rec-

ognize in the same way the importance of the African-American contribution to the culture of the United States. "Authors such as Brooks, Randolph Bourne, Lewis Mumford, and even Waldo Frank repeatedly failed to appreciate the significance of African-American culture" (98). Still, some evolutions were noticeable: Bourne enthusiastically reviewed Ridgely Torrence's *Three Plays for a Negro Theatre* (1917), which to him was "reminiscent of Synge, represent[ing] the sort of direction that Bourne felt the United States should be exploiting" (Hutchinson 104). Waldo Frank's increasing closeness to black culture, under the influence of Toomer, led him to plan "a new edition [of *Our America*] including a section on black America" (108). While many of these artists and thinkers saw the African-American contribution as only one among many, in a "transnational America" (Bourne), some envisaged it as a model for other developments; others, such as Alfred Barnes, viewed it as the only successful example of truly American culture ("America's only great music—the spirituals" [NN 21]).

4. Jean Toomer, *Cane* (1923) (New York: Norton, 1988), 12.

5. W.E.B. DuBois, "Criteria of Negro Art" (1926), *The Norton Anthology of African-American Literature,* H.L. Gates and N. McKay, eds. (New York: Norton, 1997), 752–59.

6. Nathan Huggins, *Harlem Renaissance* (New York: Oxford University Press, 1971), 64.

7. Werner Sollors, *Beyond Ethnicity: Consent and Descent in American Culture* (New York: Oxford University Press, 1986), 193–94.

8. Alain Locke himself, looking back on the Harlem Renaissance from the vantage point of the fifties, seems to have deplored such recourse to counter-stereotypes and the oversimplification of African-American life they entailed. But he admitted his own use of such "defensive, promotive propaganda" as necessary at the time ("Frontiers of Culture," Leonard Harris, ed., *The Philosophy of Alain Locke: Harlem Renaissance and Beyond* [Philadelphia: Temple University Press, 1989], 193).

For a discussion of the tension in Locke's thought between philosophical pragmatism and racial idealism, see Jeffrey Stuart's introduction to Locke's *Race Contacts and Interracial Relations: Lectures on the Theory and Practice of Race* (Washington, D.C.: Howard University Press, 1992, xxv–xxvi) and the introduction to this volume.

9. This does not mean that cultural contacts did not exist between East and West Africa. Actually, black Africa can be seen as an inheritor of certain aspects of Egyptian and Mediterranean civilizations, which were mixed with local traditions. Jean Laude argues that these influences followed the path of the diffusion of metallurgy, from Libya or Nubia or both (*Les Arts de l'Afrique Noire* [Paris: Librairie Générale Française, 1966], 128). Because Frobenius had already discovered this filiation, the concept was available to Renaissance thinkers. Yet the double remoteness of these origins—Egyptian influences on West African civilization and African survivals in America—makes the process of identification somewhat arbitrary and therefore designates it as an ideological construct. This is especially visible in the fact that it was used in a nationalistic way, rather than as a means to assert the common heritage of all Atlantic civilizations, and to question European claims to cultural supremacy in a clearly inclusive manner. Once more, history and tales of origins have to be read backwards, with a view on their present use.

10. Huggins, *Harlem Renaissance,* 301. David Levering Lewis, *When Harlem Was in Vogue* (New York: Random House, 1979).

11. Hutchinson, 9. This author makes another crucial remark on the paradoxical convergence of integration and particularism, about Locke's 1924 essay "The Concept of Race as Applied to Social Culture": "Indeed, Locke makes a point later developed by George Devereux and Fredrik Barth: that ethnicization and assimilation often go on simultaneously. That is, a group with a weak sense of racial or ethnic identity becomes increasingly race-conscious as its contacts with another group increase. Contacts lead to heightened boundary construction and racial stress, even as acculturation goes on" (91).

12. The purpose of the essay by that title, by writer and anthropologist Zora Neale Hurston (1934), is to define characteristics of African-American folk expression; however, it can also be very usefully applied to a study of Hurston's own creative artistry and that of some of her contemporaries.

13. Melville Herskovits, *The Myth of the Negro Past* (1941) (Boston: Beacon Press, 1958), 221.

14. Guy-Claude Balmir, *Du chant au poème* (Paris: Payot, 1982), 27–36 and 49–68.

15. "Characteristics of Negro Expression," *Norton Anthology*, 1,021.

16. Henry Louis Gates, "Their Eyes Were Watching God: Hurston and the Speakerly Text," H.L. Gates and K.A. Appiah, eds. *Zora Neale Hurston: Critical Perspectives Past and Present* (New York: Amistad, 1993), 154–203.

17. For an earlier discussion of the trope of syncopation, in a wider context, see Paul Gilroy, *The Black Atlantic: Modernity and Double Consciousness* (Cambridge, Mass.: Harvard University Press, 1993), 202–203.

18. H.L. Gates, "The Blackness of Blackness: A Critique of the Sign and the Signifying Monkey," H.L. Gates, ed. *Black Literature and Literary Theory* (New York: Methuen, 1984), 286–91.

19. Robert Hughes, *The Shock of the New: Art and the Century of Change* (London: Thames and Hudson, 1993), 21.

3. Oh Africa! The Influence of African Art during the Harlem Renaissance

Amy H. Kirschke

Passion for African art seized the Harlem Renaissance artists of the 1920s and '30s; it was a passion that would eventually spread across the country. This interest in African art was fueled by the architect of the Harlem Renaissance, Alain Locke, who encouraged the visual artists of the movement, as well as its writers, to express Africanism in their art forms. Locke believed that a complete development of black art could not take place without some significant artistic re-expression of African life and the traditions associated with it; as well as black talent serving art, art must serve black life. Locke encouraged artists to include the emotion and drama of African art, to make the work passionate, to move those who experienced it. He believed African art was a tangible way to teach African-Americans, indeed all Americans, about the connection of black America to Africa and Africa's rich culture.

Locke knew that Africa was one of the great fountain sources of the arts of decoration and design, and he was concerned that there was little evidence of any direct connection of black Americans with their ancestral arts. He realized that the rude transplanting of slavery, as he termed it, had broken many of the ties of black America with Africa. But Locke felt that the sensitive artistic mind of the African-American artist, stimulated by a cultural pride and interest, would receive from African art a profound and galvanizing influence. The legacy was there, with prospects of a rich yield. The cubists had exploited the beauty of African art for two decades. In Locke's view, why shouldn't African-Americans take back what was rightly theirs?

In the past, African-American artists did not have the opportunity to explore a connection with Africa. Only with the historical changes of the early 20th century—the urbanization and political empowerment in the northern United States of what had previously been a rural, isolated, and impoverished population—did there come the development of a middle-class black community interested in supporting such a search for African roots. The prospects, as well as the market, for the creation of a new identity for African-Americans, supplanting the slave-imposed identity, was now present.

For the first time, during the Harlem Renaissance, several visual artists began to incorporate Africanisms into their work. This trend did not occur just in painting and sculpture, but in illustrations as well. Illustrators had the unique ability to bring Africa to a large and varied audience. Locke explained: "It [African art] may very well be taken as the basis for a characteristic school of expression in the plastic and pictorial arts, and give to us again a renewed mastery of them . . . and a lesson in simplicity and originality of expression. Surely this art, once known and appreciated, can scarcely have less influence upon the blood descendants than upon those who inherit by tradition only."[1]

Aaron Douglas was the critical figure in the incorporation of African art during the Harlem Renaissance. Within weeks of his arrival in Harlem in 1925, Douglas was recruited by the NAACP's W. E. B. DuBois, editor of *The Crisis,* and by the Urban League's *Opportunity* editor Charles S. Johnson to create illustrations to accompany their editorials on lynching, segregation, theatre, jazz, poems, stories, and political issues. Douglas, a Kansas City highschool teacher, had chosen to join the young artists of the Harlem Renaissance after viewing a copy of *Survey Graphic,* which had devoted a special issue to Harlem and had chosen Bavarian artist Winold Reiss[2] to create a cover for the magazine. Douglas was impressed by the dignity and forthright manner in which Reiss portrayed blacks.

Within this largely literary movement, Douglas was hired to create a visual message for a public that had grown dramatically with the increase of black migration to the North during World War I. DuBois had complained often in *The Crisis,* most notably in his "Criteria of Negro Art," of a lack of black patronage and a black audience. He knew black artists found that most support for their work came from whites, who were the main patrons of the Harlem Renaissance. He believed that blacks, as an audience, needed to support their own artists. It was DuBois's hope that Douglas could reach a new, emerging black public across the United States, starting with Harlem. This was a role that only an illustrator could carry out. *The Crisis* had a wide national readership, and any illustration Douglas made, which frequently appeared on its cover, would be seen in libraries, schools, and homes across the country. Douglas tried to reach this new black middle-class public with the language of African art as one of his most important tools. Prior to Douglas, other American artists such as Meta Vaux Warrick Fuller[3] had begun to include African art in their work, but they did not use it on a regular basis.

Douglas was unsure of his abilities as an artist when he first started illustrating for *The Crisis*. He said, "These first efforts, as I recall them, cannot by any stretch of the imagination be described as masterful ... but ... they seemed to have been so readily accepted at the time. As I remember now, they were gladly received with no questions asked. They seemed to have been in a miraculous way a heaven-sent answer to some deeply felt need for this kind of visual imagery. As a result, I became a kind of fair-haired boy and was treated in some ways like a prodigal son. I began to feel like the missing piece that all had been looking for to complete or round out the idea of the [Harlem] Renaissance."[4]

DuBois realized that an artist could help relay a message. Art, according to DuBois, should have a message; as he put it, "I do not care a damn for any art that is not used for propaganda. But I do care when propaganda is confined to one side while the other is stripped and silent."[5] Douglas sought to follow DuBois's injunction by creating a new, positive, African-influenced black image for his audience. Tired of the white man's depictions of blacks, Douglas believed his work could touch the black audience in a unique way. He wanted to change the way blacks were depicted in art and to bring the language of African art to Harlem and then across the United States. He explained in a 1925 letter to Alta Sawyer, his future wife, "We are possessed, you know, with the idea that it is necessary to be white to be beautiful. Nine times out of ten it is just the reverse. It takes lots of training or a tremendous effort to down the idea that thin lips and a straight nose is the apogee of beauty. But once free you can look back with a sigh of relief and wonder how anyone could be so deluded."[6]

Douglas learned about African art through his own readings and studies, by studying the art collections of friends (including Alain Locke), by viewing published photographs, and by examining works in such prominent collections as that of the Barnes Foundation. He also saw African art at various exhibition spaces in Harlem, including at the Countée Cullen Library on 135th Street in New York City.

One can see Douglas's growth and experimentation through his magazine illustrations, where he created some of his most forceful and interesting works and evolved his artistic language, a language immersed in African art in a way no other American artist had done to that point. His illustrations are clean and bold, often just a few simple figures illustrating a basic idea or just showing images of African-Americans.

In the November 1925 issue of *Opportunity*, Douglas contributed *I Couldn't Hear Nobody Pray* to accompany Arthur Fauset's article "The Negro's Cycle of Song—a Review." This illustration features a figure, mouth open, reaching up to the heavens toward a large head, a boldly depicted God, notably with black features, and shows a rainbow on the left and a cabin (symbolizing the simpler life) on the right. Three stylized figures crouch down and hold their heads at the bottom of the composition. This is in a modest style and resembles some Winold Reiss drawings in *Survey Graphic* as well as Douglas's works in *The Crisis*, all of which were affected by Egyptian art. This drawing is straightforward and folklike, with an African influence. Douglas's work, with his magazine illustrations representing some of his most dynamic early efforts, displays the African influences, the drama, and the emotion Locke encouraged Harlem Renaissance artists in all disciplines to employ.

The first Douglas illustration to be included in *The Crisis* was his *Invincible Music: The Spirit of Africa*, a drawing specifically made for the magazine, but not accompanied by any text relating to the work nor illustrating any articles. The drawing consists of one figure, presumably male, in silhouette, with his head raised in song to the sky, his right arm holding a mallet that he uses to beat a large drum. He is in a crouching position and is clad only with a simple wrap around his waist. His position, with his shoulders parallel to the picture plane rather than receding into space in correct perspective, as well as his hair and the entire profile or silhouette of his body resemble those of Egyptian art, in which Douglas had a great interest. Here, Egypt stands for all of Africa. Douglas was also trying to simplify the human form. Two shieldlike marquise shapes are implanted in the ground behind the figure; a jagged design on the shapes resembles African-inspired patterning. The shapes symbolize plant life, as do three smaller versions which look like leaves and are placed in front of the figure. The top of the drawing includes two large, jagged shapes that represent forms of energy—perhaps the sun or stars—and a stylized stream of smoke on the right. The bottom of the drawing includes flat papyrus plants (resembling tulips) which appear to be inspired by the art deco movement. This drawing is successful because it is very simple, with large expanses of solid black and a bright white background highlighted by grayish outlines and details. The silhouette format makes it particularly forceful.

Douglas's next illustration appeared in the May 1926 issue of *The Crisis*. DuBois published the *Poster of the Krigwa Players Little Negro Theatre of Harlem* not attached to any particular play, but rather as a type of advertisement for DuBois's theatre project. This illustration is much more heavily influenced by Egyptian and African imagery. It is again in solid black and white, very boldly executed, and resembling a woodblock print. The poster shows a single figure, sitting cross-legged with his or her face turned to the side in profile. The figure is very angular, a primarily rectilinear form, with exaggerated thick lips, the appearance of tribal makeup in geometric form, an afro hair style, and a large hoop earring dangling from the only visible ear. Stylized plants and flowers, resembling both African motifs and art deco patterning, surround the figure, and a palm tree flanks him on the left. The figure's left hand holds an African mask or ancestral head. Above the figure, the influence of Egypt is everywhere, with pyramids on the left, a sun form above, and a sphinx on the right. Wave patterns form the bottom one-third of the composition, perhaps representing the Nile. The obvious inspiration is one of Africa, and the viewer can see the connections immediately (this despite the fact that the picture may have little to do with actual African imagery). DuBois wanted Douglas to re-mind *The Crisis* audience of their African ancestry and to inspire in them an interest in their common heritage. Egypt, despite its tenuous link to sub-Saharan Africa, was the common vocabulary to achieve this goal. The discov-ery of Tutankhamen's tomb had, indeed, prompted a renewed interest in Afri-can art.

In his 1943 book *Modern Negro Art,* artist and art historian James Porter criticized Douglas's Africanizing style. Porter argued that Douglas's vision of Africa was fanciful and unpredictable, searching for an "equivalent in design for the imagined exotic character of Negro life." He also attacked Douglas's portrayal of eyes as "long slits of light," seemingly unmoved or unaware of a connection to the art of the Ivory Coast. He noted that Douglas rarely placed "the Negro in a normal and plausible domestic life," instead placing his figures "whether in Africa or America, in a tropical setting or atmosphere."[7] Porter did not grasp Douglas's intention to connect African-Americans with their rich African heritage, and his criticism deeply troubled the artist.

One of Douglas's more interesting covers for *The Crisis,* in September 1927, was titled *The Burden of Black Womanhood.* This composition includes the figure of a woman in a long, Egyptian-influenced garment, with a side view of hips and frontal body silhouette; the figure is holding up a round shape: "the world." She looks up, with face in profile, with the same slit eyes that resemble African masks of the Ivory Coast, a style frequently employed by Douglas. Below the figure is included a cityscape, which resembles art deco drawings of skyscrapers, with the billowing smoke of industry behind it. One simple cabin—representing her humble beginnings—is on the far right. On the left, we see three pyramids and a palm tree, perhaps indicating her origins. The outlines of papyrus blossoms, with a deco handling, are scattered in the com-position. The cove, showing a woman bearing the burdens of the world, ap-pealed directly to *The Crisis*'s female audience.

In addition to his magazine illustrations, Douglas also attempted to create his own, more radical publication. Late in the summer of 1926, a group of Harlem artists met one evening at Douglas's Edgecombe Avenue home. Among them were Langston Hughes, Zora Neale Hurston, Wallace Thurman, Richard Bruce Nugent, and Gwendolyn Bennett. The group talked about the need for a new, exciting vehicle to express the feelings of the young artists of Harlem, one that would go far beyond *The Crisis* or *Opportunity*. The group decided to put together *Fire!!*, "A Quarterly Devoted to the Younger Negro Artists," to lash back at what they perceived as limits on their artistic freedom. Only one issue of *Fire!!* ever appeared, yet it was important because it showed an effort on the part of the organizers to break from the confines of Harlem leadership, both black and white, and express themselves freely and without censorship to a younger, separatist-in-thinking and more militant black audience.

Douglas's work on *Fire!!*—which coincided with his regular work for *The Crisis* and *Opportunity*—reflected a generation gap within the Harlem community as the younger artists felt themselves stifled by DuBois's autocratic leadership and by the political objectives of other black leaders. Indeed, in *Fire!!*, the black artists expressed their passion for art alone, but an art influenced by the sense of a special racial gift for artistic talent. *Fire!!* included uplifting poetry, short stories, essays, a play, and editorials. Douglas served as chief artist. He penned their artistic statement and contributed incidental decorations, three contour drawings, and the cover. He explained the group's goals in 1926: "I am writing this to give you a more detailed account of our project and of ourselves. We are all under thirty. We have no get-rich-quick complexes. We espouse no new theories of racial advancement, socially, economically, or politically. We have no axes to grind. We are group-conscious. We are primarily and intensely devoted to art. We believe that the Negro is fundamentally, essentially different from their [*sic*] Nordic neighbors. We are proud of that difference. We believe these differences to be greater spiritual endowment, greater sensitivity, greater power for artistic expression and appreciation. We believe Negro art should be trained and developed rather than capitalized and exploited."

The artists in *Fire!!* also attacked one of the essential underpinnings of the Renaissance—its support from whites. Showing an impatience with the compromises of an earlier generation, the young artists of *Fire!!* criticized some of the most popular manifestations of the interest in black culture, particularly musicals, and suggested that whites lacked the ability to understand authentic black cultural expression. As Douglas said, "We believe finally that Negro art without Negro patronage is an impossibility. It is true that the extraordinary rise of Negro musicals and light drama is due largely to non-Negro patronage. But this rise has been an increase of volume rather than quality. In other words, the great demand by white America for Negro entertainment, both musical and dramatic, has out run or rather precluded any attempt or demand to widen and deepen his sense of artistic expression. Popular American taste lacks discrimination and refinement. If there is any one thing more than another that we ask of our friends it is that they remove their Nordic (white folks) spectacles before they criticize or even praise our work."[8] Douglas's arresting cover for *Fire!!* was a provocative interpretation of Africanism. In its geometric simplicity, it appeared almost abstract. The viewer has to look twice to see that the background is not merely a geometric pattern; the entire cover is actually a profile of an African-looking face. The left side indicates eyes, nose, lips, and chin by simple geometric voids. On closer look, one discovers the geometric shapes on the right are an ear and earring. Finally, a sphinx lines the base of the cover, making this one of Douglas's more original creations.

Douglas's involvement illustrating Locke's book *The New Negro* of 1925 was one of his important early commissions. His drawing, *Rebirth*, is a complex work, with stronger and more numerous African images present. The composition is packed with symbols, including suns, jagged lines, plant life, eyes, and idol heads. It does not relate to the story with which it is featured; rather, it is an incidental illustration. The figures contain exaggerated features typical of Douglas's early works. His work *Sahdji* accompanies Bruce Nugent's[9] short story of the same name. Sahdji was the wife of a chieftain. Nugent described her full lips and her beautiful dark, graceful body dancing to a funeral march, an image that is echoed by other mourning wives in the background. Douglas's drawing illuminates the writing; he features Sahdji, seemingly nude, in black profile, standing on a circle amidst jagged forms that by this time were widely used in sculpture and the decorative arts. Her face is as if painted—a rarity for Douglas—a large idol head presses behind her, and three widows dance in front of her. The composition is complex and angular. One notices first the geometrics before taking in any actual details of the drawing. The essence of primitivism and of Douglas's perception of tribal ritual, it is ideal for the Nugent story.

African-American artists like Douglas demonstrated an interest in primitivism—or the celebration of primitive life—and were aware of the white fascination with the supposed primitivism of blacks and their art. Douglas's relationship with primitivism was problematic because he had no desire to confirm white stereotypes of blacks. Nevertheless, as the manifest of *Fire!!* makes clear, he and other black artists did perceive certain fundamental racial differences, and some of these were reflected in their portrayal of a more primitive and authentic African life.

Paul Morand's *Black Magic,* published in 1929 by Viking Press, also featured Douglas's illustrations. The book was translated into English just a year after its original printing in France. Douglas provided eight of his most sophisticated drawings for the volume.

Among the most notable is his drawing that accompanies the chapter "Congo." Congo is a French dancer who is extremely popular in the nightclubs of Paris. Douglas illuminates this chapter by showing a group of people, presumably at a nightclub or cafe, dancing to their hearts' content. The figures in the foreground are shown in dark silhouette, faces in profile with heavily exaggerated features. Their faces are uplifted in song. The women have tight chignons and earrings, giving them an air of sophistication. Transparent concentric circles cross the composition; behind them dancers wildly and expressively move in a much more primitive fashion than the patrons in the foreground. These background dancers have long hair, patterned and flowing, and their arms move freely. One dancer seems to be performing a back flip across the room. Douglas has contrasted sophisticated French society with the primitive expressions so popular to the time.

The third section of the book, "Africa," begins with a chapter titled "Goodbye, New York!" which chronicles a cruise from New York to Africa. Douglas depicts Africa by showing the profiles of two individuals, each with the signature slanted eyes showing the influences of Egyptian and Ivory Coast or Bakuban art, looking up toward an idol. This idol is similar to idols which appear in several of his compositions depicting Africa. Douglas could have obtained information on such an idol from the collection at the Barnes Foundation, from general art books, or even from photographs in *The New Negro* featuring African art. (The idol actually resembles a Bamana figure in the Barnes collection.) In the background, two seated figures, apparently nudes, also look up at the idol, which is surrounded by light concentric circles as are the heads of the viewers in the front, which are shown in profile. Palm trees frame the top of the composition. The two front figures are contemporary, urban figures, indicated by the women's modern hair style and earrings; perhaps they are black visitors from New York in search of their heritage. The figures in the background seem to be natives to the area. The two cultures come together, with common roots, as they observe the idol in the center of the composition. Douglas seems to be contrasting peoples of different African origins; it is therefore Pan-African in nature.

DuBois had been the crucial figure in the Pan-African Congresses of 1919 and 1921. Pan-Africanism, or the concept of a broad, racially based African unity which brought together all parts of Africa and the African diaspora in the New World, flourished as an ideology in the Harlem of the 1920s. Although the Pan-African movement was often confused with Marcus Garvey's "Back to Africa" movement—a movement disdained by intellectuals such as DuBois—the celebration of a mythic African homeland and unity had a wide-ranging impact in Harlem. Pan-African thought, which hoped to unify all peoples of African descent whether in Africa or not, had strong appeal to artists like Douglas, who wanted to celebrate such racial solidarity.

The Great Depression is often seen as ending the Harlem Renaissance, but it provided the backdrop to what many have called Douglas's masterpiece; his Marxist-inspired Works Progress Administration (WPA) murals of 1934. Douglas had always been determined to awaken the black middle class of the 1920s to the important issues of the time. The Great Depression's impact on this middle class was far more severe than on its white counterpart and radical-ized both Douglas and his audience. Douglas's large murals chronicled the struggle of the black man and woman from Africa through slavery, emancipa-tion, and their role as workers in the machine age. Despite opposition from some WPA officials, who were concerned about the murals' political content, Douglas intended the murals to appeal directly to a public suffering from the harsh conditions of unemployment and poverty.

The first of the four panels, *The Negro in an African Setting*, in Douglas's own words "emphasizes the strongly rhythmic arts of music, dance, and sculp-ture, which have greatly influenced the modern world, perhaps more pro-foundly than any other phase of African life. The fetish, the drummer, the dancers, in the formal language of space and color, recreate the exhilaration, the ecstasy, the rhythmic pulsation of life in ancient Africa."[10] The headpieces on the central figure and several surrounding figures resemble that of the king of Upper Egypt, as can be seen on the palette of King Narmar, c. 3000 B.C. This work was, in most respects, the culmination of the most creative period of Douglas's artistic career.

Douglas was not the only illustrator during these years to develop the vo-cabulary of Africa. Numerous artists who followed Douglas, including Celeste Smith, tried to emulate him. Smith created *Excelsior* for *The Crisis* and devel-oped a weaker version of Douglas's style for her figure bathed in Orphist rays of light and perched on the continent of Africa. Roscoe Wright's 1928 cover for *The Crisis*, titled *Negro Womanhood*, echoed Douglas with Africa again rep-resented by Egypt. Raymond Jackson followed Locke's message to connect to Africa in his own style for his February 1930 cover for *The Crisis*. Joyce Carrington mixed the imagery of Africa—a pyramid and African jewelry—with a very 1920s-looking woman for her untitled September 1928 cover of *The Crisis*. And Charles Cullen gave us his version of "the creation" with his art deco African man, muscular and proud, included in the September 1927 issue of the Urban League's *Opportunity Magazine*.

These illustrators demonstrated great pride in their African heritage. Douglas, however, remains unique in his efforts, providing crucial links between the literary figures of the Harlem Renaissance, its emerging Afrocentrism, and the international orientation of its thinking within the African diaspora. He was the first black artist in the United States to create racial art and as an illustrator was able to reach a large readership through black magazines. He based his works on studies of the African heritage, works which he created during a time of limited artistic freedom for African-Americans. Douglas confronted the problem of trying to reach a public that was still difficult to define and locate, had limited patronage, and was a geographically isolated audience. Despite these challenges, Douglas successfully addressed issues of importance to a growing black middle class. Black leaders sought his work to illustrate their messages, and he received regular commissions until his departure from Harlem in 1937. As the first African-American artist—indeed American artist of any race—to regularly incorporate African imagery into his work, Douglas brought African art to Harlem in a new, accessible, immediate way; then, through his illustrations, he brought it to Americans, both black and white, across the country.

Although fascinated by Africa, Douglas did not travel there until long after his work in the Harlem Renaissance. Indeed, in interviews later in his life, he admitted that in this early stage of his career, he was not as familiar with the history or purpose of the African objects he included in his work. Douglas embraced an Africa that was both Egyptian and sub-Saharan, the birthplace of civilization and home of a form of primitivism, an Africa that could provide a spiritual home to its African-American descendants. For the awakening black community of Harlem, the largest black urban community in the world, Douglas made a conscious and deliberate effort to illustrate the connection between African heritage and African-American culture. This attempt to recapture something lost in the history of slavery and segregation was as much an emotional and spiritual venture as an intellectual one. Ultimately, Douglas's message of pride in African heritage went well beyond the white fascination with primitivism and was a message that would find a rebirth in the work of later artists and subsequent movements.

NOTES

1. Alain Locke, "The Art of the Ancestors," *Survey Graphic* 6 (March 1925): 673.

2. Winold Reiss (1887–1953)—German-born painter, known for his expertise in mural painting, served on the faculty of New York University and was interested in painting blacks, among other ethnic groups, in an honest, straightforward manner. He had a powerful influence on Douglas and other black artists.

3. Meta Vaux Warrick Fuller (1877–1968)—gifted sculptor and teacher, Fuller was born in Philadelphia and trained at the School of Industrial Art of the Pennsylvania Museum of Fine Arts. She also studied with Rodin in Paris. Fuller turned to genre scenes of African-American life for her subject matter and created the famed *The Awakening of Ethiopia* in 1914.

4. Douglas, speech, "Harlem Renaissance," Box 3, Folder 3, Aaron Douglas Papers, Fisk University, Nashville, Tennessee.

5. W.E.B. DuBois, "Criteria of Negro Art," speech delivered at the Chicago NAACP conference and reprinted in *The Crisis* 32 (October 1926): 290–297.

6. Douglas to Alta Sawyer, no date but most probably 1925, Box 1, Folder 1, Aaron Douglas Papers, Schomburg Center, New York Public Library (NYPL).

7. James Porter, *Modern Negro Art* (1943; reprint, New York: Arno Press, 1969), 114–115.

8. Handwritten letter by Aaron Douglas on *Fire!!* stationery, n.d., Box 1, Folder 9, Douglas Papers, Schomburg, NYPL.

9. Richard Bruce Nugent (1906–?)—an illustrator and writer of the Harlem Renaissance, Nugent wrote prose and provided illustrations to a variety of works during the 1920s. His homosexuality led some to consider him flamboyant.

10. Notes from Aaron Douglas, October 27, 1949, Schomburg, NYPL.

4. Florence B. Price's "Negro Symphony"

Rae Linda Brown

I

Florence Beatrice Smith Price was the most widely known African-American woman composer from the 1930s to her death in 1953. She achieved national recognition when her Symphony in E Minor was premiered by the Chicago Symphony Orchestra in 1933 under the direction of Frederick Stock. The concert marked the first performance by a major American orchestra of a large-scale work by an African-American woman composer.

Florence Smith was born in Little Rock, Arkansas, in 1887, during the waning years of Reconstruction. Known as the "Negro Paradise" for the opportunities it provided to blacks, Little Rock was the pride of the South. Florence and her family belonged to the small, but significant, black upper class. Her father, Dr. James H. Smith, became the city's first black dentist when he moved there in 1886. Florence Irene Gulliver Smith, Florence Beatrice's mother, was a businesswoman and a well-trained singer and pianist.

Florence Beatrice was an accomplished pianist and organist when she graduated from high school at the age of 14. One year later, she left the South for Boston, Massachusetts, where she enrolled at the New England Conservatory of Music in degree programs in piano pedagogy and organ performance. The conservatory, which had a long history of accepting black students, was considered the proper finishing school for families of the Smiths' social standing. She graduated from the conservatory in 1906 with an artist's diploma in organ and a teacher's diploma in piano.

Although she was a piano and organ major at the conservatory, Florence Beatrice began to explore further her interest in composing. She was fortunate to be accepted as a student in the private studio of George Whitefield Chadwick, the conservatory's director. Her interest in studying with Chadwick may have been twofold. First, as a student, she had much to gain from working with the eminent composer. Second, in Chadwick, Florence Beatrice found a sympathetic teacher who inspired her to explore the use of Negro folk materials in composition. Although Chadwick never acknowledged any real interest in African-American folk music, he was often cited by contemporary music critics as a pioneer in efforts to free American expression from the Germanic style. His compositions, some of which suggested Negro folk melodies and rhythms, may have been a model for her.

If she had any serious aspirations as a performer or as a composer, Florence Beatrice laid them aside after graduating from the conservatory. Returning home to Little Rock to teach was little questioned by her; a sense of mission and service was deeply embedded in her, in part from her father's example of active involvement in black social and political issues. Moreover, the ties of family and tradition were too strong.

Like many of Little Rock's black elite, she placed importance on literacy or advanced education. After receiving training at the best colleges in the North, many blacks returned to the South to teach the masses of black children whose access to public school education was limited, or to teach in one of the city's four black colleges. Between 1906 and 1912, Florence Beatrice taught music at several black colleges. She began her career at the Cotton Plant–Arkadelphia Academy in Cotton Plant, Arkansas, and at Shorter College in North Little Rock, both church-affiliated colleges for black students. In 1910, after three years at Shorter, she left to accept a prestigious position as head of the music department at Clark University in Atlanta.

Florence Beatrice returned to Little Rock in 1912 to marry Thomas Price, an already established attorney. They had three children, a son who died in infancy and two daughters. Price set up a private music studio at her home and abandoned her college teaching career. When time permitted, she took up composing again. Still not seeing herself as a serious composer, she concentrated her efforts on writing teaching pieces for piano and for violin with piano accompaniment. For a long time, Price tried to suppress her creative impulse, but it was still there, still needing to find expression. There had been a significant gap, almost twenty years, between writing the symphony at the conservatory and when she began composing again in the mid-1920s. Even in writing the children's pieces, she could no longer deny her passion for composing; it would soon become a way of life.

In 1927, Price and her family moved to Chicago to escape the oppressive legalized social proscriptions of the South. The "Jim Crow laws," which stripped blacks of their rights and relegated them to second-class citizenship, had long been instituted, and lynching was on the rise. Although these new laws forced her to abdicate her rights, no one could take away her self-esteem. The pride instilled in her as a black woman would be there for life.

It was in Chicago in the late 1920s that Price's artistic impulses were liberated. She discovered a city full of vitality and an environment that was conducive to her creative energy. She had many opportunities, both social and professional, to interact with other artists, among them visual artists, dancers, writers, and actors. These quite stimulating convocations harkened back to Price's childhood, in the Little Rock of old, which had been an intellectually and culturally rich one for her.

By the early 1930s, she had developed into a serious composer whose skills were no doubt strengthened and accelerated by the many opportunities she had to hear her music performed. She wrote some 300 compositions, in all genres, producing works for piano, organ, voice, chamber ensembles, orchestra, and chorus, and she arranged spirituals for voice and instrumental combinations. Her music was regularly performed by a professional coterie of friends and colleagues in Chicago as well as by some of the leading concert singers of the day, including Marian Anderson, Blanche Thebom, Roland Hayes, Abbie Mitchell, Harry Burleigh, and Leontyne Price. An accomplished pianist and organist, Price premiered many of her own piano and organ compositions. Her large-scale works were being performed, too, by major ensembles including the Chicago Symphony, the Michigan WPA Symphony Orchestra, the Chicago Woman's Symphony Orchestra, and numerous professional chamber ensembles.

Price was successful professionally for many reasons, not the least of which was the supportive network she established shortly after her arrival in Chicago. The importance of women's musical groups in the 1930s and 1940s figured prominently. She retained membership in two musical organizations led by white women—the Chicago Club of Women Organists and the Musicians Club of Women. These clubs supported women as they struggled to gain hard-earned recognition in professional fields, including that of composition.

There is little doubt that Price's light-skinned complexion was also a factor which permitted her entry and acceptance into professional circles where her darker-skinned sisters were implicitly not welcome. Within the groups most active in promoting her music, she was the first African-American composer to be represented through the Illinois Federation of Music Clubs and was the first black member of both the Chicago Club of Women Organists and the

Musicians Club of Women. The fact that Price was fair enough to pass for white in no way lessens the significance of her achievements, but it attests to the key role that skin color played for Americans in attaining career goals.

Issues of gender, class, and race were ever present for black women in the first half of the century, and the inherent conflicts that were prevalent for professional women were difficult to reconcile. For this reason, Price maintained an active involvement in the National Association of Negro Musicians (NANM). It was through NANM and the *Chicago Defender,* Chicago's black-owned newspaper which covered the activities of the black community locally and nationally, that Price's name was kept before the public for the twenty-five years she resided in Chicago.

II

Florence B. Price's Symphony in E Minor was written in 1931. In a letter to a friend she wrote, "I found it possible to snatch a few precious days in the month of January in which to write undisturbed. But, oh dear me, when shall I ever be so fortunate again as to break a foot!"[1] In 1932, the symphony won the Rodman Wanamaker Prize, a national competition which brought her music to the attention of Maestro Frederick Stock who conducted the Chicago Symphony Orchestra in the world premiere performance of the work on June 15, 1933, at the Auditorium Theater. This program, which was part of the World's Fair Century of Progress Exhibition, celebrated the "Negro in Music."

Her feat is significant for several reasons. First, implicit here is the recognition that during the early years of the 20th century, African-American composers focused primarily on smaller forms of composition—art songs, solo piano music, music for violin and piano, and choral works. While the inspiration, creativity, and technical mastery to write orchestral music was there, the practical conditions were not. There was little feasibility with regard to performance possibilities, and, assured that the music would not see a publisher, it was financially impractical.

Second, this was a time in American music history when performance of symphonic music by American composers, in general, was a novelty. During the twenty-five-year period from 1925 to 1950, as observed by John Mueller in the *American Symphony Orchestra,* foreign-born Americans and Europeans made up a significant portion of contributions to the performed orchestral repertoire. No women composers were represented, and only one African-American composer, William Grant Still, the most well-known African-American composer in the first half of the century, won recognition.[2]

Price also found it difficult to obtain performances of her orchestral works.

Early on in her career, she recognized the conflict between her role as a woman and her role as a composer, and she was well aware of the polemics surrounding the female composer. In Judith Tick's article "Passed Away is the Piano Girl" in *Women Making Music,* the author outlines those traits of women composers, drawn from Goethe's concept of womanhood, which were defined through sexual stereotypes. Femininity in music was purported to be delicate, sensitive, graceful, refined, and more lyrical; masculinity in music was defined as powerful, noble, and more intellectual. Songs and piano music constituted the core of a woman composer's oeuvre; symphonies, opera, and chamber music remained the exclusive domain of men.[3]

On the one hand, Price did not subscribe to the characterization of her music as in any way inherently feminine; on the other hand, she admitted being shy and less aggressive than necessary to pursue and sustain a high-powered career as a composer. For some time, she suppressed her desires to be a successful nationally known composer of orchestral music, content to care for her family and reap widespread local acclaim as a composer of piano music, songs, and piano teaching pieces. As she gained more confidence as a composer, she tried to secure performances of her music by major orchestras outside of the Midwest—but to no avail. For example, in July 1943, she wrote to Serge Koussevitzky, conductor of the Boston Symphony:

> My dear Dr. Koussevitzky,
> Unfortunately the work of a woman composer is preconceived by many to be light, frothy, lacking in depth, logic, and virility. Add to that the incident of race—I have Colored blood in my veins—and you will understand some of the difficulties that confront one in such a position. My own detestable but seemingly unconquerable shyness have [*sic*] not served me to gain for me widespread hearing. The few times I have been able to overcome this handicap in the past and to manage to get a score examined I have met with most gratifying results. . . . In keeping with one last promise to myself that I shall no long hang back, I am now being so bold as to address you. I ask no concessions because of race or sex, and am willing to abide by a decision based solely on the worth of my work. Will you be kind enough to examine a score of mine?[4]

Price wrote several such letters to Koussevitzky. The conductor acknowledged her letters to him but he never conducted any of her scores.

III

With the June 15, 1933, concert, the Chicago Symphony celebrated the "Negro in Music" as both performer and composer. The program began with John Powell's Overture "In Old Virginia," a work which embodies much of the essence of the American nationalist movement as understood by many white composers of the era. The concert included renowned African-American concert singer Roland Hayes who sang a Berlioz aria. He also sang the then popular aria "Onaway, Awake Beloved" from the Afro-British composer Samuel Coleridge-Taylor's *Hiawatha's Wedding Feast* and two spiritual arrangements, "Swing Low, Sweet Chariot" and "Bye and Bye." The orchestra also played Coleridge-Taylor's spirited "Bamboula," which embodies African folk themes. The program also featured young African-American pianist Margaret Bonds in John Alden Carpenter's jazz-based Concertino for Piano and Orchestra. But the highlight of the concert was the historic performance of Price's symphony.

What is the context in which to evaluate a concert that included the music of Powell, Coleridge-Taylor, Price, and Carpenter? This concert took place during the height of the nationalist movement in the United States, when composers began to look to America's folk music, including jazz, for their creative source of inspiration. For many American composers, the models were the American-influenced compositions of Antonín Dvořák which were written during his sojourn in the United States from 1892–95. Dvořák raised the consciousness of American composers by urging them to create a national music using "Negro melodies and Indian chants" as their basis. Dvořák's article "Music in America," in *Harper's Magazine* (February 15, 1895), in which the composer states his views, has been quoted often. He wrote:

> A while ago I suggested that inspiration for truly national music might be derived from the Negro melodies or Indian chants. I was led to take this view partly by the fact that the so-called plantation songs are indeed the most striking and appealing melodies that have yet been found on this side of the water, but largely by the observation that this seems to be recognized, though often unconsciously, by most Americans.
>
> It is a proper question to ask, what songs, then, belong to the American, and appeal more strongly to him than any others? What melody could stop him on the street if he were in a strange land and make the home feeling well up within him, no matter how hardened he might be or how wretchedly the tune were played? Their number, to be sure, seems to be limited. The most potent as well as the most beautiful among them, according to my estimation are certain of the so-called plantation melodies and slave songs, all of which are distinguished by unusual and subtle harmonies. . . .[5]

Although Dvořák later was to broaden his views about what constituted national music, he acknowledged his profound interest in black folk music sung to him by his African-American student Harry T. Burleigh.

Dvořák's Symphony No. 9, "From the New World," was path-breaking. The composer was able to capture the pathos of many black spirituals so vividly that many people believe that the soul-stirring, faux-spiritual melody of the largo movement (which became known as "Goin' Home" when text was added to it by his student William Arms Fisher) is authentic.

The spiritual inspiration for Price's symphony came from the music of the Afro-British composer Samuel Coleridge-Taylor, who visited this country three times between 1904 and 1910. Coleridge-Taylor was keenly interested in African-American folk music, an interest which resulted from two contacts he had with black Americans early in his career. In 1897 he met Paul Laurence Dunbar, who had come to England to read some of his poems. The two men gave a series of joint programs that included musical settings of seven Dunbar poems. In 1899 the composer heard the Fisk Jubilee Singers in concert, which inspired several works including the *24 Negro Melodies, Transcribed for Piano* (1905).

Coleridge-Taylor, a nationalist composer who looked to his native Britain and to his black heritage as sources of inspiration for his compositions, was the most important composer of African descent at the turn of the century. Although he died at the age of 37, his influence as a composer and conductor was widespread. During his visits to the United States, Coleridge-Taylor gained many friends and acquaintances, including some of the most distinguished musicians of the Harlem Renaissance. Among them were poet/songwriter James Weldon Johnson, composers J. Rosamond Johnson and Bob Cole, and concert violinist Clarence Cameron White. The esteem in which American and European composers and conductors held Samuel Coleridge-Taylor warranted a generous inclusion of his music on this special concert celebrating the accomplishments of musicians of African descent.

Thus, two internationally respected composers—not coincidentally, both European—validated for both black and white American composers the beauty of African-American folk music and led the way for its use in large-scale instrumental forms. For the first time, Americans could envision the artistic viability of black music in the concert hall. It contrasted sharply with the stereotype that most Americans came to know of black music through the stage in the form of minstrel shows. The inherent subtleties of the spiritual— in rhythmic, harmonic, and melodic design—offered myriad possibilities to those who first arranged them in instrumental forms. The music of Coleridge-Taylor and Dvořák's epoch-making "New World" symphony were testimony of the universal appeal of the songs of black people.

First- and second-generation African-American composers closely identified with African-American folk material, and they eagerly appropriated it in small- and large-scale musical forms. Indigenous dance and other folk music, both sacred and secular, provided the foundation for the music of most of the black composers born before 1900. These composers, almost all nationalists, consciously turned to the folk music of African-Americans as a basis for composition. Their mission was to prove to the world the inherent worth and musical richness of this material. While expressing themselves as individuals, these composers willingly tied themselves to their historical past through the use of folk music. In the 1930s, much of this music was considered conservative, but to these composers, cultural expression outweighed any alliance with modern techniques.

The first symphonies by African-Americans to be performed by major American orchestras—William Grant Still's *Afro-American Symphony* (1931), Florence B. Price's Symphony in E Minor (1933), and William Dawson's *Negro Folk Symphony* (1934)—fall within the context of American musical nationalism. Still's *Afro-American Symphony*, composed in 1930, was written as part of a symphonic trilogy based on a composite musical portrait of the African-American. When the work was completed, the composer added program notes and appended to each movement descriptive verses from poems by Paul Laurence Dunbar. The themes in Still's celebrated and often performed work are original, but the melodic contour and flavor are wholly African-American. The primary theme of the sonata-form first movement, for example, is a twelve-bar blues, and the secondary theme of that movement is in the style of a spiritual. The third movement, a syncopated dance, is notable for its inclusion of the tenor banjo, the first known use of this instrument in an orchestral work. Dawson's three-movement symphony differs from Still's work in that it is highly programmatic; the understanding of the symphony depends, in part, on recognizing the spirituals that form the basis of the work. Dawson scored his symphony for a romantic-era orchestra, but it includes two African percussion instruments: the clave and the adawura.

These compositions also represent the musical culmination of the Harlem Renaissance or New Negro movement that emerged in metropolitan cities throughout the country in the 1920s and continued to the early 1930s. Nationalism was the backdrop from which the New Negro adapted old artistic forms into self-consciously racial idioms. This race consciousness united black intellectuals with common attitudes, ideals, and a sense of purpose.

The Negro renaissance spawned a surge of literary, artistic, and musical creativity by African-American artists. The affirmation of the values of the black cultural heritage during this time had a decisive impact on Price, Still, and Dawson, who had as their primary goal the elevation of the Negro folk idiom—that is, spirituals, blues, and characteristic dance music—to symphonic form. This elevation could be accomplished through the fusion of elements from the neoromantic (tonal music of the early 20th century) nationalist

Example 4.1: Symphony in E minor, movement 1, mm. 7-10

movement in the United States with elements from their own African-American cultural heritage. The spirit of African-American folk music provides the contextual foundation for Price's symphony and other compositions of hers written during this time period.

Originally subtitled the "Negro Symphony," Price's work assimilates characteristic African-American folk idioms into classical structures. The programmatic title was abandoned, however, perhaps for fear that it would have limited the perception of the symphony's scope.

The first movement, in E minor, is structured in sonata form. That is, two contrasting themes are presented, developed, and recapitulated. The principal theme—a bold, angular theme, played by solo oboe and clarinet—is built on a pentatonic scale, the most frequently used scale in African-American folksongs (Example 4.1: mm. 7–10). The simple harmonization of the theme—i, iv, v, i—grows out of the suggested harmony of the theme itself. The lyrical secondary theme, in G major, is played by a solo French horn accompanied by strings (Example 4.2: mm. 71–78). The treatment of the theme is markedly

Example 4.2: Symphony in E minor, movement 1, mm. 71-78

Dvořákian in its flavor and even resembles the melodic contour and orchestration of its counterpart in Dvořák's "New World" symphony.

The second movement, marked "largo," is a hymn that is first played by a brass choir (Example 4.3: mm. 1–5). This unusual instrumentation may have been inspired by Price's interest in the organ, an instrument which can produce warm and rich colorful sounds. Dvořák's second movement, from which unfolds the famous largo melody, is also framed by instrumentation that omits the strings. Both Dvořák's and Price's movements are in a tripartite form and include melodies based on pentatonic scales. Interestingly, the hymn in Price's movement is accompanied by African drums.

Always committed to African-American musical principles, Price turned directly to her roots for the third movement, titled "Juba dance" (Example 4.4: mm. 1–6). This movement is based on the sprightly, syncopated rhythms of the antebellum folk dance, pattin' juba. The lower strings maintain the "um-pah" rhythmic accompaniment, while the upper strings provide the syncopated melody. The figures that form the basis of the dance are African-derived figures that entered the juba dance by way of black banjo and fiddle music with

Example 4.3: Symphony in E minor, movement 2, mm 1-5

LARGO MAESTOSO

its percussive accompaniment of hand-clapping and foot-tapping. Referring to her Symphony No. 3, which also uses the juba as the basis of a movement, Price wrote:

> In all of my works which have been done in the sonata form with Negroid idiom, I have incorporated a juba as one of the several movements because it seems to me to be no more impossible to conceive of Negroid music devoid of the spiritualistic theme on the one hand than strongly syncopated rhythms of the juba [dance] on the other.[6]

The last movement of the symphony, marked "finale," is the most straight-forward (Example 4.5: mm. 1–7). A presto movement in E minor, its melodic and harmonic content is based on a four-measure triplet figure which ascends and descends around an E-natural minor scale. The general form of the fourth movement loosely resembles a rondo.

In writing about the Still, Price, and Dawson symphonies of the early 1930s in *The Negro and His Music* (1936), Alain Locke noted:

> But with the successful presentation of symphonies based on folk themes from each of these young composers [Still and Dawson] in the last year, the hope for symphonic music in Negro idiom has risen notably. In 1935, ten years after his enthusiastic championing of the serious possibilities of jazz,

Example 4.4: Symphony in E minor, movement 3, mm. 1-6

Example 4.5: Symphony in E minor, movement 4, mm. 1-7

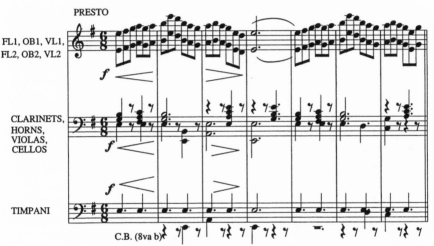

[conductor] Leopold Stokowski was able to present with his great Philadelphia Orchestra William Dawson's *Negro Folk Symphony;* certainly one of America's major contributions thus far to symphonic literature.[7]

For Locke, the symphonies of Still and Dawson, based on recognizable folk themes and idioms, no doubt seemed the proper model for works by black composers.

The absence of overt identifiable ethnic characteristics in Price's Symphony in E Minor—such as quotations of black folk themes or the use of a blues progression—caused Locke to criticize her symphony in the essay cited above. He treated the discussion of her symphony as though it had no racial references at all, asserting

> In straight classical idiom and form, Mrs. Price's work vindicates the Negro composer's right, at choice, to go up Parnassus by the broad high road of classicism rather than the narrower, more hazardous but often more rewarding path of racialism. At the pinnacle, the paths converge and the attainment becomes, in the last analysis, neither racial nor national, but universal music.[8]

Before examining Locke's criticism of Price's work, one must be clear about those particular characteristics of African-American music that distinguish it from other types of music. Call-and-response organizational procedures, dominance of a percussive approach to music, and off-beat phrasing of melodic accents have been documented as typical musical characteristics in African-American music. A predilection for a percussive polyrhythmic manner of playing and the inclusion of environmental factors, such as hand-clapping and foot-patting, as integral parts of the music event are also common characteristics.

Locke's approach to black music was based on the degree to which certain black musical characteristics were present in a given composition. While this approach is valuable, it limits the scope of the black music tradition. If one examines Price's symphony from the qualitative perspective, rather than from Locke's quantitative approach, it becomes evident that Price's music is reflective of her cultural heritage; by no means does she exclude racial elements. Price's symphony does not, however, depend on the quotation of folksongs for its ethnicity. Composer R. Nathaniel Dett explained, "As it is quite possible to describe the traits, habits, and customs of a people without using the vernacular, so it is similarly possible to musically portray racial peculiarities without the use of national tunes or folk-songs."[9]

In Price's symphony, cultural characteristics are borne out in the pentatonic themes, call-and-response procedures, syncopated rhythms of the juba dance, a preponderance of altered tones, and timbral differentiation in the second movement where the brass choir and woodwind ensemble are juxtaposed with large and small African drums. These traits in themselves may not be exclusive to black music, but in combination they are fundamental to the African-American music tradition. Price's approach to composition derives essentially from African-American musics, and the predominance of these core characteristics is the best evidence for this.

Locke's criticism of Price's symphony must also be examined from another perspective. Despite the appearance of equal participation of women in the Harlem Renaissance, in music, literature, the plastic and visual arts, patterns of exclusion were notable. Although Locke's role in the Harlem Renaissance was controversial, his ideas gave definitive shape to the New Negro movement. Locke, however, was not always generous in his critiques of works by women. His contempt for women in the classroom and disparagement of their intellect, which were carried over into his evaluations of their work, are well documented. Although Price had a supportive professional environment in Chicago, which included both men and women, one must wonder if Locke's widely read, perhaps deliberate misrepresentation of her symphony impressed her. Price never defended herself, however, against Locke's criticisms, preferring instead to let the music speak for itself.

An impartial examination of Price's symphony reveals that she does not abandon her African-American heritage. Rather, the symphony inherently incorporates many aspects of the black music tradition within a Euro-American medium—orchestral music. In a more subtle way than either Still's *Afro-American Symphony* or Dawson's *Negro Folk Symphony,* Price's compositional approach does make manifest the African-American heritage in music. Following the first performance of the symphony, Edward Moore of the *Chicago Tribune* wrote

> Mrs. Price displayed high talent both in what she did and what she omitted, each one of which is a test for a composer. She has based her work on racial folk song idioms, choosing some first rate melodies and harmonizing them fully and yet with the essential simplicity that they demand.

Racial pride was quintessential to the Harlem Renaissance and the black nationalist movement in music. It was this attitude of black pride and consciousness that permeated much of Price's music of the 1930s, and the Harlem Renaissance and the New Negro movement were the background against which she developed as a formidable composer.

Implicitly and explicitly, Price's racial heritage figured prominently in her music. Informed by her training at the New England Conservatory of Music in Boston and through her experiences growing up in the South during Reconstruction and the bitter years of Jim Crow, Price's music bears witness to the confirmation of her racial identity as an African-American. She wrote music that fuses Euro-American structures with elements from her own American cultural heritage to create an art music that, while utilizing European forms, would affirm its integrity as an African-American mode of expression.

NOTES

1. Quoted in notecard #14 of Florence Price Robinson (Price's daughter). Price Materials, University of Arkansas, Fayetteville, Arkansas.

2. John H. Mueller, *The American Symphony Orchestra: A Social History of Musical Taste* (Bloomington: Indiana University Press, 1951), 276–78.

3. Judith Tick, "Passed Away Is the Piano Girl," in *Women Making Music: The Western Art Tradition, 1150–1950,* Jane Bowers and Judith Tick, eds. (Urbana: University of Illinois Press, 1986), 336–37.

4. Florence Beatrice Smith Price to Serge Koussevitzky, July 5, 1943. Library of Congress, Music Division.

5. Antonín Dvořák, "Music in America," *Harper's Magazine* (February 15, 1895), 432.

6. Florence Price, Letter to Frederick L. Schwass, Allen Park, Michigan, October 22, 1940. Held in the Price Materials, University of Arkansas, Fayetteville, Arkansas.

7. Alain Locke, *The Negro and His Music* (New York: Arno Press and the *New York Times,* [1936] Reprint 1969), 114.

8. Alain Locke, *The Negro and His Music* (New York: Arno Press and the *New York Times,* [1936] Reprint 1969), 114.

9. R. Nathaniel Dett, "Introduction," *In the Bottoms: Characteristic Suite for the Piano* (Chicago: Clayton F. Summy, [1913] 1973), 33.

5. Ethel Waters: The Voice of an Era

Randall Cherry

Ethel Waters may be seen as one of the defining black talents of the Jazz Age. It was she who turned countless songs—ranging from "There'll Be Some Changes Made," "Sweet Georgia Brown," and "West End Blues" to "Am I Blue?" and "Stormy Weather"—into standards as she ensured her reign over Harlem nightclubs from the mid-1920s to the mid-1930s. Why, then, has she been all but forgotten?

In the words of theater and music critic Ashton Stevens, she was no less than "the greatest artist of her race and of her generation."[1] And, according to Carl Van Vechten, the white chronicler of the Harlem Renaissance, Waters's vocal style and stage persona made her one of the two authentic geniuses of the Negro movement, the poet Langston Hughes being the other one.

Hughes, for his part, exhorted the readers of his autobiography, *The Big Sea*, to "put down the 1920s for that grand comedienne of song, Ethel Waters, singing 'Charlie's elected now! And he's in right for sure'"—a line from Waters's brassy, blues-inflected "Go Back Where You Stayed Last Night." What no doubt impressed Hughes about this song was Waters's ability to put blues, jazz, and Tin Pan Alley sensibilities in masterful equipoise. Notable, too, were her irrepressible humor and inimitable half-talked, half-sung delivery—all of which was built on selectively borrowing from her contemporaries, refining and extending what she borrowed, to forge her own polished and modern style.

By tracing those most experimental years of Ethel Waters's musical career, I intend first to examine her hybrid style, viewing it as a reconciliation between two musical traditions: one black, one white. Then I shall examine how this amalgamation of musical influences has impacted her musical legacy. Essentially, I shall argue that she forged a sound that was part blues, part jazz, and part "white" popular music and that, ultimately, could not be categorized, to the dismay of specialty-conscious music critics and, consequently, to the detriment of Waters's own musical reputation.

*   *   *

Born in 1896 in a poor section of Chester, Pennsylvania, near Philadelphia, Waters first sang as a teenager under the name "Sweet Mama Stringbean" (because of her lanky physique). She traveled to black music theaters and tent shows, singing minstrel, ragtime, and coon tunes as well as vaudeville songs. While touring on the black circuit, she traveled throughout the South, Midwest, and Eastern Seaboard, singing saucy novelty numbers such as "I'm Gonna Shake that Tree Until the Nuts Come Down" and "Come Right in and Stay Awhile." She was, however, essentially a blues singer, having been the first professional female artist to sing W. C. Handy's classic "St. Louis Blues"—a seminal song that helped define the classic or vaudeville blues genre.

Until the turn of the century, blues had been a simple and functional voice-centered music, having been spawned by the work song. The emergence of vaudeville blues singers such as Bessie Smith and Waters, who followed the example of the "Mother of the Blues," Gertrude "Ma" Rainey, brought a more refined blues sound that could be sold as entertainment to blacks. The classic blues singers' sound was closer to the vaudeville tradition than to the original, more folksy blues. Although these female singers were preceded by traditional or down-home singers, who were primarily male, it was these females who would make the first blues recordings starting in 1920—on the heels of the first blues recording hit, Mamie Smith's vaudevillian "Crazy Blues," which was cut that year. Shortly thereafter, vaudeville blues would give impetus to the concept of the race record: that is, commercial recordings aimed exclusively toward blacks.

While Waters's potential as a race recording artist was spotted almost immediately—indeed, she was the fourth female blues artist to record—she was not content to just sing and cut records. Furthermore, she earned only about $100 per session, and, like her contemporaries who almost never received royalties, she tended to view recording as a promotional vehicle to draw crowds to her live performances. In any event, her appeal, as William Gardner Smith noted, lay in her stage appearances: "Perhaps [the secret of her success] was her warmth, her visible humanity. Audiences felt drawn to her, caught up by her, held by the personality which came through words and dance" (Smith 293).

It was as if her voice were merely the auditory aspect of a multifaceted professional performance. She relied on her trademark shimmy dance, monologues, attire (notably, a slinky radium dress that glowed in the dark), gestures, and every subtlety at her command to move or inspire her audience. Usually, the crowd would give immediate feedback, responding with rowdy applause or by calling out to her directly in mid-song.[2] In short, Waters's brand of vaudeville blues was built around an entirely theatrical approach.

A crucial ingredient of Waters's participatory performance lay in the force of her personality and her comic flair. As blues singer Edith Johnson recalled, "Years ago at that time blues singers on the stage were real new around here and each week at the Booker Washington they would feature some blues singer like Ida Cox or Clara Smith or Bessie Smith, Ma Rainey, Blind Lemon Jefferson and . . . my, Ethel Waters. . . . I always thought she was one of the better singers that we had. . . . If you don't have no personality with your singing, your singing is enjoyed but you are soon forgotten."[3]

Waters moved to New York in approximately 1919, eventually making her base Edmond's Cellar, a Harlem honky-tonk at 132nd Street and Fifth Avenue. She remained for several years, occasionally interrupting her regular shows there to tour in black musical revues, which included "Hello, 1919!" (in which she worked in burnt cork as a "Jane Crow" character) and "Oh, Joy!" in which she received her first top billing. In March 1921, she cut her first recording, "The New York Glide/At the New Jump Steady Ball," on the Cardinal record label. Her next recording, "Oh Daddy/Down Home Blues," was issued on Black Swan, the first black-owned and -operated recording company, which was founded by W. C. Handy's ex-music-publishing partner, Harry Pace.[4]

"Oh Daddy" and "Down Home Blues" are particularly interesting for showing how Waters excelled in putting over certain elements borrowed from white vaudeville and black vernacular and how she could turn them off and on at will. For example, Gary Giddens described "Oh Daddy" as a "vivacious minstrel-like interpretation of the blues, complete with a spoken chorus à la Jolson."[5] The recording seems to have been aimed, first and foremost, at a black bourgeois segment of the race market, based mainly in the North, which preferred a smoother mainstream sound. Were it not for the song's few hints of a real blues feeling, "Oh Daddy" could easily be confused with a song by many a popular singer of the day. Even these blues touches are perceived only fleetingly, as when Waters sings in the lower registers or when she lets loose her full, rounded moans of "O-o-o-h" in "Oh, Daddy."

To get a real understanding of Waters's prowess as a blues singer, we must look at the song "Down Home Blues" on the recording's flip side or consider later releases such as "Dyin' with the Blues," "Georgia Blues," "Handy Man," and "West End Blues." These numbers seem more clearly aimed at black fans of a grittier form of the blues. For example, although Waters relies essentially on her trademark clear elocution and immaculate phrasing as in the pop tune "Oh Daddy," on "Down Home Blues" she uses the slightest of inflections— her sense of rhythm, her occasional swoop into a lower register, her attack on the word "down home" transforming it into "down-h-o-o-o-me," or transforming "Lord" to "Lawd"—to deliver a beautiful, soulful blues. Although it may be argued that "Down Home Blues" is still a vaudeville blues in the vein of Mamie Smith's "Crazy Blues," the fact remains that each song was closer to a genuine blues than was most of what was available on recordings at the time.

On the momentum of the huge sales of "Oh Daddy/Down Home Blues" (118,000 copies were sold at a time when a 100,000-seller was considered a major hit[6]), Waters embarked on a tour of the black circuit with Black Swan's house band, the Black Swan Troubadours, which was under the direction of the then unknown Fletcher Henderson.

In the ensuing years, Waters gained renown as she toured on the black circuit and continued to perform mainly at Edmond's Cellar. The turning point in her career came in the summer of 1925 when she replaced the legendary black musical comedy star Florence Mills at the Plantation Club in New York. Waters then toured extensively in vaudeville shows, drawing accolades as the greatest comedienne of her day in Broadway after-theater clubs. She gained international fame that same year with the release of the show's hit song, "Dinah." In 1927, she made her Broadway debut in *Africana* at Daly's 63rd Street Theatre. Her triumph in that show led to headliner billing later that same year at The Palace, the mecca of vaudeville. In 1929, Waters made her film debut in *On With the Show*, the first talkie shot entirely in color, in which she introduced "Am I Blue?"

In the mid-1930s, Waters would concentrate on work in nightclubs and cabarets (introducing her signature song "Stormy Weather" at the Cotton Club with Duke Ellington's orchestra in 1933). Shortly thereafter, she emerged as a Broadway stage star. While performing in the musical comedy *As Thousands Cheer* (1933), she became the first black female star to appear in an all-white Broadway production and introduced the songs "Heat Wave" and "Supper Time."

In 1935, Waters performed in *At Home Abroad.* After scoring these Broadway triumphs, she concentrated on establishing herself as a serious actress, delivering a highly acclaimed performance as Hagar in *Mamba's Daughters* (1939). In the 1940s and 1950s, she embarked on a successful film career, appearing in *Cabin in the Sky* (1943) (having starred earlier in the successful stage version) and *Pinky* (1949) (for which she received an Academy Award nomination as Best Supporting Actress). She reached the pinnacle of her acting career, however, in her role as Berenice Sadie Brown in *The Member of the Wedding*

Figure 5.1. Ethel Waters in feathered stage costume, ca. 1928. Photo courtesy Yale Collection of American Literature, Beinecke Rare Book and Manuscript Library.

(1952). In the 1950s, she starred in the television series *Beulah*. In the 1960s, while in semi-retirement, Waters sang in Billy Graham's evangelical crusades. By the time of her death in 1977, her enormous success as a stage and film actress had all but overshadowed her years as an innovative and highly influential blues, jazz, and popular singer.

Combining "white" theatrical art with a singing style rooted in the blues tradition, Waters forged a new, fluid, part-blues, part-white vaudeville style that would have an enormous impact on a variety of singers, ranging from white vocalists Sophie Tucker and Mildred Bailey to black jazz legends Ella Fitzgerald, Billie Holiday, and Sarah Vaughan. At minimum, each owes Waters an enormous debt for making it acceptable to blend blues and jazz with the idiom of white popular song. Waters's influence is vaguely audible in, but no less crucial to, the music of most of the major exponents of jazz in the 1930s. It is worth noting, for example, that the young Ella Fitzgerald prized Waters's first hit, "Oh Daddy/Down Home Blues," as one of her favorite early race record purchases; while Fitzgerald would go on to make her name in the 1930s as a jazz improviser, Waters had already helped paved the way with her 1930 scat version of "I Got Rhythm" and her swinging renditions of "There'll Be Some Changes Made" and "Heebie Jeebies." Although the extent of Waters's influence is less readily apparent—considering Billie Holiday's inimitable vocal approach—it can be detected, nevertheless, in Holiday's "Fine and Mellow," in which she uses the lyric "love is like a faucet" from Waters's self-penned "Ethel Sings 'Em." More importantly, Waters's influence on Holiday comes across undeniably in Holiday's first recording, "Your Mother's Son-in-Law," on which Holiday—singing in a bizarre, quite uncharacteristically high register—sounds eerily like Waters!

Perhaps the best indication of how profoundly Waters influenced the most seminal of the great popular music and jazz vocalists was offered by Mahalia Jackson: she proclaimed unequivocally that Billie Holiday, Ella Fitzgerald, and Sarah Vaughan came directly from Ethel Waters.[7] Sad but true, Waters may have been partly responsible for her own obscurity in the annals of blues and jazz history. As Donald Clarke stressed, she was reputed to have a difficult personality and keen rivalry with singers she viewed as a threat—often the very people who could have helped her reputation: "The irony is that Ethel Waters has been described as 'a rotten bitch, she hated and resented everybody,' which is why although Lady, Lena, Dinah, Sarah, and all of them got something from Ethel, they never gave her any credit" (Clarke 1994, 396).

These statements notwithstanding, the question of Waters's musical legacy remains far from settled, and credit still has not been given where it is due. Although Waters once could be safely considered to rank with Bessie Smith and Louis Armstrong as one of the major jazz vocalists of the 1920s—and perhaps even surpassing them in terms of influence on the wider boundaries of American popular song—she is now the least remembered of the three. This is despite the fact that some of her jazz innovations were waxed before Smith and Armstrong recorded, making Waters the first important jazz vocalist on recordings.[8]

As Donald Clarke put it, "Ethel Waters was well known as a vocalist before Louis Armstrong. The English writer Charles Fox has described her as the first important jazz singer, because of the way she told a story. . . . [She] could transform a pop song more subtly than Bessie Smith, displaying a remarkably expressive voice, a keen understanding of how language should come across in song, and a rhythmic flexibility very rare at the time" (Clarke 1995, 133).

That view is shared by Chris Ellis, who draws attention to Waters's 1921 rendition of "There'll Be Some Changes Made." For Ellis, this tune contained flourishes which stand as hallmarks of the rise of jazz vocalizing, notably the way that "Ethel swings!"—like none of her contemporaries:

> Even Bessie Smith, herself, sounds stolid and heavy by comparison, at least until, in the twilight of her recording career, she produced such wonderful pieces of jazz singing as "Moan You Moaners" and "He's Got Me Going." This is no criticism of Bessie, rightly named Empress of the Blues. To clarify a little, no-one would claim that Bessie swings in the way that one would apply that word to Ella Fitzgerald, and indeed Ella's kind of singing is regarded as dating from the 1930s. Yet this is precisely the way Ethel was singing as far back as 1921. . . . Certainly, Ethel Waters was the first to take pop songs and turn them into jazz. (Chris Ellis, "Ethel Waters—Jazz Singer," in *Storyville* 22 [May 1969], 128–30)

More skillfully than almost any of her contemporaries, Waters embraced light popular songs written for black vaudeville and gave them a distinctive jazz or blues flavor. Notably, it was she who made a hit out of Maceo Pinkard's "Sweet Georgia Brown" and "Sugar," now standards in the jazz repertoire. In "Brown," she sings the first verse brightly, in a straightforward way befitting most Tin Pan Alley or Broadway musical tunes—that is, as if she's simply reciting a story to music. All the while, she intersperses half-spoken lines that allow her to inject her own personality: "You know I don't lie—not much!" Then, after a jazz instrumental break, we sense a slight change in her singing style and attitude. She seems to add more edge by playing up the song's suggestive possibilities, either by throwing out knowing lines with a slightly rougher touch ("Who's that mister? 'taint his Sister") or by stretching the vowels in "Sweeeeet Georgia Brown" or "She cooools them down," to ensure that no double entendre is lost on the listener. By simply adding little nuances, it seems she's improvising around the text, even if the lyrics have not changed substantially. By so doing, she also avoids singing the song as if by rote, as was the practice among most vaudeville singers of the day.

Waters similarly transformed "Dinah." When first presented with this popular song by its white songwriters, for inclusion in the *Plantation Revue*, she refused to perform it in what she perceived to be the "corny" fashion they suggested. Instead, she insisted on doing it her way. At certain moments she sings in a high, bright pitch, "Is there anyone finer in the state of Carolina?" but in the second verse she gives a slower, more drawn-out and bluesy rendition. At one point, she goes so far as to dispense entirely with a somewhat forced if not altogether "hokey" rhyme between "China" and "liner" to avoid distracting from the song's now more restrained mood. She sings simply, "If Dinah ever wandered to China, I would hop an ocean. . . . Just to be with Dinah Lee."

While "Dinah" in particular shows that Waters is clearly far removed from the more authentic blues material that Bessie Smith was recording at the time, this recording is an instance in which Waters demarcates her area of vocal authority: a popular song that draws equally on elements of blues, jazz, and vaudeville and that demands, if it is to be put over properly, a marked suppleness of voice, a deep understanding of language, a mastery of enunciation, and a sense for characterization.

By 1925, Waters's and Smith's paths had begun to diverge substantially. In fact, it would be more relevant to compare Waters's "Dinah"[9] with Josephine Baker's 1925 recording. Baker's version is much more comedic and jazzy: Clearly the music's more animated pace and Baker's exaggerated pronunciation of "Carolin-er" (Carolina), "Din-er" (Dinah) and "Chi-ner" (China) and "fin-er" and her Jolson-like take on the last line ("Just to be with Dinah Lee, Ta-da-da-tee. . . .") are in keeping with the dictates of a certain vaudeville tradition. In Baker's hands, the song is intended to be a crowd-pleaser. Waters's approach is much more subtle and demanding: Her goal is not to "wow" the audience but to slowly build a rapport with the listener who is prepared to carefully lend an ear. Waters's forte is in revealing the subtlety of language, of painting a mood.

Ethel Waters's place on the music scene of the mid-1920s to the mid-1930s must be seen within the framework of an era in which black and white elements of vocal music were no longer divided into distinct factions but had come to impact each other, giving rise to a great, modern black-and-white art form. In 1925 and 1926 alone, a number of significant developments took place which signaled that popular music had embarked upon an entirely new era: New electronic recording techniques made it possible to capture the voice more effectively, giving rise to the soft voices of crooners or torch singers while effectively rendering obsolete the exaggerated declamatory style and accenting inherited from vaudeville or imposed by earlier, cruder recording methods. These years also saw the first vocal jazz recordings by Louis Armstrong and marked Bing Crosby's recording debut. Popular music by black female artists reached its zenith when, at two extremes of the spectrum, Bessie Smith made the definitive recording of the blues classic, "The St. Louis Blues," and Waters set Harlem ablaze with "Shake That Thing" and was rocketed to international fame with the release of "Dinah."

Thanks to the success of "Dinah" and the widespread critical acclaim that would come shortly thereafter, upon her first appearance in a white theater, in Chicago, Waters would gain an enormous white following, which would continue to grow when she moved to Columbia Records' Race label. (Columbia's race catalogue proudly proclaimed, "Everybody, old and young, white folks as well as Race, flock to the theater where Miss Waters is appearing. And everybody buys, plays, and loves her records."[10])

In some important ways, Waters's assimilation into the mainstream pointed up certain preconceived ideas or outright prejudices, among blacks and whites alike, concerning the black voice. Most importantly, in the first years of black blues recordings, most companies preferred Waters's "white sound" to the earthier, gospel sound of other black singers. As Chris Albertson pointed out, even Black Swan rejected Bessie Smith's very black sound when she auditioned for the company in 1921, although it would record the "whiter sound of Ethel Waters extensively."[11]

Obviously, Black Swan's failure to recognize one of the greatest black voices of the century was inexcusable. But this slight should not be used as a license to diminish Waters's importance; nor is it fair to couch the rivalry between Waters and Smith in such starkly black and white terms. Waters's sound was ideally suited to the black audience's shift in sensibilities. There was no better proof of this than Waters's first Black Swan release, which outsold Mamie Smith and every other black artist of the time (see Thygesen, Berresford, and Shor 9).

Even after 1923, when Bessie Smith made her first recordings and her record sales began to challenge and often outstrip Waters's, *both* artists had a huge interracial appeal. Still, each singer in her own way represented a certain embodiment of blackness, as if to stand as touchstones of the black voice: While no one would argue that Smith laid claim to the crown as the greatest blues singer, Waters's sound was a better personification of an emerging urban—and racially mixed—sensibility. Thus, Angela Davis's claim that Smith "was not only the greater artist, she also more accurately represented the sociohistorical patterns of black people's lives" (A. Davis 1998, 153) must be put in proper perspective. Only if we accept that there was no one black consciousness, no single sociohistorical pattern, can we begin to understand the importance that Waters's singing held in the minds of her black audiences. As William Gardner Smith put it,

> Ethel Waters, said *Life* magazine, made her songs sound "like humanity in general." . . . The nation—and particularly the Negro people—saw only blackness in the future. Disorganized, demoralized, they longed for a voice to utter feelings and, at the same time, still some of their doubts. . . . There were people in those days who could not think of certain songs without thinking immediately of Ethel Waters. There were Negro women who could not wash the clothes or clean the homes of their white employers without thinking of the woman who sang "St. Louis Blues." . . . She personified the needs of the people of her day. (Smith 294)

The appeal of Waters's singing style also signaled, in Ann Douglas's words, that black audiences were increasingly "hungry for sophistication." This sophistication took various forms. Waters often played up black vernacular against white vaudeville. In "You Can't Do What My Last Man Did" (1925), for example, she switches from a direct, down-and-dirty talk with her "daddy" to a flawless upper-crust British accent—pronouncing "can't" as "C-A-H-N-T," adding "Come get me, Ethel Barrymore." What is more, from the earliest years of her career, Waters offered her black audiences a then new singing style that was smoother and more sophisticated than what they had been used to. In her autobiography, *His Eye is on the Sparrow*, Waters recalls the response she generated while performing at the Lincoln Theatre in Baltimore and other Negro vaudeville houses during her first season: "I would sing 'St. Louis Blues,' but very softly. It was the first time that kind of Negro audience ever let my kind of low singing get by. And you could have heard a pin drop in that rough, rowdy audience out front" (Waters 1992, 74).

While most female blues singers in those shows relied on throaty growls and moans as their trademarks, Waters developed a coyly suggestive approach, singing in soft tones. Her blues were, in her words, "sweeter" and "smoother" than those of great "shouters" like Rainey and Smith.[12] The black audiences' clearest acceptance of her new blues style occurred during a show that probably took place at the Decatur in Atlanta around 1918, where Waters was playing on the same bill as Smith. Although Smith had forbidden anyone else on the bill to sing the blues, she was forced to relent when the crowd began howling, "Blues! Blues! Come on, Stringbean, we want your blues!" Waters recalls in her autobiography, "People everywhere loved [Bessie's] shouting with all their hearts and were loyal to her. But they wanted me, too. . . ." (91–92).

By the time she debuted in Harlem's Edmond's Cellar, certain observers such as Harlem Renaissance writers James Weldon Johnson and Rudolph Fisher were quick to note how her sound, personality, and demeanor set her apart from her blues-singing black sisters. Waters showcased her flair for witty burlesque-like patter, in which she addressed the men in the audience directly. After titillating them with her sexy blues numbers and suggestive come-ons, she would set them straight with hard-hitting comeuppances, or she would mix blues with monologues in songs like "You Can't Do What My Last Man Did." Above all, she excelled in exuding a raw sexiness, but without a trace of vulgarity. Along these lines, James Weldon Johnson wrote

> Miss Waters gets her audiences . . . through an innate poise that she possesses; through the quiet and subtlety of her personality. . . . Her bodily movements, when she makes them, are almost languorous. . . . Her singing corresponds to her bodily movements; she never overexerts her voice; she always creates a sense of reserved power that compels the listener. . . . Miss Waters also has a disarming quality which enables her to sing some songs that many singers would not be able to get away with on stage. Those who have heard her sing "Shake That Thing" will understand.[13]

Rudolph Fisher echoed Johnson's assessment, but gave more insight into what set Waters apart from her blues-singing contemporaries. Waters stood out mainly because "She knew her importance. . . . Other girls wore themselves ragged trying to rise above the inattentive din of conversation, and soon, literally, yelled themselves hoarse; eventually they lost whatever music there was in their voices and acquired that familiar throaty roughness which is so frequent among blues singers, and which, though characteristically African, is as a matter of fact nothing but a chronic laryngitis. . . . Ethel took it easy," Fisher stressed. "She would stride with great leisure and self-assurance to the center of the floor, stand there with a half-contemptuous nonchalance, and wait. All would become silent at once. Then she'd begin her song, genuine blues, which, for all their humorous lines, emanated tragedy and heartbreak. . . ."[14]

Yet, for all her sophistication, Waters also reveals on some recordings that, if need be, she could occasionally evoke the kind of nitty-grittiness usually associated with her rivals. For example, there is Waters's Bessie-Smith-like performance of "Black Spatch Blues" (1924) and her hilarious self-penned send-up of both Bessie and Clara Smith in "Maybe Not at All" (1924).

By the mid- to late 1920s, Waters had basically become associated with outright popular tunes like the lilting "Am I Blue?" and "Lonesome Swallow," even as she continued to record popular blues. True to the way she had crafted her blues, her popular songs gave only the slightest hint of a gruff or raspy vocalizing. Yet, even in her bawdier, blues-inflected songs like "Shake That

Thing," "Take Your Black Bottom Outside," and "Organ Grinder," the emphasis is placed not on "roughness," but on putting over sexy double entendres while drawing on her ability to exude a kind of sophisticated mock innocence.

Waters's exploitation of these various qualities allows us to view her songs as the incarnation of what Ann Douglas described as the mongrel style of the 1920s.[15] It was a style that reflected the black-inspired Jazz Age, whose music was tempered by certain social realities: By then, paid blues performers seldom played only pure blues—this was true for musicians as well as for singers (many began to embrace popular songs as the blues craze began to fade around the mid-1920s).[16] Furthermore, blues and jazz were part of the mixed entertainment format of minstrelsy and vaudeville shows; although major black songwriters such as Clarence Williams and W. C. Handy believed the blues to be an exclusively Negro idiom,[17] they wrote and produced dozens of "whitened" blues songs and recordings in an attempt to appeal to both races.[18] The same could be said of the work of black songwriter Andy Razaf, who would write Broadway and vaudeville tunes, including love songs, such as "Sposin'" for white crooners of the day such as Rudy Vallée. Razaf would also collaborate with Ethel Waters and Eubie Black to create such memorable blues-inflected popular songs as "My Handy Man" and its follow-up, "My Handy Man Ain't Handy No More," which Waters would make famous in black musical revues at the close of the 1920s.

Despite these outward signs of musical borrowing, imitation, and blending between the races, the fact remained that racial prejudice, stereotypes, and segregation were inescapable realities of Waters's musical world. While Waters's voice and stage persona have been criticized for being "white-influenced" or "too sophisticated," her right to flaunt these qualities had been hard-won. As Waters's friend and contemporary blues-singing sister, Alberta Hunter, pointed out, black women performing on the black circuit in the North had to wear bandannas, Aunt Jemima dresses, and gingham aprons, and men wore overalls. "They wouldn't accept us Negro girls in smart clothes. . . . That's why Ethel Waters made up like a washerwoman for so many years" (Taylor and Cook 68). For as much as her first records may have been "white-sounding," it was virtually unimaginable for Waters to hope, at least at the outset of her career, that her records would reach anyone but blacks (however, even "Oh Daddy/Down Home Blues" seems to have sold among whites) or that her shows would be seen except primarily by blacks.

It was possible, however, for some black artists to circumvent the racial divisions to a certain extent: Bessie Smith, most notably, was the highest-paid black entertainer by the mid-1920s, even though she had deigned not to appear in the segregated clubs of Harlem, and performed only in a limited number of Harlem revues. Waters was well aware that to reach the pinnacle of success in New York—namely on Broadway or in white clubs—she would have to pay an enormous price. To be accepted by white audiences, blacks were expected to play the buffoon or minstrel. As Waters wrote, "I never exaggerated or overemphasized my characterizations. . . . [M]ost of the Negroes who were getting by on the white time were like caricatures of human beings and portrayed like buffoons who were lazy and shiftless beyond belief" (Waters 1992, 174). Moreover, blacks most certainly were not supposed to act "uppity," sophisticated, or white.

Rather than acquiesce to this institutional racism, which risked compromising her sophisticated performance style and vocal approach, Waters staunchly refused before 1924 to appear on "white time"—even to the point of refusing lucrative offers to appear in the Broadway hit *Chu Chin Chow*. As an explanation, or perhaps a consolation, she suggested that by working exclusively in Harlem's "Black Belt"—while earning a paltry $35 per week at Edmond's Cellar—she could remain close to the most talented black artists who were creating the music that she admired. Most of them, she added, were unknown artists who were ignored by the general public merely because they were black.

While the pressures of a segregated society clearly motivated Waters's decision to retreat to her self-imposed exile, there were other factors that were tied to Waters's temperament: "I was scared to work for white people. I didn't know very much about them, and what I knew I didn't like. The very idea of appearing on Broadway in a cast of 'ofays' made me cringe in my boots" (148). Many of her reservations stemmed from her belief that whites, and especially whites in the North, simply were not prepared for her style, could not understand her music, and were simply off the beat most of the time.

Waters would take refuge in the Black Belt until 1924 when she appeared before a white audience at a theater in Chicago. Her producer and musical partner, Earl Dancer, had urged her to perform there. He advised her to incorporate even more popular songs into her routine, instead of singing verse after verse of the blues, to build a larger white following. Dancer felt Waters did not belong to the "colored line."

In black theaters, Dancer argued, the public would tire of her in a few years, whereas whites would love her for the rest of her life—if she would only let them hear her sing. She reluctantly agreed to the engagement in Chicago, where she did a variation on the show she had done at the New York Plantation Club. To Waters's surprise, she garnered some of the greatest accolades of her entire career. Proclaiming her "the greatest black artist" or the "Ebony Nora

Bayes,"[19] critics seemed as much impressed by Waters's virtuosity as by her elegance, dignity, and class.

Waters's self-imposed exile had been, in Ann Douglas's words, a kind of "enabling act." Away from the glances and reprobation of white critics, Waters was able to develop "her special art, one more musically and theatrically varied and sophisticated, more black-and-white, than white audiences of the day would have permitted" (Douglas 338).

Not everyone was pleased with every aspect of Waters's repertoire. Some black critics viewed her "low-down" blues (which she performed primarily for black audiences) as a bad reflection on the race; still others saw them as the very essence of what was to be most treasured about black music.

Two important mouthpieces of the Harlem Renaissance, the *Messenger* and the *Chicago Defender,* described the blues as a kind of black folk music: read that as an unrefined source from which a "true" art could be built. The *Messenger* ran an editorial in which the blues were deemed "loud, boisterous, cheap, tawdry, [and] unmusical" compared to opera, which represented culture and art.[20]

Appalled as well by the blues singers' garish taste and flamboyant behavior,[21] a reporter for the *Chicago Defender* inveighed against them, claiming that "Stage folks have a wonderful opportunity to help elevate the race—help lift the stamp of inferiority. . . . Vulgarity is the yoke or burden. See it for what it is—a hindrance to our standards of respectability and success."[22] To make the point about the baseness of blues singers, the article included a reprint of a review in the *Detroit News* lambasting Waters's "unspeakably rotten blues" in her *Miss Calico* revue (Harrison 30).

Another *Defender* article presented a telling comment on how songs like Waters's "Shake That Thing" (a danceable take on "Jelly Roll Blues") were scandalizing the morals of black female listeners in particular: "Our sedate young ladies . . . , tearing down every conceivable hope of redemption, abandon themselves into such frenzied, epileptic contortions as 'snake-hip,' 'black-bottom' and the vulgar *dance de ventre,* known as the 'rhumba', to the tune of 'Shake That Thing'" (Spencer 130). Yet, for certain Harlem Renaissance intellectuals, the risqué "Shake That Thing" seemed to capture the sexual mood of the 1920s and stood as something of an anthem for the essence of Harlem club life. It was certainly Waters's great success with the song that inspired Carl Van Vechten to give it pride of place in his controversial paean to Harlem, *Nigger Heaven*—until a threatened lawsuit for copyright infringement forced him to withdraw it and replace it with lyrics specially written by Langston Hughes. The song's cause was taken up again, to good effect, in Claude McKay's 1929 novel, *Banjo.* As the hero's favorite song, which he constantly sings in his head, nostalgically calling up images of Harlem, the lyrics recur throughout the text—like a Proustian *petite musique:* "Old folks are doing it, and young folks too, / The young folks learning the old how to do, / Shake That thing, Shake That thing, / I'm getting sick and tired, but . . . Oh, SHAKE THAT THING!" (C. McKay 1957, 280).

Criticism aside, it was clear that the blues had a large black following that revered this music as an art form and its stars as great race artists.

* * *

Despite the profound impact that Waters's songs had on prominent writers and multitudes of singers and everyday listeners in the 1920s and early 1930s, the irony today is that Waters is rarely given the attention she merits in histories of the Harlem Renaissance—not to mention the history of blues and jazz. That can be explained, in part, by the fact that the Renaissance movement was led, essentially, by writers and artists—who often had little real interaction with singers. In Waters's case, she would eventually strike up friendships with at least two major exponents of the Harlem Renaissance: Van Vechten, whom she befriended in 1927, and Zora Neale Hurston, although their friendship dates from after the years of the Renaissance.

Despite the writers' clear admiration for the singer, their friendships required considerable effort. Van Vechten may have attributed this difficulty to Waters's distrust of whites and her unfamiliarity with the rarefied circle in which he lived. In Hurston's case, the problem had as much to do with the writer's being "too timid to go backstage and haunt [Waters]" as it did with Waters's feeling that Hurston "belonged to another world and had no need of her" (Hurston 1942, 244).

The friendships that eventually developed between Waters and these writers were surely an exception to one of the Harlem Renaissance's unwritten rules: other than Hughes and Sterling Brown, most writers ignored blues and jazz singers. It is perhaps not surprising then, that, aside from the short treatments by Fisher and Johnson and small biographies such as the one found in Nancy Cunard's *Negro* (actually postdating the Harlem Renaissance by a few years), Waters and others have all but escaped mention in Harlem Renaissance histories.

Today, Waters is often overlooked by scholars because they see her as more of a song stylist (a "diseuse" or "torch singer") than a genuine jazz or blues singer. True, she was a stylist, but she was also a blues and jazz singer. She did it all, which is clear when one listens to her best blues numbers or "Ethel Sings 'Em" or her most famous songs like "Dinah," "Memories of You," and "Stormy

Weather." Indeed, they all seem related to the art of diction or the creation of dramatic characterizations or emotional scenes, in a way intimately related to what Waters saw as the secret behind her vocal approach to the blues: "I . . . believe that critics were intrigued by my characterizations, which I drew from real life. . . . I'd hear a couple in another flat arguing for instance. I'd sing out their woes to the tune of my blues music. . . ." (Waters 1992, 130).

Waters grudgingly added popular songs like "Dear Old Pal of Mine," "My Buddy," "The Rose of Washington Square," and "A Pretty Girl Is Like a Melody" to her repertoire; but when she saw that blues and jazz touches gave them a new life, she was pleased: "To my surprise," she noted, "I found out that I could characterize and act out these songs just as I did my blues" (129). Next, she began to write her own blues verses while interpolating them into torch songs like "My Man" (a song which, she had been told, whites had confused with real blues) (178).

While blues critics would cry treason, Waters could be seen, in fact, as helping lay the ground for the future jazz vocalists, who would, essentially, draw upon the white popular song idiom.[23] It is therefore perplexing that, although she is a crucial figure in the making of the story of modern blues and jazz, Waters is all but excluded from serious consideration as either a blues singer in the true, folk tradition or as a true jazz singer.

In short, while Waters's reputation benefits from a sort of *succès d'estime* among blues and jazz singers (Joe Williams, Mel Tormé, Joe Turner, and Viola Wells, for example, considered her one of their earliest and most important singing influences; Bessie Smith even admitted, shortly before her death in 1937, that Waters was her favorite singer), she is rarely recognized for the paramount importance of her artistic accomplishment. As Crowther and Pinfold suggested, "Of the three major jazz voices of the 1920s, Bessie Smith, Louis Armstrong and Ethel Waters, it is the latter who must be regarded as the most influential of all. Bessie Smith is the yardstick by which all blues singers are measured; Louis Armstrong, the innovator, created a style and was the original jazz voice; but Ethel Waters transcended most positively and effectively the wider boundaries of American popular song. . . . Exactly because she sang the blues but was not solely a blues singer and because she sang jazz but was not solely a jazz singer—but sang so well in each element—her influence was preponderant. So effective was she that blues and jazz singers, vaudeville artists [and] . . . popular entertainers alike came under her spell." "It was Waters," they continued, "even more so than Armstrong, who demonstrated jazz style was adaptable to popular song" (Crowther and Pinfold 52).

Perhaps it is precisely because her influence was so widespread that she has not gotten the attention she deserves. Waters's all-encompassing output—

Figure 5.2. Ethel Waters in the 1930s. With Harlem as her base, she started as a blues singer in the 1920s and by the end of the next decade had forged a new and sophisticated black-and-white approach that influenced countless popular singers—not to mention some of the greatest jazz singers of the day. Archive Photos.

covering blues, jazz, and popular song—almost seems to defy a truly fair and comprehensive treatment. This in part explains why, more often than not, Waters is relegated to a gray area between the earlier generation of "classic" blues singers and more recent jazz vocalists such as Holiday, Vaughan, and Fitzgerald.

The truth of the matter is, Waters's reputation suffers from a problem which plagued her throughout her career. Even in the 1920s, her status was far from clear. Critics and even musicians with whom she had worked extensively disagreed on what singing style best captured her approach. Although she considered herself to be a blues singer, first and foremost, her long-time Black Swan collaborator, Garvin Bushell, said, "She didn't sing real blues, though: she was a jazz singer. She syncopated. Her style was influenced by the horns she'd heard and by church singing. She literally sang with a smile, which made her voice sound wide and broad" (Bushell 32). Van Vechten, for his part, saw her as a blues singer (Angela Davis scoffs at this notion, dismissing his as "unschooled white ears"[24]); but he was careful to point out that her dramatic blues-singing approach made her into something quite different from a genuine blues singer like Bessie Smith. In his ground-breaking series of articles on blues singers, which ran in *Vanity Fair* in 1926—boldly presenting the blues as a real art form—Van Vechten wrote, "Of the artists who have communicated the Blues to more sophisticated Negro and white public, I think Ethel Waters is the best. In fact, to my mind, as an artist, Miss Waters is superior to any other woman stage singer of her race. . . . Her methods are precisely opposed to those of the crude coon shouter, to those of the authentic Blues singer, and yet, not for once, does she lose the veridical Negro atmosphere. Her voice and her gestures are essentially Negro."[25]

If Waters's status as a singer is ambiguous, the crux of the problem springs from the fact that, as far as her musical output is concerned, she was more than the sum of her parts. The quality of her songs, while stunningly impressive on the whole, is uneven or undermined by her tendency to be too "talky" or to abruptly change the tone in mid-song, as she wavers between a ballad and a blues, such as in "Smile!" and "Home." While we may admire this tendency as part of Waters's bold sense of experimentation, it is sometimes distracting and, to say the least, makes it all the more difficult to categorize her once and for all. Even with some of her more effective numbers—such as her send-ups of Armstrong ("I Can't Give You Anything But Love"), Smith ("Maybe Not At All"), or Mae West ("Come Up and See Me Sometime")—the impact of her parodies as great vocal achievements is perhaps somewhat blunted by the sense that they owe more to vaudeville than to the subtle nuances of language now associated with jazz.

Still, on the basis of the variety of her repertoire and her virtuosity, it is hard not to be impressed by Waters's musical output. For all the variation in the quality of her music, she is hard to match in the breadth of her emotional range and her subtlety of language. She could be sultry and sexy, if not outright raunchy in popular blues like "Long, Lean Lanky Mama"; she could be stately in ballads like "I'm Coming Virginia"; and her voice could evoke a throbbing sentimentality in beautiful tunes like "Lonesome Swallow" and "When Your Lover Has Gone."

Although there have been notable studies on Waters—such as essays by Gary Giddens and Susannah McCorkle, both titled "The Mother of Us All," Allen Woll's *Black Musical Theatre,* and, more recently, Ann Douglas's *Terrible Honesty*—which have underscored Waters's importance to American blues, jazz, and popular music, far too many other studies have relegated her to nothing more than a historical anecdote or footnote. To cite only a few of the most flagrant examples, in the popular press and scholarly press alike—ranging from Angela Davis's recent survey of the most influential soul musicians ("Back to the Roots" in *Time* magazine of June 8, 1998) to Houston Baker, Jr.'s *Modernism and the Harlem Renaissance*—Waters is not mentioned at all. She is cited only in passing in Samuel A. Floyd, Jr.'s *Music and the Harlem Renaissance*— in a text whose title and subject matter would have led one to believe that Waters would have been given pride of place, insofar as she epitomized the sophisticated sound of black jazz vocalizing in Harlem nightclubs in the 1920s and 1930s.[26] Sandra Leib's *Ma Rainey: Mother of the Blues* and Angela Davis's *Blues Legacies and Black Feminism* are more typical examples of how Waters is treated by blues specialists: as a counter-example to be used to show off her rivals to better advantage. They simply dismiss her voice as "white-sounding" or not on par with that of Smith or Rainey, without considering Waters's contribution to the evolution of the blues. Waters would have been the first to admit that she was not the greatest singer, but she brought something else to the music: "Now critics have praised my voice, but I've never thought I was a good singer. That I was able to please that brass-knuckle crowd of regulars [at Edmond's Cellar] but began to draw the sporting men and downtown white people I credit to the fact that I had spunk and was also an enigma" (Waters 1992, 130). What could be heard in her new blues was her infusion of her own inimitable personality.

Leib's curious treatment of Waters deserves special attention. What matters in Leib's approach is that Waters serve as the prime example of the kind of decidedly popular blues singer whose sound stood in starkest contrast to the unmistakably black, folk voice of Leib's heroine. Implicit in texts such as Leib's is a controversy which bodes ill for the eventual reclamation of Ethel Waters's legacy. Waters's reputation is disparaged—for reasons which have less to do with music than with promoting a certain literary or political slant on "blackness" or "folk art."

In Leib's case, for example, the underlying implication is that Waters's voice, like Waters herself, somehow did not have the unmistakable stamp of "blackness" or "folksiness" that Smith's and Rainey's voices, personalities, and comportment incarnated. To make her point, Leib draws a comparison between Waters's "popular-sounding" "Oh Daddy" and Smith's and Rainey's more "down home" or "less sophisticated" renditions of the same song. But, insofar as even Waters's rendition was accepted by black audiences as a blues and was sold almost exclusively to a black record-buying public, it is perhaps fairer to say simply this: to the ears of their contemporary black listeners, the voices of Waters, Rainey, and Smith were simply variations on a black, folk voice. It is not enough to dismiss Waters from consideration as a black, folk blues singer simply because, by today's standards, one of her songs sounds blatantly whiter or more popular sounding than a rendition by her major rivals. From a sociohistorical perspective, the question of whether Waters was a true blues singer is less important than the fact that contemporary audiences, and no doubt even her greatest rivals, perceived her as such.

Moreover, from an ideological perspective, it is just as intellectually disingenuous to evaluate Waters's entire œuvre on the basis of one song à la Leib as it is to ignore what Waters's œuvre as a whole tells us—as contradictory as it all is. She sang the blues and jazz, and she was a popular singer. Her contributions in each genre were too significant to argue that she does not belong solidly in any one of these musical traditions.

Musical purity aside, we must recognize that Waters remained rooted in the blues feeling—albeit a decidedly popular blues feeling. Nevertheless, she wrote many of her blues herself,[27] and she sang them as she felt they should be righteously done. In that alone, she was true to the very spirit of the age, as defined by an anonymous jazz singer: "I wrote these blues, gonna sing 'em as I please."[28]

That motto is perhaps best summed up in the possibilities and playful options announced in "Ethel Sings 'Em" and "Maybe Not at All"—which may be seen as counterparts. In the former song, it is as if, by the sheer virtuosity of her performance, she leaves no doubt that she has lived up to the assertion in the title. She has *said* it. Indeed, she all but declares—with intoxicating exuberance and without any trace of egotism—that she is laying claim to her place as a singer who is contributing to, and helping to define, the contemporary elements that make up the blues-jazz idiom. But if "Ethel Sings 'Em" is essentially an act of affirmation, "Maybe Not at All" is nuanced by counter-statement. By first singing in her trademark "sweet" and "sophisticated" blues style, as we saw earlier, and then parodying and signifying on the earthier approaches of Clara and Bessie Smith, whom Waters mentions by name, she humorously pays homage to the tradition from which she sprang, even as she appears to be demarcating her own special place among the many available examples of blues stylization. The point is, Waters must be seen as extending blues styles—or, rather, playing them against each other—while suggesting that they might be transcended altogether. She had the right to sing the blues . . . or maybe not at all.

NOTES

1. Stevens, a celebrated, tough Chicago newspaper critic, quoted in Waters's *His Eye is on the Sparrow*, 181.

2. Daphne Duval Harrison, *Black Pearls* (New Brunswick: Rutgers University Press, 1990). Harrison gives an interesting overview of the female vaudeville or classic blues singer's classy image and stage persona.

3. From an interview with blues singer Edith Johnson (1903–1988), quoted in Jeff Todd Titon's *Early Downhome Blues* (Chapel Hill: University of North Carolina Press, 1994), 44.

4. For an overview of Black Swan's history and Harry H. Pace's account of the first time he heard Waters's "peculiar" voice, see "The Black Bourgeoisie" in *The Negro in New York,* Roi Ottley and William J. Weatherby, eds. (Dobbs Ferry, New York: Oceania Publications, 1967), 233. See also Helge Thygesen, Mark Berresford, and Russ Shor, *Black Swan: The Record Label of the Harlem Renaissance* (Nottingham, Great Britain: Vintage Jazz Mart Publications, 1996).

5. See Giddens, *Riding on a Blue Note,* 7. Various critics have noted the influence on contemporary blues and vaudeville singers of Al Jolson (1886–1950). Crowther and Pinfold point out his vocal inflections and syncopated phrasing influenced many younger and decidedly diverse singers, including Ethel Waters, Bing Crosby, and Connee Boswell. See Bruce Crowther and Mike Pinfold, *The Jazz Singers* (Poole, United Kingdom: Blanford Press, 1986), 26.

6. Helge Thygesen, Mark Berresford, and Russ Shor, *Black Swan: The Record Label of the Harlem Renaissance* (Nottingham, Great Britain: Vintage Jazz Mart Publications, 1996), 9.

7. From an interview in *Metronome,* December 1954.

8. Louis Armstrong's recordings featuring his singing would start in 1925–1926. For a general survey of the importance of Ethel Water, Bessie Smith, and Louis Armstrong to the evolution of popular music, see Henry Pleasants, *The Great American Popular Singers* (New York: Simon and Schuster, 1974).

9. Here, an interesting question arises: Would Bessie Smith have deigned to record such blatantly popular material as "Dinah?" Aside from the obvious rejoinder that the song would have been very different—and no doubt still a blues in the hands of

Smith—Giddens presents another partial response. Smith's increasing readiness to record popular songs, he contends, was certainly influenced by her rivalry with Waters's popular success. See note 16.

10. From a 1927 advertisement cited in the liner notes of the compact disc *Ethel Waters, 1926–1927*, Classics 688.

11. Chris Albertson, *Bessie: Empress of the Blues* (London: Abacus, 1975), 32.

12. Waters gives a succinct comment on her style as compared to that of her rivals: "For years [black audiences] had been used to Bessie Smith and Ma Rainey. They loved them and all the other shouters. I could always riff and jam and growl, but I never had that loud approach." Ethel Waters, with Charles Samuels, *His Eye is on the Sparrow* (New York: Da Capo, 1992), 74.

13. James Weldon Johnson, *Black Manhattan* (New York: Knopf, 1930; reprint, New York: Da Capo, 1991), 210.

14. Nathan Irvin Huggins, ed., *Voices from the Harlem Renaissance* (New York: Oxford University Press, 1995), 76–77.

15. Ironically, the term "mongrel" takes on another meaning in light of Waters's personal life. She was born out of wedlock when her mother was raped at the age of 13. She was always made conscious of this fact ("I knew I was a bastard and what that meant").

16. Giddens points out that Waters's mainstream recordings were a source of inspiration for black and white singers alike, especially white singers who had no inclination toward the blues, as well as for black singers more firmly rooted in the so-called authentic blues tradition: "It was almost certainly Waters's phenomenal success that encouraged Bessie to record as much pop material as she did. I suspect, too, that the popularity of Waters's 1928 'My Handy Man' fostered Smith's 1929 'Kitchen Man' session, as well as countless other double entendre blues records. (Andy Razaf was commissioned to write both of those songs, and Smith's rolled "r" in the "Kitchen Man" verse was as unusual for her as it was characteristic of Waters.)" Gary Giddens, *Riding on a Blue Note* (New York: Oxford University Press, 1981), 5–6.

17. According to Handy, "Blues is one of the oldest forms of music in the world. It is folk music of the purest type. It represents the full racial expression of the Negro, and its distinguishing characteristics are throwbacks to Africa." Handy quoted in Eileen Southern, ed., *Readings in Black American Music* (New York: Norton, 1983), 212–13. See W. C. Handy, *Father of the Blues: An Autobiography* (New York: Da Capo, 1991).

18. For Crowther and Pinfold, "technically, the blues is frequently (but not exclusively) a twelve-bar chord sequence in which the third and seventh notes are bent. . . . The blues can be a public celebration or condemnation. . . . It can be rural or urban, it can be art or it can be commercially exploitative. Indeed, it can be almost anything its practitioner wants it to be. . . . The blues is thus so diverse that isolating a point in time when it becomes identifiable is clearly impossible" (Crowther and Pinfold 27).

19. Nora Bayes had started in small-time vaudeville as a "coon shouter"; that is, she brought elements of minstrels and black ethnic music to a wider audience. By the twenties, she was the reigning queen of vaudeville, having popularized "Take Me Out to the Ball Game," "Over There," "I'll Be Seeing You in Apple Blossom Time," and "Shine on Harvest Moon." Waters would record "Harvest Moon" in 1931.

20. In Ted Vincent's *Keep Cool: The Black Activists Who Built the Jazz Age* (London: Pluto Press, 1995), we see that the black-white and lowbrow-highbrow music di-

chotomies were not as absolute as one might believe. A Black Swan advertisement in the *Chicago Defender* of June 2, 1923, read, "Only bonafide Racial Company making talking machine records. All stockholders are Colored, all artists are Colored, all employees are Colored. Only company using Racial Artists in recording high class song records. This company made the only Grand Opera Records ever made by Negroes. All others confine this end of their work to blues, rags, comedy numbers, etc." Vincent stresses that, in fact, Black Swan's advertising was not always based in truth. When it lost one of its concert artists, Revella Hughes, Black Swan simply recorded a white concert singer and put Revella Hughes's name on the record label.

21. Ma Rainey's trademark was her necklace made from a string of flashy coins; Bessie Smith wore a large plumed headdress. See Sandra Leib, *Mother of the Blues: A Study of Ma Rainey* (Boston: University of Massachusetts Press, 1981).

22. Quoted in Jon Michael Spencer, *Blues and Evil* (Knoxville: University of Tennessee Press, 1993), 131.

23. Admittedly, as Crowther and Pinfold point out, today's jazz singers are relying less on popular music and increasingly writing their own songs or writing lyrics to well-known jazz compositions—reversing the trend started by Armstrong and Waters (see Crowther and Pinfold 19). However, jazz diva Dianne Reeves's reliance on popular songs proves that there are notable singers who buck this trend.

24. See Angela Davis 153. Interestingly, the debate raised by Davis, Albertson, and others, regarding Waters's "white" sound and her great white following, still raged at Waters's death. In an obituary that ran in the September 10, 1977, edition of the black journal *New York Amsterdam News,* the writer noted that Waters was seen by many Harlemites as having gone "over to whitey." However that may be, there were undoubtedly many black readers—with sufficiently schooled ears—who nevertheless agreed with the piece's title, "World Mourns the Death of the Gre[a]test Blues Singer."

25. Essay reprinted in Bruce Kellner's *The Letters of Carl Van Vechten* (New Haven: Yale University Press, 1987), 163–66.

26. See Samuel A. Floyd, ed., *Black Music in the Harlem Renaissance* (Knoxville: University of Tennessee Press, 1993) and Houston A. Baker, Jr., *Modernism and the Harlem Renaissance* (Chicago: University of Chicago Press, 1987). Baker's choice to focus on Rainey as heroine of the Harlem Renaissance is worthy of comment. While Rainey's influence on the early black music scene was preponderant, and she was somewhat of a muse to certain black intellectuals such as Sterling Brown, the fact remains that Rainey's relationship with the Harlem scene was minimal. To be sure, she cut some important records in New York with Fletcher Henderson in December 1925 and played the Lincoln Theatre in New York in 1926. However, she was based in Chicago and never caught on in New York's Harlem—and certainly not to the extent that Smith and especially Waters did.

27. Waters wrote or co-wrote "Kind Lovin' Blues," "You'll Want Me Back," "Chinese Blues," "Maybe Not At All," "Ethel Sings 'Em," "Satisfyin' Papa," "Go Back Where You Stayed Last Night," "Stop Myself from Worrying Over You," "Tell 'Em About Me," and several gospel songs.

28. See Elisa Segrave's review of *Terrible Honesty,* from *The Observer,* January 28, 1996, in which these words (actually adapted from the original quote "Dis yere mah song, an I'll sing it howsoevah I pleases") are proposed as catching the spirit of the age.

SELECTED DISCOGRAPHY OF WORKS AVAILABLE ON COMPACT DISC

Ethel Waters

Ethel Waters: Her Best Recordings: 1921–1940, Classics 4013.

Although this collection provides a good introduction to Ethel Waters's career, it does not include some important songs, such as the touching "Lonesome Swallow" (1928) and one of the earliest scat songs, her rendition of "I Got Rhythm" (1930). Sadly missing, too, is her "Frankie and Johnny" (on the album *Push Out*), which is a good example of her mastery of the speech-song technique. This volume also shortchanges her impressive work in *Cabin in the Sky.* Although this collection includes the title song, recordings like "Happiness is a Thing Called Joe," "Taking a Chance on Love," and "Honey in the Honeycomb" certainly warranted inclusion.

Am I Blue? Ethel Waters, Living Era, AJ1 5290.

This is a British-made 1999 compilation of Waters's prime jazz and swing era recordings from 1925 through 1939.

Ethel Waters: Taking a Chance on Love, Definitive Records, DRCD 1114.

This compact disc, issued in 1999 by an Andorran label, includes 27 tracks of previously released recordings made for the Bluebird label from 1938 through 1946.

Ethel Waters: 1935–1940, Classics 755

Ethel Waters: 1931–1934, Classics 735

Ethel Waters: 1929–1931, Classics 721

Ethel Waters: 1926–1929, Classics 688

Ethel Waters: 1925–1926, Classics 672

Ethel Waters: 1923–1925, Classics 775

Ethel Waters: 1921–1923, Classics 688

Ethel Waters: Push Out, 1938–1939, Jazz Archives No. 1

Ethel Waters: Cabin in the Sky, Milan Jazz Classics 688

Cabin in the Sky (Motion Picture Soundtrack), Rhino Records, R2 72245

This is an excellent remastering and repackaging of an impressive soundtrack. Many of these songs appear in the previously mentioned "Classics" collection. However, the versions on this soundtrack are generally superior. The liner notes—which contain numerous interesting photos—are especially valuable for insight into the evolution of the play from stage to the movie screen. This compact disc is also notable for contributions by Duke Ellington and Louis Armstrong.

Ethel Waters: On Stage and Screen (1925–1940), Classics 688

Bessie Smith

Bessie Smith: The Collection, Columbia, 7464–44441

An Introduction to Bessie Smith: Her Best Recordings 1923–1933, Classics, 4030

Bessie Smith: 1923, Classics, 761

Bessie Smith: I'm Wild About that Thing, Object Enterprises, 0R0 102

It's hardly worth mentioning that alongside Smith's untopped "The St. Louis Blues" and "Gulf Coast Blues," many of her all-time classics—ranging from "Nobody Knows You When You're Down and Out" and "Alexander's Ragtime Band" to "Do

Your Duty"—are in fact popular songs. These collections prove that, in Smith's hands, everything became a blues.

Louis Armstrong & the Classic Blues Singers

Louis Armstrong, Volume 6, March–May 1925, Masters of Jazz, MJCD 55
   This includes Armstrong accompanying Eva Taylor, Clarence Williams's Blue Five, Trixie Smith, Clara Smith, Fletcher Henderson and His Orchestra, and Bessie Smith.
Louis Armstrong, Editions Atlas, Jazz & Blues collection, 1995
   This collection contains, most notably, "Tiger Rag" and "Black and Blue."

Ella Fitzgerald

Ella Fitzgerald, Cryin' Mood, Object Enterprise, 0R0077, 1989

Billie Holiday

Billie Holiday: The Quintessential, Vol. 1 (1933–1935), Vol. 2 (1936), Columbia, COL 450987 1 and COL 450987 2

Ma Rainey

Ma Rainey: The Mother of the Blues 1923–1928, Blues Collection (EPM), 159232, 1998.
   Granted, the recording quality is poor. But Rainey's vocal power is no less diminished. Listen to "See See Rider Blues," "Oh Papa Blues," and "Daddy Goodbye Blues."
Ma Rainey: The Paramounts Chronologically 1928, Volume Five, GHB Records, HCD-12005, 1994.
   This recording is interesting for "Daddy Goodbye Blues" and "Prove it on Me Blues." It has surprisingly apologetic liner notes, which portray Ma Rainey as a "second-tier" blues singer.

Sarah Vaughan

Sarah Sings Soulfully, EMI, CDP 7984452, 1965

Josephine Baker

Josephine Baker: Collection d'or, Super Music, SM00003, 1999
   This recording includes a rare cut of "Dinah" from *La Revue Nègre* of 1925.

Various Artists

Ida Cox: I Can't Quit My Man, Charly Records, AFS 1015, 1991
Al Jolson: One in a Million, Pilz Entertainment, 449338–2, 1993

Sippie Wallace, Storyville Records, STCD 8024, 1993

The Ultimate Encyclopedia of American Blues Classics, Proper, 40–33/1, 1997

In addition to Ethel Waters, this recording includes Ma Rainey, Victoria Spivey, male "down-home singers," and white blues singers Sophie Tucker and Mildred Bailey.

6. Oscar Micheaux and the Harlem Renaissance

Clyde Taylor

It wasn't in Harlem, and it wasn't a renaissance, according to poet Sterling Brown. Some say, cynically, that Brown dismissed the renaissance because he was left out of it. But if he, arguably the best, most essential poet of Black American literature, was left out of it, that would leave the Harlem Renaissance with a hole in it and with much less than is claimed for it.[1] A neat, coffee-table, postcard, tourist-attraction view of the Harlem Renaissance is fascinating as the one time when everyone, Black and White, can have a good time gazing into the mirror of the past, watching Black and White people having a ball.

But there is a broader inspection of the Black 1920s and early 1930s that is fuller of contradictions, snarls, and complications, yet is richer nourishment for the historical imagination. Brown affirmed his connection to an alternate historical framing, "the New Negro movement," a configuration I prefer, though I will continue to bow to the catchiness of the Harlem Renaissance. In this broader framing, it is possible to consider, as I argued many years ago, that the literary movement of the Harlem Renaissance may have been a controlled diversion to draw force away from a much more significant event: Marcus Garvey and his Universal Negro Improvement Association.[2] If the Harlem Renaissance, as this favorite Black literary-cultural moment in all of American history, cakewalks through cultural chronicles minus the presence of such potent contemporaries as Black America's greatest poet and the leader of its most popular mass movement, what else might it be missing? It is also missing one of its most prolific and successful cultural producers—film director Oscar Micheaux.

Micheaux was the front-runner of a cinematic movement that in many respects paralleled the ambitions of the literary and scholarly renaissance, yet remains marginalized in its history. The race movie industry's evolution dovetails precisely with the contours of the more celebrated movement. In an effort to establish a Black voice on the screen, in opposition to stereotypical and debasing images, the first Black independent film was produced and directed by Blacks in 1910. This development was launched in bustling Black Chicago, an outgrowth of the massive migrations from the South to the industrial North. When the New Negro movement gathered momentum from World War I and from Black military participation, Black filmmakers like Peter Jones of Chicago memorialized the contributions of Black troops in several films. One of the best remembered race movies, *The Flying Ace,* reflects that celebration.

The excitement generated in some circles around the creation of a race-movie industry carried that same pioneer ethos that fired new initiatives by Blacks in real estate, the press, education, sports, entertainment, business, the fine arts, and other fields. These were times, we should remember, when Black people were themselves intrigued by celebrated firsts. There was a drive, not only to form film production companies and produce and distribute movies but also to build or buy Black-owned movie theaters; the most lavish of these was the theater exhibition hall built by Madame C. J. Walker, the first millionaire businesswoman in U.S. history, in Indianapolis, which was the headquarters of her hairdressing conglomerate. It was in this climate that Oscar Micheaux produced and directed, from his own script, his first movie, *The Homesteader,* in 1919, at the dawn of the Harlem Renaissance, as generally interpreted by its historians.

Some of the more interesting connections between Micheaux and the Harlem Renaissance are literary. Micheaux's first artistic efforts were as a writer. When he jumped into movie-making, he had already written three novels. Why then has he been left out of the annals of the literary Black awakening of the period? One reason is that his novels are of poorer literary quality than those that marked the new notable successes; his were pop, or rather pulp, novels. Other reasons existed for the poor reception of his narratives; for example, his works showed obvious affection for Booker T. Washington's social philosophy while nearly all the Harlem Renaissance fiction writers were associated with the rival camp leg by W. E. B. DuBois. Another certain limit to his acceptance among the chosen flock is the fact that Micheaux was flamboyantly self-published. He is notorious for having formed the Micheaux Publishing Company, printing his novels, and successfully selling them door-to-door in the South and Midwest. In the official Harlem Renaissance, the definitive literary achievement was not writing well, or even winning a contest in *Opportunity* or *The Crisis*, but getting published by a mainstream White publishing house, as did Claude McKay, Langston Hughes, Countée Cullen, Jean Toomer, Rudolph Fisher, Wallace Thurman, Zora Neale Hurston, and James Weldon Johnson. Micheaux had many connections with the literary renaissance, but they were perforce mostly underground connections, or sub-renaissance efforts.

He was, however, a most literary film director. A good number of his movies were remixes of his novel plots. Others were screen adaptations of popular, ephemeral fictions of the day. For Micheaux, the literary foundation of a movie was its most important element—before direction, actors, performances, or editing. He insisted that movies were best described as photoplays. From the ideology expressed in his novels—strongly anti-urban, somewhat anti-intellectual, and hostile to race leaders of the time (with the exception of Washington)—we can assume that there was a "natural" distance between Micheaux and the reigning literary coterie in Harlem. But that distance broke down in some interesting places and ways.

The puzzle of Micheaux's creative personality is nested in the many contradictions it could sustain with serenity—a Washingtonian conservative who could at the same time make a film as explosively anti-racist as *Within Our Gates*. Micheaux apparently read himself as such a complete outsider to all cliques, formations, movements, coteries, and established institutions—not just Hollywood—that he felt justified in making up his own rules as he went along.

A bit of this existentialist freedom shows up in his appreciation of Charles W. Chesnutt. Chesnutt received the NAACP Spingarn Medal in 1928. This was one sign of his role as exemplar for the Black literary awakening of the times. He had long since silenced his pen, discouraged by the cold ear White audiences turned to his adroitly racialized portraits of the American landscape, drawn at the turn of the century. Micheaux's appreciation of Chesnutt materialized in the film he made, in 1923, of Chesnutt's novel *The House Behind the Cedars* (a film that has since disappeared). But one of the more curious events of Micheaux's career, full of quirky turns and escapades, was his rewriting of Chesnutt's novel in 1947 under the title *Masquerade*.

This was not an adventure into plagiarism. Micheaux acknowledged Chesnutt's novel in the early pages of his own version, which was not radically inferior to the original that had by then gone out of print. Thematically, Micheaux was paying tribute to a motif dear to his heart: the confusion sown in racialized America by the presence of "Black" people so light-skinned that they could, and often did, "pass" for "White." (One good reason for capitalizing these racial designations is to indicate that they signify culturally, more than biologically.) At the same time, Micheaux's rewriting of another's novel shows a complete disregard for the canons of authorship ensconced in the Western world since the 18th century. His pagan infidelity to the myth of artistic originality, which also shows up in his consistent cannibalizing of his own novels and films for later productions, is another marker of the distance that must have set him apart from the more conventional streams of the literary renaissance.

Micheaux may have understood that he was too *outré* to be warmly accepted by his Harlem Renaissance peers, but this did not keep him from trying to form some meaningful artistic connections with them. He moved the headquarters of his film production company to Harlem, on 135th Street, in the mid-1920s. Around this time, it was reported that Micheaux had a meeting with Chesnutt and DuBois. Whatever the outcome of this meeting, the fact is that Micheaux did make a screen version of Chesnutt's novel, as mentioned above, and a version of DuBois's novel *Dark Princess,* both no longer known to be in existence.

Not much has been said about this last film, or its connection to DuBois's fabulous political romance that is little read these days. But the synopsis of Micheaux's movie, *Martin Garland* (1925), which is all that can be found of it today, overlaps neatly with DuBois's scenario of a worldwide underground movement of third world intellectuals bent on revolutionary overthrow of colonialism, as background to a romance between a Black American, who reads very much like DuBois himself, and an Indian princess, as brilliant as she is beautiful and dedicated. The surviving synopsis of this movie not only suggests its title character is a fictionalization of Marcus Garvey, but also that the story reflects DuBois's fictionalization of his political antagonist Garvey in *Dark Princess.* (The Garvey character is trying to blow up a train loaded with Ku Klux Klan officials; but the DuBois character must sabotage this plot, not only because it will lead to catastrophe for the Black American community, but also because the princess is aboard.) But these creative ventures did not earn Micheaux a place in the honor rolls of the Harlem Renaissance, nor in the memoirs of DuBois or Chesnutt.

An apt question at this point is to ask what does this connection or lack of connection tell us about Micheaux and about the Harlem Renaissance? Firstly, it tells us that the phenomenon was driven by its literary manifestations, primarily and, one might say, hegemonically. All accounts of the times cite the general outflowing of creative energy among Black Americans in many diverse arenas, one testified to by many brilliant personalities such as Josephine Baker, Paul Robeson, Roland Hayes, Louis Armstrong, Jack Johnson, Bessie Smith, Earl "Snake Hips" Tucker, the Cotton Club, the distinctive vibrancy of the

Afro-American press, Andy Razaf, Florence Mills, and Duke Ellington. The movement is dated, however, by its achievements in literature: for some, by the publication of Claude McKay's poem "Harlem Dancer" in 1917. But outside the literary arena, the 1917 date makes no sense, particularly if the Harlem Renaissance were scanned through the lens of Black music, which was, of course, the most potent and original cultural achievement of Black Americans in the 20th century. The very different curvature of the Harlem Renaissance once it is viewed as a musical development, with a plethora of different dates to choose from for its origin and development and in many fertile venues outside of Harlem, suggests that the official history has the tail wagging the dog.

This contradiction has one efficient explanation, which I have already broached. What the writers did constituted a "renaissance" because they gained the recognition and imprimatur of the Euro-American art-culture system in the field that it prizes most highly—literature; this field also carries the heaviest signification of "civilized" cultivation because of the Eurocentric premium placed on literacy over orature. This is the fountainhead of a cultural hierarchy that continues to be exercised through Harlem Renaissance studies today. Musical genius follows next in this chain of respect, largely in accordance with the same principle of White audience acceptance (e.g., the Cotton Club phenomenon). But we should remember that the closer to the contemporary awakening, the more the musical triumphs celebrated by renaissancers like Locke et al. were "classical," shadowing the European symphonic and operatic repertory, the more favorably they were received. Locke, let us not forget, despised jazz and the blues, as did DuBois. The more academic and professionalized in the European mold were the media that Black people worked in during those times, the better chance their practitioners had of becoming recognized as part of the Harlem Renaissance. The other half of this selection process is an offshoot of the first: those social, educational, political, and artistic developments that were evolved by Black people and for Black people, away from the approving eye of White audience, were doomed to be neglected or derided, until reconsidered by the cultural awakening of the 1960s and '70s. For many decades, this left Oscar Micheaux and his self-taught filmmaking contemporaries beyond the pale.

But outside the official sanction of the literary renaissance, Micheaux and the race-movie tradition were very much a part of any broadly conceived notion of a Black awakening in the period. Micheaux made it a point to capitalize on the performing talents and notable figures of the day as attractions for his films. He regularly cast members of the Lafayette Players in his films, like Lawrence Chenault and Evelyn Greer. He enlisted boxing luminary Sam Langford for *The Brute,* and rising star Paul Robeson made *Body and Soul* (1924), his first movie, under Micheaux's direction. Moreover, if one wants to get some idea of what the Harlem Renaissance looked like in motion, Micheaux's movies are among the best sources available.

The motivation and themes of the race-movie movement, in fact, synchronize tightly with those of the literary awakening. The very name "race movie" highlights the racial self-consciousness and self-determination that characterized the New Negro phenomenon generally. The whole expression was fueled by the intent to override the subhuman portrayal of Black people that was axiomatic in mainstream media. One of the more conservative, bourgeois aspirations of the literary movement, as analyzed by Arthur P. Davis—the best-foot-forward motivation—is also a major sociological imperative behind race movies, as indicated by early film titles: *Realization of a Negro's Ambition* (1916); *The Colored American Winning His Suit* (1919); *The Symbol of the Unconquered* (1920), this by Micheaux; and *A Giant of His Race* (1921). By the 1940s, such titles had disappeared from race movies.

Under these titles, favorite themes of the Harlem novelists and poets were featured in the films as well. One of these, the migration from the South to northern cities, figures dramatically in Micheaux's narratives—but with a difference. In typical stories like Rudolph Fisher's "City of Refuge" or Zora Neale Hurston's tales in *Spunk*, the perils of the country hick, particularly when a woman, dealing with the machinations of a city slicker, are treated as matter for wry local colorism, not unlike the work of Mark Twain and the literary comedians dealing with the contretemps of the greenhorn on the frontier. This was a motif that Spencer Williams adopted in his movie *The Girl in Room 6*. But for Micheaux, this theme had powerfully ideological and autobiographical resonance.

The young Micheaux was convinced that the Black community of his time was seriously on the wrong developmental track, misled there by errant leadership. Setting out to build an agricultural and ranching empire in the plains region of the United States, he hoped to become a role model for Black people who were being diverted into wasteful life schemes in the urban centers by leaders who wished merely to capitalize on their miseries. In all of Micheaux's surviving films, this theme is at least subtext, and it plays a significant part in *Ten Minutes to Live, Body and Soul, Within Our Gates, God's Stepchildren,* and *Swing*. Micheaux's fusion of Greeley's slogan "go West young man" with Booker T. Washington's self-help philosophy gives bite, historical depth, and shading to a theme that was usually treated in fiction as fodder for titillation.

Micheaux's stories often melded this question of the city versus the country with the theme of miscegenation and "passing." He was not the only Black storyteller to take up this theme of race-mixing that goes back at least to William Wells Brown's novel *Clotel* (1853) and that passed from Chesnutt's novels into the 20th century. Think of Langston Hughes's several stories on this theme as well as his play and novella *Mulatto*, or Jean Toomer's story "Bona and Paul" in *Cane*, Nella Larsen's *Quicksand* and *Passing*, and Jessie Fauset's fiction. Again, Micheaux's take on this motif is both ideological and autobiographical and requires the extended and expert treatment given it by Pearl Bowser and Louise Spence.[3] Micheaux was at least as dedicated to this theme as any participant in the Harlem Renaissance, touching on it repeatedly in his 36 feature films. In this and other ways, he fully shared the narrative and thematic concerns of the Black literature of his times.

Maybe that's one reason why he came in for such profound silence and neglect from his intellectual contemporaries. Carlton Moss, playwright, script writer, and film director (*The Negro Soldier* 1944), illuminated this neglect in an extended interview for the film *Midnight Ramble*. In material that did not get used in the film, Moss talks about meeting with Micheaux and trying to apprentice with him in the late 1930s. Moss was an idealistic youth coming out of Morgan State, a historically Black college, where the drama society had developed ideas about literature needing to reflect the aspirations, problems, and obstacles of the average Black person. "And when I learned of these pictures I said, well, maybe I should go there and try to put this new thesis in this organization." Through a fortunate connection, he got a chance to work with Micheaux. In the interview, Moss commented

And I had contacted the established writers—that's James Weldon Johnson, Langston Hughes, Rudolph Fisher, and all those people within the Black renaissance. And they said forget it. Forget him. That all he's going to do is imitate what they're going to do in Hollywood and we don't want any part of it. . . . The writers weren't—the leaders weren't against Micheaux the individual. They felt that the motion picture industry's contents was [*sic*] so negative, and so far as the Black population was concerned, it would be impossible to work with him. . . . They said, what are you messing with him for? All he's doing is that same junk they do in Hollywood. They wouldn't hire you in Hollywood. That was standard. Langston, the Johnsons [James Weldon and Rosamund], all of them felt this. They felt there was a little better opportunity in the theater, but it was an open and shut case that there was no place for you in Hollywood. And you were an insult to your people to mess around with that stuff because all they're going to ask you to do is open some doors and scratch some heads. They were the ones that told me he's a joke. . . . Well, now the Black Tower people, and that's the Countée Cullenses and the Harold Jackmons and the Langston Hugheses and the Rudolph Fishers (and I had my most direct contact with Langston voicing this): As I perceive what he said and what they were saying, it was that they saw Micheaux as an illiterate person. And this they could not accept. Because the big thrust at that time was to prove that you were as literate as whoever the accepted figure was on the national scale.[4]

Micheaux as an unwelcomed ghost of the Harlem Renaissance helps us better understand this cultural moment and one of its contradictions. The Renaissance writers were more willing than Micheaux to draw characterizations in a celebratory vein of "the Negro lower down," everyday working people. But they did so in many cases to please White audiences and patrons who valued these portraits to the extent that they confirmed their fantasies of fashionable primitivism. Micheaux and his race-movie contemporaries, by contrast, made their movies with almost exclusively poorer, less educated Blacks in mind as their audience—but they consistently favored middle-class professionals as heroes and lead characters in their moral fables.

The notion of a unitary renaissance dissolves before any examination of the many crosscurrents and divergent shifts of interest, politics, class, gender, and regional issues that swam across the efforts of Black people to gain a foothold in modernity as it was developing in America at the time. The biography of Andy Razaf, sterling songwriter and lyricist of the times, contributes to this more complex understanding.

> Many today apply the "Harlem Renaissance" label indiscriminately to all that was Harlem culturally in the twenties: to the literature and the jazz music, the nightclub reviews and the ambitious poetry and painting. Razaf . . . understood that the movement largely was being orchestrated by local Black leaders like sociologist Charles Johnson as a social revolution mounted on a cultural premise: that Black America's best chance at gaining approval and, ultimately, acceptance from White America was through artistic creativity that commanded respect. For this Renaissance dream to succeed, Johnson and others believed, its substance would have to be unimpeachable—esthetically and racially neuter, as far removed as possible from that which Johnson considered to be the cliched, the stereotypical, the low-down artistic contributions of the African in America to date.

Heading Johnson's roster of unsuitables were minstrelsy, ragtime, "coon tunes," and the blues, the coarse, vulgar, bottomless blues, including everything that these various expressions of Black culture currently meant to Black theatrical and musical creativity in Harlem. This surely left Andrea Razaf and his peers well outside the Harlem Renaissance mainstream.[5]

Doubtless, race movies would be included among the unsuitables in Johnson's list, not because they were coarse in sexual reference, but because they were unpolished by the standards of White art and entertainment. The clash between Micheaux and the Harlem Renaissance illuminates a region of taste and perception found in the mass of working Black people, a region often spoken for or swept under the rug (when company's coming) by participants in the Harlem Renaissance.

The Harlem Renaissance was one part of a development of an official class of Black representation. For most of the 20th century, this class of educated Blacks steered favorable imagery of Blacks in certain directions. The NAACP, the Urban League, the several Black colleges and universities, the fraternities and sororities, widely circulating magazines like *Ebony*, all were typical of these image-steerers. And the images they promoted were such as Paul Robeson (until his radical politics made him too hot to handle), Joe Louis, Jesse Owens, Madeline Anderson, Lena Horne, Bill Robinson, Mary McLeod Bethune, Adam Clayton Powell (you could be radical in this company so long as you also had status and middle-class demeanor), Duke Ellington, and so on.

This was not a pernicious conspiracy; the images celebrated certainly deserved their respect. But, in the meantime, the unsorted populace lived, dreamed, and created in ways that have until recently escaped thoughtful attention. Two books that struck a blow to this hegemony of taste were E. Franklin Frazier's less-than-complimentary sociological analysis, *Black Bourgeoisie*, and from the same period in the late '50s, Billie Holiday's autobiography, *Lady Sings the Blues*. Baraka's book *Blues People* was one of the first to redress some of the balance away from this Black bourgeois image screen. But the proof that this culture clash continues is available in the contemporary Black middle-class distaste for rap.

Very little unites these millions of Black people who make their lives and imaginations outside of Western and Black bourgeois consciousness. From a distance, their taste seems lamentable, until you remember they sustained the creation and development of the blues, ragtime, jazz, gospel music, rhythm and blues, and the extraordinary body of Black vernacular visual art that is just now surfacing—all while the image-steerers directed attention elsewhere.

It is these pagan moderns, as I call them, who specifically supported Micheaux's movies and race films generally. The anecdotes about such audiences laughing at these films suggest they knew they were not watching masterpieces. But they had different schedules of taste and different demands to place on artists. They understood the validity of a ragged line in the blues. They were not attuned to the militaristic precision of ballet. And many of them liked Micheaux's movies for what was offered them, knowing that they were not in a position to demand more.

So it is one of the contradictions of the Harlem Renaissance that, while it uncovered some wonderful creative talents and made some fundamental gains in the erection of Afro-modernity, the concessions made to European aesthetic codes and values worked to obscure other creative ferments that were equally or even more productive. A contemporary reflection puts this cultural schism into better perspective. Looking back from 1944, L. D. Reddick, curator of the Schomburg Collection, saw the lost opportunities. "Frankly, most of the movies made by Negro producers have been of third-rate quality. Yet the success of Oscar Micheaux suggests what could be done if those who know better would help."[6] Of course Micheaux would have bristled at the notion that the habitués of the Dark Tower "knew better."

The condescension of this phrase marks the separation between Micheaux and the finer artists of the Harlem Renaissance—and Micheaux had his own way of voicing his resentment. In his novel *The Story of Dorothy Stanfield*, he draws a portrait of a motion picture producer and book publisher, Sydney Wyeth, who is a very thinly disguised representation of himself. "Wyeth is an intense race man; and while he can and does criticize the Negro in his books . . . , he is for his people at all times, regardless of the circumstances."[7] Micheaux also makes a pointed portrait of another writer clearly intended to reflect Richard Wright. Micheaux writes with disdain for the Wright character who lives outside of Harlem and the Black community with his White wife, all the while pronouncing alien ideas about that community without knowing it intimately, by contrast to Wyeth who lives in the Harlem community with his Black wife and is fully immersed in the lives of the community he portrays. The contempt Micheaux exhibited here, toward the end of his career, echoes the similar skepticism about the relevance of Black preachers and intellectuals that was evidenced in his first novel and earliest surviving letters.

The divide between Micheaux and the Harlem Renaissance could offer an occasion for moralizing and taking sides—but to what purpose? The better option is to reflect on these differences and bring to them the wonder deserving of complex lives. We should remember that by some accounts and some evidences, Micheaux could be a mean customer to deal with—rough, self-absorbed, and self-important. And we must always consider the pressure on all Black cultural performers in this period to find one groove or another in a time when the orbit of choice and free movement was severely circumscribed.

We might also reflect on the attitude of the Harlem Renaissance toward Micheaux and creative personalities of his type. While the writers of the recognized group, the best of them, identified with ordinary Black people and brought new vitality to Black writing through this identification, they apparently shied away from a personality from these ranks of the ordinary and from the poorly educated who tried to do what they did. They were, doubtless, ashamed of Micheaux because he menaced their need to gain the same respect given their White literary peers. Their attitude was much like that of Ralph

Ellison who divided writers who might be important to him into "relatives" and "ancestors." Relatives were those who were like family members, whom one could not choose. Literary ancestors were those one could choose. So Ellison saw Wright, who mentored him into writing as a craft, as a "relative," along with Langston Hughes, and reserved the role of "ancestor" for Hemingway, Eliot, Malraux, Dostoyevsky, and Faulkner.[8] The inability to embrace or at least cheerfully tolerate artists like Micheaux, who are roughnecks when it comes to reflecting the artistic values of European classicism, is a long-lasting and telling feature of African-American literature.

NOTES

1. Clyde Taylor, "The Human Image in Sterling Brown's Poetry," *Black Scholar* (February/March 1982), 13–20.

2. Clyde Taylor, "Garvey's Ghost: Revamping the Twenties," *Black World* (February 1976), 54–67.

3. Pearl Bowser and Louise Spence, "Identity and Betrayal: The Symbol of the Unconquered and Oscar Micheaux's Biographical Legend," in Daniel Bernardi, ed., *The Birth of Whiteness: Race and the Emergence of U.S. Cinema* (New Brunswick: Rutgers University Press, 1996), 56–80.

4. Transcript of Carlton Moss's interview, in author's private possession; no page numbers.

5. Barry Singer, *Black and Blue: The Life and Lyrics of Andy Razaf* (New York: Shirmer Books, 1992), 176–77.

6. L. D. Reddick, "Educational Programs for the Improvement of Race Relations: Motion Pictures, Radio and the Press and Libraries," *The Journal of Negro Education*, Vol. 13 (Summer, 1944), No. 3, 381.

7. Bowser and Spence, 72.

8. Ralph Ellison, "The World and the Jug," *Shadow and Act* (New York: New American Library, 1966), 144–45.

PART II.
"ENTER THE NEW NEGRO": SOME WRITERS
OF THE RENAISSANCE

The poetry and prose of the Harlem Renaissance can be pictured as a complex braid with three main threads, woven together in various proportions and with different emphases, but marked with a recognizable stamp. The first thread would be that of the entertainment world, marked by the success of black performers in music or on stage. In music or on the stage, in fact, the stylization that is often a structural feature of popular culture, black or white, can easily freeze into types, whether stereotypes or counter-stereotypes, and a creative influence become a deadening one. We see the second thread as linked to a remarkable increase in human-sciences research on black life, from history to folklore and sociology. This provided the grounds for a more realistic treatment of the traditional folk culture and its metamorphoses on the urban scene. The third major reference would be to contemporary modernism in its various forms, from the avant-garde cubist collage of T. S. Eliot and Pound's imagism, to the tamer and more socially concerned cultural nationalism of a Waldo Frank or Sherwood Anderson.

The constraints of a specific field also define the conditions for its creativity and innovation; what may appear as limitations are inseparable from achievement. Modernism and folk forms, as Alain Locke intuited, actually bolstered each other, bringing about an original synthesis which appears as the trademark of many works of the New Negro movement. Jean Toomer's *Cane* (1923), one of the books which is often referred to as the first and finest example of the literary renaissance in Harlem, is just such a hybrid work: it sets in motion a vertiginous counterpoint between peerless formal experimentation and rural as well as urban folk culture, between orality and literacy, between artistic alienation and communal solidarities. But the tension between these polarities was highly volatile, conducive on the one hand to synthesis and fusion and to estranging ironies on the other. The same ambivalence was to be found in Zora Neale Hurston, whose novels and anthropological works constantly hover between two concepts of reality and language: the performative drama of the black popular ethos and the arbitrary nature of Western sign and science (Raynaud, chapter 12). For both authors, this formal dilemma was also a quandary about identity.

The same dialectic of creative freedom and constraint was visible in the poetic practice of the Harlem Renaissance. The poets like Countée Cullen, who developed New Negro themes in the romantic idiom of a Keats, were criticized for aspiring to honorary whiteness; those like Claude McKay, who attempted, for greater political impact, to clothe a radical message in the easily identifiable garb of the rhymed sonnet, were kept at arm's length for their revolutionary ideas and for their conservative prosody. Langston Hughes succeeded in fusing readability and a social intent into specific African-American forms by adopting the structure of the blues; his poetic persona was constructed on a par with his intended public, thereby ideally closing the social gap between the Talented Tenth (the black elite) and the working-class majority (Michlin, chapter 13). Such a move, occurring as it did at about the end of the 1920s, ushered in the preoccupation of another group in the thirties: the impetus toward protest literature.

The comparatively disappointing crop of serious black drama—as opposed to the success of more popular entertainment—during the Harlem Renaissance is offset by the ways in which New Negro writers managed to overrun the difficulty of producing their plays. Jean Toomer integrated "Kabnis" in *Cane* as a prose piece, a piece whose structure still bears the mark of the original medium for which it was composed. Zora Neale Hurston, faithful to her own interpretation of the "Characteristics of Negro Expression," of which drama was a prominent feature, set many of her fictional pieces in a theatrical situation, complete with a store-front chorus and call-and-response between the protagonists and audience. W. E. B. DuBois wrote plays, but, with a view to imbuing his audience with a sense of history and pride in their origins, also staged pageants like *The Star of Ethiopia.*

Alain Locke's wish for a Negro school of art took the literary form of such attempts at fusing modernism with folk modes of expression and at the spelling of an alphabet of "racial" themes. References to Egypt, Ethiopia, and West Africa abound in the poetry; special places are featured in narratives and lyrics, moving up and down the migration line between the teeming life of city centers like Harlem and the heritage of the rural South (Löbbermann, chapter 11, and Boelhower, chapter 10); characters from folklore such as the conjure man or woman, the Trickster, and the ballad hero are incorporated in the fiction. Against this trend are also to be found narratives dealing, in more "genteel" form and content, with the preoccupations of the black bourgeoisie. What superficially appears as an imitation of the mainstream may also articulate original interrogations about the color line, as in Nella Larsen's *Quicksand* (Hutchinson, chapter 9).

The question of the representativeness and freedom of the artist, which was so crucial at the time, did not really fly in the face of the central premise, that of the validity of racial categories in an ethnically and culturally mixed society like the United States. This epistemological limit was the object of the many narratives of the times dealing with "passing" and biracial identity: for example, James Weldon Johnson's *Autobiography of an Ex-Coloured Man* (1912) and Nella Larsen's *Quicksand* (1928) and *Passing* (1920). Such subversive probing denies the reality of the concept, yet paradoxically recognizes its social currency (Portelli, chapter 7, and Hutchinson, chapter 9). If we remember that writers like Jean Toomer and, to a lesser extent, Zora Neale Hurston never managed to reach beyond the "hypnotic divisions" of race, either in their lives or in the reception of their writings, we might conclude that the blind spot of the Harlem Renaissance's literary and critical production still partly blurs our own vision.

7. The Tragedy and the Joke: James Weldon Johnson's *The Autobiography of an Ex-Coloured Man*

Alessandro Portelli

SIGNIFICATIONS

> I laughed heartily over what struck me as the capital joke I was
> playing.
>
> —JAMES WELDON JOHNSON, *The Autobiography*
> *of an Ex-Coloured Man*, p. 197[1]

In the beginning of James Weldon Johnson's *The Autobiography of an Ex-Coloured Man*, we are told that this is going to be the story of a joke. In summing up the motives that led him to write the story, the first-person narrator says, "I find a sort of savage and diabolical desire to gather up all the little tragedies of my life, and turn them into a practical joke on society" (*Autobiography* 4).

Let us start with a joke, then. The ex-colored man laughs because his success as a white man is enough to "disprove the theory that one drop of Negro blood renders a man unfit" (197); on the other hand, that drop still defines him to himself, an ex-ed colored man, a colored man under erasure whose identity is defined by the identity he thinks he has shaken off. So let us listen to another joke—a little folk tale about the unshakability of identity.

> Two men walk down the street. One of them is a humpback. As they walk, they talk. Turning a corner, they find themselves in front of a synagogue.
>
> One of them, the "straight" one, sighs deeply, turns to the humpback, and says, "You know, I once was a Jew." The humpback sighs back, and says: "I know, I know. I, too, once was a humpback."[2]

W. E. B. DuBois had prophetically announced in 1903 that "the problem of the twentieth century is the problem of the color line." Less than ten years later, James Weldon Johnson both confirmed and complicated that statement. On the one hand, by writing a novel about the color line, he confirmed its tragic importance; on the other hand—and this is where the joke lies—he made that line greatly problematic. In a complex game of hide-and-seek, Johnson in one motion drew the line and blurred (*ex*-ed) it to the point that, the harder one looks for it, the harder it is to locate. Yet, invisible and powerful, it's there, like the invisible, tragic hump in the old Jewish joke: you can call yourself an ex-Colored Man, or an ex-Jew, but you can no more discard the burden of cultural identity than the cripple can discard the hump on his back.

In his recent revision of Sterling Brown's image of the "Tragic Mulatto," Werner Sollors points out that "in many cases literary Mulattos were able to cross racial boundaries that were considered fixed, real, or even natural. This ability is what made them such ideal questioners of the status quo."[3] This is precisely what Johnson's formulation does: he downplays the tragedy (as in *tragic* Mulatto), and he foregrounds the ironic transgression (literally, boundary-crossing) in the form of the joke. Yet, he also reminds us that the mulatto's ironic crossing would be meaningless without the shadow of the tragedy: just as the mulatto needs to evoke the line in order to cross it (to evoke his "colored" identity in order to erase it), likewise, to play his joke, Johnson needs to evoke and exorcise the tragedy.

This takes place a number of times in the text. For instance, a potentially typical tragic-Mulatto situation arises when the narrator, at a performance of Gounod's *Faust* in Paris, finds himself sitting next to his unknowing white half-sister.[4] "I felt," he writes, "an almost uncontrollable impulse to rise up and scream to the audience: 'Here, here in your very midst, is a tragedy, a real tragedy!'" (*Autobiography* 135). And yet, although his "feelings [are] divided," he does nothing. While the tragic show goes on on the stage, the potentially tragic hero stumbles out of the theater and never mentions the episode again in his narrative.

The theatrical, and therefore implicitly contrived connotation of *tragedy* already visible in this scene is underlined by the author's definition of himself as a "spectator." This is in fact the role that he plays as he narrates, with an abundance of visual detail, the two most actually tragic episodes in the story: the killing of a widow by a jealous lover (in an interracial love story in which, however, race is ostensibly not a motive); and the lynching that scares him into finally passing for white. The word "tragic" is not used in the representation of either of these tragedies.

We find it, instead, again with theatrical connotations, in two passages in which it is linked to the comic. One is the story of the minstrel with the big mouth who carried in his heart a burning ambition to be a "tragedian." His failure to make people take him seriously is so sad that, indeed, in real life "he did play a part in a tragedy" (106). This episode is so important that it later becomes a paradigm for the quandary of black intellectuals, including himself, and the black middle class as a whole. All black people, the narrator remarks, are fixed in comic stereotypes: "A novel dealing with coloured people who lived in respectable homes and amidst a fair degree of culture and who naturally acted 'just like white folks' would be taken in a comic-opera sense. In this respect the Negro is much in the position of a great comedian who gives up the lighter roles to play tragedy" (168).

In the next move, however, the narrator complicates the line he has just drawn between tragedy and comedy. "In the same respect," he remarks, "the public is not too much to be blamed, for great comedians are far more scarce than mediocre tragedians; every amateur actor is a tragedian." Once again, his feelings are as divided as his ancestry. While he resents black exclusion from the serious art of tragedy, he suggests that the seriousness of black culture may be couched in the joke.

The essential black practical joke and serious criticism of life is called, as we know, *signifyin'*. From the very first page, Johnson's text plays a threefold game of signifying: on the racial discourse of racial boundaries; on the literary discourse of the tragic mulatto; on DuBois's political discourse of the color line. Yet, there may be more: he may also be signifying on the values and texts of the dominant culture at large. In this sense, it might pay to read *The Autobiography of an Ex-Coloured Man* not only in the context of DuBois and Frances Harper, but also in that of his contemporaries, Henry James or Edith Wharton.

The ex-colored man's practical joke on society may or may not allude to Melville's Ishmael's sense that "this strange *mixed* [my italics] affair we call life" is nothing but "a vast practical joke."[5] Yet, there is a curious symmetry, a shared symbolic ground. Ishmael feels that life's joke is upon him, while Johnson's narrator is the perpetrator of the joke on society; but they both share a keen sense of existential absurdity (Ishmael ends his musings by drawing up his will; Johnson's narrator ends his story by lamenting the loss of his heritage).

Again, one hears artfully distorted echoes of the literary canon when reading, "My mother and I lived together in a little cottage" in New England, where the outcast and unwed mother "was kept very busy with her sewing." When we hear that once a month "she received a letter," the impulse to capitalize that "A" is hard to resist—not because this may be the intention of the text, but because it is another way to remind us that what is going on in that cottage is, although apparently normal, potentially tragic.

These are one reader's inferences. On the other hand, it is a fact that Johnson's narrator is not unfamiliar with the white American canon, as shown by his reference to Mark Twain (another very serious comedian and the author of a comic novel called a "tragedy" on the color line: *Pudd'nhead Wilson*). That Johnson is bent on signifying on white discourse is also made clear by the scene in which the narrator, passing for white, listens unrecognized to the white conversation on race in the segregated parlor car. This is a classic motif in turn-of-the-century African-American literature,[6] and its power lies in the fact that it can be seen not only as a figuration of the absurdity of segregation but also as a metaphor for the presence of the black reader in the white text. The fact that this white discourse is reported by the silent and invisible black narrator is also a figure for the ironic bent that the white discourse takes on when it is filtered by the black voice.

The joke, indeed, is already intimated by the title: *Autobiography* implies a pact of referential veracity with the reader, but then the book is a work of fiction. Or, as Philippe Lejeune suggests, the genre "autobiography" is predicated on the coincidence of the names of the author, the narrator, and the main character—who in this case have no names at all. Of course, the truly savage joke is in the rest of the title—*Ex-Coloured Man.* In a society of rigid biologic boundaries in black and white, how can a colored man become an ex? Once we establish this possibility, no one is safe, no identity is sure.

Let us then go back to that little New England cottage, a "place of purity and safety" created by a mother's arms. This may very well be a late-Victorian cliché of the sanctity of maternal love and affection, and probably is—but what are we to make of the fact that this particular mother—like Hester Prynne—is unmarried and therefore, in the same Victorian cult of sainted motherhood, certainly not a paradigm of "purity"? Johnson's text situates itself on the boundary of indecision generated by this ambivalence: not just between black and white but also between piety and transgression, between middle-class uplift and popular cultural defiance—between the generation of Frances Harper and that of Claude McKay.

Does this ironic image of purity resonate in the tradition of Harriet Jacobs's statement that southern black women cannot be measured against the standards of conventional society, or does it suggest that there is a type of purity that has nothing to do with sexual mores—or does it mean that *purity* is itself a moot concept in a novel of mixing and passing?

ALL THAT GLITTERS

> I have a dim recollection of several people who moved in and about this little house, but I have a distinct mental image of only two: one, my mother; and the other, a tall man with a small, dark moustache. I remember his shoes

or boots were always shiny, and that he wore a gold chain and a great gold watch with which he was always willing to let me play. (*Autobiography* 5)

This passage, quite early in Johnson's text, introduces the figure that is the cornerstone of tragic mulatto stories, the white father. Rather than as an obsession, however, the paternal image is only a dim recollection; a later encounter generates but little emotion. The meaning of this passage is to suggest one side of the double heritage that the narrator derives from his mixed descent. The black heritage, as we learn in the next page, is represented by his mother's piano and by the talent that will make him a black musician (with a "particular fondness for the black keys");[7] the white side is represented by his father's shoes, a metaphor of inheritance; by the gold that will make a successful white businessman; and by the "shine" that throws an ambiguous bridge between the inheritance of gold and the inheritance of blackness.

I will return later to the gold. First, I would like to follow the variations that Johnson plays on "shine" throughout the first chapter. "It became my appointed duty," he goes on, "whenever he came to bring him a pair of slippers and to put the shiny shoes in a particular corner; he often gave me in turn for the service a bright coin. . . ." (5). Shine, the eponymous hero of black toasts and signifying, is also a slangy synonym for African-Americans. This is the sense in which the word is picked up a few pages later, when the narrator describes his best friend, a bright black boy, exactly in the same terms as his father's shoes:[8]

> His face was black as night, but shone as though it were *polished* [my italics]; he had sparkling eyes, and when he opened his mouth, he displayed glistening white teeth. It struck me at once to call him "Shiny Face," or "Shiny Eyes," or "Shiny Teeth," and I spoke of him often by one of these names to the other boys. These terms were finally merged into "Shiny." (14)

Just in case we missed the implications, the author gives the reader the source of these images—ironically, a mocking racist rhyme sung by white children (including the narrator, who thinks he's white) to their black schoolmates:

> Nigger, nigger, never die,
> Black face and shiny eye. (15)

"My admiration," he writes, "was almost equally divided between the watch chain and the shoes." All that shines is not gold; indeed, the symbolic web is rather intricate and all its terms are "divided." "Shiny" is both a racist slur and a term of endearment. The shoes are both a metaphor of his white father's inheritance and a bright object of blackness—polished black skin, like Shiny's face. Polishing blackness seems to be one of the narrator's missions in life, culminating in his project of polishing black music into classical form. The inheritance of gold, finally, is both a possession and a "chain," an essentially flawed gift that becomes a burden:

> I remember how I sat upon his knee and watched him laboriously drill a hole through a ten-dollar gold piece, and then tie the coin around my neck with a string. I have worn that piece around my neck the greater part of my life, and still possess it, but more than once I have wished that some other way had been found of attaching it to me besides putting a hole through it. (6)

PASSAGES

The Autobiography of an Ex-Coloured Man is a double tale of immersion and emersion. Starting from New England, the hero immerses himself in the black world of the South, emerges into New York and Europe, then plunges back into the Deep South to do folklore research, and finally finds refuge from fear in wealth and whiteness. The text hinges on two dramatic passages from one race to another, two dramatic initiations to, and one flight from, blackness.

The first passage coincides with the sudden discovery of his own conventional and institutional blackness. "That day," he writes, "was wrought the miracle of my transition from one world into another; for I did indeed pass into another world" (20–21). As Sollors points out, Johnson subverts the conventional use of *passing,* by designating a passage from white to black rather than vice-versa.[9] Thus, while he does not belittle the brutal suddenness of the revelation and its impact on the narrator as a child, this episode is more in the vein of comedy than literary tragedy.

> On one day near the end of my second term at school the principal came into our room and, after talking to the teacher, for some reason said: "I wish all the white scholars to stand for a moment." I rose with the others. The teacher looked at me and, calling my name, said: "You sit down and rise with the others." I did not quite understand her, and questioned: "Ma'am?" She repeated, with a softer tone in her voice: "You sit down, and rise with the others." I sat down dazed. (*Autobiography* 16)

This anecdote is another of the many "jokes" included in the novel. It is part of a family of humorous narratives that circulate, orally and in writing, in different traditions, in which the humor derives more from the brazen suddenness of the revelation than from the racial contents.[10] It is also a revision of the beginning of DuBois's *The Souls of Black Folk.* "In a wee wooden schoolhouse" in New England, DuBois recalls in the very first page of his book, he participated in a children's game of exchanging visiting cards, "till one girl, a tall newcomer, refused my card—refused it peremptorily, with a glance."[11] In this way, DuBois tells his discovery of his own blackness and prefaces the memorable passage on double-consciousness and the veil—a passage to which the ex-colored man also refers when he describes the impact of the discovery on himself.[12]

The episode inflicts also on Johnson's narrator a wound "which was years in healing" (*Autobiography* 19). Rather than DuBois's dark sense of being locked into place, walled-in in a "prison-house" of blackness, however, he experiences a loss of place, and is dazed. Johnson's narrator is driven not to a philosophical revision of the meaning of blackness, but to a physical revision of his own mirror image (another topos in black literature, but not in Du-Bois).[13] More importantly, while DuBois must face the discovery and its consequences by himself, the ex-colored man finds refuge and consolation in the arms of his mother. Even the tall white girl who spurns DuBois (there may be a suggestion of a sentimental rejection here, too) reappears in Johnson's novel as the older (and implicitly taller) girl with "dark hair" and "pale face" with whom the boy falls in love and plays music while she "laughingly encouraged" him (29, 31).

Though painful, this passage into blackness generates no overwhelming need for the narrator to confront his white father, nor does he pine for the white world as he lives his life as a black man. Racial identity is not a life-or-death concern to him, to the possibly mixed-blood Cubans with whom he associates in the cigar industry in Jackson, to the white sponsor who takes him to Europe, nor even to his fiancée. Unlike Rena in Charles Chesnutt's *The House Behind the Cedars*, who is brought to death by her fiancé's rejection after he discovers her racial identity, here the girl overcomes her initial shock and returns to marry him. All this implies that the barriers that made for tragedy in conventional imagination and literary formulae are not as all-important and as impassable as they are said to be.

The narrator's plunge into blackness, indeed, is clinched less by the loss of identity than by the loss of his money, and is therefore as much a matter of class as it is of race. When his money is stolen in Atlanta, he begins his picaresque journey into the world of the black working class, black "society," and the black underworld. In fact, the chapters that tell this story hinge upon a remarkable contradiction. As a character immersed in the black world, he spends and gambles his money freely; but as a narrator, who tells the story after he has already passed for white and contracted the "money fever," he accounts for it carefully, dollar by dollar. On the one hand, he writes

> I was a hail fellow well met with all the workmen at the factory, most of whom knew little and cared less about social distinctions. From their example I learned to be careless about money, and for that reason I constantly postponed and finally abandoned returning to Atlanta University. It seemed impossible for me to save as much as two hundred dollars. (83)

On the other hand, accounting for money, his own and other people's, occurs at almost every page: in New England, "the benefit yielded me a little
more than two hundred dollars, thus raising my cash capital to about four hundred dollars" (51); in Atlanta, "When we finished [eating], we paid the waiter
twenty cents each and went out" (57); in Jacksonville, "a *regalia* workman . . .
earned from thirty-five to forty dollars a week. He generally worked a sixty-
dollar job" (70), while "I was earning four dollars a week, and was soon able to
pick up a couple more by teaching a few scholars at night" (72), and later "I
was now earning about twenty-five dollars a week" (74); in Harlem, "In less
than three minutes I had won more than two hundred dollars, a sum which
afterwards cost me dearly" (95); later, "I had more than three hundred dollars,
and New York had impressed me as a place where there was lots of money and
not much difficulty in getting it" (110). Although he quickly adds that "I did
not long hold this opinion," the sense remains that money comes and goes
easily: "Some days found me able to peel ten- and twenty-dollar bills from a
roll, and others found me clad in a linen duster and carpet slippers" (114).

> A great deal of money was spent here [at the "Club"], so many of the
> patrons were men who earned large sums. I remember one night a dapper
> little brown-skin fellow was pointed out to me and I was told that he was the
> most popular jockey of the day, and that he earned $12,000 a year. This latter
> statement I couldn't doubt, for with my own eyes I saw him spending at about
> thirty times that rate. (106–107)

The spending, then, is as important as the earning; and the earning is as
easy as the spending. Thus, while class is very much on the narrator's mind,
money is not the only defining factor at this stage. He carefully draws class
boundaries: the "desperate class," the servants, the independent workmen and
tradesmen, and "the educated and well-to-do" who form a "society as discriminating as the actual conditions will allow it to be." Yet, he points out that discrimination is based as much on respectability and "distinction" as on money:

> I know personally of one case in which money to the extent of thirty or
> forty thousand dollars and a fine house, not backed up by a good reputation,
> after several years of repeated effort, failed to gain entry for the possessor
> [into society]. These people have their dances and dinners and card parties,
> their musicals, and their literary societies. The women attend social affairs
> dressed in good taste, and the men in dress suits which they own. . . . I be-
> longed to the literary society—at which we generally discussed the race ques-
> tion—and attended all the church festivals and other charitable entertain-
> ments. (82–83)

When he is accepted in this "professional" class, he is still working at a
manual job in a cigar factory, but also gains distinction as a piano teacher. His

mother's piano, always a symbol of uplift in black culture, is still more important than his father's shoes and gold. There is an important symmetry between the remark that this class has evolved "a social life of which they need not be *ashamed*" (81), and the sense of "*shame*" that finally drives him into passing after he has witnessed a lynching (191; italics mine). This is an expression of what sociologist E. Franklin Frazier has described as "status without substance": the attempt to comply with white standards of behavior without the corresponding material basis.[14] In the absence of gold, polished manners as an outward sign of education and morals, or culture "in the limited sense of 'refinement' and 'sophistication,'" as Leroi Jones put it, will have to do.[15] An illuminating parallel defines this difference.

When he is preparing to enter Atlanta University, the narrator takes a pledge "to abstain from alcoholic beverages, tobacco, and profane language" (*Autobiography* 61). When he passes for white in the end, he again renounces alcohol and tobacco ("as much as I enjoyed smoking, I limited myself to an occasional cigar. . . . Drinking I cut out altogether"), but makes no mention of profane language. The fact is that this time the pledge has less a moral than an economic significance: "I denied myself as much as possible in order to swell my savings" (195). Words, profane or not, cost nothing; and in an environment in which real money talks, respectable language is not as strictly required.

In between, there is the interlude with his "millionaire friend" (120, 124, 126, 129, and passim). Here, music and money are held in temporary balance. The relationship starts with a nightly tip of five dollars for his piano playing (116) and continues with their travels in Europe, during which he plays music and his sponsor "kept me supplied with money far beyond what ordinary wages would have amounted to" (130).

Johnson here treads the same ground as his contemporary Henry James— the international theme of Americans in Europe, always predicated on the opposition of European cultural pretense and American money: "the Londoner seems to think that Americans are people whose only claim to be classed as civilized is that they have money, and the regrettable thing about that is that the money is not English" (136). The difference between English money and American money, of course, is that the former is old and inherited, the latter is new and just made. In a number of these international narratives, in fact, American characters seem to share the embarrassment, not about money but about its sources: how exactly Christopher Newman and the sponsors of Lambert Strether amassed their wealth is always a bit uncertain. It is the making, not the having, of money that is morally suspect. James solves the problem by having his heroines inherit fortunes made by others; Johnson, by making his sponsor a millionaire whose money flows "like fairy godmother's gifts" (195).

In this way, Johnson's millionaire and James's heiresses can be as unconcerned about earning and spending money as the cigar makers of Jacksonville and the gamblers of Harlem.[16]

The difference, of course, is that the protagonist is not the millionaire who already has money, but the piano player, who must get it. Thus, the ex-colored man entirely absorbs the near obsession with money of the moneyless in a money-making world that seems so immoral when Henry James's characters strive to pass from poor to rich: "I had made up my mind that since I was not going to be a Negro, I would avail myself of every possible opportunity to make a white man's success; and that, if it can be summed up in any one word, means 'money'" (*Autobiography* 193).

> What an interesting and absorbing game is money-making! After each deposit at my savings-bank I used to sit and figure out, all over again, my principal and interest, and make calculations on what the increase would be in such and such time. Out of this I derived a great deal of pleasure. I denied myself as much as possible in order to swell my savings. . . . The day on which I was able to figure up to a thousand dollars marked an epoch in my life. (195)

It is an apt conclusion. As the autobiographical form requires, the narrated and the narrating selves finally join together, at the time when, on the threshold of one thousand dollars, the ex-colored man derives pleasure not from the spending but from the making of money. Gone are the days "when my conception of money was that it was made only to spend." He has "earned [it] by days of honest and patient work," has "carefully watched [it] grow from the first dollar." And from this he derives "a pride and satisfaction which to me was an entirely new sensation" (195–96).

And yet—the ex-colored man has passed from the "status without substance" of the black middle class, to economic substance and unsubstantial identity as an infiltrator in the white bourgeoisie. Just like the hump on the back in the old Jewish story, his native blackness cannot be leveled out but only hidden from sight. "My appearance was always good, and my ability to play on the piano, especially ragtime, which was then at the height of its vogue, made me a welcome guest"; the fact is, however, that his "appearance" is to some extent a mask, and his familiarity with ragtime derives from his immersion in the black world. "The anomaly of my social position appealed strongly to my sense of humor": just as in the parlor car, he is the invisible, and therefore threatening, black presence in the midst of confident whiteness. This is the "capital joke" he plays—but the joke may be on him, too. He smiles inwardly at the racial slurs he occasionally hears, but the humor is also a way of diffusing the frustration of being unable to speak out against them. The last page of the book is about the men who speak out for black people; the fact that he must keep silent makes him feel "a coward, a deserter," "small and selfish," and fills him with "a strange longing for my mother's people." The price he pays for the mask he wears as a "spy in the enemy's country"[17] is cultural silence: a man can pass for white, but the music can't.

MAKING RAGTIME CLASSIC

When he arrives in Atlanta, the ex-colored man is appalled at what he sees—"my first sight of coloured people in large numbers"—but is ambivalent about what he hears:

> The unkempt appearance, the shambling, slouching gait and loud talk and laughter of these people aroused in me a feeling of almost repulsion. Only one thing about them awoke a feeling of interest; that was their dialect. (*Autobiography* 56)

Both author and narrator labor under a similar contradiction. As a political figure and a leader of the National Association for the Advancement of Colored People, Johnson would later pursue a policy of uplift that is represented here by the occasionally stilted, always polished language of his narrator; as an artist, however, he was fascinated by the folk culture of spirituals and sermons and by the popular culture of the cakewalk, ragtime, and the musical stage. Likewise, his narrator—also an artist—carefully seeks distinction from the black popular classes, but seeks among them the source of his artistic expression.

The ex-colored man represents this ambivalence in his project to renovate American music by injecting in it the rhythm and harmonies of black music—while, at the same time, polishing out of black music all its antagonistic implications and formal otherness, in order to make it "classic." It is not by accident that the idea originates with a white man in a European parlor. He has played his ragtime versions of classical pieces, when another guest reverses the operation:

> He seated himself at the piano, and, taking the theme of my ragtime, played it through first in straight chords; then varied and developed it through every known musical form. I sat amazed. I had been turning classic music into ragtime, a comparatively easy task; and this man had taken ragtime and made it classic. (142)

It is another initiation, a second discovery of blackness at which he is as amazed as he had been dazed at the first. He makes up his mind "to go back into the very heart of the South . . . and drink in my inspiration firsthand" from "the immense amount of material" available there. This concept continues the ambiguity of the first encounter with the black masses at Atlanta: cultural respect for black popular and folk culture, which the narrator claims as evidence of the humanity of all black people, including himself, and class prejudice against its creators, labeled as "obtuse, simple people" (170).

This contradiction, however, derives from the fact that both respect and prejudice are the result of the same source: actual encounters with the folk and immersion in their lives. Folklore, therefore, is not depicted in abstract or local color terms, but in the context of its discovery in the course of the narrator's voyage of self-discovery. Thus, the narrator identifies with folklore as an expression of black identity, and yet is repelled by its bearers in terms of class distinction. Black working people, therefore, appear no longer as naive sources of quaint folklore, but as a tangible, sometimes threatening social presence. *The Autobiography of an Ex-Coloured Man* is perhaps the first powerful literary representation of the experience of field work as well as a pre–Harlem Renaissance voyage into the depths of the black metropolis of Harlem and the redclay roads of the South. On the strength of his own experience as a musician in show business, Johnson overcomes the academic gap between rural folklore and urban popular culture (although not the cultural hierarchies between low and high art):

> It is my opinion that the coloured people of this country have done four things which refute the oft-advanced theory that they are an absolutely inferior race, which demonstrate that they have originality and artistic conception, and, what is more, the power of creating that which can influence and appeal universally. The first two of these are the Uncle Remus stories . . . and the Jubilee songs. . . . The other two are ragtime music and the cake-walk. . . . These are lower forms of art, but they give evidence of a power that will some day be applied to the higher forms. (87)

What is important here is that the proof of black creativity is not to be found among the polished expressions of discriminating society, but among those of the unkempt masses—not those of idealized local color, but of the actual people the narrator encounters in the factories of Jacksonville or the streets of Atlanta and Harlem. Yet, the existence of these forms of expression is evoked to demand the end of segregation not for their creators, but for the respectable elites who would not have allowed any of them into their parlors.

The creators of the folk tales, folk songs, dances, and instrumental music that demonstrate the humanity of all are part of what the narrator calls the "desperate class—the men who work in the lumber and the turpentine camps, the ex-convicts, the bar-room loafers." Although he admires and wishes to learn their language and their music, he insists that "there is no more urgent work before the white South, not only for its present happiness, but for its future safety, than the decreasing of this class of blacks" (76–77). The problem is that the art created by these people is representative less of uplift and moral elevation than of anger and struggle (or, as he puts it, "hatred and degeneracy"):

> These men conform to the requirements of civilization much as a trained lion with low muttered growls goes through his stunts under the crack of the trainer's whip. They cherish a sullen hatred for all white men and they value life as cheap. . . . This class of blacks hate everything covered by a white skin, and in return are loathed by the whites. The whites regard them just about as a man would a vicious mule, a thing to be worked, driven, and beaten, and killed for kicking. (77–78)

Blues and folk songs are full of stories about oxen, donkeys, mules who refuse to be killed or worked to death, who growl, kick back, and kill their masters and drivers. In a classic 1930s performance, Josh White tells the story of a mule named Jerry, who not only refuses to work, but rebels and kicks his driver to death. A lesser known blues artist, Florida Kid, sang about a mule named Jim who was "too lazy to wag its tail." The police order him to stop hitting Jim to make him work, and he ultimately identifies with the stubborn animal who stands (or, rather, like coeval Detroit autoworkers, sits down) for his rights:

> Well, that ole mule sat down, when he heard what the police said,
> Well, that ole mule sat down, when he heard what the police said,
> That ole mule looked at me and smiled, bucked his head and crossed his legs.
>
> I don't blame that old mule, and neither could nobody else,
> I don't blame that old mule, and neither could nobody else,
> Before that darn old mule would wiggle, woo Lord, I set to hauling myself. . . .[18]

These songs are explicit metaphors for the attitudes of the dangerous class of black people: mules but—as Johnson perceives—also lions. Ironically, Johnson writes, "Decreasing their numbers by shooting and burning them off will not be successful" (*Autobiography* 77). The final solution, in this case, is the appropriation of their culture into the middle class and its refinement from rebellion to uplift.

This is what "making ragtime classic" means. The narrator's southern journey is a source of moving experience, of fascinating encounters and deep inspiration. These are some of the best pages in literature about folklore, primarily because the writer's attention is not merely focused on the notes and the words of the songs and sermons he hears, but because the writer includes the identity of the performers, the preacher John Brown or the hymn leader "Singing Johnson," the collective, social context of the performance, and their impact on the participant observer: "At the close of the 'big meeting' I left the settlement where it was being held, full of enthusiasm. I was in that frame of mind which, in the artistic temperament, amounts to inspiration" (182).

This inspiration, however, never comes to fruition. The next night, he witnesses another southern folk ritual, a lynching in which a black man is burned alive. This experience is another, traumatic initiation that promotes another, and final, passage from one race to another. In fact, the word he uses to describe his state of mind—"dazed"—is the same that he had used after his first shocking discovery of blackness. We might say that, for the first time after an adventurous but relatively sheltered life, he is now discovering what the meaning of being black in America may be:

> A great wave of humiliation and shame swept over me. Shame that I belonged to a race that could be so dealt with; and shame for my country, that it, the great example of democracy to the world, should be the only civilized, if not the only state on earth, where a human being would be burned alive. . . .
> It was shame, unbearable shame. Shame at being identified with a people that could with impunity be treated worse than animals. (187–88, 191)

At this point, playing a variation on the familiar metaphor of passing as emigration, he has already decided that "to forsake one's race to better one's condition was no less worthy an action than to forsake one's country for the same purpose" (190). Emigrants, however, must leave some of their most precious possessions at home; in this case, what the narrator cannot bring with him across the racial boundary is the music. There is no reason, technically, why he could not work at making ragtime classic while passing as a white man; after all, the idea had originated with a white man in Germany. Rather, the reason is anthropological. Folk music, and black folk music especially, is not just a formal structure of sounds and words; it is the expression of an experience, one that includes also the pain and fear and shame instilled by white violence, as well as the memory and pride of resistance. This music of historic struggle cannot be turned into harmless and fashionable sounds of uplift. Precisely because he has been so keenly aware of the social context of the music and the poetry, he finds it impossible to reproduce them once he has run away from that environment and cut off his connections to it.

As the music fades, the color of money emerges. He marries a yellow-haired white girl, and she dies giving birth to "a little golden-haired god" (209). The sense of "longing for [his] mother's people," generated by the exchange of his mother's music for his father's gold, is clinched by the color of the manuscripts in the final lines:

When I sometimes open a little box in which I still keep my fast *yellowing* manuscripts, the only tangible remnants of a vanished dream, a dead ambition, a sacrificed talent, I cannot repress the thought that, after all, I have chosen the lesser part, that I have sold my birthright for a mess of pottage. (211, my italics)

NOTES

1. Notes to Alessandro Portelli, "*The Autobiography of an Ex-Coloured Man* di James Weldon Johnson," *Studi Americani*, 18 (1972), 241–67.

All quotes are from James Weldon Johnson, *The Autobiography of an Ex-Coloured Man* ([1912] New York: Hill and Wang, 1960) (hereafter referred to as *Autobiography*). I also draw on my earlier treatments of this book in "*The Autobiography of an Ex-Coloured Man* di James Weldon Johnson," later revised as a chapter in my *Bianchi e neri nella letteratura americana. La dialettica dell'identità*.

2. Moni Ovadia, *Perché no? L'ebreo corrosivo* (Milano: Bompiani, 1996), 35. A signifying variation on this joke is in Mel Brooks's *Young Frankenstein*. When Frankenstein tells I-gor that he can operate on his shifting hump, I-gor replies, startled, "Hump? What hump?"

3. Werner Sollors, *Neither Black Nor White Yet Both* (New York: Oxford University Press, 1997), 245.

4. For a tragic development of the black brother–white sister theme, we may recall Charles Chesnutt's "The Sheriff's Children," in *Collected Stories of Charles W. Chesnutt*, William L. Andrews, ed. (New York: Mentor, 1992).

5. Herman Melville, *Moby Dick* (Harmondsworth, Middlesex: Penguin, 1988), 232.

6. For another occurrence, see Charles Chesnutt's *The Marrow of Tradition* ([1901], Ann Arbor: University of Michigan Press, 1969).

7. "My mother and I lived together in a little cottage" in which, among other furniture, the parlor sports "a little square piano." "Always on Sunday evenings she opened the little square piano and picked out hymns. . . . Sometimes on other evenings, she would play simple accompaniments to some old Southern songs which she sang. . . . When she started toward the instrument, I used to follow her and sat by her side . . . chiming in with strange harmonies. . . ." (*Autobiography* 6–8).

8. Johnson doesn't mention the color of the father's shoes, leaving to the reader the task of imaging them black, or brown.

9. Later, he further defuses the power of this word by referring to it as merely stepping from one floor to another of a house: "On passing downstairs I was told that the third and top floor of the house was occupied by the proprietor" (Sollors 97).

10. This is a version I remember reading in the *Reader's Digest* in 1960. On an aircraft carrier, a noncommissioned officer (NCO) must inform one of the sailors that his mother has died. He goes on the public address system and calls out loudly: "Sailor Brown, your old lady's dead." Everyone is shocked by his insensitive manner, and the commander tells him he must be more careful next time. When the news comes in that sailor Jones's mother is dead, the NCO assembles all hands on deck and orders: "All

those whose mothers are still alive, take a step forward. Not so fast, Jones!" Another, which I heard from the Jewish actor and storyteller Moni Ovadia at a conference in Rome in 1998, is about the man who must bring to a woman the news that her husband is dead. He knocks on the door: "Are you the widow Abramowitz?" "What do you mean, widow! My husband is alive!" "Wanna make a little bet?"

11. W.E.B. DuBois, "Of our Spirituals' Strivings," in *The Souls of Black Folk.*

12. Although he does not remark on the revision of the discovery narrative, Sollors (*Neither Black Nor White Yet Both,* 266) reads Johnson's comments on its effects as "an adaptation of W.E.B. DuBois's famous formula of the double-consciousness." Johnson's narrator later praises "that remarkable book by Dr. DuBois, *The Souls of Black Folk*" (*Autobiography* 169).

13. Mirror scenes, in which black characters scrutinize their faces, often in a context of discovery of—or escape from—blackness, are found from *The Life of Olaudah Equiano* to Alice Walker's *The Temple of My Familiar.* The classic scene in *The Autobiography of Malcolm X,* in which the narrator admires the "shiny sheen" of his straightened hair, reminds of the way in which the ex-colored man contemplates "the softness and glossiness of my dark hair that fell in waves over my temples" (*Autobiography* 18). Perhaps the passage most ironically similar to Johnson's is the beginning of James Baldwin's *Giovanni's Room,* in which the white narrator contemplates his own whiteness, again defined by the color of his hair, as reflected by a window pane. For a similar narrative of brutal discovery and self-scrutiny in the mirror, see *Volevo diventare bianca* [*I Wanted to Be White*], by Nassira Chohra, written in Italian by a French-born writer of Saharawi descent (Rome: Edizioni E/O, 1994).

14. E. Franklin Frazier, *Black Bourgeoisie. The Rise of a New Middle Class in the United States* ([1957], New York: Collier, 1962), 180ff.

15. LeRoi Jones, *Home: Social Essays* (New York: William Morrow, 1966), 107–108.

16. See my "*Freedom, Fortune, and Fancy.* Henry James e la frontiera," *Acoma,* 12 (Winter 1998), 52–61.

17. The phrase of course is Ralph Ellison's, *Invisible Man* ([1952], Harmondsworth, Middlesex: Penguin, 1978), 17.

18. Quoted in Paul Oliver, *The Meaning of the Blues* (New York: Collier, 1963), 43, from a 1940 recording.

8. "The Spell of Africa Is Upon Me": W.E.B. DuBois's Notion of Art as Propaganda

Alessandra Lorini

> *Africa is at once the most romantic and the most tragic of continents. Its very names reveal its mystery and wide-reaching influence. It is "Ethiopia" of the Greek, the "Kush" and "Punt" of the Egyptian, and the Arabian "Land of the Blacks." To modern Europe it is the "Dark Continent."*
>
> —W.E.B. DuBois, *The Negro* (1915)

Late in 1926, DuBois discussed "The Criteria of Negro Art." He was concerned that politics was abandoning the Harlem Renaissance and that the New Negro movement was turning into a mere search for recognition of its individual artists. DuBois pointed out that white publishers expected "Uncle Toms," "good darkies," and clowns as Negro characters and were ready to reward those authors providing them. He also admitted the existence of a few successful Negro artists, but in his view these were "the remnants of that ability and genius among us whom the accidents of education and opportunity have raised to the tidal waves of chance." To him, the "apostle of beauty" was "the apostle of truth." DuBois declared, accordingly:

> Thus all art is propaganda and ever must be, despite the wailing of the purists. I stand in utter shamelessness and say that whatever art I have for writing has been used always for propaganda for gaining the right of black folk to love and enjoy. I do not care a damn for any art that is not used for propaganda. But I do care when propaganda is confined to one side while the other is stripped and silent. (D. L. Lewis 1994, 103)

DuBois warned against the seductive idea that there was no use in fighting, and that creative talents should do great things and get the reward they deserved. Fighting was crucial, in DuBois's view, because the color line was still an imposing presence: that a black woman sculptress could not find a school in New York willing to accept her meant that the "Negro question," with all its unglamorous battles for the ballot, education, jobs, and housing, was still a priority (101).

In *The Crisis*, during the same year (1926), DuBois reviewed Alain Locke's *The New Negro* and made similar points. He found the book excellent but disagreed with Locke's idea that "Beauty rather than Propaganda should be the object of Negro literature and art." DuBois saw the danger that the Negro Renaissance would lead to "a search for disembodied beauty which is not really a passionate effort to do something tangible." He recognized that this controversy was as old as the world, but if Locke's thesis was insisted on too much, it would "turn the Negro Renaissance into decadence" (Aptheker 1977, 78–79).

DuBois detected a visible sign of this decadence in McKay's *Home to Harlem*, which he reviewed in 1928 in *The Crisis* together with Larsen's *Quicksand* and anthropologist Melville Herskovits's *The American Negro*.[1] Editor DuBois liked Larsen's book but found McKay's nauseating. "After the dirtier parts of its filth," a dismayed DuBois wrote, "I feel distinctly like taking a bath." Although he admitted that the book included some good stuff in the way its author portrayed characters, he could not tolerate McKay's giving in to the "prurient demand" of a "certain decadent section of the white American world" centered in New York, which longed for unrestrained passions and wanted to see them written in black and white and "saddled on black Harlem."

In the same review, DuBois praised Herskovits's work. He found Franz Boas's pupil a real scientist that is, "a man who is more interested in arriving at truth than proving a thesis of race superiority." At the end of an extensive research of physical anthropology, Herskovits had concluded that American Negroes were forming a new racial type that was a mixture of African, American, Indian, and Caucasian ancestry and were likely to remain physically distinctive for a long time. DuBois welcomed Herskovits's findings. They gave evidence that fewer than one-fourth of the Negroes in the United States were of unmixed Negro blood, and that forty percent of them had as much, or even more, white blood as they did Negro. According to DuBois, this showed the unsoundness of the argument that the Negro was an inassimilable race in the United States and the idiocy of discussing American Negroes as if they were Bantu (113–15). Anthropologist Herskovits had been influenced by his encounter with the Harlem Renaissance and the desire of black intellectuals to develop a distinctive cultural tradition rooted both in the African past and in African-American folklore (W. Jackson 1986, 95–126). DuBois saw in Herskovits's findings a good piece of social science susceptible to being used as a weapon of propaganda.

DuBois's notion of propaganda expressed the tension between DuBois the scholar and DuBois the artist, as David Blight puts it (Blight 45–71). This tension dated back to DuBois's Harvard times and was the result, in part, of how he was influenced by William James's pragmatism. Shortly before his death in 1910, philosopher William James, who was DuBois's teacher at Harvard, wrote that "philosophy is more a matter of passionate vision than logic" (Coon 73). A radical pragmatist, DuBois certainly agreed with James's latest views, which followed the philosopher's active intellectual involvement in the Anti-Imperialist League after the Spanish-American War of 1898 and his strong criticism of the growing of the impersonal, big institutions that ruled American society and threatened its pluralistic premises. It was at Harvard that DuBois turned, as he put it, "back from the lovely but sterile land of philosophic speculation, to the social sciences as the field for gathering and interpreting that body of fact which would apply to my program for the Negro" (DuBois 1968, 133). This notion of propaganda shaped DuBois's idea of *The Crisis*, the magazine he directed for twenty-four years, and his choice of pageantry as an effective form of propaganda.

THE CRISIS: SOCIAL SCIENCE AS A WEAPON

When, in 1910, DuBois resigned as professor of economics and history at Atlanta University to take charge of *The Crisis*, the official magazine of the National Association for the Advancement of Colored People (NAACP)—with no steady salary granted—he felt pleased to leave the classroom. He thought the magazine could become the intellectual tool he needed to make social science an active weapon in the struggle for racial equality.

By then, DuBois had come to realize that problems like lynching could not be aggressively attacked in the classroom, but could be thoroughly investigated and publicly exposed from the pages of a journal capable of reaching a large public. It was a shift from academic social science to propaganda, as DuBois's biographer David L. Lewis aptly puts it (Lewis 1993, 408).

DuBois made that decision in 1899 after the shocking experience of seeing parts of the body of a lynched Negro man on display at a grocery store in Atlanta, and white men, women, and children fighting over those pieces of flesh. That scene deeply affected the scholar, who later wrote in his autobiographical *Dusk of Dawn:* "I began to turn aside from my work." From then on, DuBois's double-consciousness, the struggle between his American and Negro identities, became further complicated by his awareness that one "could not be a calm, cool and detached scientist while Negroes were lynched, murdered and starved" (DuBois 1975, 67). DuBois saw an opportunity to turn the impotence of social science into an active weapon of change by asserting in the pages of *The Crisis* the centrality of the so-called "Negro question" in American democracy. The agenda of militant journalism he envisioned appeared in his first editorial: to investigate and make public "those facts and arguments which show the danger of race prejudice."[2]

Under DuBois's leadership, the magazine became self-supporting within five years, selling a total of 1,400,000 copies (Aptheker 1986, 154). "With this organ of propaganda and defense and with its legal bureau, lectures and writers," DuBois remarked, "the National Association for the Advancement of Colored People was able to organize one of the most effective assaults of liberalism upon prejudice and reaction that the modern world has seen" (DuBois 1975, 226–27). In spite of internal tensions, the early NAACP projected the public image of an effective organization, able to mobilize thousands of people to fight for the civil and political rights of the "dark races" of the world. One of the most strenuous battles of its early years was the one against *The Birth of a Nation,* David W. Griffith's technically ground-breaking movie, the script of which was based on Thomas Dixon's negrophobic *The Clansman.* In the May 1915 issue of *The Crisis,* DuBois explained to his growing number of readers the reasons for the NAACP's campaign against the screening of *Birth of a Nation.* He didn't deny that the first part of the movie contained "marvelously good war pictures," but maintained that the second half was a vicious misrepresentation of the Negro "either as an ignorant fool, a vicious rapist, a venal or unscrupulous politician or a faithful but doddering idiot." The film was a powerful weapon of racist propaganda at a time in which the lynching of black men for alleged attacks on white women was almost daily news, racial segregation of residential areas expanded, and pervasive antiblack feelings had become common culture in the re-unified United States. Yet, as DuBois acutely observed, in a way, Griffith's racist propaganda and the NAACP battle against it helped each other get public attention. Paradoxically, mobilization against the film probably "succeeded in advertising it even beyond its admittedly notable merits." Although in favor of the NAACP's legal campaign for censorship, DuBois was fully aware of the danger of limiting artistic expression. It was, in his words, "a miserable dilemma": without some limitations "civilization could not endure" (240).[3]

As a militant magazine, *The Crisis*'s main function was not the publication of creative writing. Yet it did provide a forum for young black writers such as Langston Hughes and Jessie Fauset, endorsed the NAACP's annual award of the Spingarn medal, and provided a place for a number of occasional parties and conferences. When the organ of the National Urban League, *Opportunity,* was founded in 1923 and immediately endorsed the New Negro movement, *The Crisis* increased its support to young Negro writers by offering a series of literary awards (Ikonné 97–99).

In 1924, DuBois's magazine also launched the Krigwa, a workshop for young writers and artists, which by 1926 already had six branches in different parts of the country. One of these, the Krigwa Players of New York, which was devoted to research on drama, founded the Little Negro Theatre at the 135th Street branch of the New York Public Library, which found in DuBois one of its strongest supporters. From these workshops on the theater run by *The Crisis* clearly emerged the notions that "a real Negro theatre" had to have plots revealing "Negro life as it is," that its plays had to be written by Negro authors "who understand from birth and continual association just what it means to be a Negro today," and that it had to be located "in a Negro neighborhood near the mass of ordinary negro people" for their entertainment and approval.[4] In his search for a "real Negro drama," DuBois left out those "excellent groups of colored amateurs" who successfully adapted Shakespeare or Broadway shows to black audiences. Thus the Krigwa group aimed at producing original plays that were written, performed, and enjoyed by African-Americans (Huggins 1971, 292–93).

This idea of "a real Negro theatre" was a practical development of DuBois's concept of art as propaganda—that is, an art conveying a message of racial uplifting and equality. According to the activist and scholar, the black drama was an instrument of education and uplifting, a weapon of cultural enlightenment, and a source of African-American identity. For this reason, DuBois saw in pageantry, a popular form of community theater in progressive America, a great opportunity "to get people interested in this development of Negro drama to teach on the one hand the colored people themselves the meaning of their history and their rich, emotional life through a new theatre, and on the other, to reveal the Negro to the white world as a human, feeling thing."[5]

ART AS PROPAGANDA: THE PAGEANT *THE STAR OF ETHIOPIA*

When DuBois wrote several sketchy drafts of the pageant *The Star of Ethiopia*, pageantry was in the air. One of the most significant movements of the progressive era, the pageant movement included both radical and conservative versions of humanitarian, nationalistic, Americanizing, uplifting concerns of progressive reformers. DuBois's pageant was the only one among the hundreds staged in the early decades of the century to tell the story of the Negro race both in Africa and in America. Meant to attract large crowds and involve whole communities in organizing the performance, this form of dramatic representation of history offered versions of the past that suited the goal of the celebration or national holiday for which the pageant was devised. Social workers, teachers, church leaders, grassroots organizations were all involved under the guidance of pageant masters to build a theatrical machine able to gather sometimes as many as thousands of performers. Pageantry made history vivid while promoting community solidarity through mass participation.

From its beginning, as historian David Glassberg points out, pageantry was "a blend of progressivism and antimodernism, customary civil religious rituals and the promise of artistic innovation" (Glassberg 284). In the period 1908 through 1917, more than 300 pageants were performed in the United States. Most pageants emphasized continuities between past and present generations by performing classical and biblical themes, fairy tales, medieval and Renaissance legends, and reenactment of historical events. The role that pageants played in the celebration of the Fourth of July as the national holiday in which episodes of American history and community life were represented was particularly relevant. There were two ways, at least, to turn historical reconstruction into a dramatic public ritual enhancing community cohesion. On the one hand, there was "the pageant of nations" in which "all races and nationalities" that made up an American city celebrated the contribution or "gift" of each group to America. On the other, there were those schemes that emphasized an assumed "underlying public spirit" beneath differences of class, gender, race, or ethnicity. DuBois's pageant belonged to the former group because it was constructed on the idea of "the gift of the Negro race to the world." But by the time DuBois's pageant *The Star of Ethiopia* was staged for the last time at the Hollywood Bowl in 1925, pageantry had lost its early strength. "My pageant died with an expiring gasp in Los Angeles in 1925," he recalled in *Dusk of Dawn*. It was not only lack of financial support, "but the tremendous and expanding vogue of the motion picture and the power of the radio and loud speaker" that killed pageantry. And DuBois in 1925 chose Hollywood as a stage for his pageant, hoping to turn it into a film to reach larger audiences. He did not succeed, but it "was still a beautiful thing": "It cost five thousand dollars and weeks of work; and doubt and travail, harsh words and with it, all curiously inwrought, love and wonder, a working hand in hand and heart in heart which paid" (DuBois 1975, 274).

The battle against Griffith's *Birth of a Nation* had shown how powerful movies could be as instruments of racist propaganda. DuBois wanted to create an oppositional form of propaganda, the very reversal of Griffith's epic celebration of the Ku Klux Klan (KKK). He strongly believed that reconstructing historical events in pageant form could have a greater impact than any book, exhibit, or lecture. But his pageant never reached the movie audience, although it was witnessed by tens of thousands and several thousand people were involved in its production.

A close look at DuBois's papers reveals how strongly he believed in reaching large audiences, which is why such a well known intellectual as DuBois decided on pageantry as a medium to express his ideas. Most other progressive academics did not get involved in the time-consuming and strenuous efforts necessary to organize this form of community-built theater; they simply limited their intellectual activity to writing books. Unlike most of his intellectual colleagues, DuBois, in writing and staging the first pageant on Negro history, put his notion of art as propaganda and history as weapon of change into practice by creating a "usable past" to instill pride and to foster a national black drama.

The first draft of *The Star of Ethiopia* is dated 1911, but it was not staged until two years later in New York for the fiftieth anniversary of Emancipation, where it involved 350 volunteer performers and 14,000 viewers. In 1915, the year Griffith's *Birth of a Nation* premiered, DuBois's pageant was represented in Washington, D.C., and bore proof to the mobilization of the African-American community of that city by collecting 1,200 performers and a public of 12,000. In 1916, it was staged in Philadelphia for the centennial of the American Methodist Episcopal (AME) Church, and in 1925, in Los Angeles to support the local branch of the NAACP.[6]

After seeing the large, enthusiastic audience gathered at the New York Armory in October 1913, an excited DuBois exclaimed, "The pageant is the thing. This is what people want and long for. This is the gown and paraphernalia in which the message of education and reasonable race pride can deck itself" (DuBois 1915, 91).

Central to *The Star of Ethiopia* was the idea of "gifts of the Negro race to the world." DuBois's early drafts of the pageant portrayed five scenes of African and African-American history divided into several episodes covering a period of ten thousand years. The pageant began with prehistoric times and proceeded to tell of the discovery of the art of working metals by "the Eldest and Strongest of the Races of men whose faces be Black," as the herald announced. This was, in fact, the first gift black people gave to humanity: the Gift of Welding Iron. The character of Ethiopia, the Mother of Men, was a tall, veiled woman in splendid garment, who had Fire in her right hand and Iron in her left. As she slowly proceeded on stage, the rhythmic roll of tom-toms began, the arts blossomed, wild animals were brought in, and the whole picture created a general atmosphere of merry feasting and dancing.

The second gift of black people to the world was the Gift of Civilization of the Valley of the Nile. The episode portrayed how the civilization of ancient Egypt came about. One hundred savages filled the scene along with fifty veiled figures, the Sphinx, the Pyramid, the Obelisk, and the empty throne of the Pharaoh. The Egyptians unveiled and displayed Negroes and mulattos magnificently dressed. One of the Cushitic chiefs was crowned pharaoh, and the Queen of Sheba and other African rulers paid visit. The culture of Egypt spread to Central Africa, where empires flourished from the sixth to the sixteenth centuries. Slowly, with the sound of music, all people left the stage except fifty savages, who stayed to examine their gifts. When the lights grew dim as the Egyptian culture died, the fifty savages fell asleep.

Then the light returned to herald the third gift of black people to the world: the Gift of Faith. The episode depicted how the Negro race spread the faith of Muhammad. But with Islam (which DuBois referred to as Muhammadanism) came numerous religious wars that weakened and divided black people and made them an easy prey to the slave trader.

The next scene dramatically showed Ethiopia blotted out by fire and pillaged by slave hunters. During this pillaging, two monks representing the Christian world looked on in silent acquiescence. The Muslims (referred to by DuBois as Muhammadans), forcing their slaves forward as European traders entered the stage, took gold in barter. The Negro race learned to suffer and hence gave the fourth gift to humanity: the Gift of Humiliation to teach human beings to bear even slavery and continue to live. The following scene showed the Negro race transplanted in the Americas. Hordes of slaves filed on stage. As the chorus sang spirituals, black people faced the lash, and over the prostrate and bending forms of the slaves, the Ghost of Slavery danced in and out. A group of Native Americans danced, too; as they left the stage, they vainly urged the slaves to follow them to the forests. Then the slaves' toil was interrupted by a lively Creole dance announcing the fifth gift of the black people to the world: the Gift of Struggle Toward Freedom.

Subsequent scenes portrayed the actions of Toussaint-Louverture, David Walker, Nat Turner, Denmark Vesey, Sojourner Truth, Frederick Douglass, William Lloyd Garrison, Harriet Beecher Stowe, and John Brown. Ethiopia awakened as Shango, the Thunder God, called her to duty. She rose with a glistening sword in one hand and the Star of Freedom shining brightly in the other. As black Union soldiers entered on stage, a chorus sang "Marching Through Georgia."

The last scene portrayed African-American history since the Civil War. Groups of black people were shown at work in various trades. Groups of businessmen, athletes, ministers, physicians, teachers, trained nurses, and others were shown quietly enjoying freedom in their own ways. Suddenly they were viciously attacked by the "furies" of race prejudice, envy, gambling, idleness, intemperance, and the KKK. At first, some of the groups gave in, but others stood up for themselves. The furies tried to seize the Star of Freedom, but the freedmen appealed to Ethiopia, the mother of all human beings. She called her sons and daughters all over on earth to come forth and build a Tower of Light upon which she set the Star of Freedom so high that it would be forever safe. The last gifts of black people to the world were the Gift of Laugher and the Gift of Hope.[7]

DuBois chose pageantry as the aesthetic form to bring "facts, dreams, and ideals of the colored people" together in a dramatic recital. "The Negro is essentially dramatic," he wrote after the third staging of his pageant in Philadelphia in 1916. "His greatest gift to the world has been and will be a gift of art, of appreciation and realization of beauty," proclaimed DuBois together with the dark herald of the pageant.[8] These broad generalizations were meant to counteract racist assumptions of Negro inferiority similarly drawn in monolithic and stereotypical terms. DuBois, however, was perfectly aware of how differentiated and socially stratified the people of African descent were. He spoke to the elite, to the "Talented Tenth," because he believed that "the Negro race, like all races, is going to be saved by its exceptional men" (DuBois 1982, *Writings by W.E.B. DuBois in Non-Periodical Literature*, 17). This is what *The Star of Ethiopia* celebrated. Its staging and public success were the work of genius of African-American artists and musicians and the organizational efforts of talented African-American church ministers, school principals, and teachers. At the same time, DuBois's pageant went beyond the historical reconstruction of African-American past and delivered a visionary message to the whole human race.

It was the original contribution of the Negro race that DuBois made visual in *The Star of Ethiopia*. Yet DuBois did not think that American people of African descent should Africanize America "for America has too much to teach the world and Africa," as he had already stated in *The Souls of Black Folk* (DuBois 1992, 4). Similarly, their Negro identity should be preserved from the "flood of white Americanism" because of the unique message their race had to give the world. For DuBois, racial identity was the basis of collective memory and vice versa. The history of the Negro race was an essential ingredient of black American identity that the pageant *The Star of Ethiopia* would foster.

In general, social conflicts were concealed in most pageants. In pageant schemes for the Fourth of July, for example, enslaved blacks were represented as contented and loyal workers who never tried to escape. Foreign immigrants were shown performing colorful dances, well accepted in their new country, but placed at its margins. Nearly every pageant included a scene in which white colonizers peacefully purchased native land as if it was the price of inevitable progress and not an expression of white conquest. Hence, DuBois's pageant was an ambitious attempt to offer an oppositional definition of pageantry by including it within the tradition of the black folk drama. His *Star of Ethiopia* would give history and memory to the people of African descent in America and place their experience at the center of U.S. history.

DuBois's pageant created a depiction of a structured African past and made African-American history coherently develop into an allegorical uplifting of a racial group. Yet *The Star of Ethiopia* was not simply an expression of the uplift ideology. Fascination with ancient African royalty, civilization, and unquestioned patriarchal authority was part of a popular African-American vision of Africa and African diaspora, the central element of both black nationalism and racial uplifting ideology, as Kevin Gaines has pointed out.[9] DuBois used two pieces from Verdi's opera *Aida*—whose text was a European version of Egypt[10]—but did not use ragtime. DuBois included in each representation either traditional "sorrow songs" or original music by black composers such as Coleridge-Taylor, Bob Cole, J. Rosamond Johnson, and DuBois's army friend Charles Young who were dominating the world of New York's commercial theaters, and primitivistic songs.[11] This issue of "primitivism" haunted the authors of the Harlem Renaissance. The question was how to acknowledge African-American "gifts" of singing and dancing without falling into racist stereotypes. DuBois tried to avoid this pitfall by appealing to Ethiopianism.

DUBOIS'S ETHIOPIANISM AND IMAGES OF AFRICA

Ethiopianism—with its two thematic components, the rise of Africa and the decline of the West—provided one element of Anglo-African literary tradition on which DuBois's myth-making was based. Ethiopianism assumed, as Wilson Moses points out, that Caucasians and Ethiopians were separate varieties of humanity with distinct destinies "competing for honor in the eyes of history and the world." Africans were considered special people with special gifts, and blacks were, in some ways, superior to whites. To an African-inborn genius were attributed traits like tropical dreaminess, feminine aestheticism, and a childlike love for nature. In Wilson Moses's words, Ethiopianism may be defined "as the effort of the English-speaking black or African person to view his past enslavement and present cultural dependency in terms of the broader history of civilization. It serves to remind him that this present scientific technological civilization, dominated by Western Europe for a scant four hundred years, will go under certainly—like all the empires of the past. It expressed the belief that the tragic racial experience has profound historical value, that it has endowed the African with moral superiority and made him a seer" (Moses 1978, 159–61).

Can DuBois, the militant scholar who conceived social science as a weapon for social change, be reconciled with the DuBois with a literary soul? His conception of art as propaganda, although it might appear reductive and the very denial of artistic freedom, was an attempt to reconcile the two DuBoises. Pageantry was an instrument DuBois, the sociology professor, used after he had stepped out of the "ivory tower of statistics and investigation" of the academic world (DuBois 1975, 226). In this perspective, his "double-consciousness," DuBois's "two-ness," seemed further complicated by these other sides of his divided intellectual self. Unifying attempts included DuBois's militant conception of Pan-Africanism and his literary abstraction of Africa as the "Spiritual Frontier of Humanity." Did he succeed?

DuBois's racialism compelled him to proclaim that the Negro race was "essentially dramatic," having an inborn "gift of art, of appreciation and realization of beauty," and might appear in strident contradiction with DuBois's universalism. Yet his conception of art as propaganda combined racialism and universalism in the mystical language of Ethiopianism. Expressed in all different genres of African-American culture—from slave narratives to the sermons of black ministers of the free people of color in the antebellum, urban North and to political tracts of early emigrationists such as Martin Delany and Edward Blyden—this long tradition of Ethiopianism includes DuBois. After 1896, with the victory of Ethiopian emperor Menelik II over the Italian colonizers at Adwa, the inspiring biblical prophecy that "Ethiopia shall soon stretch out her hands unto God" seemed fulfilled by Ethiopian independence from the European powers spreading over African land. To Pan-Africanists such as DuBois, Adwa became the symbol of the black defeat of white dominance over people of African descent.

In 1919, the militant scholar wrote in *The Crisis,* "The African movement means to us what the Zionist movement means to the Jews, the centralization of race effort and the recognition of a race front. To help bear the burden of Africa does not mean any lessening of effort in our own problem at home. Rather it means increased interest" (Moses 1978, 143). And in 1921, in the same magazine, DuBois wrote, "The absolute equality of races—physical, political and social—is the founding stone of world peace and human advancement. No one denies great differences of gift, capacities and attainment among individuals of all races, but the voice of science, religion and practical politics is one in denying the God-appointed existence of super-races, or of races naturally and inevitably and eternally inferior. . . ." (Aptheker 1986, 195–99). For DuBois, the cosmopolitan intellectual and creative writer, Africa was "the Spiritual Frontier of human kind." In 1924 he wrote the following:

> The spell of Africa is upon me. The ancient witchery of her medicine is burning my drowsy, dreamy blood. This is not a country, it is a world. . . .
> One longs to leap against the sun and then calls, like some great hand of fate,

the slow, silent crushing power of almighty sleep. . . . Life is slow here. . . . Life slows down and as it slows it deepens. . . . Unknown evil appears and unknown good. Africa is the Spiritual Frontier of human kind. . . . Then will come a day . . . when there will spring in Africa a civilization without coal, without noise, where machinery will sing and never rush and roar, and where men will sleep and think and dance and lie prone before the rising suns, and women will be happy. The objects of life will be revolutionized. Our duty will not consist in getting up at seven, working furiously for six, ten, and twelve hours. . . . No—We shall dream the day away and in cool dawns, in little swift hours, do all our work. (Aptheker 1985, 131–32)

Far from being a praise of *il dolce far niente*—no one can deny that DuBois was the most restless and productive scholar, editor, racial leader—this vision of Africa revealed a tension between the social scientist and the creative writer that he never suppressed. *The Star of Ethiopia* was an example of this tension between history and poetry, between social science and art. This belonged to DuBois's style, to his efforts to shape African-American memory and identity. The image of Africa as the "spiritual frontier of human kind" contained an inclusive message forcing the value of *deepness* over the shallowness of racial prejudice and the competitive values of a mass-market society that bring in the "furies" of vanity, gossip, envy, crime, poverty, ignorance, distrust, and license. In 1926, DuBois further explored this notion of spiritual frontier: "In Africa the swift, the energetic are the dead. In Africa the 'lazy' survive and live. This African laziness is several things; it is shelter from the penetrating rain; it is defense from malaria. And it brings with it leisure and dreams and human intercourse."[12]

Thus, by offering an ecological vision of Africa as a utopian resource for humanity, DuBois reversed the Victorian notion of a "Dark Continent" with no history. Yet his message did have the limits of a reconceptualization of Victorian dogmatic beliefs in progress and elite knowledge implicit in DuBois's notion of the Talented Tenth (C. West 65).

For his writing of the first draft of *The Star of Ethiopia*, DuBois could rely on various sources of African history that a few years later (1915) he would elaborate in *The Negro*. Although he could depend on those volumes written in the nineteenth century by African-American intellectuals, whose aim was to show that black people had a "glorious past," as a racial weapon against white supremacy, he did not use them.[13] Black authors of the 1830s and 1840s, such as Robert Benjamin Lewis and James Pennington, claimed that black people were the descendants of ancient and noble civilizations that had given the whole world art, literature, science, and great men. They explained enslavement by the fall of African civilizations, which occurred when black people abandoned monotheism for polytheism. But as God was the engine of human history, it was God's will to uplift the black race in both Africa and America. This interpretation, however, could not explain the enduring nature of racial prejudice that persisted and became even stronger after Emancipation. In fact, that which was commonly looked on as the "failure" of Reconstruction strongly reinforced the racist thinking that blacks were unfit for self-government. Columbia University political scientist John Burgess, for example, expressed a widely shared belief when he stated in 1902 that "a black skin means membership in a race of men which has never of itself succeeded in subjecting passion to reason, and has never, therefore, created any civilization of any kind."[14] In hegemonic racial thinking, there was no space for any notion of an African-American "glorious past": it was assumed that those colored people who had achieved something relevant were irrelevant anomalies, like those women whose intellectual capacity seemed to undermine the general assumption of the irrational behavior of the "gentle sex."[15]

More than relying on mid-nineteenth-century black authors and their linear and teleological interpretation of history, DuBois reconstructed the African past by using the lenses of contemporary social science as a weapon. As he had done with *The Star of Ethiopia* two years earlier, he wrote *The Negro* by drawing upon a few primary historical sources and a large variety of secondary sources. He made critical use of the works of the German traveler Leo Frobenius and the English liberal imperialist Sir Harry Hamilton Johnston, who both took African history seriously and rejected Hegel's view that Africa was "no historical part of the world."[16] What was new in DuBois's retrieval of the African past was his turning to contemporary social science in order to grasp the complex cultures of African peoples.

Besides challenging Hegel's assertion that Africa had no movement or development to show the rest of the world and that its inhabitants were still in the conditions of "mere nature," DuBois wanted to face the ignorant racism of eminent politicians and spokespersons at home. For example, in 1914, U.S. Senator James K. Vardaman of Mississippi declared that the Negro had never written a language, never risen above "the government of a club," never created monuments, never sailed: "He is living in Africa today, in the land where he sprang, indigenous, in substantially the same condition, occupying the same rude hut, governed by the same club, worshipping the same fetish that he did when the Pharaohs ruled Egypt. He has never had any civilization except that which has been inculcated by a superior race" (DuBois 1970, xi). By focusing his historical reconstruction on Ethiopia as the most ancient human civilization, DuBois wanted to erase this racist ignorance and give people of African descent their past by showing that with little or no assistance from external forces, black people had developed distinctive and complex cultures in Africa.

He also made the African diaspora, the outcome of the slave trade, the cause of the destruction of those West African states that were flourishing at the time when Europe was in the Middle Ages. In his *The Star of Ethiopia*, Negro slavery was made central to the American experience and notion of progress and the basis of modern imperialism, which presented itself as the rescuer of a backward and inferior race.

In 1915, with the publication of *The Negro*, DuBois made clear that historical scholarship could become collective memory by means of aesthetic stimulus. Without essentializing Africa as a monolithic entity, but by instead spending more than half of the book demonstrating the complexities of the different parts of the continent and its diverse peoples, DuBois's history of the African diaspora was a scholarly version of *The Star of Ethiopia*. Like the pageant, *The Negro* was an attempt to give Africa a historical past at a time when the world powers were scrambling to colonize the land and resources of that continent. He rebuilt the history of the descent of black people into the Valley of the Nile, the raising of a new civilization allied with Asia, and cultural developments along the Niger and in the Congo Valley; he reversed the prevailing idea that every sign of civilization in Africa at Benin, in Zimbabwe, and on the east coast were due to European or Asiatic cultures; and he called for more archeological research.

DuBois anticipated by a decade at least the findings of anthropologist Melville Herskovits, whose early work he had praised in *The Crisis*, who thoroughly researched African cultures and their relevance to black Americans. Herskovits pointed out how incorrect it was to think of Africa as having been "isolated" from the rest of the world and challenged the erroneous definition of the vast area south of the Sahara as "darkest Africa," whose peoples would have "slumbered on until awakened by the coming of the dynamic civilization of Europe." Africa fully participated in the development of human civilization, Herskovits argued. It was therefore pointless to speak of Africa as "moving into a wider world," as the continent was never out of it. Africa did not lie dormant for centuries, as the myth of its "darkness" would claim. Africa was never isolated, and its caravan routes across the desert had been known since medieval times. Africa simply had little to offer, compared to the Indies, to Europeans seeking gold, spices, silk, and other treasures. The only thing Europeans would find of interest on the African soil was a labor force in the form of slaves. It was not until the Treaty of Berlin in 1885 that the scramble began among the European powers for control of Africa.[17]

DuBois made this point in his effective article "The African Roots of the War" in the May 1915 issue of the *Atlantic Monthly*, which anticipated Lenin's *Imperialism as the Highest Stage of Capitalism* (1917). By reviewing the history of European hegemony over the continent based on technological superiority and citing Franz Boas's argument that iron was first smelted in Africa and that agriculture and commerce flourished there when Europe was still a wilderness, DuBois looked at the economic motives that led to the present conflict to achieve domination over tropical Africa: "Africa is a prime cause of this terrible overturning of civilization." In a striking parallel to Lenin, DuBois wrote of the "white workingman" who was asked to share "the spoil of exploiting 'chinks' and 'niggers'" as a force united to capitalists: "It is the nation; a new democratic nation composed of united capital and labor." Welfare concessions on the one side and threat of competition of colored labor on the other side made the West's white working class potentially available to share the spoils of the darker nations of the world: "It is increased wealth, power and luxury for all classes on a scale the world never saw before."[18] These words shed light on the profound relationship between domestic racism and imperialistic views binding together different groups of a mass democracy. This cement was made of mainstream scientific views, of preconceptions and racial stereotypes based on deep and archaic fears that by 1915 found a powerful means of popularization in a mass medium like the movies.

It was DuBois's double-consciousness, his awareness that being an American and a Negro were often two separate identities, that shaped his symbolic construction of Africa. Yet his Africa had a symbolic meaning for both white and black America. DuBois insisted, as demonstrated in *The Star of Ethiopia*, that Africa had a rich artistic and social history that was a necessary antidote to the usually absent or hostile accounts of Africa that American citizens could find in most of their libraries and schools. This rediscovery of Africa and its cultures became one of the favorite themes of the Harlem Renaissance.[19] A similar spirit of rediscovery of Africa shaped Carter Woodson's Association for the Study of Negro Life and Culture, the aim of which was to retrieve historical documents, dismissed or ignored by white historians, and to show "what the race has thought and felt and done as a contribution to the world's accumulation of knowledge and the welfare of mankind" (Woodson 1919, 274–75). This contribution was what audiences of DuBois's *Star of Ethiopia* learned and critics perceived.

Instead of rejecting the biological concept of race of his time, DuBois's historical reconstruction turned it into a definition of racial differences in which each human group was complementary and necessary to all others. DuBois's rewriting of African history departed from nineteenth-century black authors' notions of a mythical glorious past of the black people who would evolve, together with other human groups, along a common line of progress from savagery to barbarism to civilization. DuBois's rewriting of African history became, instead, a narrative of human cultural differences in line with the new scientific paradigm of cultural anthropology that explained human differences in historical, not biological, terms that DuBois had learned from Franz Boas, whom he met in 1906 at Atlanta (Lorini 76–89). At the same time, DuBois's notion of art as propaganda combined the ideology of Ethiopianism with the language of a black New England Victorian trapped in the faith of knowledge based on scientific investigation and in an assumed inner power of highbrow culture to transform for the best whoever is exposed to it, as Cornel West has remarked (C. West 57–70). Yet by extending the promise of Ethiopianism to the whole human race, this image of Africa reversed the Victorian notion of a Dark Continent with no history. There is no question that DuBois often spoke the language of an evolutionist social scientist. DuBois was a child of his time, but his vision was much larger than that of the American intellectual elite. An example of DuBois's broad vision was his shift from searching for an African usable past to shaping African-American identity, to imagining a utopian future in which all gifts of different human groups would be freely delivered to enrich a cosmopolitan world. In this perspective, this powerful message together with DuBois's notion of art as propaganda addressed the literary world of the New Negro of the Harlem Renaissance by urging that art be made "the Spiritual Frontier of human kind."

NOTES

1. Melville Herskovits, *The American Negro: A Study of Racial Crossing* (New York: Knopf, 1928).

2. W.E.B. DuBois, "Editorial," *The Crisis* 1 (November 1910), 10–11.

3. On *The Crisis* as a weapon of social change, the battle against Griffith's racist film, and DuBois's pageant, see Alessandra Lorini, *Rituals of Race: American Public Culture and the Search for Racial Democracy* (Charlottesville, Virginia: University Press of Virginia, 1999), 141–50, 219–36.

4. "Krigwa Players Little Negro Theatre: The Story of a Little Theatre Movement," *The Crisis* (July 1926), 134.

5. W.E.B. DuBois, "The Drama Among Black Folk," *The Crisis* 2 (August 1916), 171.

6. A number of typewritten drafts of the pageant are in the papers of W.E.B. DuBois (microfilmed edition of the University of Massachusetts collection), reel no. 87. DuBois's biographers have generally overlooked this pageant. Only David L. Lewis, in his masterpiece *W.E.B. DuBois. Biography of a Race, 1868–1919* (New York: Holt, 1993), 459–63, explores the pageant, which is also analyzed in Frieda L. Scott's essay "The Star of Ethiopia: A Contribution Toward the Development of Black Drama and Theater in the Harlem Renaissance," in Amritjit Singh, William S. Shiver, and Stanley Brodwin, eds., *The Harlem Renaissance: Revaluations* (New York: Garland Publishing, 1989), 257–69. See Lorini 219–25.

7. W.E.B. DuBois, "The People of Peoples and Their Gifts to Men," *The Crisis* 6 (November 1913), 339–41. This scene reconstruction is also based on the several drafts and handwritten annotations included in DuBois's papers.

8. W.E.B. DuBois, *NAACP. Report of the Department of Publications and Research, From August 1910 through November 1915* [1916], reprinted in Aptheker, 1986, 169.

9. Kevin K. Gaines, *Uplifting the Race—Black Leadership, Politics, and Culture in the Twentieth Century* (Chapel Hill: University of North Carolina Press, 1996), 109–11.

10. Edward W. Said, in *Culture and Imperialism* (New York: Vintage Books, 1994), 111–32, develops a compelling analysis of Verdi's famous grand opera *Aida* as the embodiment of "the authority of Europe's version of Egypt" and as an expression of the civilizing "mission" of the West. Verdi worked on this opera, based on a story developed by the French Egyptologist Auguste Mariette, in 1870–1871 when Egypt, although technically under the Ottoman Empire, was gradually coming under European cultural hegemony.

11. "Bamboula" from West Africa, "Take Nabauji" from East Africa, "The Imaginary Ballet," and Motherless Child" were by Coleridge-Taylor; Young wrote "Prelude Primitive," "Chant of the Savages," "When Darkness Descends," "The African Chant," and "The Welding Song."

12. W.E.B. DuBois, "The Answer of Africa," *Writings of W.E.B. DuBois in Non-Periodical Literature*, 1982, 150–55.

13. The first of these works was published in 1836 by Robert Benjamin Lewis and titled *Light and Truth: Collected from the Bible and Ancient and Modern History; Containing the Universal History of the Colored and the Indian Race, from the Creation of the World to the Present Time.* According to this author—whose background was African and Native American—the origins of many ancient civilizations were Ethiopian and Negroid, and black people were the descendants of Ham, the son of Noah. Black people, whom he named Ethiopians, had produced outstanding figures such as Scipio Africanus, Hannibal, Moses, and other ancient leaders. A similar school of thought was followed by James Pennington, who wrote *A Textbook of the Origin and History of the Colored People* (1841), in which he stressed the "glorious origins" of black people and rejected one of the common pro-slavery arguments circulating in nineteenth-century America: that they had been enslaved because of Noah's curse on Ham. The emphasis these authors gave to biblical texts was part of their attempt to establish the unity of humankind at a time when a new version of the old idea of polygenesis, namely the distinct origins of different human groups and their consequential hierarchy according to God's design, was becoming a popular pro-slavery argument in America. See George M. Fredrickson, *The Black Image in the White Mind: The Debate on Afro-American Character and Destiny* (New York: Harper & Row, 1971), 71–96.

14. John W. Burgess, *Reconstruction and the Constitution, 1866–1876* (New York: Scribners, 1902), 133.

15. For an exploration of scientific analogy of racial and gender differences in the nineteenth century, see Nancy L. Stephan, "Race and Gender: The Role of Analogy in Science," *ISIS* 77 (June 1986): 261–77.

16. Philosopher Georg Wilhelm Friedrich Hegel put into philosophical terms the attitude many Europeans and Americans shared about Africa. The mainstream argument, which justified slavery and other forms of oppression of the people of African descent, held that Africans did not have a written language, any monuments, any sophisticated forms of architecture, or any forms of civilization or government except

when inculcated under the control of a superior race. Hegel wrote that Africa had no movement or development to show the world because it was "still involved in the conditions of mere nature." In his university lectures, the German philosopher referred to "African stupidity." See Hegel, *The Philosophy of History* (1831), J. Sibree, trans. (New York: Dover Publications, 1965), 99. DuBois paid a tribute to Leo Frobenius by relying on his findings and using material from his *The Voice of Africa: Being an Account of the Travels of the German Inner African Exploration Expedition in the Years 1910–1912* (London: Hutchinson & Co., 1913, 2 volumes); he treated Sir Harry Hamilton Johnston's *The Negro in the New World* (1910; reprinted, New York: Johnson Reprint Corp., 1969) in the same manner. DuBois also respected and used the work on African history of nineteenth-century English traveler and writer Winwood Reade, *An African Sketch-Book* (London: Smith, Elder & Co., 1873).

17. Melville Herskovits, *The Human Factor in Changing Africa* (New York: Vintage Books, 1962), 3–15.

18. W.E.B. DuBois, "The African Roots of War," *Atlantic Monthly* 115 (May 1915), 704–14.

19. Theater played an important role for the New Negroes of the Harlem Renaissance. Artists, performers, organizers, and writers—such as Countée Cullen, Jessie Fauset, Nella Larsen, Zora Neale Hurston, Jean Toomer, Langston Hughes, James Weldon Johnson, and several others—explored African themes in their works. DuBois's message profoundly influenced the New Negroes. See Ann Douglas, *Terrible Honesty: Mongrel Manhattan in the 1920s* (New York: Farrar, Straus and Giroux, 1995).

9. Subject to Disappearance: Interracial Identity in Nella Larsen's *Quicksand*

George Hutchinson

The importance to the Harlem Renaissance of interracial relationships has always caused critics—including the participants themselves—to look with some suspicion on the movement.[1] This suspicion has been a dominant note in much of the scholarship on the phenomenon, while defenses of particular aspects of it and of individual authors have often hinged on playing down interracial dimensions. In fact, I believe that a tendency to scapegoat or repress interracial qualities of the Harlem Renaissance has been pivotal to prior histories of the movement and has obscured crucial aspects of its nature and importance.[2]

Yet the dynamic of repressing interracial dimensions of the movement or (more often) blaming them for corrupting it can be found, I believe, in criticism brought to bear on some of its most important literary achievements. Indeed, this critical tendency has perhaps prevented us from fully appreciating the originality and power of certain texts, thereby contributing to another charge from which the Harlem Renaissance has suffered—that the literature it produced was not really all that good. In this essay I want to begin to address such problems by way of Nella Larsen and her extraordinary novel *Quicksand* (1928), the best novel of the Harlem Renaissance until Zora Neale Hurston's *Their Eyes Were Watching God* (1937) and, in my opinion, one of the most significant in the history of what Werner Sollors has recently termed "interracial literature."[3]

I contend that Larsen's most important revelations about the nature of the modern, transnational racial labyrinth, not least her consciousness of her own entrapment within it, have been sublimated, even unwittingly repressed. Critics' desires for narrative resolutions that conform to American assumptions about "race," "culture," and identity have veiled the formal coherence, critical scope, and thematic power of Larsen's achievement.

I.

Although Larsen's novel does not fit any of the critical stereotypes of "tragic mulatto" tales, biracial subjectivity is central to *Quicksand*.[4] Yet resistance to reading the novel with this in mind has been a major impetus of much recent criticism. Critics often imply or assert that if Larsen's novel has centrally to do with interracial subjectivity, it is inherently of limited significance. Worse yet, it is often implied that such issues are only of interest to white readers who are titillated, flattered, or both by tales of mulatto tragedy.[5] If critics once dismissed the novel because its mulatto protagonist seemed to place it in the company of genteel appeals to white sympathy, the reaction against such views of the novel has resulted in a failure to recognize the issue of Helga Crane's interracial or bicultural sensibility in its full import. Moreover, emphasis on the feminist concerns of the text has so far worked to repress the distinctive racial perspective of the novel, at best assimilating Helga Crane to models of black female sexuality and psychology.[6] It seems that the specific insights or experiences of biracial women can only be perceived as metaphors for some other, more serious and important concern.

Even recent readings of *Quicksand* that acknowledge the importance of Helga Crane's biracial background—without therefore demoting the novel—suggest that by killing off Helga Crane at the point of her immersion in black culture, the novel expresses the author's and narrator's desire to kill off the ambivalent racial self that cannot repudiate connections with whiteness in the form of Helga's mother. This sort of argument exemplifies the workings of the binary white-black racial system and mirrors the longstanding popular assumption that biracial subjectivity is itself inherently neurotic, curable only by purging a "whiteness" within. The "resolution," in fact, that readers have looked for is nothing other than the elimination of the mother-daughter bond that puts the myths and rituals of race in question.[7] In contrast, the desire of the text in *Quicksand* is for a world in which races would not exist and women's bodies would not be mortgaged to them. This desire runs up against the harsh confines of fate as the modern institution—the labyrinth—of race.

2.

Larsen's novel begins in a place called Naxos, a black college in the South loosely modeled on Tuskegee, where the heroine feels lonely and misunderstood. Although critics have recognized the allusion to Greek myths of Ariadne and Naxos, they have missed its most significant resonances with *Quicksand*, which have directly to do with the pattern of the plot and with Helga Crane's "mixed" identity.[8] According to the myths, Minos of Crete annually demanded of Athens seven boys and seven girls to be devoured in the Labyrinth by the Minotaur. Theseus offered to go to Crete to deliver Athens from this oppression. While he was there, Ariadne, daughter of Minos, fell in love with him and gave him the clew of thread by which he found his way out of the Labyrinth after killing the monster. Theseus then sailed away, Ariadne fleeing with him; but he abandoned her on the island of Naxos.[9] According to the most common conclusion of the story (cited by prior students of *Quicksand*), Ariadne was found on Naxos by Dionysus, who married her and made her immortal.[10] Plutarch, however, gives a different ending, one based on local legend in which Theseus left Ariadne pregnant and she died in childbed.[11] Meanwhile, Theseus sailed to Delos and instituted a commemorative dance known as *Geranos*, "the Crane," after the bird whose movements resembled the twistings and turnings of the Labyrinth (*Oxford Classical Dictionary* 898).

The Labyrinth might well stand as a correlative to the racial maze from which Helga Crane is never able to emerge. Indeed, the Labyrinth was constructed to hide a creature of "mixed" and forbidden origins whom Minos's wife Pasiphae had conceived after having intercourse with a bull. According to Ovid's famous version in *The Metamorphoses*, "In [Minos's] absence the monstrous child which the queen had borne, to the disgrace of the king's family, had grown up, and the strange hybrid creature had revealed his wife's disgusting love affair to everyone. Minos determined to rid his home of this shameful sight, by shutting the monster away in an enclosure of elaborate and involved design, where it could not be seen."[12]

Helga Crane's story is in one sense a figure of the labyrinth in the form of an attempt to escape it, and Helga parallels the Minotaur whom the labyrinth was intended to hide. Yet just as the Minotaur is a kind of double of his half-sister Ariadne in some interpretations, so Helga Crane's story resembles that of Ariadne with its alternate endings. The version of the myth that says Dionysus/Bacchus (god of vegetation) married Ariadne and made her immortal fits Helga's hopes when, after a religious orgy of "almost Bacchic vehemence" (Larsen 1928, 113), she goes off with Reverend Pleasant Green—as she had earlier hoped she would be saved by Robert Anderson, whom she met in Naxos. It turns out, however, that Plutarch's version of the myth is the correct one in relation to Helga Crane's fate. She is not saved in the end, but rather left in childbed, possibly to die.

The myth also resonates with the relationship between Helga's parents, dealing as it does with a daughter who falls in love with a man of another people, cutting her links to her father, and then suffers abandonment. The text, with its allusions and narrative structure, identifies the mother's and daughter's predicaments as intertwined, as products of the same race and gender system. Thus the myth of Ariadne, Naxos, and the Labyrinth is a key to the narrative structure of Larsen's novel, which many critics over the years have found both puzzling and flawed.

3.

In the opening scene of the novel, Larsen stresses the play of light and shade in Helga's room at Naxos and connects this interpenetration of "white" and "black" with Helga herself: "An observer would have thought her well-fitted to that framing of light and shade" (2). But Helga is not well-fitted to the institution, in part because of her background, which complicates her relationship to everyone else at the school and confers on her an acute perception of the contradictions and hypocrisies about her: "The dean was a woman from one of the 'first families'—a great 'race' woman; she, Helga Crane, a despised mulatto, but something intuitive, some unanalyzed driving spirit of loyalty to the inherent racial need for gorgeousness told her that bright colors *were* fitting and that dark-complexioned people *should* wear yellow, green, and red" (18). Similarly, Helga finds herself wondering "just what form of vanity it was that had induced an intelligent girl like Margaret Creighton to turn what was probably nice, live, crinkly hair, perfectly suited to her smooth dark skin and agreeable round features, into a dead, straight, greasy, ugly mass" (14). Helga's recognition of the beauty of dark skin and Negroid features, and of black aesthetic values, sets her apart and, at the same time, derives from her *feeling* apart from the community as a "despised mulatto" without "family connections."

Readers have long remarked how Helga is prized for her decorative exoticism in Denmark, but Helga is prized for rather similar qualities at Naxos. Both at Naxos and in Harlem, Helga's mulatto appearance and European manners, combined with her unspeakable origins, bring status to those for whom she serves as a subordinate partner or retainer. Robert Anderson's suggestion of the reasons she is needed at Naxos—for her "dignity and breeding" (20–21)—arouse in Helga an indignant rejection of his assumptions: "The joke is on you, Dr. Anderson. My father was a gambler who deserted my mother, a white immigrant. It is even uncertain that they were married. As I said at first, I don't belong here" (21). According to the text, these comments come from a "lacerated pride." In reaction against the pain of losing her mother and suffering the racism of her white relatives, then suffering subordination to a black elite that disdains miscegenation but nonetheless models itself after the white elite, Helga has developed her own sense of ethnic honor.

Shortly after her interchange with Anderson, Helga feels shame and self-degradation for betraying her mother: "She had outraged her own pride, and she had terribly wronged her mother by her insidious implication" (23). Helga's sense of personal integrity, bound up with her relation to her mother, makes her relationship to "whiteness" different from that of her black friends. This is not a pride in white blood but a psychologically necessary identification with a primary attachment figure, complicated by the obligatory racialization of selfhood that typifies western modernity.

We can see from Helga's interactions with Mrs. Hayes-Rore, and later with Anne Grey, that the price of acceptance into their society is suffocation and self-contempt. In Kristevan terms, Helga takes on the role of abjection, revealing the complex intermingling of racial guilt and shame in the psyches of Hayes-Rore and (especially) Anne Grey. The seeming racial pride of these women, Larsen suggests—by way of Helga's relationship to them—covers up a sense of shame about being black *and* guilt about their own relationship to whiteness.[13]

Like the people of Naxos, Hayes-Rore values having a secretary with Helga's looks and refinement. At first, this bodes well for Helga, who finally confides to the older woman the mystery of her lack of family. As Helga speaks, passionately and full of tears, Hayes-Rore turns her head completely away from Helga: "The woman felt that the story, dealing as it did with race intermingling and possibly adultery, was beyond definite discussion. For among black people, as among white people, it is tacitly understood that these things are not mentioned—and therefore they do not exist" (39).

Indeed, Helga's introduction to elite black society is predicated on her denial of her mother. Before arriving at Anne Grey's home in Harlem, Hayes-Rore advises Helga not to mention that her "people are white"—"Colored people won't understand it; and after all it's your own business" (41). Hayes-Rore, then, will introduce Helga with the half-truth that her mother is dead. Helga, in gratitude, reaches out to take her "slightly soiled hand." In later years, Helga has only to close her eyes to remember her introduction to Grey under the shadow of this half-truth, having "her hand grasped in quick sympathy" and feeling "like a criminal" (42).

In exchange for acceptance—and shelter—Helga has locked her mother away. This act of concealment is the obverse of the fact that the mother's legacy has been *taken* from her by whites, "who had stolen her birthright. Their past contribution to her life, which had been but shame and grief, she had hidden away from brown folk in a locked closet, 'never,' she told herself, 'to be reopened'" (45). Briefly she feels free. But, as is typical of the rhythm of this novel and its labyrinthine metaphors, the very next chapter begins with the acknowledgment that "within her, in a deep recess, crouched discontent. . . . She felt shut in, trapped" (47). Helga needs something she cannot name, "something vaguely *familiar*" (47, my emphasis). Soon she becomes literally afraid of herself—afraid, perhaps, that a part of herself she has repressed will burst out of the closet to avoid suffocation.

Grey's obsession with the race problem particularly distresses Helga. Ironically, Helga has suffered from white racism more brutally and intimately than any of the race women in this novel, yet Grey's racial ardor begins to feel oppressive to Helga. Grey's contempt for all whites on principle betrays a kind of self-hatred, given that Grey "aped their clothes, their manners, and their gracious ways of living"—even preferred their music (48). Her name, Anne Grey, suggests the dependence of her own "black" identity on an abject whiteness within ("Miss Anne" being a derogatory term for a white woman). The very vehemence—panic almost—of Grey's reaction to possibilities of interracial sexual union reveals her racial insecurity while it alienates and wounds Helga.

Larsen draws a distinct connection between Grey's and James Vayle's abhorrence of interracial communion and their disdain for common black folk and vernacular culture. Indeed, Anne's status depends on racial segregation and class stratification within the black community, both of which have deeply wounded Helga Crane. Grey's very identity and security depend, in a sense, on the racial order that white society created, attempting in the process to make such persons as Helga Crane literally impossible.

The difference Helga feels from Grey grows acute in the cabaret scene of chapter 11, dramatized by way of their differing reactions to Audrey Denney. Significantly, Denney and Helga are similarly dressed: Denney in an extremely "*décolleté*" apricot dress (60) and Helga in a "cobwebby black net touched with orange" that Anne thought "too *décolleté*" (56). (In Denmark, Helga will be dressed much like Denney.) Grey comments that the dress gives Helga the look of "something about to fly." This comment provokes Helga's choice of the garment. Effectively, Helga *Crane* wears something like Denney's dress covered in a net, restrained from flight. Grey finds Denney "positively obscene" for inviting whites to her parties and for going to theirs. Interracial dancing disgusts her. Grey is rejecting the very conditions in which Helga was conceived; the latter thus develops "a slightly sickish feeling" and a flash of rage.

To Grey, her friends, and Helga's own escort, Denney's behavior "is outrageous, treacherous, in fact" (61–62). In contrast, Helga "felt that it would be useless to tell them that what she felt for the beautiful, calm, cool girl who had the assurance, the courage, so placidly to ignore racial barriers and give her attention to people, was not contempt, but envious admiration" (62). The narrator also equates Audrey Denney's freedom from taboos against interracial intimacy with a racial and sexual self-confidence expressed by appreciation for black aesthetic styles and an ability to dance with sensuous pleasure (4).

Audrey Denney's exotic appeal to black (and white) men foreshadows Helga's to the Danes, who wish to adorn Helga in shockingly "*décolleté*" dresses and to show her off. In essence, however, the Danish episode of the novel reveals the difference in racial culture between Denmark and the United States—a function that has largely escaped appreciation and scrutiny. The labyrinth of race takes on a new twist in Helga's mother country. A white American family could scarcely conceive of arranging a marriage between their mulatto niece and a white artist as a means of enhancing their class position. Helga's uncle in the United States effectively disowned her to avoid estranging his wife. In the United States, Helga must hide her connection to her white mother and learn to mix only with Negroes; however, a Danish purser aboard the steamer Helga takes to Copenhagen asks her to dine with him, remembering her from the earlier trip she took with her mother. Besides contrasting with white Americans' distaste for eating with Negroes, the purser's behavior suggests that only outside her own country can Helga be publicly identified with the woman who gave her birth, loved her, and raised her.

Contrary to the implications of most Larsen criticism, white American perceptions are not the same as the European fascination for Helga as "exotic" and "savage," emphasizing, even exaggerating, her racial difference. Larsen makes this point explicitly as one of Helga's first comparative cultural observations after meeting Copenhagen's high society: "'How odd,' she thought sleepily, 'and how different from America!'" (72). Their aesthetic appropriation of her also connects with the specifically Danish customs of matchmaking and marriage: "And was she to be treated like a secluded young miss, a Danish *frokken*, not to be consulted personally even on matters affecting her personally?" (71–72). Helga was kicked out of her white family in America; her European aunt and uncle are, in contrast, intent on looking after her.

Other attitudes also distinguish Danes from Americans. Aunt Katrina (Fru Dahl) tells Helga, "If you've got any brains at all they came from your father"— a pointed contradiction to American racial views of so-called mulattos. Fru Dahl brazenly probes Helga about her feelings toward Olsen, and his toward her, in the tradition of the elder woman's role in exploring marriage possibilities. The chapters on Denmark, over all, are an impressive—and unique—

comparative study of Danish and American cultures from the perspective of a young mulatto woman shuttling between them. That perspective exists only by virtue of the woman's maternal identification with Denmark.

As Barbara Johnson argues, Helga has learned to partially identify with whites' views of blacks, but she has also internalized *both* white *and* black American views of miscegenation that her Danish relatives cannot comprehend. Helga asks her aunt if she does not think miscegenation is wrong "in fact as well as principle" (78), to which Fru Dahl replies that it is a foolish question: Danes do not think of such things in relation to individuals (because such marriages, presumably, do not threaten Danish identity—the way they threaten white identity in America). To her aunt, Helga also reveals the true reason she could not think of marrying a white man: it is not, as commonly assumed, the heritage of white masters raping or prostituting black women that chiefly concerns her but the fate of the children. "She didn't, she responded [to Fru Dahl's suggestions of marriage prospects], believe in mixed marriages, 'between races, you know.' They brought only trouble—to the children—as she herself knew but too well from bitter experience" (78). Fru Dahl cannot understand this reasoning; nor is she cognizant of the differences in courtship patterns between the United States and Denmark, as she continues probing Helga about how Olsen seems to feel toward her and vice versa, hoping for evidence of a good match.

Just as the cabaret visit took place between Helga's decision to leave Harlem and her actual departure confirming it, her final meeting with Axel Olsen occurs after her feeling of a need to leave Copenhagen has already set in. By the time Olsen asks her to marry him, she has gradually become conscious of a feeling of entrapment. After proposing, Olsen asks why Helga did not respond to his earlier veiled request that she be his mistress. Her response—that "'in my country the men, of my race, at least, don't make such suggestions to decent girls'" (86)—is not only obviously false but a direct inversion of the legacy that Helga hides in shame. Helga does not know if her own parents were ever married; moreover, her father left when she was still a baby—the first abandonment she suffered that she attributes to a racial division in her family. Within weeks of rejecting Olsen's proposal, Helga *wants* an affair with Anderson and is hurt that he does not proposition her.

Helga does reject Olsen because she is not "for sale" to him or "to any white man," and thus she has decided she "couldn't marry a white man" (88). Her reasons for rejecting Olsen's hand are specific to her personal history, deriving from a feeling of personal insult at his presumptuousness and from her desire that her children should not have the difficulties she has had. Moreover, Helga fears that someday a white husband would come to be ashamed of her, "to hate me, to hate all dark people. My mother did that" (88).

Olsen's differences from white American men appear in his very incredulity about her fear that he would come to be ashamed of the marriage: "'I have offered you marriage, Helga Crane, and you answer me with some strange talk of race and shame. What nonsense is this?'" (61). Helga is at a loss to explain that, which in the United States would need no explanation. Even Uncle Poul cannot understand her reasoning, what he calls "this foolishness about race"— "'It can't be just that. You're too sensible'" (91).

Crucial to Helga's change in position is the black vaudeville act she witnesses at the Circus. What Helga initially feels in watching the show is shame: "She felt shamed, betrayed, as if these pale pink and white people among whom she lived had suddenly been invited to look upon something in her which she had hidden away and wanted to forget" (83). As the only person with a racial connection to the black performers, Helga feels exposed. A part of herself she has locked away (her black father, the "gay, suave scoundrel") is here brought up for the entertainment of European whites, for whom it epitomizes just what they are *not*. Suddenly Helga sees her relationship to them in a new light; whereas Helga imagined she had finally found her people, their interest in her, she now realizes, is predicated on her not being "one of them." This recognition precipitates an intense feeling of alienation from those around her, along with a growing feeling of connection with the father she has locked away, and a desire to reclaim her blackness.

Larsen's uses of Copenhagen pointedly revise the uses of Europe as an interracial haven in other American novels with black or mulatto heroines.[14] For Helga, Europe does not offer freedom from racism, just a different kind of racism. And returning to the United States does not represent a sacrifice of happiness for the heroism of racial uplift (as in some of Jessie Fauset's fiction, for example). Helga Crane's repatriation and brief commitment to uplift in the South lead to merely another dead end.

American novels that project Europe as haven for mixed-race people also tend to ignore class lines so important there, or rather deploy them to stress the gentility of the heroine or hero. The protagonist is typically related, engaged, or married to an aristocrat, revealing the lack of prejudices of the "highest" people in Europe—thus serving up white Americanism as a betrayal of civilized (European) behavior while showing that the American Negro is as refined as the "best" of Europe. In contrast, like a Scandinavian modernist, Larsen foregrounds the snobbishness of the Scandinavian bourgeoisie, their obsession with class status, and the role of the exchange of women in cementing class ties. Indeed, the "grid of class relations that has been so important to Europeans" (Sollors 342), combined with European customs of arranging marriages to advance the (patriarchal) family's social position, determines Helga's role in the Dahl family. Larsen's interracial, intercultural perspective accounts for the unique quality of her satire of conventions governing gender and sexuality in different national settings.

4.

Just as Helga felt on arriving in Copenhagen that she had finally come home, so she feels on arriving once again in Harlem. "These were her people. Nothing, she had come to understand now, could ever change that." She feels spiritually bound to the "fascinating, . . . lovable dark hordes," by "ties not only superficially entangled with mere outline of features or color of skin. Deeper. Much deeper than either of these" (Larsen 1928, 95). The language here echoes that used earlier to describe Helga's thoughts as she had planned her escape from Harlem: "She didn't, in spite of her racial markings, belong to these dark segregated people. . . . It wasn't merely a matter of color. It was something broader, deeper, that made folk kin" (55). Once in Denmark she had felt, "This, then, was where she belonged. This was her proper setting. She felt consoled at last for the spiritual wounds of the past" (67). Her feeling of spiritual belonging in Harlem the second time around would prove no more permanent than those feelings in Denmark. Indeed, her fascination with and rather distant love for the "mysterious" and "lovable dark hordes" of common black folk, particularly her attraction to their spirituality, set the stage for her final, most devastating decision about where to find a "home" when the shelter of the Harlem elite proves estranging. By undergoing conversion, marrying a minister, and moving to the rural South, the spiritual home of the "dark hordes," Helga moves toward the fate she will never, apparently, escape.

Helga's difficulties in Harlem arise quickly. Her friendship with Grey wanes because Grey distrusts and patronizes Helga for having lived too long with Nordics and for being too tolerant of them. Helga is made to feel in many ways that she does not fit in. In his conversation with her, James Vayle hints that Helga is not part of the "we" that connotes "colored people." To her retort, "I'm a Negro too, you know," he responds that she was "always a little different" (102)—a point that becomes more evident as the conversation continues. Vayle dislikes the interracial social scene of New York and, like Grey, detests the sight of a black woman talking socially to a white man at a party. Helga probes him further on the point "with polite contempt" until he exposes the heart of his dissatisfaction: "'You know as well as I do, Helga, that it's the colored girls these men come up here to see. They wouldn't think of bringing their wives'" (103). In fact, however, they have brought their wives (as Helga quickly points out), one of whom is dancing with a Negro even as Vayle speaks. Larsen directs her satire not just at stereotypes of interracial intimacy but also at the common ethic of racial "ownership" of women's sexuality. Vayle presents a eugenicist argument that middle-class Negroes are duty-bound to propagate the race: "Don't you see that if we—I mean people like us—don't have children, the others will still have. That's one of the things that's the matter with us. The race is sterile at the top" (103).

Vayle's contention that white men come to Harlem seeking affairs with black women is particularly ironic in that within moments Helga finds herself in the arms of the married Anderson: "He stooped and kissed her, a long kiss, holding her close. She fought against him with all her might. Then, strangely, all power seemed to ebb away, and a long-hidden, half-understood desire welled up in her with the suddenness of a dream" (104). After this event, strangely enough, Helga loses all her envy of Grey's recent marriage to Anderson even as she hopes for a passionate rendezvous. As Helga's desires become fully conscious, Larsen returns to the metaphors of the labyrinth:

> Abruptly one Sunday in a crowded room . . . she knew that she couldn't go [back to Copenhagen], that she hadn't since that kiss intended to go without exploring to the end that unfamiliar path into which she had strayed. . . . A species of fatalism fastened on her. (106)

However, Anderson does not offer the recognition she craves. Abandoned "forever," like Ariadne, Helga looks into an "endless stretch of dreary years" that is her only conceivable future.

The plot pivots at this point, as in Ariadne's Dionysian salvation after abandonment by Theseus. Anderson's rejection of Helga, his loyalty to Grey, drive Helga into a storefront church amid "the writhings and weepings" of a Pentecostal service—an ironic narrative reply to Helga's initial feeling of liberation upon returning to Harlem, which the narrator described in a revealing simile: "It was as if she passed from the heavy solemnity of a church service to a gorgeous carefree revel" (96). Now finding herself in a revel *cum* church service, Helga discovers that the worshipping women want her soul, calling her a "scarlet 'oman. Come to Jesus, you pore los' Jezebel'" (112). (These entreaties recall the portrait Olsen, her Danish suitor, once did of her and his comment that Helga has "the soul of a prostitute.") Weary of her *self*, Helga is easily hypnotized by the lyrics of the hymn, "Less of self and more of Thee." The scene is also erotically charged. "Little by little the performance took on an almost Bacchic vehemence" (113).

Larsen's scene, with its protagonist's two vain efforts at escape, recalls Ovid's *Ars Amatoria* (1.535–64), the source of many artistic attempts to render realistically the surreal moment of Ariadne's frightening yet compelling "salvation" by Bacchus, accompanied by his maenads and satyrs.[15] The ceremony seems to work: "Gradually the room grew quiet and almost solemn, and to the kneeling girl time seemed to sink back into the mysterious grandeur and holiness of far-off simpler centuries" (Larsen 1928, 114). Moreover, the logic at work in the scene conforms to the general labyrinthine design of the narrative. Helga Crane had come to long for the emotional expressiveness of Negroes, as opposed to the restrained atmosphere of Denmark. It was precisely the undertone of "Swing Low, Sweet Chariot" in Dvořák's "New World Symphony," derived from enthusiastic, southern African-American religious ceremony, that had made her conscious of her longing for black America. In this state of mind, she had forgiven her father his "rejection, his repudiation, of the formal calm her mother had represented" (92); she could sympathize with his "facile surrender to the irresistible ties of race" (92), and "it was *as if* in this understanding and forgiveness she had come upon knowledge of almost sacred importance" (my emphasis; 93). In the black church, Helga gets far more than she has bargained for—as she has each time she has moved to what seems a greener pasture.

Although Helga convinces herself that she has given herself up to faith, in reality, "Her religion was to her a kind of protective coloring, shielding her from the cruel light of an unbearable reality" (126). Helga "passes" for a Christian. She also uses her "deliberate allure" to snare the Reverend Pleasant Green. Looking for some "Power" to help her, she decides to "make sure of both things, God and man" (117). She still, that is to say, has the "soul of a prostitute"—perhaps like Mary Magdalene, as the final literary allusion of the text will suggest.

Helga's experience among the "lovable dark hordes" of the deep South disabuses her before long of her rather condescending as well as romantically idealized views of them. She tries to find her vocation in the very sort of racial uplift she had earlier rejected. And indeed it proves both wrong-headed and unsatisfying. Nor does it provide her with a sense of belonging. Helga retreats increasingly into herself until, after the birth of her fourth child, she nearly dies. She emerges without a shred of respect for her husband, her faith gone. In this state, and pregnant for the fifth time, she asks to be read Anatole France's story "The Procurator of Judaea," a story that has attracted remarkably little attention from *Quicksand* readers.[16]

"The Procurator of Judaea" articulates the relationship between racial ideology, empire, patriarchy, and the control of sexuality for procreative purposes, the reproduction of race and the imperial state. It is composed of two conversations between Pontius Pilate and Aelius Lamia, an old acquaintance from when Pilate had been the procurator of Judaea. Pilate speaks of how hard the job was, the Jews being rebellious and contemptuous of Romans, believing them an unclean race. For his part, Pilate thought the Jews barbarous and stupid. Constantly fighting each other over doctrinal points, intolerant of any diversity of opinion within their "race," they repeatedly demanded that Pilate execute one of their heretics. Rome, which tolerated a kind of cultural pluralism to help secure its empire, required Pilate to uphold their customs; ultimately he lost his job because of Jews' complaints about his intercessions on behalf of the accused. (Thus he let Jesus die as a palliative, in a vain attempt to stave off his own political demise.) Aelius Lamia, a cosmopolitan wanderer and Epicurean philosopher, is more tolerant of the Jews and begins to reminisce about the beauty of the Jewish women. He remembers particularly a beautiful Jewish dancer who joined the group surrounding Jesus—clearly Mary Magdalene, a woman with "the soul of a prostitute," to use the phrase Axel Olsen applied to Helga Crane. Pilate reproves Lamia for adultery and "miscegenation." In his view, sex between Romans and people of other nations is wrong:

> Marriage from the patrician point of view is a sacred tie; it is one of the institutions which are the support of Rome. As to foreign women and slaves, such relations as one may enter into with them would be of little account were it not that they habituate the body to a humiliating effeminacy. . . . [W]hat, above all, I blame in you is that you have not married in compliance with the law and given children to the Republic, as every good citizen is bound to do.[17]

Pilate's patriarchal view of women and sex is inextricable from his racism and his abhorrence of race-mixing—attitudes mirrored by the Jews themselves.

"The Procurator of Judaea" has to do with the way concepts of racial difference—connected with patrician practices of empire-building, slavery, and national chauvinism—contribute to the oppression of women and repression of sexuality except for purposes of producing "racial" subjects for the state. As do the Ariadne legends, this story applies not only to Helga Crane's fate, but to her white mother's, as well.

Quicksand ends with Helga Crane in childbed, feeling asphyxiated once again, knowing that she must escape or die. But the thought of leaving her children holds her fatally in place: "To leave them would be a tearing agony, a rending of deepest fibers. She felt that through all the rest of her lifetime she would be hearing their cry of 'Mummy, Mummy, Mummy,' through sleepless nights. No. She couldn't desert them" (135).

Critics wishing for a different kind of feminist conclusion to the novel have missed the tragedy and power of this scene, unable apparently to recognize that the voice Helga hears is her own, crying for the Danish mother that "race" in America has stolen from her. Thus, the reason Helga Crane cannot save herself in this conclusion that has disappointed so many has everything to do with her interracial origins. Helga takes responsibility for her catastrophe, and she abstains from self-pity. To many, she will seem more pathetic than tragic, her fate just another turn of the screw. But what she suffers is out of all proportion to her flaws; it seems inexorable as well. Larsen thus lines up with the naturalist, Ibsen, rather than with the classical dramatists, for fate is not above and independent of human institutions but largely determined by them.

The racial bifurcation of "black" from "white" in American national ideology—which much American literary scholarship has only reinforced—stands in for fate. The conclusion is an implicit comment on the labyrinth of race along with the patriarchal structures that support it and that it supports. *Quicksand* marks the threshold where she, whose being forms the radical "other" to the racial symbolic, disappears—or rather, is perpetually sacrificed on the altar of the color line.

In place of the Oedipal drama and the incest taboo (as ubiquitous in tragic mulatto tradition as in psychoanalysis), Larsen turns to a female-centered drama figuring the abandonment of woman under patriarchy, death in childbirth, the enslavement of the body to procreation of racial subjects alienated from themselves and their mothers by national ideologies of racial and class identity. Never embracing Jean Toomer's dream of a "new race," neither does Larsen simply dismiss race as a "fiction," for she recognizes it as a formative feature of contemporary experience. She rather exposes the violence of racialization as such in the effort to make it ethically insupportable—like fate in classical drama—an affront to humanity.

NOTES

1. This essay is a revised version of one published under the title "*Quicksand* and the Racial Labyrinth" in the journal *Soundings* 80 (Winter 1997): 543–72. I thank the editors of *Soundings* for permission to reprint portions of that essay here.

2. See *The Harlem Renaissance in Black and White* (Cambridge, Mass.: Belknap/ Harvard University Press, 1995). This is not, of course, to say that interracial dimensions of the movement should be uncritically celebrated or other dimensions of it dismissed.

3. Sollors used the term "interracial literature" to signify texts centrally concerned with "love and family relations involving black-white couples, biracial individuals, their descendants, and their larger kin" (*Neither Black Nor White, Yet Both: Thematic Explorations of Interracial Literature* [New York: Oxford University Press, 1997], 3).

4. For a critical discussion of the development of what has become a scholarly stereotype about "tragic mulatto fiction," see Sollors, 220–45.

5. Hortense Spillers, for example, regards the "mulatta" as a white male invention to serve his dominance; this character allegedly "covers up . . . the social and political

reality of the dreaded African presence" ("Notes on an Alternative Model—Neither/ Nor," in *The Difference Within,* Elizabeth Meese and Alice Parker, eds. [Amsterdam: John Benjamins, 1989], 166). Critics who have read Larsen's novel as an extension of the "tragic mulatto" tradition include Hirako Sato, "Under the Harlem Shadow: A Study of Jessie Fauset and Nella Larsen," in *The Harlem Renaissance Remembered,* Arna Bontemps, ed. (New York: Dodd, Mead, 1972), 63–89; Saunders Redding, *To Make a Poet Black* (Chapel Hill: University of North Carolina Press, 1939); Hugh Gloster, *Negro Voices in American Fiction* (Chapel Hill: University of North Carolina Press, 1948); Barbara Christian, *Black Women Novelists: The Development of a Tradition, 1892–1976* (Westport, Conn.: Greenwood, 1980); and Amritjit Singh, *The Novels of the Harlem Renaissance: Twelve Black Writers, 1923–1933* (University Park: Pennsylvania State University Press, 1976). Houston Baker's is the most recent instance of sharp criticism of the novel for its focus on a mulatto; for Baker, "Mulatto . . . is a sign of the legitimacy and power of . . . white male patriarchy"; by concerning herself with mulatto characters, Larsen reinforces that legitimacy rather than undermining it (*Workings of the Spirit: The Poetics of Afro-American Women's Writing* [Chicago: University of Chicago Press, 1991], 36).

6. See, for example, Deborah E. McDowell, "Introduction" to Nella Larsen, *Quicksand and Passing,* McDowell, ed. (New Brunswick: Rutgers University Press, 1986), xvi; Mary V. Dearborn, *Pocahontas's Daughters: Gender and Ethnicity in American Culture* (New York: Oxford University Press, 1986), 59; Jacquelyn Y. McLendon, "Self-Representation as Art in the Novels of Nella Larsen," in *Redefining Autobiography in Twentieth-Century Women's Fiction,* Janice Morgan and Colette T. Hall, eds. (New York: Greenwood, 1991), 153; and McLendon, *The Politics of Color in the Fiction of Jessie Fauset and Nella Larsen* (Charlottesville: University Press of Virginia, 1995), 71–93; Ann E. Hostetler, "The Aesthetics of Race and Gender in Nella Larsen's *Quicksand,*" *PMLA* 105 (1990): 35–46; Barbara E. Johnson, "The Quicksands of the Self: Nella Larsen and Heinz Kohut," in *Telling Facts: History and Narration in Psychoanalysis,* Joseph H. Smith and Humphrey Morris, eds. (Baltimore: Johns Hopkins University Press, 1992); and Cheryl A. Wall, *Women of the Harlem Renaissance* (Bloomington: Indiana University Press, 1995), 89.

7. Thadious Davis, *Nella Larsen, Novelist of the Harlem Renaissance: A Woman's Life Unveiled* (Baton Rouge: Louisiana State University Press, 1994), 262; Claudia Tate, "Desire and Death in *Quicksand,* by Nella Larsen," *American Literary History* 7 (1995): 234–60; Kimberly Monda, "Self-Delusion and Self-Sacrifice in Nella Larsen's *Quicksand,*" *African-American Review* 31 (1997): 23–39.

8. McDowell, in a note for her edition of the novel (243, n. 2), does gloss the Ariadne myth in part and cites, in recent printings, the argument of Missy Kubitschek regarding myths of Dionysus as the child of the "double door."

9. Deborah McDowell presents some of this information in her note to the Rutgers text (243, n.2), but she does not mention either of the two versions of the myth's conclusion.

10. Missy Kubitschek makes good use of this version in her *Claiming the Heritage: African-American Women Novelists and History* (Jackson: University Press of Mississippi, 1991), 102–103.

11. *Oxford Classical Dictionary,* M. Cary, et al., eds. (Oxford: Clarendon/Oxford University Press, 1949), 88.

12. Ovid, *The Metamorphoses,* Mary M. Innes, trans. (London: Penguin, 1955), 183.

13. My phrasing here borrows from Arnold Rampersad's paper at the Paris conference, "Racial Shame and Racial Guilt in the Harlem Renaissance."

14. Sollors points out that in much American interracial literature, escape to a European country allows "a happy alternative to a tragic America" (338, 339).

15. Mark P.O. Morford and Robert J. Lenardon, *Classical Mythology* (2nd ed; New York: Longman, 1977), 389–90.

16. Two exceptions are McDowell, in a note to her edition of the text (245, n. 14), and Monda (37).

17. Anatole France, "The Procurator of Judaea," *Golden Tales of Anatole France* (New York: Dodd, Mead, 1927), 23–24.

10. No Free Gifts: Toomer's "Fern" and the Harlem Renaissance*

William Boelhower

> Here we have brought our three gifts and mingled them with
> yours: a gift of story and song . . . ; the gift of sweat and brawn
> . . . ; third, a gift of the Spirit.
> —W.E.B. DuBois, *The Souls of Black Folk*

Perhaps the best account of what it was like to enter Harlem for the first time in the early 1920s is that of Langston Hughes. Hughes arrived September 5, 1921, and in his autobiography *The Big Sea* he describes his emergence from the subway at 135th Street as follows:

> 135th STREET. When I saw it I held my breath. I came out onto the platform with two heavy bags and looked around. It was still early morning and people were going to work. Hundreds of coloured people! I wanted to shake hands with them, speak to them. . . . I went up the steps and out into the bright September sunlight. Harlem! I stood there, dropped my bags, took a deep breath and felt happy again.[1]

By the end of the twenties, this experience had become ritualized in fiction as the Harlem entrance topos; rare was the writer who passed up the opportunity to record the initial impact this "city within a city"[2] had on him or her as evidence of an authenticating participation. Hughes's little scene—the instinctive act of holding his breath and then letting it out again once he is sure he is breathing Harlem air—is dramatically constructed. Twice he resorts to exclamation: first, when he notices the crowd of colored people around him and then when he emerges from below into the morning light. Now his response is a simple outburst, an ejaculation in which the linguistic matter is a place-name, perhaps the only form of acknowledgment capable of expressing his spreading sense of happiness.

---

* Copyright William Boelhower

In fact, there is really nothing more for him to say. The place-name says it all by condensing the whole scene into a single world-creating word. There is also a hint of fascination and liberality in the sudden exclamation of "Harlem!" that captures the magnificence and splendor of seeing and then merging with his own people. His explosive "throw-out" (for such is the meaning of *ejaculari*) also expresses his sense of gratitude to the city which is now literally inside him thanks to the "deep breath" that measures his joy. His desire to speak to and shake hands with the hundreds he meets is a spontaneous gesture of reciprocity signaling a symmetrical relation between him and his fellow Harlemites. He immediately feels one of the crowd and willing to seek his fortune there: "I didn't want to do anything but live in Harlem, get a job and work there" (BS 81–2).

By the early twenties, this "race capital"[3] was already on everybody's lips, a byword for those fed up with the racial violence and hostilities of white America. What Hughes's entrance scene celebrates, however symptomatically, is his *"andare al popolo"* (going to the people), as Antonio Gramsci would say. Its purpose is to show young Hughes throwing in his lot with Harlem— both place and people. Although we see only his exuberance and the cause of it (the hundreds heading to the subway platform), his coming to Harlem is an eminently political gesture, one that myriad other migrants from the South were eager to share. In fact, in the early 1920s, the population of Harlem was growing like that of no other place in America. Southern blacks in particular were voting with their feet. Between 1910 and 1920, the black population of New York increased 60 percent (from 91,709 to 152,467), with 73,000—or two-thirds of Manhattan's black population—living in Harlem. By 1930, the black population of Harlem had swollen to 164,566 (Osofsky 123–30).

A real mobilization was under way, and a "vast racial formation" (D.L. Lewis 1994, xxviii) was coming into being in the expanding area of Harlem. For those who journeyed to this "Promised Land," as the Rev. Dr. Adam Clayton Powell, Sr., called it, Harlem meant "racial independence" (Osofsky 128, 175). New York, it should be remembered, was not an open city; as the population swelled, Harlem also became increasingly crowded. But in spite of high rents, congestion, lack of political representation, and an extensive informal economy, pre-Depression Harlem was confident and upbeat because something new really was taking place, namely the genesis of the African-American people as an effective biopolitical constituency. It is certainly the latter's visibility that led Alain Locke, in his foreword to *The New Negro* anthology, to apply the language of energetics when documenting the cultural and social presence of the New Negro: "a new force," "quickened centers," "racial awakening," "nascent movements," "the resurgence of a people," "founding new centers," "an unusual outburst" (NN ix–xi). Such language points directly to a semiotic reading of a people *in statu nascendi,* and it is this physiological—or *primitive*—process that Hughes celebrates as "bare life."[4] Significantly, while Locke and others were engaging in the language of biopolitics, various newspapers supporting entrenched white Harlemites were using the language of war to recount the same phenomenon: "invasion," "captured," "black hordes," "invaders," "enemy" (Osofsky 105).

Occasionally like Hughes in spirit, Helga Crane, the heroine of Nella Larsen's novel *Quicksand,* "gave herself up to the miraculous joyousness of Harlem," for "[t]he easement which its heedless abandon brought to her was a real, a very definite thing" (Larsen 1928, 95–6). It is this act of giving oneself up, or, if you will, the heuristic principle of the gift which Marcel Mauss elaborated in 1923–1924, that I would now like to bring into play in order to more fully understand that intrinsically fuzzy category "the people" as it bears upon the territorialization of black migrants in Harlem. According to Hughes, the people, the anonymous mass of ordinary blacks, had not even heard of the Harlem Renaissance. On the other hand, as he also notes, they were it (BS 1,285). So it is this mass that demands further attention not only as a symptom— the scene of entrance mentioned previously—but also as a sharply focused and site-specific object: the people as a biotope, in which inhabitants, habitat, and habitus form part of the same act of dwelling. (In fact, all three biotopic components derive from the Latin verb *habitare.*)

If we look at Hughes's and Crane's desire to merge with the people from the perspective of the gift, we cannot but be struck by the consistent occultation of this largely unconscious structure of the social system in studies of the Harlem Renaissance. Rather than pointing saliently to the discourse of primitivism (Lemke), acts of participation and liberality like Hughes's and Crane's raise the much broader issues of political sovereignty, social reproduction, and the fundamental existence of an anti-economic economy. Such apparently slight scenes as the ones in which a fascinated Hughes spontaneously seeks recognition among the workers and a deluded Crane seeks affective relations among Harlemites *en masse* need to be viewed in the light of what Mauss in 1923 defined as "a total social fact."[5] In other words, the moments just cited are actually part of a rich symbolic order that requires a more sophisticated form of attention if we hope to seize the various strata of meaning contained in such acts of prodigality.

As always, when dealing with the phenomenon of a swelling mass, we feel, above all, that we are being confronted with an exuberance, a plethora, an excess.[6] To exemplify the importance of the etymon "*ple-*" (which is the shared root of both plethora and plebs and is strictly related to the category of the people,[7]) here is Ann Petry's close reworking of the subway scene in Hughes's autobiography, only now the street is 116th Street, between Seventh and Eighth Avenues, the time is an evening in 1944, and the sense of "going-to-the-people" is more fully sketched in:

> [S]he never felt really human until she reached Harlem and thus got away from the hostility in the eyes of the white women who stared at her on the downtown streets and in the subway.
> Up here they are no longer creatures labeled simply 'coloured' and there-fore all alike. She noticed that once the *crowd* walked the length of the plat-form and started up the stairs toward the street, it *expanded in size*. The same people who had made themselves small on the train, even on the platform, *suddenly grew so large* they could hardly get up the stairs to the street together. She reached the street at the very end of the crowd and stood watching them as they *scattered in all directions, laughing and talking* to each other.[8]

The scene is very close to Hughes's in theme. Again, we have the ritual of entrance (here a re-entrance), the crowd, the locus of the subway, and a racial border-crossing involving both physical transportation and a form of psychic transport. While Hughes's crowd is in the process of compressing itself or making itself smaller as it heads downtown, Petry's returning crowd is in the act of swelling and scattering. Moreover, while in Hughes the people are ap-parently subdued, in Petry they laugh and talk. The sense we get of the crowd in the preceding passage suggests that once again the semiotic fullness of the people is experienced as a force and an energy. It "expanded in size" as it fanned out across Harlem.

In reality, Hughes and Petry give us two different but complementary as-pects of the people. They both present us with a transitional glimpse of a work *force*, but while Hughes's crowd is in the process of assuming the guise of a reductive formation, Petry's is in the act of breaking form, in that it is abandon-ing its productive role within the capitalist economy and transmuting into something much larger, an ethnos. Again, because Hughes's crowd is heading downtown, it consolidates into the regimented ranks of workers. Petry's, on the other hand, scatters freely, transforming itself into a sovereign multitude in confident possession of the six square miles of Harlem turf. Paradoxically, it is Petry's and not Hughes's crowd that is an expression of primitivism and of political sovereignty. For while the people are a political category only insofar as they can be reduced to some representational form or subjected to a process of *reductio ad unum,* the real source of political authority lies beyond this ficti-tious form. It goes without saying that full sovereignty can only be achieved through political representation, but the realm of inalienable rights goes be-neath and beyond politics, embracing the people as an unrepresentable biologi-cal multitude, an irrepressible mass of individuals.

Petry captures this morphological primitivism intrinsic to the political category of the people. Thus, when Alain Locke availed himself of the language of energetics to project what he perceived to be happening in Harlem in the mid-twenties, he was, perhaps unwittingly, very close to identifying the source of black sovereignty in "bare life." At any rate, his contributions to the *New Negro* anthology indicate he understood very well the significance of the symbolic moment in which a people assumes political sovereignty through a foundational "outburst" or "awakening." Since Jefferson's *Declaration of Independence,* our self-evident and inalienable rights have been extended to the biological sphere of human life (expressed in the Greek *zoe*) rather than being limited just to a politically upgraded or qualified status of life (as in the Greek concept of *bios*). It is the former sphere of bare life[9] that Claude McKay's protagonist Jake Brown, in *Home to Harlem,* is talking about when he exclaims, "Harlem! Harlem! Where else could I have all this life but Harlem? Good old Harlem! Chocolate Harlem! Sweet Harlem!"[10]

As Lutie, the protagonist of Ann Petry's novel, points out, she does not feel human until she gets to Harlem, where she can finally shake off the hostility of downtown and feel part of the same communal spirit Jake finds there. From the perspective of Mauss's gift principle, what Hughes, Crane, Jake, and Lutie are talking about is the symbolic value of hospitality and an economy of reciprocity and prestige. Perhaps Jake's idea of sweetness, which derives from the racially connoted "chocolate," says it best. When Lutie notes in the preceding passage from Petry that the people "could hardly get up the stairs to the street together," we can construe this physiological surging of the crowd as a biopolitical analogue to the inalienable right to equality. At the beginning of *Home to Harlem,* when Jake and Felice go for a walk along Lenox Avenue and "she was intoxicated, blinded under the overwhelming force" (HH 12), the force that possesses her is a mingling of Jake's exuberance and that of the people on the avenue. The sumptuary display and the "easement" of the avenue suggest a "totalized competitive giving"[11] that is of the essence of political democracy. "Force" in *Home to Harlem* is invariably about the issue of sovereignty. When Petry's crowd reaches the street and begins to laugh and talk, it indirectly answers Jake's own rhetorical question, "Where else could I have all this life but Harlem?"

The first thing Jake does after arriving by subway is leave his suitcase "behind the counter of a saloon on Lenox Avenue" (HH 10) and go for a stroll down Seventh Avenue just off 135th Street, not far from Hughes's own point of entry. And like Hughes, McKay's narrator says of his protagonist, "He thrilled to Harlem" (10). To thrill to something is to be affected emotionally by it, to have a shivering or tingling sensation, "to act, move or pass into such a manner as to provoke a sudden wave of emotion" (*Webster's Third New International Dictionary*). The force that pierces (as the etymon of thrill would have it) Jake and overwhelms Felice is indeed a biological, a primitive, force; but such is our paradigm of democratic sovereignty that it would be useless to try to separate this shiver of bare life from the notion of life constituting the political category of the people. In what is perhaps one of the strongest outbursts in the novel, Jake makes this equivalence between the two most explicit: "White folks can't padlock niggers outa joy forever" (336). Condensed into a few words, this is what the making of Harlem is about.

Thus, in a sense we are back to where we started, namely with the *ejaculatio*—the brief prayer—of "Harlem!" as a rhetorical winking at the quickened site of the African-American people. But Jake Brown does not stop with the simple exclamation that spent Hughes's single deep breath. Nor does he stop with Crane's somewhat chastened "Harlem, teeming black Harlem, had welcomed her and lulled her . . ." (Larsen 1928, 43). No, in his mouth the place-name takes on the magical effect of an abracadabra as it expands into a verbal cornucopia, as the rhetorical figure is called.[12] And yet, Jake's response is no more than a simple act of reciprocity, his way of spontaneously thanking the people on Seventh Avenue for exhibiting "a life comparable to that of other people."[13] As Richard Wright reminds us in his essay "Blueprint for Negro Writing," "No theory of life can take the place of life."[14] Likewise, the palpable atmosphere of liberality that galvanizes street life like an electric current in *Home to Harlem* expresses the gift principle in modern society better than does Mauss's famous essay. Evidently, Jake felt obliged to answer abundance (*copia rerum*) with abundance (*copia verborum*). The fifty dollars that goes back and forth between him and Felice and leads to their falling in love with each other show that "[m]oney still possesses its magical power."[15]

To focus more closely on the methodological value of Mauss's essay of 1923–1924, I now would like to turn to "Fern," a sketch from Jean Toomer's *Cane* that has received a great deal of commentary but still remains exquisitely elusive and underinterpreted. Not only does "Fern" convincingly embody the gift economy, but inasmuch as it does, the sketch's methodological implications make it a helpful key to understanding the central object of the Harlem Renaissance, namely the symbolic order of the people as "a field of possibilities" (Baker 1988, 81) and that cultural movement's principal semiotic capital. As Locke said of "the great masses" in his essay "The New Negro," "they stir, they move, they are more than physically restless." And a little after that, "In a real sense it is the rank and file who are leading, and the leaders who are following. A transformed and transforming psychology permeates the masses" (NN 7).

In a fundamental way, "Fern" gives us a new opportunity to see how the making of Harlem led to a social and cultural reincorporation or *mise-en-forme* of the African-American people. Before trying to identify the gift principle in

"Fern," however, I would like to describe the narrative conditions and restraints we must respect before we can begin to understand the sketch's meaning. This preliminary work has almost always been neglected even by Toomer's best critics.

"Fern" is made up of four relatively equal blocks of text, each one set off from the others by a blank space. The final block is much shorter than the others and functions as a coda. While the first two are expository and meditative, the last two concern a specific experience in which the narrator was directly involved: "One evening I walked up the Pike on purpose . . ." (Toomer 30). It is this singular involvement of the narrator, recounted in the third block, that provides the nucleus of "Fern" and the one I am most interested in here; it is also the most difficult to understand. As a sketch, this apparently informal, but actually highly wrought, descriptive study reflects its painterly origins in the Italian word *schizzo*, the infinitive of which means to splash or squirt. In "Fern," the linguistic equivalent of squirting assumes the form of the leitmotif, which is the basic compositional unit of *Cane* as a whole. I will have more to say about it subsequently.

The narrator's light and rapid study relies primarily on visual imagery. Indeed, Fern's eyes are the central object and agency of fascination. Seeing, sight, and insight motivate the sketch's narrative economy. The physical act of seeing gives way to the spiritual act of vision, although it is not immediately clear what that vision is. Thanks to a strategy of repetition, the sketch's main effect is above all iconographic. We end up with a forceful, hieratic image of Fern eternally sitting on the railing of her porch at the intersection of the railroad tracks and the Dixie Pike Road. She is leaning against a post and her head is tilted forward because there is a nail in the post at the level of her head. Twice the narrator catches a glimpse of her in a "quick flash, keen and intuitive" (29), although of the two descriptive figures he employs in elaborating his study—prosopopoeia and ethopoeia—it is the latter, with its focus on a character's spiritual values and talents, that interests him the more. Physically, Fern is considered a seductive figure, but the narrator is interested in her spiritually. Thus, it is her eyes that intrigue him. He follows them as they look now "where the sun, molten and glorious, was pouring down," now "at the gray cabin on the knoll from which an evening folk-song was coming," now at "some vague spot above the horizon" (27). It becomes evident that for the narrator, Fern's eyes are a conduit to other levels of reality, and the oft-used verb "to flow" signals the act of transport he is concerned with.

But "Fern" is only secondarily a sketch about a beautiful southern black woman. What complicates our familiarity with her is the narrator's first-person presence as a character in the events he describes in the second half of his study.

Thus, there are two intersecting focal points. The first, which is embedded in a frame and therefore mediated by it, concerns what took place between Fern and the narrator the night they walked down the Dixie Pike together—in other words, that encrypted scene in the canebrake. The second, which is the narrative frame, concerns the narrator's relation to the reader and is rendered in the present tense. At this level, the sketch becomes a dramatic monologue and, more importantly, an autobiographical act of witnessing: "picture if you can" (28), "[y]ou and I know" (28), "I ask you, friend" (29), "[y]our thoughts can help me, and I would like to know" (30), and then at the very end, to underscore the readerly pact of testimony, "And, friend, you?" (33).

Then, in the very last words, he gives us her full name, perhaps to suggest the moral importance of identity over (the narrator's) anonymity. The familiar tone of "Fern," therefore, is due to the contract the narrator establishes with his reader, designated implicitly as African-American male. In addition, this pact or contract goes beyond the sketch itself and burdens the reader with the ethical task of interpreting the cultural significance of the intense little scene in which Fern dances and sings. Ultimately, it is the narrator's metanarrative gesture, encoded in the pact of intimacy between him and the addressee, that is of the essence here; it involves us in a circuit of obligation we dare not interrupt without risking our own prestige. For now we, too, as readers, live in the shadow of Fern's name.

The master clue to the heuristic principle of the gift is provided by the narrator himself, in the refrain he frequently repeats, "Something I would do for her" (28, 29, 30, 33). In the first textual block of "Fern," he mentions that all the men who come into contact (above all, sexual) with her "felt bound to her" (25), and this contact is such that it commits them to her forever: "it would take them a lifetime to fulfill an obligation which they could find no name for" (25). In the narrator's case, this sense of obligation is eminently spiritual and involves his very dreams (28). In the end, it seems that no gift is adequate, and the narrator observes resignedly, "Nothing ever came to Fern, not even I" (33). Because of such evidence, Nellie McKay sees a failure on the narrator's part to understand Fern and her song and suggests that the psychological and gender aspects of the sketch are paramount (McKay 1984, 111–12). McKay does not show much concern for the symbolic order in which these aspects are inscribed. But it is this order alone that allows us to appreciate the full semiotic richness embodied in the exchange between a virgin (Fern) and a writer (the narrator).

Far from being a failure, their encounter can be read essentially as an act of politesse. It is in the crucial third paragraph that the narrator and Fern meet, and no convincing explanation has as yet been given about what happened that evening in the canebrake when they did. One thing, however, is certain: it is governed by the gift economy. When the narrator goes up the Pike to call on Fern one evening, he is following the social etiquette of paying her a visit. The script is ceremonial and formally takes place during leisure time, that is, outside the time of work. Visiting is the exact opposite of a relation governed by economic exchange as we now know it. When the narrator calls on Fern, therefore, she gives her time freely and willingly. They both do. Furthermore, the time they spend together can be called rich time, characterized by dalliance and wastefulness, and thus is completely nonproductive. In this sense, their time together is symbolically a special time in which the rules of the formal economy are momentarily inverted. We now enter the atmosphere of the gift, which we can further define as a force-field that orients the narrator and incites him to circumscribe the space in which he will deploy his conduct.[16]

After sitting on the porch awhile, Fern and the narrator take a walk down the Pike, go through a canebrake, and decide to sit under a sweet-gum tree next to a partially dammed creek. Dusk is setting in, and there is "a purple haze about the cane" (Toomer 31). At this point, the atmosphere is such that the narrator says, "I felt strange, as I always do in Georgia. . . . I felt that things unseen to men were tangibly immediate. It would not have surprised me had I had vision . . ." (31). The moment is evidently a very special one. The heightened atmosphere (Toomer's trademark throughout *Cane*) has become the very atmosphere of the gift, which Mauss says is the sign that we are in the presence of a total social fact. No one thing by itself can be said to define the gift: neither Fern nor the cane nor the site nor the narrator. It is the whole scene—Mauss's total social fact[17]—that counts. Then, ready to surrender himself to the moment, the narrator takes Fern in his arms, and all of a sudden it becomes, for lack of a better word, Fern-time.

Whatever occurs next is entrusted to the narrator alone, who becomes the obliging steward of the scene. Instead of explaining or analyzing what happened, he assumes the privileged role of guarding their encounter as if it were a religious secret. And it is as a secret or cryptogram that we are implicitly asked to receive the scene, given that we readers are prevented from entering it directly or from reestablishing some positive form of continuity between the configurations the narration describes and the actual event. The third textual block remains irretrievably liturgical and becomes itself an inexhaustible source of surmise and interpretation, as it undoubtedly is for the narrator himself. On the other hand, this is part of the liberality of the gift principle insofar as it generates in the person under obligation the desire to continue and strengthen the relation established.

There are a few more observations about the gift as method that deserve our attention before we try to move into the eventfulness of the encounter under discussion. The fact that the narrator of "Fern" feels indebted to her means not only that the threefold obligation of the gift economy—that of giving, receiving, and reciprocating (39)—subtends his narration of their encounter, but also that Fern, as donor, has power over him. Thus, the precondition for interpreting the scene is our acknowledgment of the fact that the opening gift is Fern's. Her prestige derives from it, and the purpose of the narration is essentially to dramatize its power. The heart of the gift principle in "Fern" lies in the narrator's obligation to reciprocate. Whatever he received from Fern— whatever the transport of symbolic matter[18]—we can say without hesitation that it totally possesses him and exercises some kind of power over him.

Furthermore, the sketch makes it clear that Fern is not an isolated figure. She is very much part of the community, is protected by it (32), and now has the special status of virgin, after having had many men. She receives the narrator in the midst of her family, on the front porch, and when they walk together down the Dixie Pike, it is under the watchful eyes of her neighbors. We might say her value and her power lie in her situatedness. Fern belongs where she belongs, the narrator suggests, and it would be useless to carry her off to Harlem or some other city. If he is nomadic, she remains fixed, and it is her very centeredness that allows her to represent the folk, as we shall see. The point is, in the gift economy, it is the community that oversees the obligation of exchange.

As anthropologist Mary Douglas notes in her preface to Mauss, "A gift that does nothing to enhance solidarity is a contradiction."[19] And again: "The theory of the gift is a theory of human solidarity."[20] This may help explain why the narrator chose the kind of contract with his reader that he did, one which would necessarily expose him but which would also enhance the bond of intimacy he requests from his reader. The incident embedded in "Fern" is exemplary, because the forces that are condensed in her gift are essentially those that circulate among the folk. Her embodiment of these forces—the very stuff of the gift exchange—gives her a special status within the community, which is a folk-status.

Let us now move on to the scene itself and see if we can understand the dynamics at work here: "Her eyes, unusually weird and open, held me. Held God. He flowed in as I've seen the countryside flow in. . . . I must have done something—what, I don't know, in the confusion of my emotion" (32). Fern's eyes are all-important as they "hold" the narrator, God, and the landscape momentarily together inside her. They seem to cast a spell over the narrator and charm him, as is implied by the word "weird," which introduces a supernatural, unearthly, even prophetic dimension. Her eyes are conduits; "open," they allow things to flow in, so that "hold" may also mean *contain*. Perhaps, then, the narrator momentarily fell into Fern's eyes, that is, lost himself there.

There are analogues elsewhere in *Cane* which suggest this same act of merging or communion. In "Kabnis," for instance, "[t]he sun-burst from her [Carrie's] eyes floods up and haloes him [Lewis]. . . . Fearlessly she loves into them [his eyes]" (205), although she suddenly pulls back because of what she sees in them. As Dan in "Box Seat" reminds us, "It hurts to look into most people's eyes" (125), and maybe this is a clue to what leads the narrator in "Fern" to react in emotional confusion. In "Kabnis," for example, "He [Kabnis] sees the nascent woman [in Carrie], her flesh already stiffening to cartilage, drying to bone. Her spirit-bloom, even now, touched sullen, bitter" (205). In another instance later in the play, Lewis's eyes look at the old man and he "merges with his source and lets the pain and beauty of the South meet him there. . . . A force begins to heave and rise . . ." (214–15). For Lewis, the reader will recall, the old man is "symbol, flesh, and spirit of the past" (217).

Whatever the reader may draw from these analogues, however, the narrator's emotional confusion in "Fern" introduces an important note of caution. The scene as a whole must be dealt with in symbolic terms and not in terms of simple representation. In other words, the difficulties we encounter in reading it must themselves become the prime focus of interpretation, inasmuch as they express not the semantics but the dynamics of the scene. It is this readerly obligation to address the symbolic order of "Fern" that leads us to identify it with the economy of the gift. The elusive leitmotif of "flow" not only carries out the work of symbolic investment in the sketch but also alludes to the force-field of the gift, which Mauss describes as a continuous flow.[21] Thus, we have here a homology between the dynamics of narration ("Fern" as a *schizzo*) and that of the threefold obligation to give, receive, and reciprocate. The very etymon of motif, *motus*, means "to move," although the Greek word for motif, *kinetikos*, serves our purpose even better: that which moves, provokes, determines a behavior or an action. Persuasive power in "Fern," whether it be discussed in terms of narration or in terms of the gift principle, is in both cases unleashed by the verb *to flow*.

What happens next in the scene under discussion is an intense moment of symbolic condensation, and the narrator relies on his kinesthetic imagination to recount Fern's "exemplary histrionics":[22]

> She sprang up. Rushed some distance from me. Fell to her knees, and began swaying, swaying. Her body was tortured with *something* it could not let out. Like boiling sap *it flooded* arms and fingers till she shook them as if they

burned her. *It found* her throat, and *spattered* inarticulately in plaintive, con-
vulsive sounds, mingled with calls to Christ Jesus. And then she sang, bro-
kenly. (32, my emphases)

"Something," some force, possesses Fern and transforms her, as it were. It
is this vortex of behavior[23] that the reader is at a loss to interpret, as there is no
sufficient textual substratum to explain it. While the narrator does not reveal
what the "it" is that runs through Fern, he does very ostentatiously place it:
"When one is on the soil of one's ancestors, most *anything* can come to one
. . ." (31, my emphasis). The suspensive end punctuation is the narrator's, as is
the sudden switch to the use of "one" from an otherwise totally intimate narrative voice. Such extreme pronominal formalization (from "I" to "one") is a way
of tipping us off to the essentially liturgical nature of the impending action.

By alluding to the soil, the narrator establishes a metonymic relation between it and Fern's behavior. In short, the scene is site-specific. It takes place
in a canebrake, in what Linda Wagner-Martin suggests we call "a surround."[24]
Fern, in other words, occasions a symbolic conjuncture of the narrator, the
landscape, and the community to which she belongs. Her role is that of go-
between or gift-bearer. In order to fathom this symbolic order of the gift structure, Mauss advises us to adopt an archaeological approach.[25] The preceding
scene should be handled as if it were a stratified site, one with many different
layers. The canebrake, which is such an important *locus classicus* of African-
American literature, is much more than a rhetorical topos. It also evokes the
antebellum world of slavery and all it implies.

Using Edward Casey's helpful neologism, we might more satisfactorily call
the narrator's encounter with Fern a "topocosm," which conflates the words
topos and cosmos.[26] In the light of this concept, the symbolic atmosphere of
the canebrake comes to bear the mark of an awesome absent presence. As the
very epigraph to *Cane* implies, cane is an axial image, an *axis mundi.* Uprooted,
it becomes the sacred flute, also a mystic figure which feels removed from God
and through lament and song expresses its desire to return to Him.[27] In the
scene witnessed by the narrator, there is a force, a puissance, that belongs not
only to Fern but also to the canebrake, even though it is Fern who acts it out.
It is this saplike energy that constitutes the symbolic order mentioned previously and that requires us to become archaeologists. Fern's very name, evoking contiguity with the soil, is yet another clue to the kind of application
needed.

Fern's performance was evidently so stunning that the scene was indelibly
burned into the narrator's imagination. As he recounts it, it calls to mind these
words of Kabnis: "Th form thats burned int my soul is some twisted awful
thing that crept in from a dream, a godam nightmare, an wont stay still unless

I feed it" (224). Kabnis's crisis is due to the fact that the "form" possessing him is completely beyond his control and is also cut off from any specifiable meaning. Fern's ur-scene echoes Kabnis's plight and goes to the heart of the Harlem Renaissance. Like Kabnis, the narrator of "Fern" is a northerner and shares the same condition of the majority of those who participated in the Great Migration. But the issue is not really North versus South, country versus city; rather it is about the difference between generations.

As Osofsky points out, "The Negroes who came north now [1910s and 1920s] were the first descendants of former slaves. They had listened to tales of slavery . . . , but had not experienced and lived its blight—the denial of full manhood" (Osofsky 23). The encounter between Fern and the narrator stages this unbreachable difference, and it is the topocosm of the canebrake that expresses the symbolic order of the original violence of slavery resulting in more than the denial of manhood. The bare life that the descendants of former slaves shored up in Harlem was a radical response to the absolute brutality of slavery and to the continued terrorism of white society. For young African-American men and women of the twenties, the horrors experienced by their parents and grandparents had become a question of collective memory. They were, in effect, critically removed from the time of slavery.

Those who had gone north were twice removed from their past. Thus, Toomer, a northerner, could respond to this new critical condition by saying of the experience that provided him with the material for "Fern":

> Georgia opened me. . . . I received my initial impulse to an individual art from my experience there. For no other section of the country has so stirred me. There one finds soil, soil in the sense the Russians know it,—the soil every art and literature that is to live must be embedded in. (NN 51)

Here it is Toomer, and not Fern, who is "open." But for author, narrator, and character, the soil is perceived as belonging to the atmosphere of the gift. As a "surround," the canebrake itself represents the inside of an environment of African-American memory, and its atmosphere imposes on the narrator the obligation to remember. Fern's dance is a dance of memory; the spirit of place is the spirit of the past.

If we implode the topocosm of the canebrake, we inevitably enter into the atmosphere of obligation its *genius loci* imposes. Under slavery, African-Americans were subjected to biopolitical conditions similar to those of the Jews in the concentration camps of the 1940s: becoming a people foreign to itself, without form, denied self-definition, and incapable of myth.[28] But as Ralph Ellison observes, a people is "more than the sum of its brutalization" (Levine 445). It is under such annihilating conditions of absolute violence that African-

Americans founded their own social system and kept alive a vernacular (or gift) economy over and against the nonconsensual economy of slavery. In this context, we might also recall DuBois's three gifts cited at the outset, especially the third, "a gift of the Spirit." For it is this "Spirit," this intangible force, with its inextricable network of obligations, reciprocities, and acts of politeness, in short a "system of total services,"[29] that allowed enslaved African-Americans to be a people with people.[30]

The atmospheric environment of "Fern" is about this DuBoisian puissance. By going down the Dixie Pike and into the canebrake, Fern and the narrator enter the originary place of the Spirit and the originating Spirit of the place. True to the heuristic principle of the gift, this DuBoisian place-spirit, through Fern, obliges the narrator and the reader to perpetual anamnesis. Fern's swaying and her song act out this obligation. By opening herself to the force of the inspirited site of the canebrake, she holds the place open as a site of memory. In Edward Casey's words, "the basis for the inclusive power of place is to be found in the body."[31] In short, Fern's is an act of living memory.[32]

Emptying herself in a gesture of extreme and total abjection, she puts herself at the service of "something" that dances and sings her, for her actions are both hers and not hers. She is a conduit. That is what possession means. Seizing on the sorrow she expresses, Houston Baker calls Fern a victim (Baker 1988: 27), while Nellie McKay reminds us that *Cane* is "a work about the pain and struggle wrung from the soul of a people and . . . the meaning of that awful reality" (McKay 1984, 177). We might, therefore, call Fern a vessel of spectrality (a term suggested to me by Guyanan writer Wilson Harris) and ask ourselves what is "awful" here. It is Helga Crane, in Nella Larsen's novel *Quicksand,* who alerts us to "those skeletons that stalked lively and in full health through the consciousness of every person of Negro ancestry in America" (Toomer 96). But not all the descendants of former slaves care to remember. That is what "Fern" is about.

That Fern's performance has to do with an attempt to embody real horror, the narrator himself intimates at the very beginning of the sketch, when he notes that her song has the effect of making his own sorrow seem trivial (24). While she was singing in the canebrake, it seems to the narrator as if "she were pounding her head in anguish upon the ground" (32). This gesture offers the reader another somatic index to the symbolic order. His response suggests how deeply moved he was: "I rushed to her. She fainted in my arms" (32). So his narration of the terrible "little" drama in the canebrake ends with a powerful image in which she and he merge in an iconic reversal of Michelangelo's *Pietà.*

If the narrator can go no further in his response to Fern's uncommon liberality (she has surrendered herself to him), it is not because he does not understand what her sacrificial expenditure means, but because he cannot understand. Nor can any young Harlemite who has not actually lived through the horrors of the slave camps. In effect, while Fern's own performance witnesses to or puts us in touch with one of the most abysmal sites of American cultural history, it remains unequivocally an act of substitution. The awful reality of slavery, ultimately unrepresentable, lies beyond Fern's sacrificial dance. In short, the scene is liturgical. This does not mean that Fern does not penetrate the negativity of the site. On the contrary, she dialecticizes the DuBoisian "gift of sweat and brawn" and, in so doing, is sovereignly sublimated in the very force that devastates her.[33]

As far as the narrator and the reader are concerned, however, the horror embedded in the scene is left to itself. Still, the former's communion with the unrepresentable force embodied in Fern's ritual dance is real, as far as it goes. This is evident from the counter-gift he makes. Namely, through Fern he too has learned to give himself up. How? By using his narrative as a form of self-sacrifice, a counter-gift. His decision to cast it in the form of a confession indicates that he is ready to surrender himself in sketching Fern. If he had not done so, he would have failed to sketch her. Herein lies the act of reciprocity the narrator's autobiographical account seeks to express. By transmuting the force that possessed Fern into an aesthetic economy, he is in a position to extend the circuit of obligation to the reader. Through the act of reading, we help distribute Fern's prestige. And because her prestige is in turn a gift of the people, we are also in the presence of the latter's puissance, what DuBois called "a gift of the Spirit." Having transmitted his experience of Georgia to *Cane*, Toomer in effect made it possible for Fern to travel to Harlem. Once interest in "Fern" is aroused, a credit process is begun among those involved in shoring up the informal social democracy of Harlem's streets.

As Locke affirmed of the "quickened centers" of Harlem in his groundbreaking essay "The New Negro," "A second crop of the Negro's gifts promises still more largely" (NN 15). It is natural to assume his "more largely" was also meant to embrace the fundamental notion of largesse, which Starobinski traces back to the adjective *largus*, meaning that which flows in abundance, as from the source of a river.[34] Ultimately, it is to a total social fact that Locke is alluding as he is even "more largely" interested in the "channels opening out into which the balked social feelings of the American Negro can flow freely."[35] The channels Locke is speaking of are indeed many. They include the Lafayette Theater of Rudolph Fisher's "Miss Cynthie"; the "flowing," "eddying," "swirling" of Toomer's "Seventh Street"; the street scenes of Eunice Hunton Carter's "The Corner"[36]; and numberless other loci celebrating the bare life of Harlem's people. As Nellie McKay reminds us, "[B]lack survival in America has always been political and . . . the black folk culture is a manifestation of radical politics" (McKay 1984, 176).

For the narrator to free himself from Fern, there is no other alternative but to give in return. And, of course, this gift then requires another, on into infinity. It all comes down to a question of prestige, and I hope it is now clear that this, in reality, concerns the broader issue of civility or civics. As Mauss says in the closing sentence of his famous essay, the gift principle "allow[s] us to perceive, measure, and weigh up the various aesthetic, moral, religious, and economic motivations, the diverse material and demographic factors, the sum total of which are the basis of society and constitute our common life, the conscious direction of which is the supreme art, *Politics*, in the Socratic sense of the word."[37] In short, there are no free gifts, not even in free-flowing Harlem in those swell years of the 1920s.

NOTES

1. Langston Hughes, ed., *The Big Sea: An Autobiography* (London: Alfred A. Knopf, 1940), 81 (hereafter referred to as BS).

2. Jessie R. Fauset, *Plum Bun: A Novel Without a Moral* (London: E. Mathews & Marrot, 1929), 98.

3. Alain Locke, ed., *The New Negro, An Interpretation* (1925; reprint New York: Johnson Reprint Corp., 1968), 7 (hereafter referred to as NN).

4. Giorgio Agamben, *Homo Sacer, Sovereign Power and Bare Life,* Daniel Heller-Roazen, trans. (Stanford: Stanford University Press, 1998), 119–35.

5. Marcel Mauss, *The Gift,* W.D. Halls, trans. (London: Routledge, 1990), 78.

6. Elias Canetti, *Massa e potere,* Furio Jesi, trans. (Milan: Adelphi, 1981), 33–36, 129–35.

7. Emile Benveniste, *Il vocabolario delle istituzioni indoeuropee,* Mariantonia Liborio, trans., 2 vols. (Turin: Einaudi, 1976), 1:280–81.

8. Ann Petry, *The Street* (1946; London: Virago Press, 1986), 46 (my emphases).

9. Giorgio Agamben, *Homo Sacer, Sovereign Power and Bare Life,* Daniel Heller-Roazen, trans. (Stanford: Stanford University Press, 1998).

10. Claude McKay, *Home to Harlem* (1928; reprint Boston: Northeastern University Press, 1987), 14 (my emphasis). This book is hereafter referred to as HH in citations.

11. Mary Douglas, Foreword to Marcel Mauss's *The Gift,* ix.

12. Heinrich Lausberg, *Elementi di retorica,* Lea Ritter Santini, trans. (Bologna: Il Mulino, 1969), 40, 46; Jean Starobinski, *A piene mani,* Antonia Perazzoli Tadini, trans. (Turin: Einaudi, 1995), 13–25.

13. Richard Wright, "Blueprint for Negro Writing," in Gates and McKay, ed., *The Norton Anthology,* 1380.

14. Richard Wright, "Blueprint for Negro Writing," in Gates and McKay, ed., *The Norton Anthology,* 1384–85.

15. Marcel Mauss, *The Gift*, W.D. Halls, trans. (London: Routledge, 1990), 72.

16. Bruno Karsenti, *L'homme total* (Paris: Presses Universitaires de France, 1997), 405.

17. Marcel Mauss, *The Gift*, W.D. Halls, trans. (London: Routledge, 1990), 78.

18. Bruno Karsenti, *L'homme total* (Paris: Presses Universitaires de France, 1997), 408.

19. Mary Douglas, Foreword to Marcel Mauss's *The Gift*, vii.

20. Mary Douglas, Foreword to Marcel Mauss's *The Gift*, x.

21. Marcel Mauss, *The Gift*, W.D. Halls, trans. (London: Routledge, 1990), 20; Bruno Karsenti, *L'homme total* (Paris: Presses Universitaires de France, 1997), 412.

22. Joseph Roach, *Cities of the Dead* (New York: Columbia University Press, 1996), 27.

23. Joseph Roach, *Cities of the Dead* (New York: Columbia University Press, 1996), 28.

24. Linda Wagner-Martin, "Toomer's *Cane* as Narrative Sequence," *Modern American Short Story Sequences,* J. Gerald Kennedy, ed. (New York: Cambridge University Press, 1995), 28. Wagner-Martin's coining of this term is a felicitous confirmation of Mauss's notion of atmosphere in the gift economy.

25. Marcel Mauss, *The Gift*, W.D. Halls, trans. (London: Routledge, 1990), 4.

26. Edward S. Casey, *The Fate of Place* (Berkeley: University of California Press, 1997), 21.

27. Jean Chevalier and Alain Gheerbrant, *Dizionario dei simboli,* Maria Margheri Pieroni, Laura Mori, and Roberto Vigevani, trans., 2 vols. (Milan: Biblioteca Universale Rizzoli, 1989).

28. Roberto Esposito, *Nove pensieri sulla politica* (Bologna: Il Mulino, 1993), 200.

29. Marcel Mauss, *The Gift*, W.D. Halls, trans. (London: Routledge, 1990), 5–6.

30. Roberto Esposito, *Nove pensieri sulla politica* (Bologna: Il Mulino, 1993), 200.

31. Edward S. Casey, *The Fate of Place* (Berkeley: University of California Press, 1997), 476, n.12.

32. Joseph Roach, *Cities of the Dead* (New York: Columbia University Press, 1996), 26.

33. Jean-Luc Nancy, *Un pensiero finito,* Luisa Bonesio and Caterina Resta, trans. (Milan: Marcos y Marcos, 1992), 238.

34. Jean Starobinski, *A piene mani,* Antonia Perazzoli Tadini, trans. (Turin: Einaudi, 1995), 13.

35. Jean Starobinski, *A piene mani,* Antonia Perazzoli Tadini, trans. (Turin: Einaudi, 1995), 13–14.

36. Eunice Hunter Carter, "The Corner," in Roses and Randolph, 1990.

37. Marcel Mauss, *The Gift*, W.D. Halls, trans. (London: Routledge, 1990), 83.

11. Harlem as a Memory Place: Reconstructing the Harlem Renaissance in Space

Dorothea Löbbermann

The topographical center of African-American modernism, 1920s Harlem, reaches out in many directions: spatially, into the international African diaspora (within the United States and outside it); temporally, into the African and American pasts, and—both with its utopian force and from our contemporary retrospective position—into the future. Its symbolic power is thus firmly established in space and time. It is this aspect that I want to keep in mind when I look at Harlem as a memory place.

As a memory place, Harlem is the spatial representation of a certain part of the (African) American cultural memory; it shapes this memory and is, in turn, shaped by it. Harlem has been the carrier of memories ever since the Harlem Renaissance. This fact is already expressed in the name of the era that ties the notion of place (Harlem) to the notion of time and memory (renaissance). In this combination, the Harlem Renaissance's concept of a cultural renewal through the remembrance and reconstruction of an influential past is situated in the space of Harlem, the modern urban center of the New Negro movement. Harlem Renaissance writing abounds in references to the South and to Africa as culturally and spiritually significant places of the past, as, for instance, Melvin Dixon has shown in his article "The Black Writer's Use of Memory."[1] At the same time, Harlem has continuously originated memories of itself and constructed new images for the cultural memory of black America. These images are based in the urban space of New York. I want to inquire into this relationship of place and memory by investigating the memories of Harlem and the spatial images through which they manifest in texts.

Harlem in the 1920s has been repeatedly reconstructed in fiction, during the Harlem Renaissance itself and in later texts. James de Jongh, in his study on the international literary appropriation of Harlem, *Vicious Modernism,* points out that it is important to identify Harlem as a literary motif and not simply as the (realistic) setting of novels, plays, stories, and poetry. This motif has been consciously chosen for a given text in order to refer to a significant historical place. The way the motif is designed and organized shapes the place and gives it meaning, clearly within the text but also outside it. Thus, the place's significance is not only referred to, but also further established and reinterpreted. Through these acts of interpretation, the motif becomes a field of debate on the meaning of the Harlem Renaissance—and often, by extension, on the state of African-American life.

In the fictional (re)constructions of Harlem, the achievements of the New Negro were celebrated, visions were expressed, history was assessed, and cultural identities were negotiated. In the early twenties, Harlem was still *terra incognita* on the map of African-American fiction. However, the intensive attention of black—and white—newspapers, as well as traveling blues singers and other public and private dissemination, had established Harlem well on the cultural landscape, both as the respectable center for racial uplift and as the notorious center of the jazz age that was attracting blacks and whites alike. Consequently, writers about Harlem, even in the 1920s, were already reacting to a strong and contradictory public image. A naive "description" of Harlem has, therefore, never been possible. Rather, the place had to be perceived through the multitudinous reflections of it, causing a perspective split between myth and fact. The utopian force behind Harlem brought about a nostalgic view even as Harlem was still growing.

The diverse nature of this image of Harlem and its constant repercussions in popular culture made the Harlem Renaissance a very self-conscious movement, which helps to explain the problems of representation with which many of the artists saw themselves confronted. The Harlem Renaissance writers had to develop their motifs and modes of representation against the overdetermination of the image of Harlem. Authors of later ages additionally faced the temporal distance and, most importantly, the fact that over the course of its further development, Harlem had ceased to stand as a symbol of African-American achievement and was now viewed as emblematic of black inner-city problems. Although this is a significant difference between the two groups of writers under consideration, I want to stress the similarities of their situations: both groups deal self-consciously with the overdetermined state of Harlem, both apply a nostalgic view as well as a critical (re)interpretation of the place and era, and both groups, finally, (re)construct Harlem as a memory place for the American consciousness, black or white.[2]

The various interpretations of Harlem from the 1920s through the 1990s form a net of images, an intertextual literary space that is reconstructed from the topographical space in New York. With the exception of Jean Toomer, all writers of the 1920s chose Harlem as a motif for at least one of their projects: Claude McKay, Carl Van Vechten, Nella Larsen, Jessie Fauset, Countée Cullen, Wallace Thurman, Langston Hughes. In each of their projects, Harlem is scrutinized in its function as "City of Refuge," to quote the title of Rudolph Fisher's famous short story. Fisher even concentrated exclusively on Harlem as a setting for his novels and stories. To him, Harlem is sufficient in its own right as a portrayal of black life; its diversity makes it a cosmos unto itself. At the same time, Fisher draws attention to the limitations of the utopian place and envisions solutions to them, as in his 1927 story "Blades of Steel," in which all of these aspects are dealt with through the image of Harlem's topography. I will analyze it in subsequent text as an example of the spatial imagination of the Harlem Renaissance.

More recent portraits of Harlem can be found in Ishmael Reed's *Mumbo Jumbo* (1972), Toni Morrison's *Jazz* (1992), or Samuel R. Delany's "Atlantis: Model 1924" (1995). Although each of these works pursues different strategies and different aims, all of them use the image of 1920s Harlem to comment on their respective present; Reed especially uses the 1920s as an analogy to his contemporary 1960s. In their works, all of these authors reshape the place: Reed, in an act of parody, exaggerates the received stereotypes of the era and places Harlem in the center of a worldwide culture war, ranging from the beginnings of time to the 1960s; Morrison deconstructs modernist aesthetics and notions of the city, a "City" she personifies in order to explore its usefulness for the African-American community; and Delany juxtaposes a middle-class Harlem with the gay aesthetics of classical modernism. All texts strongly deconstruct essentialist notions of ethnic identity (or ethnic origins), meaning, and memory; all texts engage in complex strategies of intertextuality.

Morrison keeps most in line, perhaps, with her Harlem Renaissance precursors in that she explores Harlem from the southern rural perspective of her migrant protagonists, describing the wonders of the city and its dangers. With a highly sophisticated reflection on the problems of memory and narrative authority, *Jazz* investigates the meaning of Harlem for the African-American community then and today. I will analyze Morrison's image of the streets as an example of a more recent fictional account of Harlem, comparing her spatial construction to that of Rudolph Fisher, and thus will establish a correspondence between the two portrayals of Harlem's streets. With their differences and continuities, they serve as examples of a never-ending reinterpretation of Harlem that occupies all eras since the Harlem Renaissance. All texts, I claim, investigate the possibilities of the (re)construction of 1920s Harlem. Moreover, both the Harlem Renaissance writings and the later texts can be seen as components of the architecture of a cultural memory, the memory of Harlem that we have at our disposal today.

HARLEM AS *LIEU DE MÉMOIRE* AND AS MEMORY PLACE

Space and memory have been linked since the days of classical mnemotechnics, the antique orators' method for memorizing speeches that, as Frances Yates has shown in *The Art of Memory*, have influenced European culture up to the seventeenth century. Only recently, Pierre Nora's article "Between History and Memory: *Les Lieux de Mémoire*" opened up a new discussion on the practices of cultural memory that proved very productive for African-American studies, as demonstrated by the volume *History and Memory in African-American Culture*, edited by Geneviève Fabre and Robert O'Meally.[3] Nora's *lieux de mémoire*—sites of memory—can be geographical sites, such as battlefields or monuments, although they are not limited to geography: books or calendars, for example, can serve as *lieux de mémoire* as well, sites which connect the past to the present, the individual to the group, the real to the imaginary. The concept of *lieu de mémoire* offers a valuable explanation of Harlem's status as a site of memory in the American consciousness. One of the characteristics of the *lieu de mémoire*, according to Nora, is its overdetermination. This excess of meaning can be found, for example, in the symbolic space of the cabaret which integrates many diverging positions, as I will sketch out subsequently.

The *lieu de mémoire*, however, does not necessarily take into account the topographical qualities of the place. It is in perusal of the topography, of the spatial imagery, that I want to return to mnemotechnics and their notion of a memory that is structured spatially. This idea is expressed in the concept of the "memory place," whose founding myth, the legend of Simonedes, is narrated by—among others—Cicero.[4] This legend, a spatial story in itself, initiates the relationship of place and memory that, if applied to the space of Harlem, enables us to understand the inner structure of the construction of Harlem as a *lieu de mémoire*.

According to the legend, the singer Simonedes, hired to perform at a banquet, had just left the hall when its roof fell in and crushed hosts and guests of the party. The bodies were so dismembered that it was impossible to tell them apart for their burial. Only Simonedes could remember the position that the individuals had had at the table and could therefore identify them. In this story, the destroyed room with the unrecognizable bodies represents the catastrophe of forgetting, and the identification of the bodies for an orderly burial, the art of memory. Cicero infers from it that we can remember things by imagining them in space. The images, stored in the memory places, can be retraced by their position in that space. In fact, for Cicero, the images function like letters on a writing tablet (*De Oratore* II.85.352–54).

Harlem, like the crushed banquet hall, is such a memory place. The texts written about it form images of it and position them in its topography. Harlem, in a sense, becomes the writing tablet onto which its stories are written. The streets, buildings, and other spatial features of the real, historic place become, in fiction, carriers of ideas through which Harlem and the Harlem Renaissance can be remembered. These ideas are remembered exactly *through* their spatial concretization and within the space of the individual text, in which they hold their specific positions.

As an imaginary space that can be entered—one in which things can be deposited, lost, found, and altered—the memory place examines how the site of memory is constructed. Stressing the power of the image, it is a concept that reflects the mechanisms of memory as a creative act and its nature as a process. The memory place is never only a container, but is also always characterized by the dynamics of the act of memory and by its structure, by the ever-changing relationships among its images. In this sense, it is a perfect image for the function of literature, both as an imaginative space and as an element of cultural memory.

All the different elements of Harlem—the streets and buildings, foods and smells, clothes and colors, the sounds, the weather, the bodies—form the fabric of the literary place. The metaphor of the fabric is a significant element in the most recent fictional reconstruction of Harlem, Samuel Delany's "Atlantis: Model 1924," an intertextual web that ties together Harlem, Atlantis, and the Brooklyn Bridge in one great "tapestry" of memory and forgetting. In reconstructing a (to a considerable extent, autobiographical) past, Delany uses the image of Harlem as a focus through which he portrays not only modernism and the Harlem Renaissance, but also the intertwined strategies by which they are remembered or, almost more importantly, forgotten.

The fabric—and "fabric" is the literal meaning of "text," as Delany points out elsewhere[5]—will be woven differently in every fiction. Likewise, the corresponding fabric that the reader produces, the memory he or she constructs from the text, will be different. Thus, texts and readers produce spaces that in their sum weave the intertextual space of Harlem that is under consideration here, and in which I will continue to follow some representative threads.

THE SYMBOLIC SPACE OF THE CABARET

The task of the Harlem Renaissance writers can be described as the appropriation of the new territory of Harlem for an African-American cultural memory, the creation of symbolic spaces that express an African-American consciousness and sense of community. As Günter Lenz has shown, the cabaret, the crowded street, and the polluted airshaft have become symbolic spaces in the literature of the Harlem Renaissance, spaces of the city that create and express *communitas*, knots in the web of a cultural memory (Lenz 309–45).[6] These spaces can be charged with highly contradictory meanings; what makes them symbolic spaces—and, retrospectively, *lieux de mémoire*—is their repeated use. The cabaret, for example, became a symbolic space that was highly contested. Its role in the innovation of expressive form (jazz music, dance, or the urban blues) promised a new communal expression of the new African-American experience. This promise, however, was countered by the old and new stereotypes that quickly flocked around the cabaret—those of blacks as "natural" entertainers (for a white audience) and as people governed exclusively by sensuality and passion.

The reconstructions of the cabaret in Harlem Renaissance fiction cover a wide range of approaches. Poet Langston Hughes embraces it emphatically as the generic African-American space in which the ethnic vernacular of music and dance, and the contradictions of black life, find an urban expression. This expression he again renders into a poetic language that feeds on the rhythmic and tonal qualities of that vernacular ("Harlem Night Club," "Jazzonia").

Prose fiction exhibits more complicated attitudes toward the cabaret. Although most writers try to catch its sensuality and syncopated aesthetics, their efforts at jazz prose are always framed in a more linear narrative, which does not grant the assertive freedom a poem can claim. W. E. B. DuBois, who continually fought with his contemporaries about the function of literature in shaping social realities, accused Carl Van Vechten (*Nigger Heaven* 1926) and Claude McKay (*Home to Harlem* 1928) of exploiting the exotic appeal of the cabaret and Harlem in general. In fact, both authors test the representational value of the cabaret in a larger field of symbolic places of Harlem—Van Vechten in a more didactic manner; McKay problematizing the power of perennially existing stereotypes.[7] Repulsion by or ambivalence toward the cabaret's "primitivism" is protagonist Helga Crane's reaction to the place in *Quick-sand*, whose author Nella Larsen explores the construction of black femininity in various places of African-American life in the South of the United States, in Europe, and Harlem (1928).

In more recent fiction, the interest in the cabaret has declined. It no longer seems to serve as a site of memory, no longer seems to represent the black experience. Obviously, the act of placing a cabaret in a story on Harlem has become a stereotype in itself, no matter how it is evaluated; therefore, contemporary writers tend to avoid the topos altogether. With an elderly couple as protagonists, Morrison's *Jazz* focuses on the survival in Harlem beyond the young immigrants' embrace of the "City" and its attractions. The cabaret "Mexico" is conjured up once, by youthful Dorcas, but dismissed by Joe as "too loud" (Morrison 1992, 39[8]). Delany's "Atlantis: Model 1924" stages the repression of memories and of erotic experiences rather than the sexual abandon that is connected to the cabaret. Thus, the cabaret is conspicuously missing from the abundance of symbolic places that stimulate his protagonist's fantasies (the subway and other underground places and, most centrally, Brooklyn Bridge). For his part, Ishmael Reed is generally more interested in types, phrases, and images from popular culture than in the description of places. *Mumbo Jumbo*'s central metaphor is a play upon the received notion of jazz as an epidemic, but "Jes Grew"—the erupting craze for music, dance, and sex that governs the plot of the novel—is taken out of the confined place of the cabaret into the world at large.

CONSTRUCTING THE MEMORY PLACE: THE STREETS OF HARLEM

Harlem has more symbolic spaces than the cabaret, however. Already its streets offer themselves to be incorporated into the cultural memory. Examples of this are the many descriptions of the sidewalks, crowded with a multicolored and multifaceted mass, that fascinate the newcomer when he or she emerges from the subway. The "great race-welding" that, as Alain Locke prophesied, was to be achieved through the "first concentration of so many elements of Negro life" in Harlem has been projected onto Harlem's topography a number of times (Locke 1986, 7, 6[9]). But the streets are not only memory places in that they *contain* the images of the crowd; they themselves serve as images for the structural relationships in Harlem. I want to show this in the analysis of two very different treatments of the image of the street, one by Rudolph Fisher (from his short story "Blades of Steel") and one by Toni Morrison (from her novel *Jazz*). Both texts construct Harlem as a memory place for the African-American consciousness; both texts take the streets as an image, but they connect their images very differently to the memory place, and they construct very different kinds of memories from it.

Fisher uses the topography of Harlem to portray its structure of class distinctions—and to express a vision of community that echoes Locke's. "Blades of Steel" starts with the view of a map, followed by a general characterization of the nature of its streets:

> Negro Harlem's three broad highways form the letter H, Lenox and Seventh Avenue running parallel northward, united a little above their midpoints by east-and-west 135th Street.
>
> Lenox Avenue is for the most part the boulevard of the unperfumed; "rats" they are often termed. Here, during certain hours, there is nothing unusual in the flashing of knives, the quick succession of pistol shots, the scream of a police-whistle or a woman.
>
> But Seventh Avenue is the promenade of the high-toned dickties and strivers. It breathes a superior atmosphere, sings superior songs, laughs a superior laugh. Even were there no people, the difference would be clear: the middle of Lenox Avenue is adorned by street-car tracks, the middle of Seventh Avenue by parking.

The construction of an opposition between Seventh and Lenox Avenues is a stock characteristic of any fiction or nonfiction description of Harlem. Fisher uses it to satisfy—even parody—the expectations of an audience used to the spectacle of Harlem, a spectacle of extremes that knows no middle ("scream of a police-whistle" and "superior songs"). But like many Harlem writers, Fisher saw the instability of a community that consisted mainly of "rats" and "dickties"—the poor and the rich—without much of a middle class to keep it together. While he explicitly calls for a stronger middle class elsewhere, most notably in his novel *The Walls of Jericho* (1928), in this story he solves the conflict spatially, through a third street:

> These two highways, frontiers of the opposed extreme of dark-skinned social life, are separated by an intermediate any-man's land, across which they communicate chiefly by way of 135th Street. Accordingly 135th Street is the heart and soul of black Harlem; it is common ground, the natural scene of unusual contacts, a region that disregards class. It neutralizes, equilibrates, binds, rescues union out of diversity. (Fisher 1987, 132)

With the image of the letter H (for "Harlem" and "heart"), Fisher connects the spatial representation of class frontiers, represented by the parallel avenues, with a space of community, represented by "communicative" 135th Street. The "union out of diversity" it "rescues" echoes Alain Locke's program for Harlem as the "laboratory of a great race-welding," a "common area of contact and interaction" (Locke 1986, 6). The streets form a letter through which they communicate with one another and with their readers: Fisher's Harlem spells its own name, it speaks its own text. The image of the "H," in this case, literally functions as a letter on a writing tablet, as Cicero described the mnemonic role of images. At the same time, the self-referential foregrounding of text, however playful, voices a distrust in the utopian aspect of Harlem: maybe it is only in writing that the utopian community is established.

Fisher's image of the streets is a response within his contemporary context, a response to the ongoing discussion about the meaning of the Negro Renaissance. The "H" is a concise image that explains the complicated present and formulates a vision for the future.

Toni Morrison's novel *Jazz* responds not only to the 1920s, but also to the subsequent history of Harlem and African-American culture. Its 1992 perspective takes into account the whole range of the city's development and reflects Harlem's significant position in cultural memory. This position, which in the 1920s was still a vision, is now a fact; but it has become more complex than the Harlem Renaissance contemporaries could have foreseen. As a site of memory, Harlem now refers both to the glory of the Harlem Renaissance, to its decay into a criminal slum, and to its consolidation as a community and resurrection as a symbol of power since the 1980s.

Morrison looks back on the 1920s as the phase in African-American culture in which inner-city life had a positive, promising meaning. Although her narration is limited to the perspective of the first two decades of the century, she voices—in her distrust of the city's benevolence—her knowledge about Harlem's social decay and the ongoing inner-city problems. Her Harlem becomes the generic "City," personified as a seductive and authoritarian power. This power is expressed through the streets:

> (I)f you pay attention to the street plans, all laid out, the City can't hurt you. . . . All you have to do is heed the design—the way it's laid out for you, considerate, mindful of where you want to go and what you might need tomorrow. (Morrison 1992, 8–9)

The street plans direct the inhabitants, they control their movements. What is taken as a sign of love and protection as the protagonists arrive in Harlem, soon becomes a sign of danger. When Joe Trace remembers his youth as a hunter in Virginia and goes on the track for Dorcas, his youthful lover who has discarded him for a younger man, the city's streets and the seductive music, its voice, are united in the image of the jazz record with its grooves:

> He is bound to the track. It pulls him like a needle through the groove of a Bluebird record. Round and round about town. That's the way the City spins you. Makes you do what it wants, go where the laid-out roads say to. All the while letting you think you're free; that you can jump into the thickets because you feel like it. There are no thickets here and if mowed grass is okay

to walk on the City will let you know. You can't get off the track a City lays
for you. (Morrison 1992, 120)

Morrison's streets spin Joe in a circle; the New York grid on which Fisher's
Harlem is based rolls itself up into the grooves of a jazz record. The image
of the circle reflects the characters' obsessions in which they are dangerously
imprisoned (Joe will eventually shoot Dorcas); it reflects the characters' and
narrator's obsessions with the "City," a city that they have not yet made their
own but which they admire for its apparent perfection and strength; it reflects
the fate of the African-American city that has too soon been glorified. All
of this is projected onto Harlem's topography. While Fisher's "H" is a fixed
oppositional system that nonetheless leaves room for growth and hope, Morrison's tracks are an encircling power that can only lead to catastrophe. The
catastrophe happens on the level of story (murder and its consequences) and
on that of narration (the narrator loses control over the story; he or she cannot
produce an unambiguous memory of what happened). Both these catastrophes
lead to a "redemption" of sorts; to a certain extent, the characters learn to come
to terms with their past and to form the "village community" in the city that
Morrison holds specific for African-American fiction of urban life;[10] and the
narrator surrenders to an open text whose final version depends on the active
intervention of the reader ("make me, remake me" [229]). The communities
that city and text can provide can only be achieved against the topographical
and aesthetic structures supplied by the "City." The spinning groove thus represents the futility and danger of an urban representation that does not take
into account the well-being of the community. Like Fisher, Morrison is interested in a stable African-American community in Harlem; unlike him, she
does not see the vision written into the city itself. While Fisher manages to
express the problems and hopes of Harlem in the image of the streets, Morrison uses the streets, ultimately, as a sign of warning of the city.

For all these differences, both authors use the streets of Harlem to construct memory places from them, places into which they lead their readers' imagination, places through which they express their respective images of Harlem.
However, while Fisher's image of the "H" contains the diversity of the symbolic meaning of Harlem, Morrison's circle expresses the complexity of a retrospective representation of the Harlem Renaissance: its meanings are hurled off
the spiral, the memory place no longer contains all there is to say. Instead, the
memory place of *Jazz* is a matter of constant re- and deconstruction.

All of the retrospective Harlem versions reflect the textual construction of
1920s Harlem to a very high degree. After all, the central motif of Reed's
Mumbo Jumbo is the search for the "original text," a text whose ultimate de-

struction frees the present from a fixed written structure to perform its memories of the past according to contemporary needs and forms. Delany's "Atlantis:
Model 1924" makes visible the interplay of dreams and fears, of memory and
forgetting, of poetry, fiction and history in the (re)construction of the Harlem
Renaissance. Nevertheless, textual self-reflexivity is not only the (post-modern)
domain of authors from the 1960s onwards. The Harlem Renaissance writers
were already well aware of the problems of representation of a place that served
as a symbol to so many different interest groups (African-Americans of all nations and classes; white slummers, patrons, anthropologists; black and white
gay men and lesbians—all found in Harlem a place that reflected their particular interests). Fisher's "H" and his explicit surrender to the stereotypes of
Lenox and Seventh Avenues reflect both this overdetermination of the symbol
and its status as a text.

Fisher's and Morrison's examples help us read other conspicuous places in
Harlem literature and their positions and functions in their respective texts.
The mutual production of space and text which is foregrounded here is decisive
for the construction of the reader's memory of Harlem, of the construction
of Harlem as a *lieu de mémoire*. The focus on the spatial quality of Harlem,
of Harlem as a memory place, enables us to follow the process through which
Harlem becomes a text. With every new text, and every new reading, the
crushed banquet hall of Simonedes is reconstructed, each time with a different
emphasis on the process of reconstruction and on the meaning of the place.

NOTES

1. Fabre and O'Meally 18–27.
2. This study differs from a number of studies on the changing image of Harlem
in that it only addresses fictional accounts of Harlem in the 1920s. For analyses of the
symbolic power of Harlem through the 1960s and 1970s, see Günter H. Lenz, "Symbolic Space, Communal Rituals, and the Surreality of the Urban Ghetto: Harlem in
Black Literature From the 1920s to the 1960s," *Callalloo* 11 (Spring, 1988), 309–45;
A. Robert Lee, "Harlem on My Mind: Fiction of a Black Metropolis," *The American
City: Literary and Cultural Perspectives,* Graham Clarke, ed. (New York: St. Martin's
Press, 1988), 62–85; James de Jongh, *Vicious Modernism: Black Harlem and the Literary
Imagination* (New York: Cambridge University Press, 1990).
3. Cf. Fabre and O'Meally, which also reprints Nora's article "Between Memory
and History: *Les Lieux de Mémoire*" (284–300).
4. My idea of the "memory place" relies heavily on Renate Lachmann's *Gedächtnis
und Literatur. Intertextualität in der russischen Moderne* (Frankfurt: Suhrkamp, 1990),
which develops this term from Frances Yates's *The Art of Memory* (London and Henley:
Paul Kegan, 1966).

5. Samuel Delany, "Appendix A," *Triton* (Toronto: Bantam Books, 1976), 333.

6. The concepts of "symbolic space" and "*communitas*" refer to Victor Turner's model of cultural anthropology.

7. W.E.B. DuBois, "Books," *The Crisis* 24 (December 1926), 31–32 (on *Nigger Heaven*), and "The Browsing Reader: Review of *Home to Harlem*," *The Crisis* 35 (June, 1928), 202. On stereotypes in Van Vechten and McKay, see Astrid Franke, *Keys to Controversies: Stereotypes in Modern American Fiction* (Frankfurt and New York: Campus and St. Martin's Press, 1999).

8. All further quotations from this source refer to this edition.

9. All further quotations from this source refer to this edition.

10. Cf. Toni Morrison, "City Limits, Village Values: Concepts of the Neighborhood in Black Fiction," *Literature and the Urban Experience*, Michael C. Jaye and Ann Chalmers Watts, eds. (New Brunswick: Rutgers University Press, 1981), 35–41.

12. "A Basin in the Mind": Language in *Their Eyes Were Watching God*

Claudine Raynaud

> ... when [Nanny] gained the privacy of her own little shack she stayed on her knees so long she forgot she was there herself. There is a basin in the mind where words float around on thought and thought on sound and sight. Then there is a depth of thought untouched by words, and deeper still a gulf of formless feelings untouched by thought. Nanny entered this infinity of conscious pain again on her old knees. (TE 43)[1]

In the preceding quotation, the narrator tells the reader that the character enters the depths of consciousness precisely at the moment when language fails and formless unutterable feelings take over.[2] Conscious pain is beyond words because it belongs to the realm of feelings that have nothing to do with sound (the aural) and sight (the visual). Shapeless, these feelings blend in with the most primary of the senses: smell, taste, and touch.[3] Only through a convoluted three-tiered simile organized along the primary relationship between container and contained does Nanny, the heroine's grandmother, get in touch with this infinity of sorrow. Like the scream that signals regression toward the origins of language, Nanny's gradual descent into the abyss of conscious suffering is a mental operation that leads to a region beyond the verbal.[4] How can the metaphoric process ultimately encounter the olfactory, the oral, and the tactile? How can metaphor be in touch with the corporeal?

Nanny is not going through this experience for the first time. Yet, this instance does not refer back to another precise occurrence. The suspended analepsis leaves the reader to conjecture its referent. Slavery and the rape of Nanny's daughter Leafy come to the reader's mind as various possibilities. The repetition of the meditation, akin to a stage-by-stage process of religious meditative practice, makes the grandmother forget that "she was there herself." Singular subjective experience is transmuted into communal formless experience, beyond individual consciousness and personal history. The very indeterminacy of the referent defines that experience as *collective* memory. What seems to be at stake in the conception of the metaphor displayed in the foregoing excerpt is nothing less than its link, not so much to Hurston's style, but to the language of the folk. Folk language is conjured up in its relation to an impossible act of remembering *and* to the loss of a language of origin.

If one follows the text, metaphor would be shaped against the formlessness of repressed memory, a memory that is "untouched by words," beyond utterance. As such, it announces Morrison's notion of "unspeakable things unspoken" or the "unuttered thoughts" that Stamp Paid hears in *Beloved* when the three women finally find themselves together in 124 Bluestone Road.[5] While the shapeless, the formless, the sensory constitute one concept of "poetic" language, another modulation emerges. In opposition to this substratum of primary feelings, metaphor can also find itself closely linked to the object it represents. It is then grounded in the real of things, the material. The analogical link is as strong as possible, like the iconic relationship between the portrait and the face. I would consequently venture to say that the unutterable, the unspeakable, in their link to the preverbal, can be contrasted with the "iconicity" of the metaphor.[6] Two valences of the same understanding of language, both tell differently the ambivalence of the poetic process in front of the loss of language. In the best cases, this loss must be counterbalanced and eventually annulled by recovery. However, to retrieve the lost language might first mean to dream of close-fitting metaphors where things and words are still united.[7]

TO SEE BEYOND SEEING

The oral quality of Hurston's language, together with the insistence on the gaze, have been repeatedly praised and analyzed. A core concept of Lacanian psychoanalysis, the gaze might be defined as follows:

> The gaze is thus a call to the Other: any gaze is begging for something . . . And what is it begging for, if not a return gaze from the Other? On the one hand, it is linked to desire—meaning that it belongs to a register of the drives that is linked to the desire of the Other; but, moreover, it echoes this supplication under the shape of a *demand* to the Other that the oral drive stands for: one can thus say that there is such a thing as scopic "greed."[8]

However, Lacan's opposition between the look (the eye) and the gaze must be combined in Hurston's terminology with a third element: watching.[9] The gaze is a *"captation"* (a seizure, a ravishing, a rape) of the other, an attempt to make him or her a captive of desire. It is desire itself as the object "a". In Lacan's terminology, lowercase "*a*" stands for the "other" as opposed to the "Other," or language, among other things.

Their Eyes Were Watching *God* [emphasis mine], declares the title of Hurston's novel. In the act of "watching," the subject as the origin of the gaze is somewhat emptied of his or her libidinal intentionality. For the gaze includes an investment into the other as desired object that "watching" partially leaves out. At the same time, the power relationship between the two parties, the watcher and the watched, is brought to the fore in that very act. Watching implies intensity and duration, as well as a questioning of the other that the concept of the gaze ("*le regard*") does not entirely cover.[10] One watches, supervises—oversees—or questions, or all three, another whose deeds, encompassed by the look, escape the watcher. Through the gaze ("*re-garder*," or to keep guard again) watching insinuates a link to the Law, to the Father, to God.[11]

How can one watch God without indicating at the same time that it is an impossible act? Watching God would be an answer to God in His capacity as the One who sees all, a provocation in the shape of an interrogation because watching establishes a rupture between the subject and the watched other. It would signal neither the hope nor the desire for a return gaze, but the chasm of dead eyes directed toward an oblivious other, indifferent to the watcher's fate. Watching God might then refer to what Paul-Laurent Assoun finally formulates to enlarge his definition of the gaze: "The gaze is what forever 'hidden behind the world,' since 'Creation,' has been gazing at the subject who, because he risks existing in the visible world, risks exposing himself to *the invisible and empty gaze of night and death.*"[12]

The introductory paragraph of *Their Eyes* alludes to the Watcher in its distinction between two kinds of men—those who collect the fruit of their expectations, represented by the sailing ships, and the others: "For others [ships] sail forever on the horizon, never out of sight, never landing until the Watcher turns his eyes away in resignation, his dreams mocked to death by Time" (TE 9). The word "Watcher" finds itself close to the paternal figure of "Time" in the grammar of the text. To watch, or to keep guard like the sentinel or the vigil, slips into its other meaning: to keep time, to be the measure of time. The Watcher finally relinquishes his expectations in the face of man's mortal fate. Man's helplessness in front of death—"the life of men" (TE 9)— is thus transformed into a questioning of his destiny, an impossible observation of Being (or nothingness?).

While the Watcher of the introductory paragraphs looks away when his dreams die—in Hurston's words, "[the Watcher] turns his eyes away"—the dead, or those who are about to die in the hurricane, "are watching God." The reversal of the subject of the gaze defines a religious position that puts providence into question. The central chiasmic structure that opens the text is thus that of the gaze.[13] The title states the mirroring transgression of God's and man's respective roles while the text's introductory paragraphs restore a realistic vision of men's confrontation to death. It also asserts women's utopian position vis-à-vis desire. For women, in opposition to men, "the dream is the truth" (TE 9).[14] As many critics have underlined, sexual difference is the other structuring division in this first page. Women's desire is grafted onto memory and to a willful act.[15] The first two paragraphs may be said to define the link between memory and desire in relation to seeing and watching, as well as in relation to sexual difference. Men's dreams are easily defeated by their looking away, by temporality, while women refuse that the real of death put an end to their desire; they act on their dreams. They thus symbolically join the dead blank stare of the migrant workers during the hurricane, workers oxymoronically described as "permanent transients" (TE 196).

The beginning depicts the heroine Janie's return from those dead: "the sudden dead, *their eyes flung wide open* in judgment" (TE 9, emphasis mine). The narrator reinterprets the void of consciousness, the empty gaze caused by death as a judgment of God's ways. The apocalyptic hurricane, which freezes the gaze into an everlasting stare, has left the dead watching God: "They seemed to be staring at the dark, but their eyes were watching God" (TE 236). Further in the text, the wording becomes more precise in its metaphoric allusion to judgment: "six eyes were questioning God" (TE 245). Still further on, an ultimate modulation on the introductory allusion provides Hurston's own definition for watching: "Some dead with fighting faces and *eyes . . . flung open in wonder.* Death had found them watching, trying to see beyond seeing" (TE 252, emphasis mine). Logically linked to seeing, watching starts where seeing stops.[16] The act of watching must be thought of in the rapport established with the other side of life, the realm of the dead. This relationship of the human to the underworld runs through Hurston's novel.[17] Watching must constantly be articulated to the invisible as unseeable.[18]

MIND PICTURES

In the wake of Henry Louis Gates's ground-breaking analysis of the "speakerly text," my earlier research focused on the "grain" of the voice: what is left as traces in the text, or comes in excess of the written text and lingers there as sound and body. Since then, my attention has been drawn, notably by Maïca Sanconie's essay "Symbolisme du regard," to the visual imagery present in the novel via the look and the gaze.[19] Any emphasis on voice either leaves out the repeated reference to "pictures" and to "crayon enlargements of life" (TE 81) or avoids analyzing their articulation.[20] These references to the visual arts clash with the descriptive quality that one might expect them to entail. *Their Eyes Were Watching God* contains no "description" per se in the sense of a descriptive discourse. Allusions to pictures and drawings are set metaphors, clichés.[21] Hurston uses them to encapsulate the stories or "lies" told on the store porch by the villagers:

> When the people sat around on the porch and passed around the pictures of their thoughts for the others to look at and see it was nice. The fact that the thought pictures were always crayon enlargements of life made it even nicer to listen to. (TE 81)

The "crayon enlargements of life" are fixed, isolated images.[22] Metonyms for the folk's imagination, the "thought pictures" iconize the process at work in the stories Hurston collected and whose ultimate referent is the "lies" of the folklore. The novelist-anthropologist displays the "lies" in her own fiction and her drama by quoting them, integrating them into the structure of her texts through direct dialogue or free indirect discourse.[23] A case in point is the story of Matt Bonner's yellow mule (TE 81 *et passim*) or the creation myth (TE 138–39) which recalls those listed in Hurston's *Mules and Men* (ZNH 33).[24]

The expression "mind-*pictures*" occurs after the depiction of Nanny's meditation quoted at the beginning of this essay: "Old Nanny sat there rocking Janie like an infant and thought back and back. *Mind-pictures* brought feelings and feelings dragged out dramas from the hollow of her heart" (TE 32, emphasis mine).[25] Hurston's "mind-*pictures*" link the visual to thinking and to writing in such a way that the concreteness of the metaphor turns it from image to icon, and more literally to picture.[26] The term "pictures" actually summarizes Mrs. Tyler's and Who Flung's sad story that comes to "pay [Janie] a visit" when Tea Cake disappears: "The thing made itself into pictures and hung around Janie's bedside all night long" (TE 179). Hurston's neologism announces Morrison's thought pictures in *Beloved.* At the beginning of the novel, the ex-slave Sethe tells her surviving daughter Denver that memories do not go away; they remain:

> Oh, yes. Oh, yes, yes, yes, yes. Someday you will be walking down the road and you hear something or see something going on. So clear and you think it's you thinking it up. A thought picture. But no. It's when you bump into a rememory that belongs to someone else.[27]

Imagination is linked to collective memory, and hence to history. Where Hurston has Nanny commune with the collective pain of slavery or the Middle Passage and the relation of both these momentous events to traumatic episodes of her own life ("dramas"), Morrison underlines the concreteness of these loci. These scenes, total destruction cannot eradicate. Their otherness—they are the product of an other's memory—is precisely what makes them resilient to erasure. Like Hurston, Morrison links the individual thought process to collective memory.[28] Violence is residual. It produces irreducible traces, a remainder that interpellates individual consciousness.

In the expression "mind-pictures" or "thought pictures," the articulation of language foregrounds the visual and displays a concurrent regression of the verbal. Hurston's use of language could then be analyzed against the double articulation of language explained by Roland Barthes in an interview titled "Visualization and Language," which clarifies the partition between analogy and arbitrariness. The questions asked of Barthes bear on the differences between the visual arts (photography, cinema) and language; they can thus be relevant to our investigation into the visual and the metaphoric in Hurston's writing. Barthes states the following:

> In the system of signs that constitutes our articulated language, signs are doubly divided, if one may say so. At the level of the word, the link between the signifier and the signified is unmotivated. . . . Next to our doubly articulated system, i.e., language, there exist other systems of communication where the relationship between signifier and signified is this time analogical. That's the case, for example, of photography. . . . One must truly understand that, because of the different nature of the sign in each of the systems (analogical and arbitrary), each system, each code, refers to a mental process, to an apprehension and a mapping-out of reality that is different.[29]

The concreteness of the metaphor might be another way of apprehending Hurston's insistence on the visual image that the word conjures up. The analogical—the relation of resemblance—is thrust forward in what might be termed an iconography of writing.[30] Hurston's own wording for the language of the Black American is that "he thinks in hieroglyphics" (ZNH 831). In her expression, the image is still present, and the analogical link remains very strong; the allusion to Egypt, in fitting with the spirit of the Harlem Renaissance, points both to the African heritage and to the difficulty of deciphering the language of the other.[31] Roland Barthes tried to define the particular relationship between the image and language—the analogical and the arbitrary—in a text written for the catalogue of Marthe Arnould's exhibition of Egyptian hieroglyphics in 1966:

> There are two ways of founding a sign: either by making its two terms, the signifier and the signified, move closer to each other through an analogical image (semiologists call it an *icon*); or by establishing a purely conventional

link between a cluster of sounds and a concept (this is, properly speaking, the *sign*). Hieroglyphic writing, at times figurative, at other times phonetic, combines both systems. . . . hieroglyphic writing is the only one, among signifying systems, to present frontally and with such mastery the profound ambiguity between figure and sign, that precisely between "life" and "thought."[32]

The opposition between life and thought recalls the definition that Hurston gave to words in the language of the folk. She insisted that words of the dialect were "action words" in her essay "Characteristics of Negro Expression," published in Cunard's *Negro* anthology:

The Negro's universal mimicry is not so much a thing in itself as an evidence of something that permeates his entire self. And that thing is drama. His very words are action words. His interpretation of the English language is in terms of *pictures*. One act described in terms of another. Hence the rich metaphor and simile. (ZNH 830, emphasis mine)

In the language of the folk, a chair is a "sitting chair," an axe becomes a "chop-axe." Visualizing the action redoubles the noun. Hurston calls these words "double descriptives" (cf. ZNH 832). She explains, "So we have 'chop-axe,' 'sitting-chair' and 'cook-pot' and the like because the speaker has *in his mind the picture* of the object in use" (ZNH 830, emphasis mine). The iconicity of certain metaphoric elements matches the spare quality of the folk language, the vividness of the metaphors actually used by the folk.[33]

A similar process of extreme figuration, which might be termed "iconization," takes place in *Their Eyes* in the sustained use of a metaphor (the hair, the horizon, domestic objects, etc.) or through the direct quoting of a character's speech which contains such a metaphor. When Janie is married to Jody, Janie's body is described as a store, the very store in which she is forced to work by her husband.[34] The store, which is included in each day and which includes Janie, is first included in the universe: "Every morning the world flung itself over and exposed the town to the sun. So Janie had another day. And every day had a store in it, except Sundays. The store itself was a pleasant place if only she didn't have to sell things" (TE 81). The inclusion moves from the cosmic to the domestic in a sweeping gesture of infinite regress. Her soul, her inside, then becomes one with the inside of the store:

She stood there until something fell off the shelf inside of her. Then she went inside to see what it was. It was her *image* of Jody tumbled down and shattered. But looking at it she saw that it never was the flesh and blood *figure* of her dreams. Just something she had draped her dreams over. . . . She had an inside and an outside and suddenly she knew how not to mix them. (TE 112, emphases mine)

Janie's objectification is gradual and thorough: she is a store complete with shelves. The paronomasia which links "self" to "shelf" works as the textual locus of a dénouement. As she becomes disillusioned with her marriage ("The spirit of the marriage left the bedroom and took to living in the parlor") Janie eventually "[puts] something [in her bedroom] to represent the spirit like a Virgin Mary image in a church" (TE 111). Although the term of the comparison is explicit, the process of iconization is at work. It leads to a further objectification, that of her desire for her husband, because her love for Jody is then pictured as a shattered image which had once stood on that shelf.

Unraveling the process of objectification to which she has been submitted helps Janie distinguish the false object, the dead object, from the object of desire, the "flesh and blood figure." The image had been constructed in the real of everyday life. The drape, also a domestic object, acquires the status of a metaphoric veil that stifles desire. The image of Jody has become a fake, a false icon in contradistinction to the image of the Virgin Mary.[35] Iconization, which cunningly echoes the poetic process, is here denounced, from the point of view of the character, as the creation of a breakable image. Such objectification leads to a dead end, to the fall of the icon. This moment is epiphanic in the sense that Janie can name the process of iconization which leads to depicting herself for what she has been taken to be, a store, and her image of her husband for what it is. The artifice of domesticity—placing a picture of her husband on a shelf—points to the materialization of her life. These objects and their materialness (the store and the shelf, the image and drape) are opposed to the oneiric. She discovers that she had deluded herself. As she lifts off the veil, she recovers the figure of her dreams. The flesh and blood—the bodily—are (in) the dream; they belong to the register of desire. Janie's self-division into inside and outside is so thorough that she sees herself doing things. Like Nanny, who at the close of her meditation forgot that she was there, Janie stands outside of herself, splits herself into two. This "self-difference," to borrow Johnson's word, allows her to literally step beyond the "close-fitting" metaphor; the drape is removed.

Janie's split is further developed: "Then one day she sat and *watched* the shadow of herself going about tending store and prostrating itself before Jody, while all the time she herself sat under a shady tree with the wind blowing through her hair and her clothes" (TE 119, emphasis mine). While "prostrating" takes up the metaphor of the false icon, Janie's division allows her some freedom. She watches her other self, a shadow of her real self.[36] Meanwhile her "real" self stands in the "natural" shade. The fact that she is *watching a shadow*—i.e., not her original self—duplicates the split. At the same time, the omniscient narrator pictures her in the *shade* of a tree. The *figural* shade supplants the metaphoric shadow. Housebound Janie is a ghost of her real self with hair untied and clothes billowing in the wind. She gradually detaches her self from that shadow. Janie's watching a shadow (of her self) may also be contrasted with the stare of the eyes watching God.

At that moment of the consciousness of her inner division, Janie confronts the world with fresh yet firm resolutions: "She starched and ironed her face" (TE 135). The metaphors borrowed from domestic activities that are Janie's quotidian can be taken as another example of iconization. Janie is said to impose on her face the same treatment to which she submits her household—and husband's—clothing. Starch functions as appearance, facade; it is, after all, her *face* which is starched; her face is a piece of clothing. Other connotations further intensify the objectification. Starch is white, while traces of enslavement linger in the word "iron." The distance between shadow and shade is "compressed" into the metaphor of ironing, a domestic metaphor that equates her being to an object. The reader moves back and forth from "starch" to "stark" and "Starks," Jody's name. The words are "action words": activity is brought to the fore because the two verbs are coined on the utensils to which they refer. The paradox lies in the fact that the icon, the fixity is here contradicted by the consciousness of the character. Using a domestic metaphor, referring to a female domestic task, Janie escapes domesticity because that materialization of her body, of her face, helps her find another space. Paradoxically, reification—the reduction of the subject to an object—which names itself as such, allows subjectivity to emerge.

As is evident from such examples, metaphor and the self-consciousness that it involves are actually the source of a deeper self-awareness. Domestic metaphors are not limited to occurrences in the narrator's prose. Hurston described her rewriting process as "rubbing a paragraph with a soft cloth."[37] In such a trivial expression that equates dusting to polishing one's style, she both names the servitude of the black class and signals, by signifying upon it, her mastery over writing.

Indeed, references to domestic labor call to mind the Marxist notion of reification. Women literally become the domestic utensils they use; they are made one with the material world in which they live. Nanny, Janie's grandmother, tells her, "Put me down easy, Janie, Ah'm a cracked plate" (TE 37). Earlier, she had referred to the threat that "menfolks," white or black, might make a "spit cup" out of Janie in case she did not follow her advice of marrying early (TE 37). Yet as is evident through Janie's mastery of the metaphor, knowing that she uses these words, "[saving] de text" (TE 32), first points to reification. This foregrounding unsettles its materialness to put forth a dynamic that transgresses this tendency. The grandmother's suffering was all contained in the metaphor of the plate, so was her vision of Janie as spittoon; little did she know that her granddaughter would do better than be entrapped in the salvaged text.

THE KISS OF ... MEMORY

One of Hurston's statements from "Characteristics of Negro Expression" sums up her position: "The primitive man exchanges *descriptive* words" (ZNH 830, emphasis mine).[38] Hurston supports and puts forward a version of primitivism when it comes to metaphor. In this case, however, she defines "descriptive" as "close-fitting," which she opposes to detached ideas, degrees of abstraction. Thinking, which is notional, gives way to the image of the thing described; the relationship between signifier and signified is established through reference to action. The symbolic process borrows a certain dynamic from these close-fitting metaphors. Indeed, Janie must relearn the "maiden language all over again" (TE 173) when she meets Tea Cake. Virginal—original—language is unadulterated, unmediated, close-fitting. The analogical process on which Barthes insisted is reinforced by yoking, in the metaphor, the most concrete with the most abstract. This conjunction means an insistence on the real; it also creates polar opposites such as house vs. horizon, which structure the novel in the same way as they structure language.[39]

To follow the way in which Hurston works with metaphor, one might want to focus on a recurrent symbol. The many references to Janie's hair—a site of ambivalence because she is a mulatta—trace its change into a symbol of her freedom. She unties, liberates it when Jody dies. The recurrence of the symbol frames the narrative. The space of the text is mapped out by these occurrences. Likewise, the horizon is a rope which Nanny had pinched to such an extent that she might have strangled Janie with it (TE 138). It is a shawl ("I got a rainbow tied around my shoulders. It ain't going to rain Lawd, Lawd it ain't going to rain" [TE 252]). It is a fish-net (TE 286). This metaphor incorporates the blues singer's voice in the same way as the episode of the pear tree might be said to integrate it and to work on it (TE 51). The explicitness of the eroticism comes from the fact that the code could be easily deciphered. Hurston talks about honey and honeycomb. Later Tea Cake will be "a bee to a blossom" (TE 161). The lyrical voice of certain passages, such as the episode of the pear tree, might be thought to escape the mimesis of the folk voice. Yet this voice of yearning could be called Hurston's blues voice. As such, it fully partakes of the quality of the folk voice.

In "Characteristics" Hurston also notes redundancy ("decorating a decoration," [ZNH 834]) as representative of Negro expression. The Negro's "urge to adorn," however, stands in contradiction to the spare quality of the domestic metaphor, both the opposition between inside and outside and the gatepost as barrier delineating these two spaces.[40] "The stark, trimmed phrases of the Occident seem too bare to the voluptuous child of the sun, hence the adornment" (ZNH 833). Yet, redundancy is present in Hurston's reference to "crayon enlargements of life." This expression signals excess, caricature, or what she herself describes in her essay when she notes, "Every phase of Negro life is highly *dramatized*" (ZNH 830, emphasis mine). The excess already stressed in the repetition and displacement of the funeral of Matt Bonner's mule, framed by the allegory of the buzzards, is also present in the apocalyptic and epiphanic moment of the flood when the world is turned upside down and a dog is seen riding a cow. In this instance, the accents are biblical. The discrepancy between the genres of the novel, the drama, and the poetry found in Hurston's text, which borrows from all three, can thus be linked to another of the "Characteristics of Negro expression" that she lists: asymmetry, angularity: "The pictures on the walls are hung at deep angles" (ZNH 834). For *Their Eyes* is anything but a balanced and smooth narrative.[41]

The very ending illustrates the type of metaphoric process present throughout *Their Eyes* and brings the work of remembering to a close: "The kiss of [Tea Cake's] memory was making *pictures* of love and light against the wall" (TE 286, emphasis mine).[42] In direct opposition to the biblical reference, pictures, and not writing, are on the wall.[43] Janie does not need to decipher these pictograms through the prism of the memory of her love. Concrete and abstract exchange places in a chiasmus typical of the poetics of the novel. It is not the memory of Tea Cake's kiss(es) that Janie recalls, but the kiss of his memory which comes to comfort her. The poetic metaphor, a yoking of the physical and the sensual (the kiss) with imaginary material (memory), achieves a concrete representation (pictures) in the light projected on the wall. The poetics of language, the flicker of alliteration, contribute to create an ambivalence between love and light.[44]

The metaphoric process of the novel mimics that of the folk. Symbolism might seem heavy-handed; it is iconic rather than diffuse, structured rather than diluted, direct rather than allusive. It is easily observable. It borrows its strength from the original material of the tale, hence its highly metaphoric charge that reverberates the allegorical thrust of the folktale. The disjunction felt in the reading proceeds from Hurston's adoption of a novelistic mode when her writing project incorporates other speech acts and modes. *Their Eyes* is poetic drama.

NOTES

1. Zora Neale Hurston, *Their Eyes Were Watching God* (Chicago: University of Illinois Press, 1978), with an introduction by Robert Hemenway (hereafter referred to *Their Eyes* and in parentheses as TE followed by the page number).

2. Karla F. C. Holloway, *The Character of the Word: The Texts of Zora Neale Hurston* (Washington, D.C.: Howard University Press, 1987), signals these borrowings on page 87.

3. Tea Cake is effectively pictured as "a glance from God," but before that metaphor, his whole being is linked to smell (TE 161).

4. It is easy to assimilate this feeling to Julia Kristeva's "semiotic" and "*génotexte.*" See Kristeva, *La Révolution du langage poétique* (Paris: Seuil, 1974).

5. See Morrison, "Unspeakable Things Unspoken: The Afro-American Presence in American Literature," *Michigan Quarterly Review* 28, 1 (Winter 1989), 1–35, and *Beloved,* 199.

6. More work would be required in order to refine the articulation of my reflection to Pierce's notions and to critiques of the notion of iconicity such as Umberto Eco's.

7. Michel Foucault, *Les Mots et les Choses* (Paris: Gallimard, 1966). This dream is the dream of an Adamic language, a dream of creation.

8. Paul-Laurent Assoun, *Leçons analytiques sur le regard et la voix,* Tome I (Paris: Anthropos, 1995), 97 (italics in original).

9. See Jacques Lacan, "Le regard comme objet a" in *Le Séminaire,* Livre XI, *Les Quatre concepts fondamentaux de la psychanalyse* (Paris: Seuil, 1973), 67–112.

10. The Oxford English Dictionary definitions of "watching" first list "keeping vigil" then "keeping guard."

11. Law enters the plot of the novel via Janie's trial when she is judged and acquitted by an all-white jury. See Gwendolyn Mae Henderson, "Speaking in Tongues: Dialogics, Dialectics and the Black Woman Writer's Literary Tradition," in *Changing Our Own Words,* Cheryl Wall, ed. (New Brunswick: Rutgers University Press, 1991), 16–37 (emphasis added).

12. Assoun, *Leçons,* 97.

13. Lacan's construction of the object "a," "Le regard comme objet a," unveils the chiasmic structure at the center of the gaze.

14. Toni Morrison's analysis, during her Fall 1994 seminar at the École Normale Supérieure (rue d'Ulm, Paris), of the dead gaze of the spiked head at the end of Melville's *Benito Cereno* could serve as counterpoint to this exploration of the gaze in general, the "gaze" of the dead black man, and subjectivity within a racial context.

15. Toni Morrison defines memory as "an act of willful creation": "Memory, Creation and Writing," *Thought* 59 (1984), 385–90.

16. In Lacan's seminar, the eye and the gaze are opposed (*"l'œil et le regard"*). Translators have chosen to oppose the look to the gaze.

17. Numerous critics have equated Janie to Persephone, but the relationship is more evident in *Dust Tracks;* see Françoise Lionnet, *Autobiographical Voices: Race, Gender and Self-Portraiture* (Ithaca, New York: Cornell University Press, 1989), 97–129.

18. The extension into this beyond of the senses must be thought of conjointly with the orgasmic experience under the pear tree when Janie hears "the inaudible voice of it all" (TE 24).

19. This expression refers to Barthes's *le grain de la voix* (1972), 1436–43 (Roland Barthes, *Œuvres complètes 1966–1973*, Eric Marty, ed., Tome 2 [Paris: Seuil, 1994]), but also plays on the line "fingering the jagged grain."

20. Maïca Sanconie, "Symbolisme du regard" in *Jean Toomer's* Cane *and the Harlem Renaissance*, Françoise Clary and Claude Julien, eds. (Paris: Ellipses, 1997), 120–35; and Claudine Raynaud, "'Words Walking without Masters': *Their Eyes Were Watching God* de Zora Neale Hurston," in the same publication, 95–109.

21. As such, they must be articulated to the reference to photography which constitutes Janie's "mirror-stage" (TE 21). Another pivotal moment in the narrative is her contemplating herself in the mirror at Jody's death (TE 134). An apt counterpoint to this moment of negation is Tea Cake's summons for her to enjoy her own mirror image (TE 157).

22. See Henry Louis Gates, Jr., *The Signifying Monkey: A Theory of African-American Literary Criticism* (New York and London: Oxford University Press, 1988). Gates defines the speakerly text as follows: "It is literary language, meant to be read in a text. Its paradox is that it comes into use by Hurston so that discourse rendered through direct and indirect, or free indirect means may partake of Hurston's 'word-pictures' or 'thought pictures' as we recall she defined the nature of African-American spoken language. . . . The speakerly diction of *Their Eyes* attempts to render these pictures through the imitation of the extensively metaphorical medium of Black speech, in an oxymoronic *oral hieroglyphic* that is meant only for the printed page" (215, emphasis mine).

23. On the concept of imaging, see my Ph.D. dissertation, "Rites of Coherence: Autobiographical Writings by Hurston, Brooks, Angelou and Lorde," The University of Michigan, Ann Arbor, 1991.

24. A thorough assessment on Hurston's use of previous material in terms of narrative structure and speech levels still needs to be made. The references to Hurston's other works are to Cheryl Wall's two-volume edition in The Library of America (New York, 1995), hereafter referred to as ZNH.

25. Another instance of the descent into the abyss of feelings takes place when Tea Cake is absent for a long time: "He did not return that night nor the next so she plunged into the abyss and descended to the ninth darkness where light has never been" (TE 163).

26. See Lynda Marion Hill, *Social Rituals and the Verbal Art of Zora Neale Hurston* (Washington, D.C.: Howard University Press, 1996). The critic insists on the fact that Hurston is "staging" folklore and quotes Hurston's own defense (181).

27. Toni Morrison, *Beloved* (London: Picador, 1988), 36. Another occurrence appears on page 201: "Seems like I do rememory that."

28. The expression "collective memory" refers more precisely to Maurice Halbwachs, *La Mémoire collective* [1950] (Paris: Albin Michel, 1997).

29. Barthes, "Visualisation et langage," in *Œuvres complètes*, Tome 2, 112.

30. In this analysis of language, I move very close to Hill's reading of Hurston's work in her *Social Rituals and the Verbal Art of Zora Neale Hurston:* "My rereading of Hurston demonstrates how performance is iconographically inscribed in her texts and why Baker designates her 'the intimate *home*, the imagistic habitation of poetic space of the spirit in which works of mythomanic transmission can take place'" (153). Baker's discussion of Hurston is to be found in *Workings of the Spirit: The Poetics of Afro-American Women's Writings* (Chicago: Chicago University Press, 1991), 69–101.

31. See Hill, *Social Rituals,* 127–65.

32. Barthes, "Exposition Marthe Arnould," in *Œuvres complètes,* Tome 2, 55.

33. "Vividness" might create a confusion with Paul Ricoeur's *La Métaphore vive* (Paris: Seuil, 1974). In this case, the link with the nonreferential is precisely the opposite of what Hurston achieves when she quotes metaphors from the folk language. The whole question of lyricism must be raised within the context of folk culture and particularly in relation to the blues.

34. See Barbara Johnson, "Metaphor, Metonymy, and Voice in *Their Eyes Were Watching God*" in *Black Literature and Critical Theory,* Henry Louis Gates, Jr., ed. (London and New York: Methuen, 1984), 205–19.

35. Johnson, "Metaphor," reads the movement of a chiasmus between the placing of the image of the Virgin Mary in the bedroom and the shattering of Jody's image: "What we find in juxtaposing these two figural mini-narratives is a kind of chiasmus, or cross-over, in which the first paragraph presents an externalization of the inner, a metaphorically grounded metonymy, while the second paragraph presents an internalization of the outer, or a metonymically grounded metaphor. In both cases, the quotient of the operation is the revelation of a false, or discordant 'image'" (212).

36. See Mary Helen Washington, "Zora Neale Hurston: A Woman Half in Shadow" in Alice Walker, *I Love Myself When I Am Laughing . . .* (Old Westbury, New York: The Feminist Press, 1979), 7–25.

37. See Claudine Raynaud, "Rubbing a Paragraph with a Soft Cloth? Muted Voices and Editorial Constraints in *Dust Tracks on a Road*" in *De/Colonizing the Subject: Women's Autobiographical Writings,* Sidonie Smith and Julia Watson, eds. (Minneapolis: University of Minnesota Press, 1992), 34–64.

38. For a reference to primitivism, Black writing, and the Harlem Renaissance, see John Lowe, *Jump at the Sun: Zora Neale Hurston's Cosmic Comedy* (Urbana, Illinois: University of Illinois Press, 1994) and Sieglinde Lemke, *Primitivist Modernism: Black Culture and the Origins of Transatlantic Modernism* (Oxford and New York: Oxford University Press, 1998).

39. That the horizon is a recurrent symbol in Hurston's novel has been stressed by numerous critics. See, among others, Missy Dhen Kubitschek, "Tuh De Horizon and Back: The Female Quest in *Their Eyes Were Watching God,*" *Black American Literary Forum* 17, 3 (Fall 1983), 109–14.

40. On the gatepost episode, see my forthcoming article, "Subjectivité migratoire et figures du seuil? La barrière-biographème de Zora Neale Hurston" in *Migrations,* Andrée-Anne Kekeh et Hélène Le Dantec-Lowry, eds. (Paris: l'Harmattan, 2000).

41. *Their Eyes* was written over a period of seven weeks.

42. This kiss of Tea Cake's memory must be contrasted with Johnny Taylor's kiss given across the gatepost, which, as Gates notes in *The Signifying Monkey,* establishes "the text's opposition between truth and dream" (185).

43. See Daniel 5:5: "In the same hour came forth fingers of a man's hand and wrote over the candlestick upon the plaister of the wall of the king's palace: and the king saw the part of the hand that wrote."

44. As such, this epiphanic moment can be opposed to another moment of sadness in Janie's life : ". . . mostly she lived between her hat and her heels, within her emotional disturbances like shade patterns in the woods—come and gone with the sun" (TE 118).

13. Langston Hughes's Blues

Monica Michlin

Of all the poets of the Harlem Renaissance, Langston Hughes was the one who recognized the blues as a major art form.[1] From his first book of verse, *The Weary Blues,* which showed his intent to present his poetic voice as a blues voice, to "The Backlash Blues" (1967), Hughes stood by the blues as an expression of what was most vital, most resilient, most dynamic, and most painful at the heart of the African-American experience.[2] In this, he distinguished himself from the aesthetics of most writers of the Harlem Renaissance by looking not toward European high culture, but toward contemporary black popular culture as the only basis for truly African-American art.

When applied to a literary form, the word "blues" raises a number of questions. How can a poem *be* a blues? Can Hughes's blues aesthetic be reduced to the use of song-like patterns and stanzas, poems in deliberately "song-transcript" form? Or are the vast majority of his poems, written in more standard poetic form and simple standard English, to be read as a "transfusion" of blues into his writing? Does Hughes's blues aesthetic successfully subvert the notions of high and low art, of oral or primarily written lyrics and literature? And finally, is the be-bop of *Montage of a Dream Deferred* a rejection of the blues? Or, on the contrary, is it proof that Hughes's blues aesthetic was dialectical and that it never ceased to find new forms of black song to denounce racial oppression—not in terms of lament, but in terms of struggle—with literary weapons that wished themselves accessible to all?

As early as the first line of "I, Too" (1925)—"I, too, sing America"—Hughes's poetry connects the black poetic voice, committed literature, the

American literary tradition, and *song*. Through the allusion to Whitman—the poet who wished to give a voice to the forbidden voices of America[3]—Hughes was pointing to the paradox that the black voice was excluded from America and yet could sing it, too. In his search for the aesthetic that would allow the identification of his poetic voice, and of the working-class voices of black America, Hughes quickly realized that the only artists who were speaking and singing the actual reality of the black masses were the blues singers of his day. Not only could Hughes effect a *mise-en-scène* of the poet-figure in portraying the blues singer or the jazz musician, but the blues themselves seemed the most contemporary form of black culture that truly committed black poetry could portray. Thus, Hughes initially wrote *about* the blues; but as he did, he found that the vernacular, the rhythm, the imagery, the bitter-sweetness, the sadness, and the resiliency of the blues themselves could enrich his poetry—that it would not be poetry *on* the blues, but poetry *of* the blues, poetry infused with the blues.

The first poem Hughes called "blues" was "The Weary Blues" (written in 1923). Before that, Hughes had already taken jazz music as a theme for his poems "Jazzonia" and "Cabaret," which he had not dared to write in black dialect—although he did represent black speech in the poem "Negro Dancers" (44).[4] While this poem translated the energy of black dancers doing the Charleston, it could also be suspected of a *plantation school* use of dialect, show-ing the Negro dancers to be "primitive," in the debasing sense of the term, as they danced and spoke ungrammatically. The inclusion of the lines "White folks, laugh! / White folks, pray!" (44) seems to indicate that Hughes was iron-ically deflecting the white gaze, excluding the whites from an all-black world of uninhibited dancing and singing, but the very inclusion of the white audi-ence was a disruption, one which disappears in "The Weary Blues."

The title, "The Weary Blues," is somewhat misleading because it is pri-marily a poem *about* the blues, about a blues song of the same name, which is quoted in the text. Beyond quotation, however, the poem is saturated with the blues, not only in its vocabulary, but in its use of rhyme and rhythm: for instance, it repeats a complete line ("He did a lazy sway . . . / He did a lazy sway . . .") to recall a blues song. Of course, in a true blues song, the *initial* lines of each stanza are repeated; Hughes was to import this into later blues poems, when he started to write in the form of song lyrics, in the first person, and in black dialect.

In 1923, he was probably anxious to show both the proximity and the difference between his written poetic voice and the voice of the blues; he did so by using sophisticated literary effects such as the poetic voice's lofty vocabulary contrasted with the singer's black dialect, or with constant alliteration and assonance ("Droning a drowsy syncopated tune") to aurally imitate the lazy sway of the music. The irregular (or syncopated) rhyme pattern, with its open sounds, was also carefully composed to convey the plaintive melody, in a *mise-en-scène* of sad music ("mellow croon," "sad raggy tune," "melancholy tone," "piano moan," "melody").

Yet this was already a true blues poem in that Hughes was fusing the blues with poetry by making the bluesman's voice the emblematic black voice, one that reflexively celebrates itself throughout the poem ("O Blues"; "Sweet Blues!"; "O Blues!"). These exclamatories *about,* or apostrophes *to* the blues, can be read as the musician's own cries as he plays, in the tradition of call-and-response of blues performers on their own song or music; or as the poet's response to the bluesman, the poem acting as chorus to the invisible song; or, finally, as the poet's own reflexive exclamations on his "Weary Blues" poem[5] as he writes it; or all of these combined. The ambivalence at the heart of the blues, which seeps through the two lines "Sweet Blues!" and "He made that poor piano moan with melody," is the cornerstone of all of Hughes's blues poetry. Although the poem seems to conclude on a note of despair, on the image of the alienated musician who, with the weary blues echoing in his head, sleeps "like a rock or like a man that's dead" (the song brings about no epiphany, no change, no better tomorrow), there are already signs of Hughes's subversion of the blues into the poetry of political protest.

The first indication of this is the use of black and white symbolism ("With his ebony hands on each ivory key / He made that poor piano moan with melody"). This heralds the use of color in a poem such as "Daybreak in Alabama" (1940), in which the poetic voice uses the *mise-en-scène* of musical composition ("When I get to be a composer / I'm gonna write me some music about / Daybreak in Alabama") to sing the song of the happy daybreak in which white and black shall be friends. He blurs the color line by calling up all of the colors black and white people really are: "red," "poppy colored," "brown." When he reverts to black and white, it is to catch the words in a pun, in which they read like the black and white hands playing the black and white keys of the piano side by side ("black and white black white black people"), so that the words of the poem are those keys, performatively playing this song of love beyond white racism.

"The Weary Blues" is also truly a blues poem in its use of black idiom to describe, in the same words, the rapture of music and the sadness of life ("He played that *sad raggy* tune like a musical *fool*" [my emphasis]). Although the sustained reflexive quality of the poem is lost in its ultimate stanza, when the musician sleeps and the poem continues, the oxymoron "Sweet Blues / Coming from a black man's soul" is already the celebration of what Hughes saw in the blues, as a popular art form expressing the soul of black America and as the ultimate material for the poet who wanted to speak for his people.

Very quickly, though, Hughes was confronted with a double problem. On the one hand, his most beautiful poems so far had been lyrical, in a blue tone, but not in a blues form—the Afro-American poems on the African heritage, in the vein of *négritude,* such as "The Negro Speaks of Rivers" (1921), "Negro" (1922), or "My People" (1923)—or the politically committed lyrics on lynching, such as "The South" (1922). There are several ways of explaining the fact that the poems on the African heritage could not be written in the blues mode, but the most obvious is that the blues was an American musical form, the product of the symbiosis between African rhythms and harmonics (such as blue notes, the twelve-bar pattern) and American instruments, and Hughes felt that it would have put a "local color" twist on what was to be the universal black voice.[6] The second point was ideological: could the blues, as a popular cultural form—as one indissociable from the working-class idiom, from everything that the old guard of the Harlem Renaissance considered unworthy of representation, from all that was "low culture" (the portrayal of the marginal, but also of the poor, of the working class: i.e., of the vast majority of black people)—serve to represent *all* of the aspects of black life? Had not dialect-writing in African-American poetry previously led to a complete discredit of black speech as playing into the hands of the minstrel tradition? Was not the story of dialect-writing in black poetry that of the reinforcement of debasing stereotypes? Langston Hughes realized the risk of writing dialect poetry in the manner of poets of the plantation school such as Dunbar (whose serious and proud poems were written in standard, even lofty English, not in dialect); but like Sterling Brown, he was convinced of the beauty of black speech per se and of the rejuvenation that it could bring the written black word.[7] Because black speech was inseparable from black working-class rural and urban culture, this also meant embracing the validity and beauty of that popular culture above the bourgeois criteria of *literate* literary writing. In "The Negro Artist and the Racial Mountain," Hughes made his racial commitment clear, as he condemned the black poet who would like to write like a white poet, and raised a battle cry for a black aesthetic: "Let the blare of Negro jazz bands and the bellowing voice of Bessie Smith singing Blues penetrate the closed ears of the colored near-intellectuals until they listen and perhaps understand," the last paragraph of the essay proclaimed.

This did not mean that all of Hughes's poems were in black dialect, nor that they were obviously blues inspired, nor that all of those on the working class were in either one or the other mode. When representing the black American working class on the job, Hughes sometimes used the dialectal voice—in "Elevator Boy" (1926: 85)—sometimes not: "Brass Spittoons" (1926: 86) simply uses the "chorus" of the white man giving orders to the black, through the leitmotiv "Hey, boy!" to denounce class and racial oppression. Neither of these poems is in blues form, although metaphorically they sing the blues; on the other hand, "Hard Luck," written during the same period in time, is a blues poem on poverty, as was "Po' Boy Blues." This shows how Hughes embraced the many aesthetic possibilities opened by his essential theme: the condition of black America.

Although Hughes never thought of black dialect as too *trivial* to speak about the most tragic aspects of black life in the United States, the blues mode could not apply when what he aimed for was a song of unmitigated pain and tragic accusation because, although the blues sing a song of despair, they wear a mask of laughter. The blues are potentially full of irony and double entendre, of self-deprecation and boasting, of shifts from pathos to comedy; they are based on "laughing to keep from crying" as well as on "crying to keep from dying," so to speak. As a consequence, Hughes's blues poems are about the same themes as "real" blues songs:[8] heartbreak, jealousy, imprisonment, travel, poverty, forced migration to the North—because some subjects were too absolutely tragic to be dealt with in blues-style. Thus, the poem "Song for a Dark Girl" (1927), which is a song of mourning after a lynching, is written in the deceptively simple language not of the blues but of the spirituals, as it raises its heartbroken voice ("break the heart of me") for the broken black body.[9]

The second aesthetic reason Hughes did not systematically write in blues form was to allow both the black voices he spoke for and his own literary creativity greater recognition, by showing, through the contrasts in style and variations in tone, how differently a theme could be treated (within the same committed black perspective). There are thus a number of instances in which Hughes dealt with a theme both in a blues and in a more standard, written form of poetry, either to prove he could do both or to experiment with the freedom and test the limits of each form. Such a piece as "Bound No'th Blues" (1926), which deals with the Great Migration—and whose last stanza reads, "Road, road, road, O! / Road, road . . . road . . . road, road! / Road, road, road, O! / On the no'thern road. / These Mississippi towns ain't / Fit fer a hoppin toad" (76)—contrasts with a tragic poem in standard English such as "The South," which ends on "So now I seek the North— / The cold-faced North, / For she, they say, / Is a kinder mistress, / And in her house my children / May escape the spell of the South" (27). The first poem actually *sings* the road, or rather bemoans and celebrates it in the same breath, as the repetition of "road" and "oh" expresses how endless the road North seems; how it hurts to be exiled;

yet how good it is to leave Mississippi behind, and how dangerous the road itself is. In other words, simple tricks of repetition or punctuation allow a great level of expressiveness and of plurisignification, where the vocabulary itself seemed too simple to allow much elaboration. But this requires more reader participation, and greater cultural decoding, than does the reading of the puns in the second poem on "mistress" (meaning lover *and* slave-owner), "cold-faced" (the North's climate is cold, and its social climate is hostile to black people), and "spell" (attraction and dangerous *white* "black magic"). In other words, the blues allowed greater identification with the traveler, but the use of a more sophisticated literary form seemed better suited to a poem that, after all, was mainly addressed to a white audience—which made it as politically committed, but not as culturally immersed, as Hughes's later poems would be.

For a long period in the 1920s, many of Hughes's blues poems were written as if they were mere transcriptions of actual songs, meaning that they are set out as blues lyrics, with a repetition of the initial two lines of each stanza, with a simple rhyme pattern (ababcb), and with irregular lines of verse, which, from a standard literary viewpoint, made them, in the eyes of many critics, "trash."[10] Whereas the critics were shocked at the crude—i.e., realistic—aspect of the themes, today's readers most often object to the fact that such excellent blues "songs" as "Lament Over Love," "Life is Fine," "Midwinter Blues," "Gypsy Man," "Listen Here Blues"[11] are written as if they were lyrics to a musical score but have no such score; thus they are *lacking*. The specific musicality of poetry (the rhyme pattern, the rhythm, the euphony) still functions, but the form points to music outside the text. What matters when one reads these poems is "the blues one is playing" (to paraphrase Hughes) in one's head—the blues one loves; these poems carry with them all of the blues ever sung by black voices.

Why did Hughes go so far as to imitate the blues, in this transcript form? Although the radical politics of the artist is the obvious explanation, an additional benefit Hughes reaped was instant access to the female persona because the blues recordings of the 1920s were dominated by women: Ma Rainey, Bessie Smith. Another indirect gain was the recasting of Hughes's own blue streak in the jauntier tone and frame of his female-persona blues. Many of Hughes's blues are saturated, as were real songs, with the adjective "weary."[12] Yet this is only one side of the blues: they are as much about resilience as about lament. The use of the black vernacular paired with the female persona enabled Hughes to rephrase the suicidal aspect of his early poems into a voice of excess, conflict, and ultimately a celebration of life, as in "Suicide" (1926). This blues poem on abandonment by a "sweet good man" turns into a raw, assertive act of self-definition through the rhetorical strategies of repetition, declaratives, elision, and dialect.

This does not mean that the blues mode *automatically* indicates resilience. A song like "Lament Over Love" (1926), which is also in the blues-lyrics mode ("I hope my child'll / Never love a man," 69), is truly a lament, which ends on an image of suicide—but the speaker criticizes herself for being a lovesick fool. If Hughes were trying to voice heartbreak in a *gay* context, it seems logical that he should connect the child-figure, which he so often uses for himself, with love for a man; but the other explanation for the expression "never love a man" is that it reintroduces sexuality where the idea "fall in love" is more tritely romantic. The blues poem "Life is Fine" (1949) takes up the criticism of romantic love precisely where "Lament Over Love" leaves off, criticizing the message of the initial poem in the call-and-response mode: each time the speaker decides to commit one form of suicide, what should kill turns out to reanimate. This paradox is expressed each time in colloquial form, in a separate, italicized voice of comment; for instance, when the protagonist tries to drown, the voice comically cries out: "*But it was / Cold in that water! / It was cold!*" The reader immediately understands that this is one of the staple jokes and tall tales of the heartbroken blues, one summarized by the lines "I could've died for love— / But for livin' I was born." The celebration "Life is Fine," then, is merely the flip side of any "Lament Over Love." The blues mode allowed Hughes to balance out the element of sadness with the glorious "Hey! Hey!" of defiance and triumph.

"Blues Fantasy" (1926) summarizes this aspect of the blues and of Hughes's blues aesthetics. This poem unveils the *signifying* which Hughes sought in the blues, even while he believed in their significance as art form of the masses. The self-deprecation shown in the use of the interjection "hey," which turns into a loud laugh ("hey hey" as "ha ha") at the end of the poem, is also at work when the speaker pretends to believe that blues songs are "minor melodies." Of course, the whole poem is built around the premise that these melodies *seem* minor but carry a major message of life, humor, irony, and resistance to hardship. This woman speaker belies Peetie Wheatstraw's "C & A Blues" ("When a woman gets the blues, she hangs her head and cries / When a man gets the blues, he flags a freight train and rides") significantly: Hughes is acknowledging the voice of the female blues singer as performatively creating a space of utter freedom, including from the constraints of gender roles.[13] The language in the poem is deliberately oblique and ambiguous in the third stanza, when one slides from the meaning that the singer is weary and full of trouble and pain, to the fact that she is weary *of* trouble and pain—which launches the transition into taking the train to that "somewhere" where the sun shines and where the blues can be cast aside. The built-in call-and-response pattern, with the encouraging "Sing 'em, sister!" shows Hughes's talent not only for mirroring an actual blues performance, but for breaking down the barriers between the inside and the outside of the poem: he seems to be encouraging the singer (even if this voice is *also* that of a black audience within the poem) while the ultimate lines could be the female speaker's address not merely to her inset audience, but to Hughes's readers. In other words, blues poetry brings with it a feeling of community, in a way only black oral speech had ever done before—in sermons, political oratory, or song.

In seeking to keep all that was most vital in black oral culture—the use of dialect, of signifying, of black humor, of call-and-response patterns—without remaining prisoner to the conventions that were the backbone of authentic blues lyrics, Hughes eventually came to a compromise in his literary re-creation of the blues in the "Madam" ballads of the 1940s (after a decade of radical epic poetry which was the negation of Hughes's own poetic voice, although it was an assertion of his revolutionary politics). These ballads all revolve around the figure of Alberta K. Johnson, who refuses to have her name shortened or tampered with in any way and who tells the census man "I'm *Madam* to you!" (356) in an assertion of black dignity (not letting the white person talk *down* to her) and a symbolic reclaiming of her name.[14] But the phrase "Madam to you" is also an allusion to a famous blues. Indeed, Madam's words echo the song "Miss Brown to You."[15] This "initiate" aspect is fundamental to reader participation in the Madam poems, as they mock authority in all its forms ("Madam and the Insurance Man," "Madam and her Madam," "Madam and the Phone Bill," "Madam and the Rent Man," "Madam and the Minister," etc.) and represent a wish-fulfillment of rebellion against white oppression.[16] In this, they are committed poems in the trickster tradition of the Br'er Rabbit folk stories, or of the black hero blues songs, because Madam always wins in the end. Madam's theatrical asides, her use of exasperated italics or of incredulous and mocking capital letters, her control of speech are all forms of empowerment, even if she is sometimes (and affectionately) the butt of satirical irony. What Hughes effected was to give the working-class black people an assertive, self-authenticating, irrepressible voice in poetry, as a compensation for the pathos (and realism) of some of his other poems for the black working class—a voice only to be found until then in black oral culture.

Hughes also kept the core of the blues by moving from a *transcription* of blues lyrics to a literary *transposition*. The dialectical movement that allowed Hughes to raise black popular culture to poetry also made him turn this idea around and transform black poetry, enriching it aesthetically by finally giving it self-authenticating cultural references and linguistic material, its existential content and political thrust. To illustrate how Hughes came to transpose the orality of the blues, one can reread "Trumpet Player" (1947), one of Hughes's most lyrical poems, which creates the piercing sadness of a trumpet solo through anaphoric repetition of the lines "The Negro / With the trumpet at his lips." The pain in this poem is explicitly that of being black in America: the "dark moons of weariness" under the musician's eyes become the trace of the "smoldering memory" of the middle passage and of the "crack of whips"; the trumpet player's "vibrant hair / Tamed down / Patent-leathered now" summarizes in brilliant metaphor the dehumanization at the hands of white America which has turned the free (Afro-style), living, musical hair into something "patent-leathered." Yet the poetic voice does not stop there, in denouncing alienation, past and present; it *celebrates* the musician, his martyrdom and his dignity—his hair turns into a "crown" of jet, to be read both as the crown of thorns and as a sign of regal pride, despite the sordid surroundings of the nightclub. The beauty of the music the bluesman plays turns into burning pain, then sweetness, while the images "liquid fire" and "distilling" not only refer to the process of alchemy, or to the metaphorical depiction of desire as a flame, but to the use of alcohol and of drugs. The trumpet player functions as a real subject for the poetic voice, as a lyrical depiction of the jazz musician, and as the allegorical figure of all black people, as the emblematic figure of the *collective* pain of being black and blue, and the beauty which that pain can give rise to, and which in turn, purges the pain. This is captured in the ultimate stanzas, when it is clear that the poetic voice is the ultimate trumpet—the "golden note" not only refers to the golden trumpet, or to the music the trumpet player plays, but to the poem itself, which ends on the open sounds of "soul," "throat," and "note," the sharp inflections brought by the punctuation and the numerous dashes (which represent the injection of heroin into the body, of music into the soul) being superseded, in these last lines, by the spilling out of the tune, the golden note, over the short line "trouble." This use of the term "trouble" is, of course, heavily coded because so many blues songs use it as a euphemism to talk about misery, heartbreak, poverty, abuse; Hughes was reinscribing his poem within the lexical field of the blues itself, even while writing it in lyrical, yet un-blues-like stanzas.

Almost thirty years after Hughes had written his first blues poems, little had changed in the living conditions of African-Americans, and "blues" had come to be associated with the idea of resignation and passivity. Hughes's intent was to write a book of poetry along the lines of "What did I do to be so black and blue?" not to sing "I'm white inside," but "I'm black and proud." The musical paradigm of his time had followed this same historical evolution through criticism of the older jazz and blues forms by the young generation of be-bop musicians; hence, the dialectical process Hughes's own poetic voice went through as—rooted once again in the contemporary black music of his day—it emerged in the "Montage of a Dream Deferred."

The epigraph to the book of the same name reads as follows:

> In terms of current Afro-American popular music and the sources from which it has progressed—jazz, ragtime, swing, blues, boogie-woogie, and be-bop—this poem on contemporary Harlem, like be-bop, is marked by conflicting changes, sudden nuances, sharp and impudent interjections, broken rhythms, and passages sometimes in the manner of the jam session, sometimes the popular song, punctuated by the riffs, runs, breaks, and distortions of the music of a community in transition. (387)

Hughes explicitly introduces the book as a literary rephrasing of black music, while using a vocabulary that brings to mind social conflict as much as it does musicality—a way of foregrounding how the aesthetics of the contemporary black popular music and those of the poems cannot be dissociated from a feeling of community in a context of struggle and self-definition. Thus we will be looking at the *Montage* as a development of Hughes's blues aesthetics, as a *Montage* of conflict aesthetically controlled through the paradigm of be-bop. Conflict within the collective black voice is staged in every way imaginable, between rich and poor ("Low to High" and "High to Low"), between generations, between sexes—all against the backdrop of racial segregation that gave birth to the ghetto, and which exacerbates all of the other conflicts, because each relationship, each moment of life is poisoned by the exclusion of black people from the American Dream. What grows as one reads is the "boogie-woogie rumble" of the dream deferred, the rumble of all of these black voices rising in frustration and rage. The connection between the blues and be-bop in Hughes's aesthetic is clear: when blues raises its fist, it becomes be-bop. In this book, Hughes introduced techniques he had never used before. For example, the actual printing of the book makes the montage visual: a vertical gray band runs down each page, creating the impression that this is a master tape (or a reel of film). Just as this graphic element forces the reader to connect all the poems, specific literary effects also make them echo and comment upon each other, in a politically forceful reappropriation of the idea of dialectics, and through a *mise-en-scène* of all aspects of black speech, from dialect to call-and-response, the dirty dozens, signifying, and oblique meaning structures in general.

The *Montage* starts with "Dream Boogie." A quick commentary of this poem can show how complex it really is. The initial address posits the reader's black identity and immediately addresses him in dialect, using the musical euphemism of the "boogie-woogie rumble" to signal the incipient rebellion due to the "dream deferred." For the moment, no explanation is given for this image. The political thrust of the poem comes from the fact that the voice which addresses the reader is teaching him or her to read again ("listen closely"), to literally read between the lines, to feel that the blanks between the stanzas are the figuration of that rumble which threatens to drown everything out. The threat is made palpable by the use of the disturbing italics, which raise questions and give no answers, and which eventually carry the poem off in interjection ("Hey, pop!" is a familiar variation on the initial "Good morning, daddy"). As for the use of onomatopoeia, it also acts as a symbol of the energy of rebellion, which resists even the poetic language that would express it, carrying away speech into the swift song of the montage: the apparent meaninglessness of the interjections embodies subversion, not absurdity. This is the signifying aspect which adds itself to the call-and-response pattern of the two types of print used for the two voices. The voice which denies that anything is wrong ("Sure / I'm happy!") is a parody of the "happy black" voice: it is exposed as the black mask worn before white people. The systematic self-interruption of the voice which tells us to listen to the rumble[17] of the dream deferred forces the reader to supply the missing terms: what do the feet beat? what is the suppressed sound? The image and the sound patterns and the repetition of "beating and beating" call to mind the pattern of marching, of a call to arms, and are full of the historical memory of the black parades (victory parades, protests against lynching, protests against segregation) Harlem had known, just as the rumble evoked all the riots that had taken place since 1919. The signifying aspect of the poem, then, lies in the apparently innocent music which takes over at the end, but which seems to say that behind the enforced subservience ("mop"), revolt ("re-bop") is imminent, and that the poetic voice is calling for it, *now*.

The *Montage* stages Harlem as a polyphony of conflicting voices to avoid the didactic aspect of the poems of the 1930s, but also to show that only through the acknowledgment of these voices' friction and the reader's active participation in a critique of their varying perspectives can community be reaffirmed, can "Harlem" be defined. For instance, "Children's Rhymes" stages an older black person shocked by the racial bluntness of black children's rhymes (*"By what sends / the white kids / I ain't sent / I know I can't / be President"*) and commenting in standard type what the children chant in italics. There is no unifying poetic voice to resolve the conflict—or rather, the voice purposefully wears the mask of "be-bop" writing, reverting to onomatopoeia, which leaves the reader, implicitly, bopping to the children's voices. The same technique of conflicting voice is used in "Sister," in which a black man bemoans that his sister goes out with "trash"; a voice in italics acts as the voice of reality in the face of moralism, stating that the cause of this is poverty. As this voice puts down the brother's complaints (*"Did it ever occur to you, boy / that a woman does the best she can?"*), an anonymous voice arises to close the poem, quite brutally, in the last rhyme: *"So does a man"* (391). The title "Sister" thus embodies the opening up of vision from the narrow definition of family to the assertion of collective racial solidarity.

The poems do not deny the alienation caused by poverty even when they use the wry sense of humor inherited from the blues. A poem like "Necessity" can illustrate this with its use of boasting and deflation, of exaggeration akin to the dozens, its deliberate use of the absurd ("I don't have to do nothing / but eat, drink, stay black and die") in a way that collapses together very different forms of necessity in parodic laughter, before ending on the fact that the high cost of rent is the ultimate necessity, which does in fact entail the necessity for work, thereby contradicting the initial assertion of the poem. Realism prevails: "Ballad of the Landlord" (402) deals with the outrageous price of dilapidated housing in the inner city. In it, the tenant's voice at first reads like one of the earlier "Madam" ballads, "Madam and the Rent Man" (1943), which ends on a humorous note when Madam says she will not pay: "He said, Madam, / I ain't pleased! / I said, Neither am I. / So we agrees!" (276). In "Ballad of the Landlord," however, the tenant's voice is drowned out by the landlord's (so that the poem's title is made clear in retrospect: it *is* the ballad of the landlord). There is no call-and-response pattern: the landlord addresses himself to the police; and the tenant's arrest is then described in a series of short phrases in telegraphic style, the poem ending on the headlines in the press, in capital letters:

MAN THREATENS LANDLORD
TENANT HELD NO BAIL
JUDGE GIVES NEGRO 90 DAYS IN COUNTY JAIL. (403)

The effect of this montage-within-the-montage is that one reads the different headlines as forming a pattern of (oppressive) poetry. The reduction inherent in headline writing is transformed into a critique of the racist media, of the journalists who reverse the terms of the situation, presenting the landlord as the victim.

All of the aspects of Harlem life are portrayed and sung in the *Montage*, most of them emphasizing poetry in the trivial, subverting the voice of authority, singing out the word "wino" into two words "Wine-O" to "rehabilitate" the use and abuse of alcohol, by rewriting it in its context of deprivation and resistance to annihilation. The selection of voices and of types of speech deliberately encompasses street signs, letters, silent thoughts, comments on street curbs, the music in the nightclubs; the poetic voice picks up momentum with each poem. These are connected by Hughes's use of *scatting* (or onomatopoeia) and of *scattering* of the title throughout the *Montage:* this seems a key to the overall composition of the book. The initial images of dancing ("boogie"), marching, dreaming, introduced by the first poem are echoed throughout; after "Dream Boogie" comes the poem "Parade," which takes up the image of the marching feet; "Juke Box Love Song" stages the "rumbling" of Harlem traffic; "Easy Boogie" compares the bass of a jazz orchestra to the sound of marching feet. Similarly, the *mise-en-scène* of the montage leads to a collage of the night-club neon lights ("Neon Signs") in which name after name appears in capital letters, before the poem reverts to onomatopoeia ("re-bop"). This "bopping" of the names reads both as a demystification of Harlem-the-exotic-nightspot and as a straightforward celebration of the vitality of the black population in this city-within-the-city. The use of scatting cannot be separated, then, from the political significance of the *scattering* of the words *Montage of a Dream Deferred* as they are disseminated, like the seed that threatens to explode, from the first poem to the last.

Indeed, the poem "Tell Me" reads "Why should it be *my* loneliness, / Why should it be *my* song, / Why should it be *my* dream / deferred / overlong?" (396). This simple lyric combines what we have seen at the heart of Hughes's blues aesthetics. The tone here is that of a painful question, not a threat. The dream deferred next reappears in the poem "Boogie: 1 a.m." By now, the voice that opened the montage says, "I know you've heard," commenting on its own process of educating the reader, once again addressed as "Daddy." To show that time has elapsed, that the reader is literally progressing, the voice has shifted from "Good morning" to "Good evening." It still continues to tantalize, refusing to explain didactically *what is* the dream deferred. This mimetic process of deferring meaning is part of the signifying at the heart of the collection of poems.

Clarification occurs in the poem "Deferred" (413), which lists all of the frustrations and hopeless postponings of achievement—from a formal education to a white enamel stove, buying two new suits at once, a bottle of gin, finishing payments on the furniture, going to heaven, having a television set, a radio, taking up Bach—the chorus of voices rises as a polyphony of the deferred black dreams in white America. The poetic voice then concludes: "*Montage / of a dream / deferred. /* Buddy, have you heard?" (414), the didactic intent—belatedly giving this poem its real name, in its conclusion—being relieved by the continued dynamic of built-in reader participation. The pathos and indignation of this poem are reversed in the next to take up the image of the dream deferred: "Passing." Passing is only described as the loss of the "sunny summer Sunday afternoons in Harlem." The paradox is that to be deprived of the collective bitter dream is worse than individually crossing the color line to have a false dream turn true.[18] The *Montage* then makes the cause of deferral appear in "Nightmare Boogie." The nightmare is *white people:* "dead white" is the central pun on the deadly force of white supremacy over the black dream. The "boogie-woogie" of the "catgut" bass strings echoes the implicit image of the white whip and of all that destroyed black bodies. Now, within the poem, catgut is being made to resonate with the cry of the black spirit, of black resistance through the triple medium of black dialect ("them faces"), of black music, and of the poem which contains those black forces.

The entire phrase "Montage of a dream deferred" re-emerges in the poem "Dime" (420), in which a child asks for a dime from her grandmother—even a dime is an impossible dream. Although the poem is based on a call-and-response pattern, it also is based on echoes of Hughes's earlier poetry. For instance, the first line ("Chile, these steps is hard to climb") is a reminder of the central image developed by all of "Mother to Son" (1922): "Life for me ain't been no crystal stair" (30). The use of dialect, once again, is the mark that this is the voice of the Harlem community; at this point, Hughes introduces the central poem of the *Montage,* "Harlem." The poem starts with a loaded question, the burden that the whole montage has been carrying so far, the "heavy load" of the United States' broken promise to black America. The rest of the poem is visually "deferred" through the layout of the lines and the use of ominous blanks and suspensions that materialize the precarious peace or "syrupy sweet" crust before the explosion, the imminent threat of explosion, in italics. The force of the similes that take the reader to this last line is that they are practically synaesthetic and are bursting with the cumulative force of enumeration, accumulation, and transtextual allusion. From Steinbeck's recontextualization of the biblical grapes of wrath to Hughes's raisin in the sun, what Hughes adds is the association of the raisin and of blackness, of the grape which seems to turn back into a seed . . . of revolt. The image of the sore, of the rotten meat, of the load are all violent, unusually sordid, and beautiful all at the same time; and they all carry the sedimented significance of black bodies destroyed in lynching, death at war, death in riots; of the shoddy food sold to poor blacks; of the back-breaking work and the poverty which are their load generation after generation. The ultimate line, delayed overlong to seem practically unexpected, finally explodes the whole web of imagery in its ultimate openness, its deviation from normal type, its absolute dynamics of explosion. The *Montage* could end there; but it does not; because there are so many Harlem voices yet to be heard.

Indeed, the next poem, "Good Morning"—a short oral history of black people's migration to New York from the South, but also "up from Cuba Haiti Jamaica" (426)—ends on the gates of the dreamed paradise turning into the prison gates of the ghetto: "The gates open— / Yet there're bars / at each gate. / What happens / to a dream deferred? / Daddy, ain't you heard?" (427). Should the reader still not understand the principle of the montage, the following poem, "Same in Blues," foregrounds the idea that the poems can only be read as commenting upon each other and that this is the essence of the blues, of all the black vernacular, caught up in a web of signifying that makes the most innocuous poems part of the polyphony of a "simmering" Harlem. The "blues" announced in the title is not a "transcript"; it is blues-like in that the message seems trivial, personal, the rhyme is doggerel-like, the characters speak colloquially, they address each other as they would in a blues song. The innovation in this poem and the political use of the call-and-response pattern lie in the fact that each of the blues stanzas in normal type is followed by a translation in italics of each seemingly light grievance of the black characters into one of the grimmest aspects of the dream deferred. The poetic voice thus functions as a chorus, as a literal burden (in the "heavy load" sense of the term), and as a guide as to what blues language really *means* as it moves toward the close of the *Montage*, and the ultimate poem, "Island [2]." "Island" ends on the *mise-en-scène*, which structured the entire *Montage*, by describing Harlem as an island ("Chocolate-custard / Pie of a town"), while the poetic voice comments in italic: "*Dream within a dream, / Our dream deferred*." The poem then ends on the address that makes the whole montage loop back to its beginning: "Good morning, daddy! / Ain't you heard?" (429). The extraordinary achievement of the *Montage* is that it theorizes its use of the be-bopping blues voice and decodes it, rephrases all of the forms of black speech, from letter-writing to passing comments and song, to create this polyphony of Harlem. It marks out poetry as ultimately successful in its capacity to be speakerly, to be on the move, to be constantly as alive as music and . . . revolution.

The dream deferred is an image which is also reflexive, for Hughes repeatedly stated his aesthetic goal—to give a voice to the blues within himself, but also to black people and oppressed people everywhere—in terms of the poet being the dreamer to and through whom the multitudes could speak. One of his earliest poems, "Dream Variations" (1924), combined the dream of freedom and the dream of being embraced by that blackness which could replace the absent mother figure. This poet-dreamer figure reappeared in "The Dream Keeper" (1925), which relevantly fused the notion of song, dreams, the color blue, and poetry. "As I Grew Older" (1926) ended on the double belief in the performative force of language and of the love of blackness, in oneself and in others, to break through the alienation imposed by white power—a power

Hughes did find in the blues, even if when his first book of blues poetry came out it was decried by black intellectuals precisely because it was in black vernacular.

African-American literature since then has more than vindicated Hughes: all of the most vital black poetry of the sixties—even in the case of poets, such as Sonia Sanchez, who rejected the blues as form because it was too vocal in its pain, too silent about its anger—was born of this anchoring of black art in African-American oral and popular culture. As for the charge that Hughes's poetry is anti-intellectual, people who oppose intellectuals and popular culture generally believe that literature's highest aim should be to change the history of literature; poets like Langston Hughes believe that it must try to change the world. That, fundamentally, is the dream. The prejudice in favor of the writer's writer and poet's poet is a class bias in favor of difficulty which makes literature—art in general—inaccessible to the majority of people. Those critics who look down on poets like Hughes also consider painters like Jacob Lawrence and William H. Johnson too naive, too primitivistic, while feeling fascinated by the *obvious* complexity of Jean Toomer or Aaron Douglas. These oppositions are simplistic; Hughes, like Lawrence, like Johnson, chose an "aesthetic of simplicity" (Rampersad, 1986: 146), and such choices *redefine* what art means, critics' resistance notwithstanding. This is not to say that many of Hughes's poems are not facile; but facile and *easy to read* are not synonymous, just as facile and hermetic are not antonymous.

Hughes's "blue" and black voice was not always that of the blues: it was sometimes one of primitivistic imagery reversed into political statement ("Now they've caged me / In the circus of civilization") or of the simple lyric statement "black is beautiful" decades before it became a slogan ("The night is beautiful / So the faces of my people"),[19] or the voice of the hyphenated African-American identity ("Afro-American Fragment"). But all along, his was the voice of a poet who sought *in black culture* the words, the images, the inflections, the rhythms to express what it was to be black and proud in a racist society. That meaning of "soul," which already appeared in "The Negro Speaks of Rivers" (1921)—"My soul has grown deep like the rivers" (23)—was at the heart of Hughes's aim as a poet, which he stated again in 1966:

> *Soul* is a synthesis of the essence of Negro folk art redistilled . . . particularly the old music and its flavor, the ancient basic beat out of Africa, the folk rhymes and Ashanti stories—expressed in contemporary ways so definitely and emotionally colored with the old, that it gives a distinctly Negro flavor to today's music, painting or writing—or even to merely personal attitudes and daily conversation. *Soul* is the contemporary Harlem's *négritude*, revealing to

the Negro people and to the world the beauty within themselves. (Rampersad 1988, 403)

Thus, Langston Hughes stands as the poet of the Harlem Renaissance who, in writing poetry aesthetically infused with black music, not only brought recognition to black popular culture and to the vernacular black voice, but transformed American poetry, its song, and its song of America as he wrote as a black poet. From his blues-transcript-style lyrics, to the militant use of patterns of speech, music, and poetry in *The Montage of A Dream Deferred*, from "The Weary Blues" to "The Backlash Blues," Hughes constantly sought to fuse the vitality of popular black culture with the energy of political commitment at the sides of the black masses.

Since Langston Hughes's death, new musical forms have appeared, which could make the blues seem outfashioned. That Hughes's poetry is still so utterly contemporary is perhaps due to the rediscovery of blues classics over the past ten years, but also, tragically, to the unchanged or worsened conditions of inner-city black America, which make the *Montage of a Dream Deferred* easy to imagine as a montage in rap, soul, hip-hop, or whatever blues one is playing. So many lines of Hughes's poetry have already become the titles of other black works that the blues tradition of oral transmission lives on. Whether or not literary history eventually judges Langston Hughes's blues to have been minor melodies, the poet, in his embracing of black speech and music, did not hesitate to break free from all of the conventions of African-American poetry in the 1920s; in this, he enacted the famous line on which he ended "The Negro Artist and The Racial Mountain": "We build our temples for tomorrow, strong as we know how, and we stand on top of the mountain, free within ourselves."

NOTES

1. Many of the blues poems that appear in *The Collected Poems of Langston Hughes* are lesser known. Some poems written as blues songs are not labeled such: "Gypsy Man" (66), "Ma Man" (66), or "Wide River" (71), to name a few. See Stephen Tracy's article in Trotman, 1995. (I unfortunately was not able to get a copy of Tracy's *Langston Hughes and the Blues* [Urbana: University of Illinois Press, 1988] in time for this article.)

2. A younger generation of African-American artists was by this time criticizing the blues as a form of lament and passivity. For example, poet Sonia Sanchez's "liberation/poem" about Billie Holiday, which starts with the lines "blues aint culture / they signs of oppression," can be taken not only as a (loving) critique of the singer herself, but also as criticism of the poet—Langston Hughes—who wrote the "Song for Billie Holiday."

3. See *Leaves of Grass* and particularly Section 24 of *Song of Myself:* "Through me

many long dumb voices, / Voices of the interminable generations of prisoners and slaves, / Voices of the diseased and despairing and of thieves and dwarfs. . . ."

4. All page numbers refer to *The Collected Poems of Langston Hughes,* edited by Arnold Rampersad and David Roessel (New York: Alfred A. Knopf, 1994).

5. One need only think of Gertrude Rainey singing "Blues, Oh Blues": "Blues, oh blues oh blues / Blues, oh blues, blues oh blues / I'm so blue, so blue, oh, mama dont know what to do."

6. As a matter of fact, all of Hughes's *négritude* poems are, in their blue tone, in their love song for black people everywhere, a form of blues: a form of "soul" (see Rampersad 1988, 400).

7. Many excellent studies show the conflicts among the Harlem Renaissance intellectuals and writers on this point. For a study of the problems connected to the use of dialect in poetry, see Gates, *Figures in Black* (all of chapter 6).

8. On the blues repertoire see both Levine and Oliver.

9. The poem implicitly reminds one of the way the cross of crucifixion is called the tree in spirituals, as it speaks of the black young lover hanging from the "crossroads tree," and as it denounces, simultaneously, the "white lord Jesus" who does not strike down the lynchers.

10. See Rampersad, 1986, 140–41, for the critical reception of *Fine Clothes to the Jew,* which contained such blues poems as "Midwinter Blues," "Gypsy Man," "Listen Here Blues."

11. This poem is practically a twin, in form and content, to a blues sung by Bessie Smith called "Preachin' the Blues."

12. "Po Boy Blues" repeats it six times, "Lonesome Place" seven times.

13. Much of Angela Davis's study revolves around the way the "blues woman challenged in her own way the imposition of gender-based inferiority" (36), on how women's blues "redefine black woman as active, assertive, independent, and sexual" (75).

14. Because a black person's name in America carries the scar of the lost African name, the significance of the "K," which does not stand for any other name but which is her given name, is obviously *central* to Madam's identity as she *reclaims* herself from any normative white naming, which the census hyperbolically symbolizes.

15. Sung by Billie Holiday, in an unusual gender transgression: "Who's coming to town / You'll never guess who / Lovable, huggable, Emily Brown / Miss Brown to you / Why do you think she's coming to town? / Just wait and you'll see / The lovable huggable Emily Brown / Miss Brown to you / Is Baby to me."

16. Indeed, Hughes was trying to retain that orality of the stand-up comedy of his *Simple* stories (which reverse many of the conventions of the minstrel fool).

17. This seems an allusion to the spirituals which herald apocalypse as an end to white oppression.

18. The use of "bitter" calls to mind the closing line of the song "Strange Fruit," recorded by Billie Holiday in 1939, which ends its description of the lynched black bodies hanging from the southern trees with the words "Here is a strange and bitter crop." This made the word "bitter" a particularly loaded term in black art.

19. "Lament for Dark Peoples" (39); "My People" (36).

PART III.
THE NEGRO MIND REACHES OUT: THE RENAISSANCE IN INTERNATIONAL PERSPECTIVE

The relation between the Harlem Renaissance and world developments is a particularly complex one. The third group of essays in this volume tries to highlight certain aspects by studying the involvement of Harlem Renaissance personalities in cosmopolitan artistic and literary trends and by studying political implications of those involvements. We examined the international setting, the intricate process through which ideas and talents are exchanged, acknowledged, or misunderstood, transplanted and translated among three continents, between the New World and the Old, among several cultures and languages.

Many New Negroes were citizens of the world, eager to travel, to test their ideas, and to participate in wider currents. The more radical, like Claude McKay, saw the international implications of the race violence encountered in the United States; W. E. B. DuBois articulated the necessity to expand the struggle for civil rights to a thorough examination of the colonial situation in Africa. Garvey himself, as a West Indian and an advocate of a return to Africa, was anxious to give that international scope to his movement. Artists looked for greater freedom than the racial mountain would allow. All shared the conviction that the race problem was a world issue that concerned many nations and that out of the confrontation with other situations and encounters with other black people would emerge a new idea of race. Paradoxically Paris, the capital of a colonialist country, became the center of this new diasporic geography and consciousness, vying with this other capital and black Mecca, Harlem. These transnational claims, the many activities into which "Harlemites," West Indians, Africans, and Europeans were engaged encouraged us to see the Harlem Renaissance in this wider setting, to question the assumption that it was exclusive and parochial and revolved round its own dark tower, and to reconsider its nationalistic inclinations. Paris and other European cities became the new sites of meetings, debates, and forums, international conventions, conferences, and Pan-African congresses where black voices were heard, a springboard for new political and artistic adventures.

In Paris, the term "*nègre*" or "*noir*" appeared, as an interesting parallel and complement to "Negro," to designate artistic, literary, musical, ideological movements, and also magazines, journals, shows, and places: *Ligue de la défense de la race nègre, Paris noir*, or *Le cri des Nègres*, Blaise Cendrars's *Anthologie nègre*, and the famous West Indian dance hall, *Le Bal Nègre*. Renaissance writers made their work known and got acquainted with Francophone literatures. Paris became the center of new publications, shows, and productions, a multilingual and multicultural stage for another renaissance and the frame for the *négritude* movement. It was important to examine this complex scene: the West Indian presence within and without the Harlem Renaissance (Charras, chapter 15, and Pedersen, chapter 14); the New Negro's amazing mobility and curiosity for what was happening elsewhere; the various layers of the encounters with Africa, with the Francophone transnational world (Fabre, chapter 17, and Edwards, chapter 16); the consequences of these shifts in locus and focus; the discursive and institutional structures that this new diaspora received; the unifying or universalist claims made.

Several questions are raised in this volume whose third section documents these activities, fluxes, exchanges, and responses: to what extent was the construction of this diaspora more an imagined community, more a utopian project than a reality? How does it relate to the New Negro project? Can it be approached as one of its extensions, giving it also much larger scope? Does it reverberate upon it and force it to reconsider some of its premises? More pragmatically, did it succeed or fail in establishing new networks, reciprocity, and mutual understanding, in translating ideas and images among groups, movements, and cultures?

14. The Tropics in New York: Claude McKay and the New Negro Movement

Carl Pedersen

> Bananas ripe and green, and ginger-root,
> Cocoa in pods and alligator pears,
> And tangerines and mangoes and grape fruit,
> Fit for the highest prize at parish fairs,
> Set in the window, bringing memories
> Of fruit-trees laden by low-singing rills,
> And dewy dawns, and mystical blue skies
> In benediction over nun-like hills.
> My eyes grew dim, and I could no more gaze;
> A wave of longing through my body swept,
> And, hungry for the old, familiar ways,
> I turned aside and bowed my head and wept.
> —CLAUDE McKAY, "The Tropics in New York" (1922)[1]

The poem "The Tropics in New York" appeared in Claude McKay's first collection of verse published in the United States, *Harlem Shadows;* along with Jean Toomer's *Cane, Harlem Shadows* is often cited as marking the beginning of the burst of artistic creativity known as the New Negro or Harlem Renaissance. The first stanza of the poem teems with the lushness and color of the Caribbean, with its litany of fruits such as bananas, avocados, tangerines, and mangoes evoking the fecundity of the land. The immediate sensory experience produced by the first stanza is undermined by the second, which places these fruits behind a window in a shop in New York. The fruit of the Caribbean has become a part of memory, detached commodities no longer a part of the land. But the memory of the Caribbean trees, hills, and skies is persistent and prompts the pangs of longing the poet feels for his homeland. The poem ends with the poet weeping over what he feels has been lost to him forever.

Seen in isolation, this poem could be construed as emblematic for the displacement and alienation felt by McKay, and by extension all Afro-Caribbean immigrants, in exile in New York. However, I would argue that the relegation of the tropics as pure display, detached from its roots, is more characteristic of the critical assessment of McKay. He has traditionally been co-opted into an American New Negro movement or Harlem Renaissance rather than seen as part of a postcolonial Caribbean tradition. By exploring what I would like to call a Caribbean continuum, I will attempt to resituate McKay as part of a Caribbean as well as a global African diasporic tradition.

The term *Harlem Renaissance* evokes a hermetic entity, a centripetal force drawing African-Americans from the South together within the narrow confines of a great metropolis. In this scenario, the international character of the New Negro movement sometimes gets lost. And yet, in 1927, *Opportunity* magazine offered one of the most succinct assessments of the global forces that had come together to create this movement.

> The Anglo-African, that is the English-speaking Negro, both in America and in the British possessions, is becoming internationally minded with regard to his blood brethren. The World War, the Pan-African Congresses, fostered with prophetic vision by Dr Burghardt DuBois, the phantasmagoria of the Garvey program, René Maran's *Batouala*, increase in European travel, had forced the international thought both upon the Negro intellectuals and the Negro masses.[2]

Paul Gilroy has expressed his regret that the parochial nature of much of African-American studies downplays these important connections, citing specifically the neglect that W. E. B. DuBois's German education and Richard Wright's Paris exile have suffered in much African-American literary criticism (to be fair, I think Gilroy overplays this neglect somewhat and fails to take into account the recent biography of DuBois by David Levering Lewis and Michel Fabre's important work on Wright). In the case of Wright, Gilroy speculates that the lack of attention to Wright's work in France is in part due to the fact that it "resists assimilation to the great ethnocentric canon of African-American literature."[3] Much the same could be said of McKay, who has been effectively co-opted into the African-American canon as opposed to the Afro-Caribbean canon.

Echoing Gilroy, scholars of border cultures are seeking to identify a distinctive postcolonial, Pan-American consciousness that, in the words of José David Saldívar, would chart "an array of oppositional critical and creative processes that aim to articulate a new, transgeographical conception of American culture—one more responsive to the hemisphere's geographical ties and political crosscurrents than to narrow national ideologies."[4] One important aspect of this postcolonial, Pan-American consciousness is the notion of the extended Caribbean used by Peter Hulme in *Colonial Encounters*,[5] his study of European encounters with the Caribbean from 1492 to 1797, and Stelamaris Coser's *Bridging the Americas*,[6] which focuses on the work of Gayl Jones, Paule Marshall, and Toni Morrison. The extended Caribbean stretches from Jamestown, Virginia, to Bahia in Brazil in the era of colonial encounters and even further to New York City in African-American literature in the latter part of the twentieth century. In the period of the New Negro movement, the extended Caribbean as a discursive and historical entity spans Eric Walrond's Guyana, the Trinidad of Eric Williams and C. L. R. James, the Martinique of Aimé Césaire and René Maran, the Haiti of Jacques Roumain and Jean-Price Mars, the Jamaica of Claude McKay and Marcus Garvey, the Danish West Indies of Hubert Harrison and Nella Larsen, Zora Neale Hurston's all-black community of Eatonville, Florida, Jean Toomer's rural Georgia, and on up the coast to Harlem.

This Caribbean can be extended even farther, to the United Kingdom, where Garvey and Walrond spent their last years, and to France, where Césaire and Léon Damas first encountered the work of McKay and where Maran wrote his anti-colonialist novel *Batouala* (1921). Situating McKay and other Caribbean intellectuals in this extended Caribbean of the Western Hemisphere as well as of the Black Atlantic broadens the scope and impact of the New Negro movement and sees it as a continuum that informs Caribbean postcolonial fiction and historiography to the present day. I would like to follow this trail of the extended Caribbean by focusing on several key sites of this transnational, borderless map: Trinidad, Haiti, Harlem, Marseilles, and Jamaica.

As I pointed out, the concept of an extended Caribbean has a deep past and a resilient present, from the time before the first encounters between native Caribbeans, conquering Europeans, and transplanted Africans to present-day musical transmigrations of hip hop, reggae, and jungle music between the Caribbean, the United States, and the United Kingdom. The period I intend to focus on stretches from the end of the nineteenth century to the beginning of the 1940s. In literature, it spans the early work of McKay and H. G. De Lisser and the beginning of an Anglophone Caribbean literary tradition at the turn of the century to the publication of Césaire's *Notebook of a Return to the Native Land* in 1939. In history, it emerges with the counter-discourse of J. J. Thomas and James A. Froude and is consolidated with C. L. R. James's opus on the Haitian Revolution, *The Black Jacobins,* in 1938.

Responding to *The English in the West Indies*,[7] a 1888 travelogue on the Caribbean written by the eminent British historian James A. Froude and a thinly disguised diatribe against the dangers of an emancipated peasantry in the British West Indies following the example of Haiti, the Trinidadian J. J. Thomas in *Froudacity*[8] laid bare Froude's colonialist bias and refuted the contention that the Caribbean was without history. Turning his gaze from history to language, Thomas published a short work, *The Theory of Creole Grammar,* that sought to legitimize the Caribbean *patois* that had traditionally been regarded as a bastardized English.[9] Thomas's work serves as a useful framework in which to place McKay, arguably one of the founders of modern Caribbean literature, and Williams, who, with C. L. R. James, changed the course of Caribbean historical writing. McKay's dialect verse, collected in the verse collections *Song of Jamaica* and *Constab Ballads*—both published in 1912, the year he left Jamaica—reveals the depth of McKay's knowledge of what the linguist Frederic Cassidy has called "Jamaica Talk" in his study of the same name. Examples from McKay's verse and *Banana Bottom* appear throughout Cassidy's book, a testimony to the lasting influence of McKay's experiments in dialect. As Cassidy points out, perceptions of Caribbean *patois* as a somehow inferior language persisted even in the 1970s. Consequently, the early efforts of McKay to legitimize Caribbean speech are perhaps all the more admirable. Indeed, it could be argued that McKay's dialect verse provided an example of an indigenous form of speech that J. J. Thomas had attempted to identify with his Creole grammar.[10] Edward Kamau Brathwaite continued this tradition of exploring the contours of indigenous speech patterns in his *History of the Voice* from 1984, in which he argues that what he calls a submerged nation-language constantly intrudes on the language of the imperial center. Whereas McKay's early work can be seen as a confirmation of Thomas's notion of a Creole grammar, Williams's writing on historiography, particularly *British Historians and the West Indies*, take Thomas's critique of Froude a step further in the attempt to define a true Caribbean history.

Before C. L. R. James, and no doubt spurred by the American occupation, McKay articulated a defense of the Haitian Revolution that subverted the traditional, colonial paradigm of Haiti as the repository of chaos and savagery. The Haitian scholar Michel-Rolph Trouillot, in *Silencing the Past: Power and the Production of History*, expresses his consternation that the Haitian Revolution has been largely neglected in traditional and contemporary African-American scholarship. He argues that "the silencing of the Haitian Revolution . . . fit the relegation to an historical backburner of the three themes to which it was linked: racism, slavery, and colonialism."[11] However, as Michael Dash has observed, during the New Negro movement there seemed to have been a "latent solidarity . . . between black Americans and Haitians" which was directly linked to the circumstances of the U.S. occupation of Haiti from 1915 through 1934.[12] Indeed, Haiti as a symbol of black resistance looms large in the work of Caribbean intellectuals from McKay to James and Williams. It is no accident that the expatriate Afro-Caribbean protagonist Ray in McKay's first two novels, *Home to Harlem* and *Banjo,* is from Haiti, and not Jamaica. In *Home to Harlem,* Ray provides Jake with a diasporic interpretation of black world history by talking of the cultures of Dahomey, Benin, and Abyssinia, of an African civilization with a complicated and rich past (in much the same terms as Hubert Harrison used), and of the Haitian Revolution which created the first black republic in the Western Hemisphere. Ray left Haiti after his father had been jailed for speaking out against the occupation of Haiti by American troops. His brother had been killed by U.S. Marines. McKay highlights this link between the triumph of the Haitian Revolution and the injustice of the current American occupation. Although European imperialism had been crippled by the war, the specter of American hegemony in the Caribbean loomed on the horizon.[13] McKay's assessment of the historical significance of the Haitian Revolution and the threat that American hegemony posed to the Caribbean anticipated the work of C. L. R. James, who published his influential study of the Haitian struggle for independence, *The Black Jacobins,* in 1938. *The Black Jacobins* in turn had an impact on Williams's thinking on Caribbean nationalism. In his autobiography, *Inward Hunger,* Williams wondered "[if] Haiti's isolation, poverty and tyranny after independence represented one lesson to West Indian colonials, did the land of Toussaint Louverture pose yet another lesson—that West Indian colonials were destined to graduate from European colonialism to American?"[14]

The impact of the Caribbean went beyond the reconstruction of a usable past to the formulation of a revitalized black nationalism by Caribbean intellectuals in Harlem in the first decades of the twentieth century. In an editorial in *Favorite Magazine* in December 1919, the poet Fenton Johnson expressed his belief that "this Negro renaissance is due largely to the aggressive mind of our brother from the islands."[15] Similar pronouncements about the potential leading role of Caribbean immigrants came at about the same time from DuBois and the expatriate Guyanese writer Eric Walrond. In retrospect, this assessment of the role of Caribbean immigrants came to be seen as overly optimistic, if not downright wrong-headed. Harold Cruse, in his influential *The Crisis of the Negro Intellectual,* argued that, because Caribbean immigrants to the United States came primarily from the educated upper classes and were conditioned politically by their status as a majority population in colonized societies, they failed to address African-American concerns. Instead of responding to the indigenous African-American nationalist tradition, they blindly adopted European Marxism.

Both perspectives ignore the complex connections between the Caribbean intellectual community and black American intellectuals and fail to address the issue of how cultural discourse in the period immediately following World War I gave rise to new formulations of black nationalism that combined a postcolonialist sensibility with the African-American nationalist tradition. It is worth noting that this reformulation was undertaken by Caribbean radicals and black American radicals often working together in organizations and journals in the postwar period. A casual glance at the publications of the time reveals fascinating networks of cooperation: W. A. Domingo, a leading Jamaican active in the Socialist movement, contributed to *The Messenger,* edited by A. Philip Randolph and Chandler Owen; T. Thomas Fortune and William Ferris served as editors of the Jamaican Marcus Garvey's *Negro World.*

In his 1937 autobiography, *A Long Way From Home,* and in a letter to Max Eastman written in 1923, McKay recounts two meetings held in the offices of the radical journal *The Liberator* (which he co-edited at the time with Michael Gold) that brought together an amalgam of black and white, American and Caribbean radicals: Domingo; Robert Minor, the cartoonist for *The Liberator;* the Danish West Indian Hubert Harrison, who had joined the Socialist party upon arriving in the United States in 1911; Grace Campbell, an African-American member of the Socialist party; the Barbadian Richard Moore, who edited *The Emancipator* with Domingo; Otto Huiswoud of Dutch Guiana, who would be the Communist party's official delegate to the Fourth Congress of the Comintern; and Cyril Briggs from Nevis, the founder of the African Blood Brotherhood and the editor of its organ *The Crusader.* According to McKay, the first meeting was ostensibly devoted to "making the Garvey Back-to-Africa Movement . . . more class conscious." Apparently nothing concrete came of these meetings, but they nevertheless demonstrate the ties among the American Socialist party, Caribbean intellectuals, and the Greenwich Village white radical set.[16] *The Crusader* was especially important in charting the role of Caribbean intellectuals in Harlem in the postwar period. It was originally established in 1918 as the journal for the Hamitic League of the World. In 1921, it became the journal of the African Blood Brotherhood, founded by Briggs. The Hamitic League of the World counted among its founders Briggs; the bibliophile and journalist John E. Bruce; George Wells Parker, whose pamphlet *Children of the Sun* (1918) expressed a proto-Afrocentric philosophy; and Duse Mohamed Ali, an African of Egyptian-Sudanese descent whose *African Times and Orient Review,* a leading Pan-African and Pan-Orient magazine, had published several of Garvey's articles while he was in England in 1912.

Three currents of thought, which intermesh, can be discerned in the pages of *The Crusader:* the promotion of what Parker called race patriotism (arguments for the African roots of Greek civilization that anticipate those of Cheikh Anta Diop); a call for African independence and self-government for blacks; and the need for a reformulation of black nationalism in Africa and in the diaspora in the wake of the World War, which is linked to nationalisms in Ireland, the Middle East, and Asia.

The Crusader was sensitive to the political implications of postwar nativist sentiment on the one hand and to New Negro assertiveness on the other, but tended to interpret them as a cultural conflict between racial purists and the collective unity of Africans, Africans in the diaspora, and people of color around the world. The dire prediction of the decline of the West promulgated by nativists and racial theorists, and arguably functioning as a subtext in U.S. government investigations of radical organizations, expressed the fear that the collapse of the center would result in the chaos of peripheral cultures, a multiplication of Haitis. I would suggest that the rise of Bolshevism in Russia was perceived by Caribbean intellectuals in these terms, and even Bolsheviks like Trotsky regarded Russia's backwardness in part as a result of its semi-colonial status rooted in its dependence on Western capitalist markets. Early on, *The Crusader* had drawn a parallel between an empowered Japan as a leader of liberation movements in Asia and a Liberia strengthened by African-American liberation as the vanguard of struggle for African self-government. With the waning of the prospect of world revolution in the early 1920s, the mongrelized, colonial cultures of Africa and the African diaspora, the former Russian empire, and Asiatic nations could forge an alliance of peripheral (or in nativist terms, barbaric) cultures against a collapsing center.

It is important to note that these were not exclusively the concerns of Caribbean intellectuals. Rather, they were part of a larger formulation of an African diasporic sensibility that went beyond the boundaries of Harlem and that can be found in the writings and political activities of African-Americans such as DuBois, A. Philip Randolph, Chandler Owen, and Benjamin Brawley, and the Caribbeans Garvey, Harrison, Briggs, and McKay. What emerges from this cultural critique of postwar Western society is a reconfiguration of black nationalism that constructs ideological positions of Afrocentric education, diasporic race unity, and African independence which were motivated by postwar shifts in geopolitical power and the rise of nativism, and which combined a post-colonialist perspective with the tradition of black nationalist thought.

The reformulation of black nationalism was complemented in McKay's work by the proliferation of African diasporic cultural interchange centered not in Harlem, but in Marseilles. In a review in *The Crisis*, DuBois claimed that Claude McKay's second novel, *Banjo*, offered nothing less than an "international philosophy of the Negro race."[17] It is my contention that this "international philosophy" was based in large measure on the dissemination of Africanized musical expression outside of Africa, the Caribbean, and the rural and urban black communities in the United States, and that the French port of Marseilles served as a conduit to facilitate this dissemination. The rhythm of the city, with its polyglot and constantly changing population, reinforced the rhythms of the various forms of musical expression that were being played in the bars and cafés of Marseilles.

From the plantations of the South, the maroon enclaves of the Caribbean and Brazil, and the rural areas of Africa, black music was in the process of being heard in mainstream society in the United States and in Europe. In her recent study of the development of "mongrel Manhattan" in the 1920s, Ann Douglas argues that white America was repudiating Europe as a cultural model at the same time as African-Americans were asserting their role in the realm of culture. Music was of course an integral part of this emerging Africanization of American culture. McKay, anticipating the work of Gilroy, expands this development by giving it a transatlantic dimension.

It is the politics of cultural dissemination and not social organization that are paramount in this particular conception of a Pan-African sensibility. The links among Africans, West Indians, and African-Americans are forged by folk and music tradition and not by political ideology. This tradition, extending from Africa to the diaspora, is characterized by rhythmic variations, not by rigid ideological doctrines:

> They played the "beguine," which was just a Martinique variant of the "jelly-roll" or the Jamaican "burru" or the Senegalese "bombé." . . . "Beguine," "jelly-roll," "burru," "bombé," no matter what the name may be, Negroes are ever so beautiful and magical when they do that gorgeous sublimation of the primitive African sex feeling. In its thousand varied patterns, depending so much on individual rhythm, so little on formal movement, this dance is the key to the African rhythm of life. . . .[18]

Indeed, the repertoire of the group could be characterized as a form of proto-world music, drawing on a variety of musical traditions originating in Africa: Banjo's group performs "Cordelia Brown," a calypso tune from Trinidad; "Stay Carolina Stay," a folk song from Sierra Leone; and "Yes Sir That's My Baby," a Tin Pan Alley standard. *Banana Bottom* is often regarded as the novel in which McKay resolved the dilemma of elite versus folk culture in the character of Bita Plant and the setting of his native land, Jamaica. However, it is perhaps McKay's recognition in *Banjo* of the constantly changing, hybrid cross-cultural connections among the United States, the Caribbean, Europe, and Africa, exemplified in musical transmigrations, as an integral feature of a modern age that stands as McKay's lasting contribution to an "international philosophy of the Negro race." Lilyan Kesteloot has emphasized the impact *Banjo* had for Francophone African and Caribbean intellectuals in France in the 1930s. The formulation of a *négritude* ideology defined by Césaire as "a taking charge of one's destiny as a black man, of one's history and culture" owes a debt to

McKay's formulation of a diasporic ideology. In this sense, Leopold Senghor could, with some justification, call McKay "the true inventor of *négritude.*"[19]

McKay's intellectual and spiritual odyssey came full circle in the last fifteen years of his life. In the short stories set in Jamaica in *Gingertown* (1932) and especially in his last novel, *Banana Bottom* (1933), McKay, from a distance in time and space, returned to his native land to once again confront its culture and history, as he had done in his dialect poetry before he left the island. It is useful to look at *Home to Harlem, Banjo,* and *Banana Bottom* as a trilogy that explores the lives of blacks in the diaspora in the twentieth century: from the postwar urban culture of Harlem, to the mixed cultures cast together in a European port of commerce in the 1920s, and to the rural culture of post-Emancipation Jamaica at the turn of the century.

Banana Bottom is a critical meditation on the conflicts that drive post-Emancipation society: the waning influence of missionaries such as the Craigs; the foiled aspirations of the new colored middle class, embodied in the tragi-comic figure of Herald Newton Day; and the resilience of the black peasantry, echoed several years later in Zora Neale Hurston's *Their Eyes Were Watching God* (1937). In *Banana Bottom,* Bita Plant, a precursor of Jamaica Kincaid's *Annie John,* has been educated abroad and finds herself, upon her return to Jamaica, increasingly intolerant of the narrow-mindedness and artificiality of her sponsors, the Craigs, and drawn toward the indigenous culture of the island. Unfortunately, McKay injects Squire Gensir, a thinly veiled Walter Jekyll, into this scenario, and in doing so robs Bita of full independence from the colonial center. For, however sympathetic, Gensir still represents the kind face of imperialism, like Jekyll adopting a patronizing attitude toward his protégée, whom he must continually goad to realize her intimate connection with the people.

In *The Negro in the Caribbean,* Williams argued that "For studies of African survivals . . . the islands are a great unexploited laboratory," anticipating his later support for the study of black folkways in Trinidad. He believed that only changes in the political structure of the Caribbean would lead to the success of peasant ownership.[20] McKay did not address these issues, focusing instead on the purported cultural strengths of the black peasantry. However, he fails to present more than a romantic stereotype of the Jamaican black peasantry, much the same as he had in his early essay, "When Black Sees Red and Green," in which he compared the Irish peasantry and the Jamaican peasantry in a paean to the culture of the soil.[21] In spite of these flaws, *Banana Bottom* is at times an incisive portrait of a Jamaica in a period "of inquietude," caught between the colonial legacy of the past and the rapid social and economic changes of the present, where some inhabitants of Jubilee leave the island to work on the Panama Canal, and where the peasants fall victim to the vagaries of a fickle world market, much the same as the motley group in Marseilles owes its fate to world commerce.

In his foreword to Williams's *The Negro in the Caribbean*, Alain Locke expressed the hope that "this study will furnish a closer and sounder bond of understanding between the Negro-American and his brother West Indian, known all too limitedly as a migrant rather than with regard either to his home background or with reference to our common racial history and problems."[22] I have attempted to show that McKay had already made substantial contributions to this understanding. Furthermore, a deeper understanding of the Caribbean and diasporic dimension of McKay's work reconfigures the New Negro movement in time and space. It is ironic that in 1942, the same year that *The Negro in the Caribbean* was published, McKay had applied for a Rosenwald Fund grant in order to write a book about Caribbean immigrants in New York. It was to be titled "The Tropics in New York." His application was rejected, and the book was never written.[23] McKay never returned to his native land. Thus was the torch passed to a new generation of Caribbean intellectuals, many of whom would build on his work.

NOTES

1. "The Tropics in New York," in Hill et al., 1998, 883.

2. Michael J. Dash, *Haiti and the United States* (New York: St. Martin's Press, 1988), 47.

3. Gilroy (London: Verso), 183. See also Lewis's *W.E.B. DuBois* and Michel Fabre, *The Unfinished Quest of Richard Wright* (New York: William Morrow, 1973).

4. José David Saldívar, *The Dialectics of Our America: Genealogy, Cultural Critique, and Literary History* (Durham: Duke University Press, 1991), xi.

5. Peter Hulme, *Colonial Encounters: Europe and the Native Caribbean 1492–1797* (London: Routledge, 1986).

6. Stelamaris Coser, *Bridging the Americas: The Literature of Toni Morrison, Paule Marshall, and Gayl Jones* (Philadelphia: Temple University Press, 1994).

7. James A. Froude, *The English in the West Indies, or the Bow of Ulysses* (London, 1888).

8. J.J. Thomas, *Froudacity* (Trinidad, 1889).

9. See Williams, *British Historians* 130–46. See also Wilson Harris's perceptive comments on Froude and Thomas in his essay *History, Fable, and Myth in the Caribbean and Guianas* (1990; reprint, Wellesly: Calaloux, 1995).

10. J.J. Thomas, *The Theory of Creole Grammar* (Trinidad, 1887).

11. Michel-Rolph Trouillot, *Silencing the Past: Power and the Production of History* (Boston: Beacon Press, 1995), 98.

12. Dash, 46.

13. Claude McKay, *Home to Harlem* (1928; reprint, Boston: Northeastern University Press, 1987), 131, 134.

14. Eric Williams, *Inward Hunger: The Education of Prime Minister* (London: Andre Deutsch, 1969), 65.

15. Fenton Johnson, "Editorial," *Favorite Magazine* 3 (December 1919).

16. McKay, *A Long Way From Home* 109. McKay's letter to Eastman is reprinted in Cooper, *The Passion of Claude McKay* 89.

17. DuBois quoted in Melvin Dixon, *Ride Out the Wilderness* 49.

18. McKay, *Banjo* 105.

19. Kesteloot, *Black Writers in French* 56–74.

20. Williams, *The Negro in the Caribbean* 9.

21. McKay, "When Black Sees Red and Green" in Cooper, *Passion* 57–62.

22. Williams, *The Negro in the Caribbean*, n.p.

23. Cooper, *Claude McKay* 349–50.

15. The West Indian Presence in Alain Locke's
The New Negro (1925)[1]

Françoise Charras

The Great Migration of the Negro rural population from the South was the important demographic factor that made possible the Harlem which became the locus of the New Negro Renaissance. Yet, according to Irma Watkins Owens, of the 340,000 black residents who were living in Upper Manhattan by 1930, some 40,000 (i.e., 20 percent of the Negro population in Harlem) were English-speaking Caribbean migrants of African descent.[2] This foreign black migration played a significant role in the political, cultural, social, and economic life of the African-American community, a role that far exceeded its demographic importance. The impact of this West Indian population is clearly evidenced by the debate that has developed concerning its activities in Harlem during the first three decades of the twentieth century.[3] Owens's study, based on formal sources as well as on personal interviews, thoroughly documents the historical importance of these black immigrants who arrived in the United States between 1911 and 1924. In her introduction she deplores that, contrary to contemporary observers of the New Negro movement, "more recent research rarely emphasizes Harlem's diverse origins and [rarely] explores the intraracial ethnic dimension as an important dynamic in African-American community life" (Owens 1).

Contrary to Owens's feeling that "In part this oversight might be due to the attention most Harlem scholars have given to the community's importance as a center of cultural production during the 1920s" (1), this chapter will emphasize, as a stage of the intraracial and ethnic debate, the cultural presence of West Indian writers and intellectuals in *The New Negro*. Their participation in what claimed to be the manifesto of the New Negro Renaissance constitutes more than a mere introduction to the cultural production of the ethnic minority they were meant to represent.

Claude McKay, Eric Walrond, James A. Rogers, Arthur A. Schomburg, and W. A. Domingo were not discovered by the "midwives" of the Harlem Renaissance. They had actually been there, on the scene, and had already contributed to the proclaimed political and cultural emergence of the New Negro.[4] W. A. Domingo was a well-known orator of the "young firebrands" soapbox and stepladder type described by J. Anderson (Anderson 106). First an active member of the Socialist Club, Domingo had, by 1919, joined Cyril Briggs's African Blood Brotherhood (founded in 1917) and was publishing his own magazine, *The Emancipator*. By 1920, J. A. Rogers had moved to Harlem and gained some fame as "the people's historian." He had already published his *From Superman to Man* (1917), which was described in *The Negro World* (to which he was a frequent contributor) as "the greatest book on the Negro we have ever read" (Owens 161). Arthur A. Schomburg—who had also been a frequent contributor to *The Negro World* (T. Martin 353)—already was a well-known historian and librarian. In 1922, *The Negro World* published two accounts (by Eric Walrond and by Zora Neale Hurston) of a visit to Schomburg's famous personal library (316, 369). By 1925, Eric Walrond, who had joined *The Negro World* in 1920, had just moved to *Opportunity*, and C. S. Johnson's essay in *The New Negro* clearly indicates Claude McKay's confirmed symbolic position as "the young Negro poet, [who] caught the mood of the new Negro in this [the new spirit of resistance], and molded it into fiery verse which the Negro newspapers copied and recopied" (NN 296).

Although the West Indians' various contributions do not loom large in number, their artistic and intellectual presence in Locke's *The New Negro* indicates the significance of the Caribbean immigration on this movement and points to the tensions and conflicts that it contained. Thus are foregrounded such oppositions as the reality of a Harlem multiculturalism almost ignored by the prevailing black nationalism, the complexity of the issue of race in a multicultural black community, and the definition of African America in relation to the larger black diaspora.

This chapter is an attempt to emphasize and assess the significance of the Caribbean immigration in the text of *The New Negro* through the formulations of its non–West Indian contributors as well as in the texts of those writers or intellectuals who had themselves come from the Caribbean. By such a double-sided presentation I do not mean to emphasize oppositions or suggest that conflicts will be at the center of this study (even though they cannot be ignored), but rather that tensions are inherent in the complexity of the project of

The New Negro's cultural nationalism and in the subsequent interpretations it gave rise to.[5] Continuing in the spirit of Owens's research, my approach concurs with her contention that "ethnic relations are not [to be] viewed in terms of conflict alone, but as an integral dynamic in Harlem's formation" (Owens 1). Insofar as through its contents and purpose it continues the debate on the definition of a larger and more open African-American identity, I will conclude this analysis of the West Indian intellectuals' contribution to the New Negro construct by a short presentation of the 1926 *Opportunity* issue on the Caribbean.

People of Caribbean descent such as Nella Larsen (not included in Locke's collection), W. E. B. DuBois, or James Weldon Johnson might have been considered in this study, inasmuch as they deemed their Caribbean ethnic origin meaningful enough to comment upon it in their own writings. However, this article will focus only on the five authors who actually came from the Caribbean: my purpose is not to look for a Caribbean entity as an essence that would be detectable through several generations of Americanization, but rather to insist on the Caribbean immigration's continued significance in the history of African America. In his article "Gifts of the Black Tropics" (NN 341), Domingo recalls this long history:

> West Indians have been coming to the United States for over a century. The part they have played in Negro progress is conceded to be important. As early as 1827 a Jamaican, John Russwurm, one of the founders of Liberia, was the first to be graduated from an American college and to publish a newspaper in this country.[6] . . . Prior to the Civil War, West Indian contribution to American life was so great that W.E.B. DuBois, in his *The Souls of Black Folk*, credits them with main responsibility for the manhood program presented by the race in the early decades of the last century. (NN 344–45)

The West Indians who contributed to *The New Negro* came from various parts of the Caribbean: from Puerto Rico came Arthur A. Schomburg, who arrived in the United States in 1891 and was part of the political immigration from the Spanish Caribbean colonies prior to the Spanish-American War; from Jamaica came Joel Augustus (or James A.) Rogers in 1906, Wilfrid Adolphus Domingo in 1910, and Claude McKay in 1917; and from Guyana, via Barbados and Panama, came Eric Walrond in 1918. One might also add, in absentia, Marcus Garvey. None of these men were part of the restless black peasant masses—whether southern or from the West Indies—that, according to Charles S. Johnson of *Opportunity*, were attracted to Garvey (296). Nor was the major part of the West Indian immigration (contrary to more recent waves of migrants from that area) predominantly peasantry, as Owens makes clear in her criticism of DuBois's more ideological than precise social definition of these migrants.[7]

All these men had, at one point, been part of what Tony Martin sees as Garvey's vanguard Harlem Renaissance.[8] They all had already published in Garvey's *New World* although, by 1925, they had dissociated themselves from Garveyism, if not from Garvey himself. Walrond and McKay are both characterized in Martin's study as "Garvey's defectors" (*Literary Garveyism* ch. 7). *The New Negro* appeared in the aftermath of the anti–West Indian reactions that accompanied the "Garvey Must Go" campaign in which Domingo, as he himself openly declares, was most instrumental[9] (NN 348).

This political episode has been largely defined in terms of the conflict of leadership among the various civil rights organizations, the socialist *Messenger,* and the Garvey movement. It has also been very negatively described by Harold Cruse who, in his analysis of the impact of the radical and communist West Indian activists, ironically comments about "the West Indian criticism of the inability of the American Negro to achieve the kind of nationalist unity *as a minority* that the West Indians could not achieve *as a majority at home,* and never have to this day" (*The Crisis of the Negro Intellectual* 47; my emphases).[10] However, as this article deals with the text of *The New Negro,* I will only indirectly address the larger context of Caribbean or, more precisely, West Indian/African-American political relations, only insofar as it appears in Locke's collection. I will, however, as indicated previously, refer to the 1926 Caribbean issue of *Opportunity* which, continuing this intraracial debate beyond the limits of the marginalization of Harlem's West Indian migrant community, displaces the problematics of the New Negro into the larger issue of American hegemony in the Caribbean.

As A. Rampersad remarks, "*The New Negro* exudes a sense of racial pride and yet also ignores the most important mass movement in black America of the 1920s, which was led by Marcus Garvey."[11] In spite of this conspicuous absence, at the very moment when the populist leader had been indicted and was in jail, Garveyism could not in fact be completely disregarded. It is repeatedly evoked in section 3 of *The New Negro,* underpins Domingo's article, and also surges up in various references to Garvey in several articles by non–West Indian authors. Only to that extent is it referred to here and only to the degree to which it supports the idea of a West Indian resilience within (and in spite of) the African-American nationalism of *The New Negro.*

In "The New Frontage of American Life" (NN 279–98), for instance, Charles S. Johnson very leniently refers to this conflict in relation to the recent Negro commercial development in northern cities—an attitude that may be explained by *Opportunity*'s less stringent approach to that issue:

> Mr. Marcus Garvey has been accused of inspiring and leading a movement for the "re-exaltation" of things black, for the exploitation of Negro resources for the profit of Negroes, and for the re-establishment of prestige to things

Negro. As a fact, he has merely had the clairvoyance to place himself at the head of a docile sector of a whole population which, in different degrees, has been expressing an indefinable restlessness and broadening of spirit. The Garvey movement itself is an exaggeration of this current mood which attempts to reduce these vague longings to concrete symbols of faith. (295–96)

Charles S. Johnson then concludes that this "mood" has found "a middle ground in the feeling of kinship with all oppressed dark peoples . . . and takes, perhaps, its highest expression in the objectives of the Pan-African Congress," thus reinstating Garvey's movement into a continuum that brings together the various trends of an almost all-inclusive New Negro movement in face of white violence (296).

Charles S. Johnson's interests as former social researcher for the National Urban League may account for his detailed analysis of the social and economic trends at work in the Negro community.[12] His article even suggests that the pervading optimistic tone of *The New Negro* is but another "grinning mask":

> With all the 'front' of pretending to live, the aspect of complacent wantless-ness, it is clear that the Negroes are in a predicament. The moment holds tolerance but no great promise. Just as the wave of immigration once swept these Negroes out of old strongholds, a change of circumstances may disrupt them again. The slow moving black masses, with their assorted heritages and old loyalties, face the same stern barriers in the new environment. They are the black workers. (290–91)

Such a grim description of this transformation of the "small increments of population" that for forty years "have been dribbling from the South, the West Indies, and South America" (284) finds an echo in the polysemous variations suggested by the article's new title.[13] The "frontage," which also suggests a new advance of the American frontier into the "promised land," opens upon the dubious future of "the melting pot of the city" (284)—a merely intraracial affair—as well as to the following observation: "the new *frontier* of Negro life is flung out in a jagged uneven but progressive pattern" (297; my emphasis). Charles S. Johnson is not the only *New Negro* contributor to make use of this Turnerian phraseology.[14] Paul U. Kellog's article "The Negro Pioneers" (271–77) abounds with references to the American Frontier thesis, which also impregnates Locke's first essay (even though, as shown by Hutchinson, their viewpoints are very clearly antithetical).[15]

Charles S. Johnson's article reads as a sort of counterpoint that denies the enthusiastic metaphors of the New Negro's Americanization process as related by Alain Locke. Such emphasis on the necessity of a "frontage" to oppose the social and racial forces that may disrupt the uniting process at work is made explicit in the following remark:

> If the present Negro New Yorker would be analyzed, he would be found to
> be composed of one part native, one part West Indian and about three parts
> Southern. If the tests of the army psychologists could work with the precision
> and certainty with which they are accredited, the Negroes who make up the
> present population of New York City would be declared *to represent different
> races*, for the differences between South and North are greater than the
> difference between whites and Negroes. (284–85; my emphasis)

In a description that somehow repeats many of the alienating stereotypes
that make for the exclusion of the so-called "West Indian" population (*The
Making of a Ghetto* 131–35), Osofsky later claimed that the coexisting ethnic
and racial groups turned Harlem into "the battleground of intra-racial antagonisms between American Negro Nativism and West Indians" (134). Similar
remarks are constant in *The New Negro*, where the majority of the references
or allusions to the West Indians emphasize their alienness,[16] while paradoxically their pregnant presence in the anthology indicates a de facto recognition
that they were a constituting part of Alain Locke's project—the "sort of leaven
in the American loaf" humorously described by Domingo (NN 348).

As has often been indicated, West Indian exception—if not exclusion—is
early signified in *The New Negro*. Indeed, in the very first short story of the
anthology, "The City of Refuge" (57–74), Rudolph Fisher plays upon various
ethnic stereotypes in the comic plot as well as in the language. Ethnic difference is also central to Jessie Fauset's essay "The Gift of Laughter"; yet, conversely, she explains how it contributed to the construction of the New Negro's
positive dramatic stature. She points out that Bert Williams's very foreignness
and identity as the West Indian outsider made possible the transformation of
the Negro on the stage from a comic freak or clown stereotype to a full-fledged
character.[17] Explaining how his color "would probably keep him from ever
making the 'legitimate'" stage career, J. Fauset adds:

> Consequently, deliberately . . . he turned his attention to minstrelsy. Natively
> he possessed the art of mimicry, intuitively he realized that his first path to
> the stage must lie along the old recognized lines of "funny man." He was as
> few of us recall, a Jamaican by birth, the ways of the American Negro were
> utterly alien to him and did not come spontaneously, he set himself therefore
> to obtaining a knowledge of them. For choice he selected, perhaps by way of
> contrast, the melancholy out-of-luck Negro, shiftless, doleful, "easy"; the
> kind that tempts the world to lay its hand none too lightly upon him. The
> pursuit took him years, but at length he was able to portray for us not only
> that "typical Negro" which the white world thinks is universal but the special
> types of given districts and localities with their own foibles of walk and speech
> and jargon. (163–64)

J. Fauset's ethnic reflections on the essence of Negro laughter may explain what
separates the comic realism of Fisher, and his almost traditional use of the

trickster/con man, from the different modes of irony and bitter humor that may be seen as characteristic of Walrond's or McKay's fiction. Their easygoing use of the vernacular seems more natural, less rigidly stultified in the stereotypes, or African-Americans' reactions to the stereotypes, of dialect and of black American minstrelsy.

In "The Paradox of Color," Walter White also emphasizes differences in racial divisions and hierarchies between the two societies. To the dual black-white racial opposition of the United States, he opposes a "tripartite" West Indian societal structure (whites, blacks, and mulattos). Thus, cultural difference is seen to explain racial psychological attitudes that create "color lines within the color lines" and, consequently, underlie the black supremacy stance that prevails among West Indian Negroes and is best illustrated in Garveyism (366–67).[18] Yet as White's own article tends to show, racial reality is certainly more complex than this ethnic explanation would suggest. "Passing," a recurrent theme in Harlem Renaissance fiction and a practice, of course, vigorously denounced by White, negatively signals the existence of similar social and color hierarchies in the African-American community. Conversely, the racial confusion described in Eric Walrond's short story "The Palm Porch" denies the simple tripartite division that would characterize Caribbean societies.[19] Moreover, because race pride is at the core of the New Negro Renaissance, color is the object of lyrical descriptions by both African-American and Caribbean authors who exalt the richness and beauty of blackness in its various shades.

The tensions that arise from this ambivalence in the West Indians' status point to similar tensions between a Negro American nationalism and the larger definition of the Harlem Renaissance's concept of *négritude*. This is most interestingly seen in Locke's various articles describing the Americanization of the Negro and the impact of the New Negro Renaissance in the democratization of American racial attitudes (see, for instance, 10–12). Locke's descriptions of this period of transformation rely in part on his recurrent and ambiguous use of the word "*gift*," which conveys the two different meanings of "offering" and "talent," signifying the almost contradictory implications of an innate racial genius and a conscious cultural construct—as, for instance, when he writes, "The South has unconsciously absorbed the *gift* of his folk temperament," or "A second crop of the Negro's *gifts* promises still more largely" (15; my emphases).

This image is mostly developed in his second article, "Negro Youth Speaks," which opens with "The Younger Generation comes, bringing its *gifts*. They are the first *fruits* of the Negro Renaissance" (47), in which, from a mention of "the *instinctive gift* of the folk spirit" (51), we are led to the following ambiguous assertion:

Art cannot disdain the *gift* of a natural irony, of a transfiguring imagination, of rhapsodic Biblical speech, of dynamic musical swing, of cosmic emotion such as only the *gifted* pagans knew, of a return to nature, not by the way of the forced and worn formula of Romanticism, but through the closeness of an imagination that has never broken kinship with nature. Art must accept such *gifts* and revaluate the *giver.* (53; my emphases)

This gift metaphor, which is obviously central to Locke's cultural Negro nationalism,[20] is to be found in various titles and in several articles by other contributors, who are somehow reflecting Locke's (or DuBois's) ideas on the New Negro. The first paragraph of J. Fauset's "The Gift of Laughter," for instance, also plays on the ambiguous meaning of the word:

The black man bringing *gifts,* and particularly the *gift* of laughter, to the American stage is easily the most anomalous, the most inscrutable figure of the century. All about him and within himself stalks the conviction that, like the Irish, the Russian, the Magyar, he has *some peculiar offering* which shall contain the *very essence* of the drama. Yet the medium through which the unique and intensely dramatic *gift* might be *offered. . . .* (162, my emphases)

The gift metaphor thus appears as providing an imaginary space for the tensions resulting from the American black cultural nationalism that sustains the collection.

Herskovits's essay "The Negro's Americanism" betrays similar tensions in the presentation of a cultural theory that emphasizes a process of acculturation: "All racial and social elements in our population who live here long enough become acculturated, Americanized in the truest sense of the word, eventually." Yet, two paragraphs before, adopting a more essentialist view of race, Herskovits claimed, "Even the spirituals are an expression *of the emotion of the Negro* playing through the typical religious patterns of white America." Insisting on this innate specific trait, he then paradoxically adds

But from *that emotional quality in the Negro,* which is *to be sensed* rather than measured, comes the feeling that though strongly acculturated to the prevalent pattern of behavior, the Negroes may, at the same time, influence it somewhat eventually *through the appeal of that quality.* (359; my emphases)

However, no such ambiguity prevails in Elise Johnson McDougald's "The Task of Negro Womanhood," which opposes the usual racial stereotype and, in a distorted echo of Herskovits's acculturation process, pointedly claims that the Negro woman's *"emotional and sex life is a reflex of her economic station.* The women of the working class will react, emotionally and sexually, similar to the working class woman of other races. . . . Sex irregularities are *not a matter of race, but of socio-economic conditions. . . .* There is no proof of *inherent* weakness in the ethnic group" (379; my emphases).

The tensions thus revealed in various expressions of Locke's cultural nationalism also involve the internationalism contained in his construct of the New Negro. Described as an "outlet" for the American Negro's revived energy, it develops with his "consciousness of acting as the advance-guard of the African peoples in their contact with Twentieth Century civilization" (14) and gives rise to a missionary spirit of leadership that becomes even more explicit in Locke's evaluation of Garveyism.

> With the American Negro, his new internationalism is primarily an effort to recapture contact with the *scattered peoples* of African derivation. Garveyism may be a transient, if spectacular, phenomenon, but the possible role of *the American Negro* in the future development of Africa is *one of the most constructive and universally helpful missions* that any modern people can lay claim to. (15; my emphases)

In this all-englobing vision, the American South is seen as evolving from the Negro "peasant matrix" into an acculturation process that almost reverses Herskovits's claim of the Americanization of the Negro inasmuch as, according to Locke, "The South has unconsciously absorbed the *gift* of his [the Negro's] folk-temperament." The southern Negro is then made into the symbol of the tropics, to the point of incorporating, in Locke's description, Domingo's *leaven* metaphor mentioned before (348): "In less than half a generation it will be easier to recognize this, but the fact remains that a *leaven* of humor, sentiment, imagination and *tropic nonchalance* has gone in the making of the South from a humble, unacknowledged source" (15; my emphases throughout). The multi-ethnic composition of the New Negro is almost denied in Locke's *The New Negro,* in which the Negro Renaissance has effectively come to be seen as a purely African-American messianism.

However, in spite of James Weldon Johnson's description of "Harlem: The Culture Capital" (301–11), which projects a multicultural American image of the social and ideological context, and in opposition to the New Negro image presented by the various African-American contributors, W. A. Domingo's article (341–49) makes clear that the Americanization of the West Indian remains problematic. If America has played its "usual role in the meeting, mixing and welding of the colored peoples of the earth" (341), and the West Indians, "unlike others of the foreign-born, . . . are inevitably swallowed up in Black Harlem" (342), they still remain foreigners within the African-American community. Such a situation is explained by the residential concentration and the economic success of the West Indian immigrants, also evoked in James Weldon Johnson's article (307), and is here described by Domingo as the "Gifts of the Black Tropics."

Domingo's portrait of the West Indian community mildly but firmly insists on the particularities of the West Indian experience, offering as "*a gift*" (an offering, not an innate talent) of these "black tropics" another different history of racial consciousness. It is indeed the history of a racial majority, which reveals a political awareness that looms high in its spirit of revolt and protest. This West Indian tradition of resistance—which Houston Baker also evokes at length in his treatment of *marronnage* (*Modernism and the Harlem Renaissance)*—is seen as symbolized by, or symbolic of, McKay's poetry. The last two lines of McKay's poem "If We must Die" are quoted by Domingo as the conclusion of his essay and as an illustration of the West Indians' "dominant characteristic . . . of blazing new paths, breaking the bonds that would fetter the feet of a virile people—a spirit eloquently expressed in the defiant lines of the Jamaican poet, Claude McKay" (349).

Through this vindication of a West Indian's ethnic identity, Domingo also suggests a broadening of the role of the African-American in the world as well as in the political independence of the foreign Negro communities subjected to European rule. Domingo's Pan-Africanism, here evoked in its West Indian developments (whatever its Garveyite avatars), leads to DuBois's vision in "The Negro Mind Reaches Out" (385), which concludes *The New Negro.*

In contrast to the emphasis put on the Negro's Americanization in the great majority of the essays presented in the anthology, this opening onto the world scene is what most characterizes the West Indian intellectuals' contributions to *The New Negro*.[21] This "reaching out of the Negro's mind" may be found in Schomburg's emphasis on the significance of the concept of Negro history in "The Negro Digs up his Past" (231) and in the presentation of his bibliographical research, both of which aim at enlarging the knowledge of the Negro beyond the confines of the United States. It is also occasionally present in Rogers's article "Jazz at Home," in his references to a larger tradition and sense of rhythm as, for instance, in his evocation of Jamaican music. According to N. Huggins, such a larger outlook may be set in opposition to the African-American provincialism that explains some of the failings of the Harlem Renaissance[22] and, in its most puritanical form, has resulted in the utter rejection of Walrond's or McKay's prose fiction as voyeuristic or sexist exoticism.

Induced by the Caribbean political and economic situation or, for the intellectual, by the isolation of the islands,[23] the more or less forced migrations of the West Indians certainly account for this opening upon horizons wider than the limited vision of the common American Negro experience might allow. Beyond the individual personality and experience, it is this West Indian trait that apparently makes for the restlessness and vagrancy common to McKay's and Walrond's lives and themes; yet, for very similar reasons that may have more to do with personality and race than ethnicity, L. Hughes's "I Wonder as

I Wander" echoes McKay's "All my life I have been a troubadour wanderer, nourishing myself mainly on the poetry of existence" that concludes *A Long Way from Home*,[24] or the feeling of uprootedness that characterizes Walrond's *Tropic Death*.

Domingo's use of the phrase "Black Tropics" indicates an extension of the West Indian entity to the whole region—thus avoiding the use of the pejorative "West Indian" denomination. Resisting the fragmentation that is the historical heritage of the Caribbean colonial past, the West Indian entity is here recurrently denominated and defined as regional: "the Black Tropics." Foreign to the American scene, as shown in McKay's "Tropics in New York," this ethnicity cannot be reduced to the mere innate "tropic nonchalance" that, to Locke, characterizes the southern Negro (15).

Walrond's short story "The Palm Porch" is not only *foreign* but also directly antagonistic to Locke's vision of the construction and Americanization of the New Negro, which is expressed in the metaphor of a dam. To Locke,

> The racialism of the negro is no limitation or reservation with respect to American life; it is only a *constructive effort to build the obstructions in the stream of his progress into an efficient dam of social energy and power.* Democracy itself is *obstructed* and *stagnated* to the extent that any of its *channels* are closed. . . . Fortunately there are *constructive channels* opening out into which the balked social feelings of the American Negro can flow freely. (12–13; my emphases throughout)

In contrast to Locke's metaphorical construct and in a more real setting, Walrond's short story describes the building of the Panama Canal and the ensuing destruction of the original landscape by the Americans' intrusion that symbolically announces a "Tropic death."

> Before the Revolution it was a black, evil forest-swamp. Deer, lions, mongooses and tiger cats went prowling through it. Then the Americans came . . . with saw and spear, tar and Lysol. About to rid it . . . molten city . . . of its cancer, fire swept it up on the bosom of the lagoon. Naked, virgin tree; limbless. Gaunt, hollow stalks. Huge shadows falling. . . . Dredges in the golden mist; dredges on the lagoon. Horny iron pipes spouted over the fetid swamp. Noise; grating noise. Earth stones, up from the bowels of the earth, rattled against the ribs of scaly pipes like popping corn. Crackling corn. Water, red, black gray, gushed out of big, bursting pipes. For miles people heard it lap-lapping. Dark as the earth, it flung on its crest stones, pearls, sharks' teeth . . . jewels of the sunken sea. Frogs, vermin, tangled things. . . . (115)

Walrond's *Tropic Death* evokes a Gothic world of colonial and imperial decadence which has been seen to draw its inspiration from Lafcadio Hearn and Conrad.[25] Set in the context of Locke's anthology, the Gothicism of this first version of "The Palm Porch" is not only "pessimistic," as J. Berry defines it (299), but also reads as a bitter and sharp provocation.[26] Berry's analysis, however, concurs with my interpretation of this passage in relation to the different uses of the frontier imagery in *The New Negro:*

> Walrond also comments on imperialism and on the effects of modernization and technological advancement on undeveloped countries. "The Palm Porch" opens with a harsh and ironic comment, replete with traditional American images, such as the new frontier and the virgin land. He equates the construction of the Panama canal with the expansion of the American frontier. (299)

Walrond's alleged morbidity has often been set in contrast with Toomer's elegiac stance, thus opposing the Caribbean writer's artificiality to the African-American purer style. Although the *New Negro* version of Walrond's story, for some unclear reason, seems to adopt and reproduce Toomer's modernist techniques, Walrond's overly decorative baroque style and irregular rhythms in "The Palm Porch" are again *foreign* to Toomer's controlled and self-contained descriptions in "Fern" and "Carma." Like other short stories in *The New Negro,* "The Palm Porch" presents an abundant number of suspension dots that signal the impact of Toomer's imagist style. These, however, have disappeared in the book version of Walrond's story published in 1926, where narrative and characters are more consistent, the plot less obscurely elliptic, as if the author, changing models (or away from Locke's supervision), was coming closer to what would now be called *surrealistic realism.*[27] For this reason and because of the choice of its themes, *Tropic Death* may not so much relate to an American imagist modernism, or a French literary tradition of exoticism, as it announces the South American literature that will come out of the *modernismo,*[28] or even more so, the work of recent Caribbean writers from Guyana, such as Edgar Mittelholzer or Wilson Harris.

"The Palm Porch" was not included in the 1925 *Survey Graphic,* "Harlem, Mecca of the New Negro," although Walrond had played a part in the famous dinner that gave birth to this first journalistic event, and its inclusion in Locke's *The New Negro* obviously came as an afterthought. As early as 1923, however, *Opportunity* had begun publishing short stories by Walrond who, in 1925, joined the staff of *Opportunity* as its business manager.[29] As Owens notes: "It was during this period with *Opportunity* that the wealthy Virgin Islander and numbers banker Casper Holstein offered financial support for the journal's writers contest" (Owens 157). This dual West Indian influence can be seen in the Caribbean *Opportunity* issue that came out one year after *The New Negro* and offered a more bitter and radical interpretation of the intraracial debate, thus bringing to light some of the ambiguity of the West Indian intellectuals' stance in the New Negro political and cultural debate.[30]

Although it follows the pattern set up by Locke—alternating literary pieces and analytical essays—the Caribbean *Opportunity* issue, if less ambitious, is also essentially more informative than illustrative, in conformity with the journal's tradition.[31] By reason of this factual presentation, this issue somehow defeats the purpose of *The New Negro*—and perhaps its own purpose. Addressing American-born Negroes, it intends to bring out differences which, if ignored, make for misunderstanding and conflicts between peoples "of the same blood, and in the United States of the same status," who are living in a society in which "the single inexorable presence of race . . . proceeds on the assumption that being alike, they are the same" (Caribbean issue of *Opportunity* 334). The editorial board (with Walrond's assistance) no longer claims an emergent New Negro culture in which the West Indians would be participating by offering their tropical gifts, but rather aims at "an essential friendship through [the] conviction that friendships usually follow the knowing of one's neighbors" (334).

The journal accordingly proceeds to describe the historical and geopolitical context of the Caribbean in relation to the United States. In the three articles by Domingo and Virgin Islanders Judge Malmin and Casper Holstein, this description actually turns into a stringent denunciation of the drastic effects of American military occupation and hegemony in the Caribbean. Recurrently the authors evoke the situation in Puerto Rico, Haiti, and the Virgin Islands, in contrast to a more open and less destructive Danish, or British, colonial domination. Just as pointedly, they bring up the question of the United States' restrictive immigration legislation and its denial of citizens' rights in the Virgin Islands under U.S. Navy rule. In a second series of two articles, W. Malliett and A. Schomburg describe the intellectual, professional, and artistic achievements of the West Indies as a contribution to the American New Negro culture, but, even more so, as evidence of a Caribbean inviolate cultural entity.

Almost paradoxically set in the middle of this radical context of ethnic domination and exclusion, E. Franklin Frazier's essay makes a return to the American scene with a sociological analysis of Garvey's leadership. Set between these two exclusively Caribbean sections, Frazier's essay places Garvey's movement in the historical context of a Negro community dominated by the black church, where it no longer appears as a West Indian epiphenomenon, but as the only African-American mass movement.

Similarly, but also more ironically, Waldo Frank's "In *our* Language" (my emphasis) presents a review of Walrond's *Tropic Death* as one of the West Indies' cultural achievements. This essay appears as a muddled attempt to define an all-englobing American language that might include and thus redeem Walrond's "unaccountable" ethnic style: "Mr Walrond who, for all I know may be a subject of the King, *is* in his language an American. And I hereby claim him!" In that context Frank's ethnocentrist conclusion rings with almost racist overtones, revealing an utter blindness to the West Indian reality described at length in the issue and also betraying a simplistic disregard of Caribbean culture. In a narrow interpretation of the American modernist ideals of a return to a true and original "folk culture,"[32] Frank patronizingly reminds Walrond that "Perhaps one of your ancestors was a Caribbean peasant. When he wielded the hoe or the knife, did he not grasp it loose in his brown hand? Do you likewise with your language. Let your fine instrument lie easy in a palm half-open" (352).

In spite of "A Symposium," which, as a conclusion, presents successively two personal views on this ethnic conflict and ends on a note of noncommittal wishful thinking, the *Opportunity* Caribbean issue reads as the expression of a dissonance that had been more or less muted in *The New Negro*. It brings forth the reality of intraracial and ethnic tensions that cannot be ignored in the light of the conflicts resulting from American hegemony in the Caribbean. From a cultural point of view, it also reveals the precarious status of Walrond and McKay as vanguard writers from the Caribbean in the United States.[33]

Indeed, Walrond and, to a lesser degree, McKay are most often evaluated by American critics within the American literary context and tradition, to the detriment, at least, of the former who has been dismissed as too foreignly exotic. From a Caribbean perspective, Walrond and, to a lesser degree again, McKay are defined as those "lost West Indian writers" "who ran away,"[34] thus estranging themselves from their native literary tradition. They are then seen in contrast to a later generation of Caribbean writers who managed to build up a literary front and organization in their London exile in the 1950s and 1960s. New waves of migration from the Caribbean to the recent poles of attraction of the United States and Canada may help bring about a stronger recognition of those writers whom Frank Birbalsingh defines, in the title of his 1996 book, as being on the *Frontiers of Caribbean Literature in English*.

In a later period of redefinition of the African-American identity, the special issue of *Freedomways* on "The People of the Caribbean Area," published in 1964, may be seen as an effort to reenact, in defense of the Caribbean people, the attempt previously made by the 1920s civil rights leaders to advance the African-American cause through Locke's manifesto. It also echoes, however, many of the claims and bitter criticisms made, some forty years before, by the West Indians intellectuals in *The New Negro*, or even more so in the Caribbean issue of *Opportunity*, thus attesting to the difficulty of breaking down the barriers that define a national, racial, or cultural territory.

1. All references to *The New Negro*, henceforward abbreviated as NN, refer to the 1992 edition presented by A. Rampersad.

2. See, in Irma Watkins Owens, the following figures quoted from the U.S. Bureau of the Census and other demographic sources: "There were 20,336 foreign-born blacks in the United States in 1900; 73,803 in 1920; and 98,620 in 1930. Only 8,500 entered the country between 1925 and 1930, reflecting the effect of the 1924 law. Many of the latter individuals were the immediate family members of naturalized citizens. However these do not include migrants from the U.S. Virgin Islands or the estimated 43,452 native-born black persons of foreign-born parentage. By 1930 the number of the foreign-born or the children of foreign-born was 150,000. Approximately 50 percent of these individuals lived in New York City" (186–87 n.11).

3. See particularly Harold Cruse's rather ferocious indictment of the West Indian community's political role in Harlem. This conflictual situation is also mentioned in G. Osofsky's and N. Huggins's studies; D. Lewis and G. Hutchinson focus more specifically on the cultural and literary significance of the West Indian writers and intellectuals who were active in the Negro Renaissance movement; even more so, J. Anderson's *This Was Harlem* devotes a whole chapter to the West Indians of Harlem. A more pro-Caribbean viewpoint is offered in the W.B. Turner and J. Moore Turner presentation of Caribbean militant P.B. Moore's life in Harlem and, as previously indicated, Irma Watkins Owens provides a most useful sociological and cultural analysis of Harlem's Caribbean migrant community between 1905 and 1925. Winston James's book on Caribbean radicalism offers a detailed and fully documented criticism of Cruse's thesis. For full citation of these works and the following, see the bibliography of this volume.

4. Joyce Turner remarks, "I still find it fascinating that Cyril Briggs wrote in 1918 that his magazine, *The Crusader*, would be dedicated to a 'renaissance of negro power and culture throughout the world'" (W.B. and J.M. Turner 34–35 and 14 n.19).

5. See G. Hutchinson's "Producing *The New Negro*: An Interpretation" in *Harlem Renaissance in Black and White* (432–33).

6. As W. James indicates, however, "Recent scholarship runs against this accepted notion," because Russwurm was not the first, but the third, black person to get an American college degree (296 n.7).

7. Owens quotes a September 1920 article in *The Crisis*, in which DuBois foresees the role of this "mass of peasants" whom he claims have "among them very few illiterates or criminals. . . . It is not beyond possibility that this new Ethiopia of the Isles may yet stretch out hands of helpfulness to the 12 million black men of America." Owens underlines that, on the contrary, within the Caribbean migration, "Only 14 percent entering between 1901 and 1935 were classified as agricultural workers according to the *Reports of the Commissioner of Immigration*," and that this "mass," in fact, constituted "a small but visible educated elite—a Caribbean 'Talented Tenth'" (3).

8. See Martin's two studies, *Literary Garveyism* and *African Fundamentalism*.

9. However, Domingo, as did other West Indians, reacted to the xenophobia that accompanied this affair. In a letter to *Opportunity* in 1923, he violently criticized the insulting xenophobic stereotype used by A. Philip Randolph against Garvey (the famous "Jamaican jackass"). In opposition, Domingo mentioned DuBois's avoidance of ethnic references concerning this painful affair in *The Crisis* and in a letter to him. This

letter is mentioned by W. James out of context and only in relation to DuBois's pride in his West Indian descent as well as to the American Negroes' deep obligations to the West Indians (James 2). This conflictual intraracial debate would continue after the publication of *The New Negro* in the November 1926 *Opportunity* issue on the Caribbean under Walrond's editorship.

10. Although this fact is totally ignored in Martin's two books mentioned previously, W.B. Turner and J. Moore Turner show that "Domingo had served as editor of [Garvey's] *The Negro World* from its inception in August 1918 to July 1919 and as contributing editor of *The Messenger* commencing with the July 1919 issue." They also indicate that "he and Moore launched *The Emancipator* in March of 1920 with the assistance of other socialists." "*The Emancipator* is notable not only for its radical stance but for its attacks on Garvey. By 1920 the widening ideological differences between the socialists and Garvey had resulted in open conflict. A movement to remove Garvey from the scene had been initiated by such figures as Randolph, Owen, and Domingo, and *The Emancipator* was one of several periodicals that attempted to expose Garvey" (W.B. and J.M. Turner 32). The same data is presented from a very critical perspective by Cruse in section II, chapter 1 of his book and appears as a recurring theme throughout his book. See also W. James's refutation of Cruse's thesis (262–91).

11. See his introduction to the recent edition of *The New Negro* (1992), pages xx to xxi, in which he quotes Garvey's "gallant message" to the *Survey Graphic* issue on Harlem and also quotes Levering Lewis's comments on the exclusions that characterize the almost noncommittal political stance of the anthology.

12. In his essay on C.S. Johnson in *Harlem Renaissance Remembered* (223), Patrick J. Gilpin describes the large range of topics related to racial politics in the United States and in the rest of the world that were debated in *Opportunity*. Owens insists on Walrond's influence on Johnson's larger global perspectives and sees Walrond as largely responsible for suggesting publication of the *Opportunity* Caribbean issue of November 1926 (Owens 157).

13. The *Survey Graphic* version of this essay was less figuratively entitled "Black Workers and the City."

14. Franklin W. Knight, in his introduction to the biography of B.P. Moore, also uses similar American ideological images: referring to the Caribbean emigration of West Indians to the United States in the 1820s, he compares them to "a Caribbean counterpart to Manifest Destiny" (5)—an interesting contamination of American ideological metaphors.

15. These stylistic remarks do not exactly corroborate Hutchinson's analysis of Locke's racial theory, as developed in part I, chapter 3 of the former's book.

16. As Jervis Anderson comments in *This Was Harlem*, "The view among their critics in Harlem was that while they enjoyed the privileges of residency, they were content to shirk the burdens and responsibilities of American citizenship" (303). On this issue, see Owens (82–86).

17. See also J. Anderson's description of this comedian (*This Was Harlem* 36–43).

18. Owens also comments on White's interpretation of the color issue in Harlem, noting that "a predominantly light-skinned African-American elite held on to leadership positions and denied the color issue validity in political discourse" (215 n.37).

19. On the racial confusion in "The Palm Porch," G. Hutchinson remarks, "Walrond . . . consciously *flouts* the North American obsession with racial definability" (409;

my emphasis), without mentioning that Walrond's attitude to color was, in fact, very much Caribbean.

20. Yet Locke here seems to have followed DuBois's lead in the ambiguous use of this word. See, for instance, DuBois's chapter 14, "Of the Sorrow Songs," in *The Souls of Black Folk* (1903), his *The Gift of Black Folk* (1924), and his *Survey Graphic* article, "The Black Man brings his Gifts."

21. A point also emphasized by F.W. Franklin, for whom the interests of the West Indian "small, vocal, active community of radicals centered in Harlem . . . were without national boundaries" (in W.B. and J.M. Turner 9). Yet, according to W. James, Schomburg's stance regarding race was "rather anomalous" among the Puerto Rican political refugees (101). In contrast, the bibliographical references concerning magazines established by Locke does not list any of the Harlem West Indian periodicals (NN 450).

22. See Huggins's various interpretations of this trait in reference to culture, the arts, and music, which are summed up in his introduction (8–9).

23. See Owens, ch. 2: "Panama Silver meets Jim Crow."

24. Michael B. Stoff, in "Claude McKay and the Cult of Primitivism" (*Harlem Renaissance Remembered* 142–43), presents an interesting analysis of McKay's "troubadour wanderer."

25. Robert Bone in *Down Home* (185–93) analyzes Hearn's personality and influence on Walrond.

26. In the same way, McKay's "Baptism" can be read as a subversion of the melting pot theme. As will be seen subsequently, in the *Tropic Death* version of the story, this bitter indictment of American imperialism is very much reduced.

27. See the purposefully long excerpt from the introduction of the story in the version previously quoted. It has almost completely disappeared in *Tropic Death*, and what remains of it is a much more realistic description of the setting of the story, which has almost entirely lost its previous symbolic function.

28. See G. Hutchinson's comment on the Harlem Renaissance writers' relation to modernism and *modernismo* (118–20). Analyzing Walrond's *Tropic Death*, he defines it as "a far more complicated case of the American [!] pan-African reach of The New Negro" (408–10). He also comments on Waldo Frank's review of *Tropic Death*, which reads strangely paradoxical in regard to Frank's former appreciation of Toomer's *Cane* (see the correspondence between the two writers [1922–1923] and Franck's introduction to the first edition of that work). Hutchinson, however, does not consider Franck's review in the context of the Caribbean *Opportunity* issue in which it was published.

29. By 1926, five of Walrond's short stories had appeared in the National Urban League's journal. The last of this series, "The Voodoo's Revenge," was awarded a third prize in the magazine's literary contest of 1925 (J. Berry 296).

30. Neither H. Cruse nor W. James mentions this *Opportunity* issue, their focus being mainly on West Indian radicals. Hutchinson and Owens deal more precisely with certain specific aspects of the journal, respectively, as concerns Waldo Franck's criticism of *Tropic Death* and Eric Walrond's Caribbean influence as a journalist.

31. See Hutchinson 57. All the West Indian intellectuals who participated in *The New Negro* are also represented in *Opportunity*, except for J.A. Rogers, whose name however appears in the "Who's Who" of the contributors, and Walrond who acts as the *deus ex machina*. In *Opportunity*, however, they all serve different functions. New contributors are Judge Lucius J.M. Malmin and Casper Holstein with essays on the

Virgin Islands, and the Jamaican journalist A.M. Wendell Malliet, who presents "Some Prominent West Indians."

32. See Hutchinson 84.

33. As shown by Franck's review of *Tropic Death,* Walrond's case, much more so than McKay's, has become central in this issue on the Caribbean.

34. See Kenneth Ramchand's 1970 article ("The Writer Who Ran Away: Eric Walrond and *Tropic Death,*" *Savacou,* vol. no. 2). Ramchand had made a passing reference to Walrond in his *The West Indian Novel and its Background* (London: Heinemann, 1983), quoting Robert Bone's brief bibliographical remark on some Negro novelists who, because of their national origins, had not been included in his study *The Negro Novel in America* (New Haven and London: Yale University Press, 1958). Curiously enough, both these critics later on came back upon their first bypassings of the "Guyanese" novelist and devoted fuller attention to the author of *Tropic Death.*

16. Three Ways to Translate the Harlem Renaissance

Brent Hayes Edwards

Whether in the words of Alain Locke, Hubert Harrison, Jane Nardal, or W. E. B. DuBois, the point that the modern phenomenon of the New Negro is international resurfaces time and time again in black expression between the world wars. In *The New Negro,* Locke goes so far as to claim that the Negro's newness is closely related to his "new internationalism," which represents one of the few "constructive channels" for black expression beyond the "cramped horizons" of postwar U.S. racism and brutality.[1] New Negro internationalism, evidenced for Locke by the proliferation in the 1920s of a multilingual and "cosmopolitan" black print culture and by transnational organizations like the Pan-African Congress, "is primarily an effort to recapture contact with the scattered peoples of African derivation" (NN 14–15).

But correspondence and "recaptured" contact among peoples of African descent is only one strategy in what Nathan Huggins has described as the "post-war effort to thrust Negro social thought into an international arena."[2] Black intellectuals and activists were especially eager to participate in the institutional discourses of internationalism that developed in the West after World War I, particularly through the League of Nations. For instance, DuBois conceived of the Pan-African Congress in part as a means to influence the Versailles Peace Conference meetings on the question of former German colonies in Africa, intending to interject a black voice into the growing discourse of international civil society because he was certain that institutions such as the League would be at the center of postwar global power. "I went to Paris because today the destinies of mankind center there," he told the readers of *The Crisis.*[3]

Likewise, the radicalization of Marcus Garvey was rooted not just in the race riots of the "Red Summer" of 1919, but also in the international implications of that unrest, particularly in terms of labor revolts in the Caribbean. This concern led directly to the emergence of the "Magna Carta" of the Universal Negro Improvement Association (UNIA), the "Declaration of the Rights of the Negro Peoples of the World" adopted at the 1920 international convention, and also to the UNIA's many attempts throughout the decade to organize transnationally, both in the Americas and in Africa itself (in Liberia in particular).[4] The point is that even given their pronounced political differences, interwar black intellectuals such as Locke, DuBois, and Garvey shared what we might term an internationalist imperative, continually articulating the "race problem as a world problem."[5]

This imperative is belied by much of the scholarship on the period, which has tended to emphasize seemingly nation-bound themes of cultural nationalism, civil rights, and uplift in the "Harlem Renaissance."[6] This essay will be a necessarily preliminary attempt to come to terms with the reminders of a handful of scholars such as Michel Fabre, Melvin Dixon, and Robert Stepto that "the Renaissance was international in scale both in terms of where its contributors came from and in terms of its being merely the North American component of something larger and grander. . . ."[7] Although black intellectuals in the period do not explicitly use the term, I understand this facet of the Renaissance as the emergence of a complex black discourse of diaspora in the interwar period—a discourse arising out of the Old Testament metaphorology that Locke, for one, alludes to in charting the "effort to recapture contact with the scattered peoples of African derivation," and in arguing more pointedly that "As with the Jew, persecution is making the Negro international" (14).

Rather than simply investigate the ways that U.S. black intellectuals imagined the African diaspora, however, I will take up this theme by reading three flash points of a particular conjuncture of black internationalist discourses—the long-running dialogue between United States–based English-speaking writers and their Francophone counterparts. Although the few critics who have engaged this issue have generally concentrated on the ideological differences and representational conundrums that fracture any articulation of diaspora, I will pay particular attention to the work of language difference among groups of African descent, which (as much as ideology or representation) is at the root of what Kenneth Warren has called "the ambiguities that inhere in diasporic thought—ambiguities that make diasporic visions possible."[8]

It has already been recognized that one way to consider the diasporic stirrings in the Renaissance is to consider the black presence in France.[9] About 200,000 African-Americans served in the segregated U.S. armed forces during the First World War, and more than half spent at least some time in Europe.

There, working mainly on the docks and in supply units, they were introduced to a scarred French countryside not at all reminiscent of the Jim Crow South. Along with a warm reception from the French people, African-American soldiers encountered the tangible presence of soldiers of color from throughout the French Empire (tens of thousands from the French Caribbean and more than 135,000 from French West Africa alone by 1918) and colonial workers imported into France throughout the war (about 300,000, both from elsewhere in Europe and from the colonies). Although France repatriated the great majority of the colonials, in 1926 there were still about 10,000 Caribbean students and workers and 1500 black African workers in Paris alone.[10]

This is nowhere near the concentration of peoples of African descent in Harlem, but was still the seeds of a vibrant cosmopolitan black community. After the war, tales of encounter and connection, forged in the trenches and on the docks, traveled back to the United States with the American fighting forces. Some U.S. blacks stayed in France to study or to perform, most gravitating to Paris—for Paris had simultaneously come to appreciate jazz and *l'art nègre*, partly through the performances of military music units like James Reese Europe's 369th Infantry Regiment "Hellfighters" Band, and postwar musicians such as Louis Mitchell's Jazz Kings, Palmer Jones's International Five, Cricket Smith, Eugene Bullard, Ada "Bricktop" Smith, and Florence Embry Jones.[11]

The literary culture of the Renaissance emerges to a significant extent in the transnational circuits of black culture that flourished after the First World War, particularly through France. When one considers the extensive travels of the New Negro culture makers, the exceptions are those who did not travel. Not even to mention musicians, performers, and visual artists, almost all of the major literary figures of the period—including Anna Julia Cooper, Claude McKay, Walter White, Gwendolyn Bennett, Countée Cullen, Langston Hughes, Alain Locke, James Weldon Johnson, Jessie Fauset, J. A. Rogers, Jean Toomer, Eric Walrond, and Nella Larsen—spent time abroad (and in France in particular) in the 1920s. It is often overlooked that early Francophone intellectuals were equally mobile: René Maran was born in Martinique and educated in Bordeaux, and was a colonial officer in central Africa before settling in Paris after publishing his prize-winning novel *Batouala* in 1921.[12] The Dahomean lawyer Kojo Tovalou Houénou, the founder of the journal *Les Continents* and the *Ligue Universelle de Défense de la Race Noire* in 1924, gave a speaking tour in the United States in 1924 (in New York, he appeared at the convention of Garvey's UNIA), published in *The Crisis* and *Opportunity*, and shuttled between Paris and Porto-Novo, often delivering copies of U.S. publications such as Garvey's *Negro World* to West Africa.[13] Louis Achille, the Martinican scholar, taught at Howard University in the early 1930s and later founded a choir in Lyon that specialized in Negro spirituals. Tiemoko Garan Kouyaté, the black radical who was born in the French Sudan (now Mali) but studied in Senegal before coming to Europe, moved as a propagandist and labor organizer between Paris, the South of France, Hamburg, and Moscow. Many of these figures invested in one way or another in the notion of Harlem as a worldwide black culture capital, and yet many of them met and exchanged ideas in Paris, which came to function as a kind of "gateway to Africa" for African-American intellectuals. Tyler Stovall describes this dynamic well:

> The part played by Paris in the African-American rediscovery of Africa was both fascinating and deeply ironic. After all, the city was the seat of one of the world's great colonial empires, a place where anonymous French officials supervised the subjugation of millions of black Africans. . . . Outside of Marseilles, London, and some other British cities, one could not find a more diverse black population anywhere in Europe. More so than in the United States, even New York, African-Americans found that in Paris the abstract ideal of worldwide black unity and culture became a tangible reality. . . . French colonialism and primitivism thus paradoxically combined to foster a vision of pan-African unity. (Stovall 1996, 90)

A vision of internationalism, perhaps, though not exactly "Pan-African unity": for the "black counterculture of modernity" (in Paul Gilroy's phrase) emerging between the two world wars must be read, perhaps most importantly, to be counter to itself, necessarily affected by the paradoxes Stovall signals. In these transnational circuits, black modern expression takes form not as a single thread, but through the often uneasy encounters of black peoples with each other. If during the 1920s, black discourses and cultural artifacts can be said to proliferate strikingly as products in motion, this exchange is never a neat and happy call and response between blacks in different places in the diaspora. It is equally shaped by a profound series of misapprehensions, misreadings, persistent blindnesses, and solipsisms, a series of self-defeating and abortive collaborations, a failure to translate even a basic grammar of blackness.

In part, black and brown encounters on the Seine were uneasy because of the African-American habit of thinking about Paris as a liberating cosmopolis, as free of racism, at precisely the height of French colonial exploitation. McKay took the Harlem Renaissance literati to task on precisely this issue:

> The good treatment of individuals by those whom they meet in France is valued so highly by Negroes that they are beginning to forget about the exploitation of Africans by the French. . . . Thus the sympathy of the Negro intelligentsia is completely on the side of France. It is well-informed about the barbarous acts of the Belgians in the Congo but it knows nothing at all about the barbarous acts of the French in Senegal, about the organized robbery of native workers, about the forced enlistment of recruits, about the fact

that the population is reduced to extreme poverty and hunger, or about the total annihilation of tribes. It is possible that the Negro intelligentsia does not want to know about all this, inasmuch as it can loosely generalize about the differences in the treatment of Negroes in bourgeois France and in plutocratic America.[14]

This blindness allowed the Harlem Renaissance intelligentsia to glorify in its own vanguardist myths, as it employed the putative universality of the French "Rights of Man" to decry U.S. racism. In effect, this rhetorical move uses France as a trump card, a reminder that the roots of the Declaration of Independence lie within the "anti-racist" democratic philosophy of the French Revolution. In other words, race is traded in for a certain kind of national currency, an "anti-racism in one country" by default, a complacent U. S.–centrism which McKay finds indefensible.

What is seldom recognized in the numerous condemnations of the Harlem Renaissance as a failure—as myopic, elitist, or insufficiently radical—is the degree to which such failings are in fact constitutive of black modern expression in general, which is shaped to a significant degree by what Kenneth Warren has termed the "necessary misrecognitions" (Warren 404–405) of diasporic discourse. Attempts to foster links among populations of African descent, articulating race as a world-changing force that transcends the boundaries of nation-states and languages, are necessarily skewed by those same boundaries. Diaspora, in other words, is an epistomology of fracture, a "thought whose closure cannot be seen by any one individual nor imagined by any single text" (405). But this characteristic distorts not just the many versions of black internationalism, but also the expressive culture of the Renaissance in general. One sees its impact, for example, even in the ways the movement positions itself in Harlem, the culture capital of the black world. The changing metaphors of Harlem as diasporic center reflect and refract these cracks, resonating with suggestive ambivalence. Harlem is often described with a metaphor that alludes to the different and contemporary prestige of cities in Western modernity: "Overcrowded, vulgar, and wicked, Harlem was Afro-America's Paris," as David Levering Lewis writes.[15] But such metaphors backfire on themselves, clashing with their historical referents, when we are told that the Paris quarter of Montmartre is really "an Afro-American colony," as black figures such as James Weldon Johnson and Noble Sissle claimed (Lewis 85).

The field of black modern expression between the wars is to a large extent shaped by this kind of metaphoric chiasmus. What happens when metaphors clash, when one figurative capital of blackness is defined oddly as a "colony" of another, which in turn defines the essence of the first? To be sure, there is a certain innocence to such talk of African-American camps and colonies in the heart of old Europe: Paris is a kind of outpost of an African-American cultural vanguard whose Harlem-based glory can only be compared to Paris. But one should not ignore the unevenness of these interlocked metaphors, which misrecognize the center of the French empire as itself a "colony." They bend into a configuration where *Paris Noir* is paradoxically pictured as having nothing to do with black French culture, with the Francophone African and Antillean workers, performers, and students who were in the metropole—and it certainly has nothing to do with the black cultures of the French colonies.

In tracking the effects of this transnational context on the literary culture of the Renaissance, the question is not simply who traveled when and where. Instead, one must account for the ways the black modern imaginary of the movement is itself inherently shaped by the ambiguities of diaspora. Consistently, the literary expression of the period engages diaspora, even the texts that are often considered to be paradigmatic articulations of Harlem—as though certain moves, certain arguments and epiphanies, can only be staged beyond the confines of the United States, and even in languages other than English. In other words, what would Nella Larsen's *Quicksand* be without Copenhagen? What would McKay's *Banjo* be without Marseilles, or *Home to Harlem* without its Haitian protagonist, Ray? What would Fauset's *Plum Bun* be without that Paris ending, or her *Comedy: American Style* without its final section set in the South of France? Why does James Weldon Johnson's *The Autobiography of an Ex-Colored Man* place in Berlin the narrator's realization about the possibilities of using folk materials in musical composition? One thinks equally of Hughes's *The Big Sea* or "Jazz Band in a Parisian Cabaret," elaborating a black transnational culture circuit in Europe and Africa, or DuBois's *Dark Princess*, so fascinated with the corridors of international power and intrigue, or Eric Walrond's *Tropic Death*, unraveling the intricacies of imperialism and labor migration in the Caribbean basin.

Similarly, the periodical culture that explodes in the period on both sides of the Atlantic in a steady stream of journals, newspapers, and pamphlets is remarkably interwoven and constantly concerned with the international implications of the "race problem." While stopping through Paris, McKay profiles Houénou for *The Crisis*, while Duke Ellington is interviewed by Jacques Fray in *Documents*. Parisian journals such as *La Dépêche Africaine* and *Europe* publish French versions of key Harlem texts, while the black press in the United States publishes a stream of translations from French and Spanish. *La Race Nègre*, the most important radical newspaper in Paris in the late 1920s, quotes articles from Garvey's *Negro World*. Two of the most vibrant monthly journal columns of the Harlem Renaissance—Cullen's "The Dark Tower" and Gwendolyn Bennett's "The Ebony Flute," both published in *Opportunity*—give almost as much space to events in Europe as to the goings-on in Harlem, reporting on Josephine Baker, French journals such as *La Voix des Nègres*, McKay in the south of France, the *Bal Nègre* in Paris (the Martinican dance hall which featured the beguine), and early Francophone literature. With such a complex outernational host of examples, it would seem difficult to read the Renaissance as structured by a simple center (Harlem) and national periphery.

TRANSLATING THE "NEW NEGRO"

To read the print culture of the Renaissance as constituted by diasporic concerns, one might turn to any number of periodicals, from *The Messenger* in Harlem to *La Voix du Dahomey* in Cotonou, from *Wasu* in London to the *Diario de la Marina* in Havana, from *Le Cri des Nègres* in Paris to *La Revue Indigène* in Port-au-Prince. My first example here is culled from one of the moderate black newspapers in interwar black Paris, Guadeloupean Maurice Satineau's *La Dépêche Africaine*. The inaugural issue of the journal in February 1928 featured an article by Jane Nardal, a Martinican student in Paris, who was as concerned with black participation in international civil society as was DuBois, Locke, or Garvey. Her "L'Internationalisme Noir" (Black Internationalism) opens with a forceful invocation of the world-straddling ambitions and cultural forces of the postwar period:

> In this postwar period, the barriers that had existed between countries are being lowered, or are being pulled down. Will the diversity of frontiers, tariffs, prejudices, customs, religions, and languages ever allow the realization of this project? We would like to hope so, we who affirm the birth at the same time of another movement which is in no way opposed to the first. Negroes [*noirs*] of all origins and nationalities, with different customs and religions, vaguely sense that they belong in spite of everything to a single and same race.[16]

Jane Nardal finds the sources of this developing black internationalism in the cultural and political events of the postwar period: whereas previously, there had only been mutual miscomprehension—with the "more favored" black populations in the Americas looking down on Africans as savages, and the Africans themselves thinking of New World blacks as no more than slaves, subjugated "bétail" (cattle)—in the 1920s another kind of consciousness began to become possible, largely due to the advent of the *vogue nègre* in France and the increasing popularity of the spirituals, jazz, and African art. She concludes her summary history with an espousal of the "birth of racial spirit" in the metropolitan Negro intellectual: "From now on, there will be a certain interest, a certain originality, a certain pride in being Negro [*nègre*], in turning back toward Africa, cradle of the Negroes [nègres], in recalling a common origin. The Negro will perhaps have to do his part in the concert of races, where until now, weak and intimidated, he has been silent."

In theorizing this Negro internationalism, this new diasporic consciousness, however, Nardal is not willing to turn to a language of rootless nationalism that would deny her background and upbringing—what her sister Paulette Nardal elsewhere termed her "formation Latine" [Latin education]. And thus Jane Nardal turns to a neologism:

> For new ideas, new words are required, and thus the meaningful creation of new terms: Afro-Americans, Afro-Latins. These confirm our thesis while throwing a new light on the nature of this black internationalism. If the Negro [nègre] wants to be himself, to affirm his personality, not to be the copy of some type of another race (as often brings him resentment and mockery), it still does not follow that he becomes resolutely hostile to any element from another race. On the contrary, he must profit from acquired experience, from intellectual riches, through others, but in order to better understand himself, to assert his own personality. To be Afro-American, to be Afro-Latin, means to be an encouragement, a comfort, an example for the blacks [noirs] of Africa by showing them that certain benefits of white civilization do not necessarily drive them to deny their race.

One notes the ingenuity of the term "Afro-Latin," which strikes an intriguing parallel to "Afro-American": it is not directly a profession of loyalty to a nation-state or empire, France, but instead an appropriation of a wider cultural heritage of which republican France is a part. Oddly, though, it implies that American and Latin are somehow parallel terms—apparently as both regional and cultural distinctions within a broader Western space. This is not a position espousing biological assimilation or miscegenation (Afro-Americans and Afro-Latins are both "racially" nègres) but one of cultural acculturation within a context of colony-metropole migration ("certain benefits of white civilization do not necessarily drive them to deny their race"). Although Jane Nardal was not a colonial apologist, as were many of the other contributors to La Dépêche Africaine, there is little doubt that her invention of Afro-Latin expresses a political moderation that she shared with the circle that would later coalesce around the bilingual journal La Revue du Monde Noir, founded in 1931 by her sister Paulette and the Haitian dentist Léo Sajous.

In fact, Nardal's conception of Negro internationalism is not unlike that of Locke—above all, in the persistence of its New World Negro vanguardism.[17] One way to comprehend the complexity of this transnational context, of course, is to be attentive to issues of translation, and it should come as no surprise that Jane Nardal had written to Locke at Howard University in 1927, requesting permission to translate The New Negro for the French publisher

Payot, apparently under the title *Le Nouveau Noir*. But for unknown reasons, the project was never carried out. Although *The New Negro* in its original edition remained a touchstone text for the black intellectuals involved with journals such as *La Dépêche Africaine* and *La Race Nègre* in the late 1920s and early 1930s (mainly through the mediation of the intellectuals who read English, such as the Nardal sisters and René Maran), it did not appear in French until the journal *Europe* published a translation of Locke's introductory essay by Louis and Renée Guilloux in 1932, under the title "Le Nègre Nouveau."

What forces are at work in this heterological slippage among the most basic terms of racialization, from *nouveau noir* to *nègre nouveau* over the space of five years? Ultimately, such vexed translation issues are the traces of an argument about the shape of black modernity itself: the ways diasporic thought "crosses," is carried over, and in the process is necessarily re-formed. In the Francophone context, Jane Nardal's "Nouveau Noir" contends most specifically with the radicalism of Communist Party–affiliated African intellectuals such as Lamine Senghor, who was elaborating an anticolonial diasporic vision in part by reclaiming the formerly derogatory term "nègre."[18] Critics such as Henry Louis Gates, Jr., and Lawrence Levine have identified a struggle around the political valence of the appellation "New Negro" among U.S. black intellectuals: the socialist journal *The Messenger* espoused A. Philip Randolph's vision of an irrepressible, militant nationalist "New Negro," while *Opportunity* came to adopt a very different version of that phrase in the image of Locke's cosmopolitan cultural sophisticate.[19] Such competing variations on the New Negro share an internationalist imperative, however, as *The Messenger* and *Opportunity* were both keen to read the "race problem" as a world problem, tracing the development of black modern expression on a global scale.[20] Thus Nardal's nouveau noir (emphasizing uplift, race consciousness, and cosmopolitanism) and the nègre nouveau of leftists like the Guilloux and Lamine Senghor (emphasizing anticolonialism and black radicalism) take up the diasporic thought already inherent in the New Negro in a Francophone jousting over the way the phrase is to be carried over—contesting the particular ideological valence of its translation into the French colonial context. If the Renaissance is indeed international, such debates are not at all secondary, simple echoes, or extensions of Harlem. They are the record, in translation, of the ways the ambiguities of diaspora constitute the very notion of the New Negro.

TRANSLATING "FRANCE"

A more pointed example of the necessary misrecognitions of diasporic thought in the Renaissance is an exchange published in *Opportunity*. In the January 1924 issue, Locke wrote an article called "The Black Watch on the

Rhine," a report of his visit to see French African troops serving to guard the border with Germany after the First World War.[21] "My title is no misnomer," he begins, and immediately goes on to make extravagant claims for the significance of the *tirailleurs sénégalais* watching over the frontier: "the first troops I saw on entering the occupied territory, and the last I saw on leaving, were colored—and a very impartial observer, let us say the traditional Martian, would have jotted down in his diary that a polyglot, polyracial African nation had in alliance with France conquered Germany" (Locke 1924, "The Black Watch" 6). Locke, surprised at the sight of such a large contingent of integrated African and Antillean soldiers comporting themselves responsibly and with more autonomy than would be imaginable in the U.S. armed forces, gushes in the article about the putative nonracist policies of France in relation to its colonies. He writes:

> [M]ere social miracle as it may seem to the Anglo-Saxon eye, they are not merely French soldiers, they are French citizens, comrades not only in arms but in all the basic human relationships. . . .
>
> The instinctive social logicality of the French mind has made a clean sweep of the whole field [of prejudice], and in spite of its handicaps of militarism and colonial imperialism, France has here worked out a practical technique of human relationships which may very possibly earn for her world-mastery as over against her apparently more experienced and better equipped competitors. (8)

Moreover, Locke commends the "human quality" of the French military ("other armies are machines, the French is human" [8]), noting with pleasure the diversity tolerated in its colonial ranks. Latin justice and tolerance are set implicitly against the racism and segregation of the U.S. "Anglo-Saxon" military model (6), as might be expected, in what is ultimately a propaganda piece in the context of U.S. civil rights and anti-lynching struggles. Of course, the choice of example itself is significant, because in the early 1920s, German propaganda (and parts of the international media) had been attempting to incite U.S. opposition to the French occupation of the Rhine by portraying the African soldiers there as "savages" and "rapists"—with a logic explicitly indebted to U.S. lynch mobs. But Locke wants not so much to dispel racist myths about the comportment of black soldiers in Europe as to criticize the resurgence of racism in the United States after the war. Slyly, Locke writes, "I am not going to discuss motives in this article—(that makes another article, if you please)" (6), and yet his own motives are nonetheless clear. Above all, his discussion of the ways "Anglo-Saxon and Latin ways . . . differ widely" uses a fawning depiction of French military "humanism" to decry—indirectly, by juxtaposition—the terrors and inequities of racial oppression across the Atlantic.

Later that year, *Opportunity* published a remarkable exchange of letters stemming from Locke's article. René Maran, the Martinican novelist, wrote an "Open Letter to Professor Alain Leroy Locke," initially published in the June issue of the Paris-based journal *Les Continents*, which had been founded in the spring by Houénou.[22] Maran, writing that "it grieves me to shatter your illusions," critiques the blindnesses of Locke's "Rhine" piece, telling Locke that he had confused the "true France" of the republican Rights of Man—the potential France, the rhetorical France—with the "official France" of imperialism and colonial oppression equal to the British. "The benevolence of France toward subject races," Maran remarks bitingly, "is a matter of theory and official pretense. It is little more than a subterfuge" (Maran and Locke 261). "One must not be confused about the conditions of 'codified slavery' in the colonies, nor about the violent history of forced conscription and forced labor instigated by the French during the war" (262). Maran suggests that Locke "take pains to read" (and to have translated into English) some of the critiques of French colonial policy, such as Lucie Cousturier's remarkable *Les Inconnus de Chez Moi*, a 1920 meditation on the training camps for African soldiers near Fréjus in the south of France, and colonial literature such as the Tharaud brothers' 1922 *La Randonnée de Samba Diouf*.[23] "Reading them," he continues,

> will make clear our position and creed. . . . You will then understand that the black, brown and yellow soldiers [*les volontaires noirs ou jaunes*] did not come to the French colors as the little children come to Jesus. Far from it. On the contrary, either by express order, or at least with the tacit approval of the Colonial Administration, in certain of the colonies government officials under one pretext or other of recruiting actually engaged in seizure and man-hunting. Thus, summarily, do the official representatives of France superimpose civilization. France well understands that job. (262)[24]

Maran concludes by calling for an international strategy of collaboration to expose the hypocrisy of the French colonial system: "Europeans, Asiatics, Negroes [*nègres*], we must work assiduously in the same cause. We must gather, bit by bit, the evidence of these things in irrefutable fact. And one by one they will be exposed in the French parliament . . ." (262). While this call is notable in itself, and a fascinating example of an attempt at articulating a political project among diasporic black intellectuals, we should not overlook the tenor of Maran's critique: his "Open Letter" is a way of telling Locke not to use blacks "elsewhere" in the service of African-American civil rights struggles in the United States. The letter is the diaspora writing back, as it were: it contests Locke's strategy of prioritizing national integration over international anti-racism and anti-imperialism. Maran's critique, of course, is first of all a contestation of Locke's translation of "France," his strategic representation of a particular version of events in Europe in the pages of *Opportunity*. Here, in contrast to Nardal's *nouveau noir,* the translation is ideological rather than lin-guistic, but Locke's "France" is no less an attempt to carry a key sign of a di-asporic geography over into English.

In his reply letter, which is addressed to Maran as "Dear Friend and Kins-man" (262), a scrambling Locke admits his U.S.-focused motives. Retreating from the claims of his article, Locke explains that his "firing-range was set from our own trenches and for a very special purpose. I was not discussing French policy in Africa, but merely the French treatment of her Negro soldiers in Europe. At the time I was primarily concerned with contrasting this treat-ment of the man of color in the armies of France with that of our own Ameri-can army . . ." (262). The military metaphor is pressed to the breaking point as a means of claiming common purpose between them:

> The need for international coordination among us is imperative; that is why, no matter what you might say, the very sound of your voice is welcome. . . . But the essential thing, my dear Maran, is not that we should have common tactics, but common counsel. We cannot all wear the uniform of the same national loyalty, or carry the weapons of the same social philosophy. But we can and must coordinate our efforts, and share our burdens as we hope also to share our victories. (262)

The military metaphor seems oddly inappropriate in a discussion of military policy toward troops of color. In fact, it allows Locke the seemingly active dis-course of "commands" and "enlistments" and "barrages," while at the same time excusing him from the possibility of discussing an international race-based alli-ance that would place global democratic rights and anti-imperialism before civil rights in one country—such a step is "impossible," for "we cannot all wear the uniform of the same national loyalty."

In many ways, Maran's "Open Letter" calls the bluff of another article pub-lished by Locke in *Opportunity,* the February 1924 "Apropos of Africa," in which Locke had called for the attention of African-Americans to the educa-tional, economic, and political affairs of Africa in the postwar period. "Ameri-can Negroes," Locke writes, are "culturally the heirs of the entire continent" of Africa. "As the physical composite of eighty-five per cent at least of the African stocks," he claims, "the American Negro is in a real sense the true Pan-African . . ." (Locke 1924, "Apropos" 37). Although the "Africa interest" among African-Americans is a kind of necessary vanguardism for Locke, it is important to recognize that it is also a kind of necessary anti-Americanism, an emphatic privileging of the diasporic over and above the national: "[I]t is rather *against* than within the wish of the interested governments, that the American Negro must reach out toward his rightful share in the solution of African prob-lems and the development of Africa's resources" (37; emphasis added). This pronounced theme in Locke's work is seldom noted, but it is one of the more influential articulations of internationalism in the period—an argument in the vein of what Locke termed "cosmopolitan humanism."[25] Even as Locke wrote in the service of civil rights in the United States, he (like DuBois) was hedging his bets, arguing for an explicit strategy that would use the channels of international arbitration available after World War I to influence and override U.S. racial debates. In one interview, Locke went as far as to describe the seat of the League of Nations, Geneva, as "the Mecca of the liberal and progressive elements of all nations."[26]

In the most remarkable section of that essay, however, Locke not only advocates such a black internationalism, but also begins to temper his vanguardism with a call for what he terms "reciprocity" in African diasporic politics.[27] In his view, the "best channels of cooperative effort" lie in educational exchanges and economic investment projects, precisely because black internationalism in politics gives rise to "inevitable contentiousness and suspicions" (37). The spirit of emerging black *political* internationalism, then, must for Locke be reciprocal, rather than provincial or condescending (the notion of some "civilizing mission"), because that internationalism is necessarily a politics of difference—a dialogue among blacks placed unevenly in transnational political environments. "We must realize that in some respects we need what Africa has to give us as much as, or even more than, Africa needs what we in turn have to give her," Locke instructs. He continues:

> [U]nless we approach Africa in the spirit of the finest reciprocity, our efforts will be ineffectual or harmful. . . . [T]he meeting of mind between the African and the Afro-American is dependent upon a broadening of vision and a dropping of prejudices from both sides. The African must dismiss his provincialism, his political-mindedness, his pride of clan; the Afro-American, his missionary condescension, his religious parochialism, and his pride of place. The meeting of the two will mean the inauguration of a new era for both. (37)

As he envisions this model for a truly "Pan-African" politics, Locke argues that (in part through the work of the Garvey movement) "the first great span in the archway, communication, exchange of thought and information between American Negroes and their brothers in the West Indies" has already in large part been established (38). But Maran's "Open Letter" stakes out a challenge to this model from the perspective of the Caribbean, in the voice of a Martinican intellectual, around the issue of the African presence in the French military (and from a Parisian journal edited by a West African, Houénou), in criticizing Locke's strategic misrecognition of French colonialism. In *this* case of black international politics, Maran reminds Locke, there is no way to consider the "American Negro" to be "the most disinterested party," as Locke would have it

(38). Locke's commitment to civil rights in the United States is as context-bound, as "parochial," as Maran's commitment to the ideals of French universalist humanism.

Maran's intervention is black internationalism as reciprocity, in other words. One should note that reciprocity is not quite the same as call and response, that structure of antiphony which we so often associate with black expression. Reciprocity is less an originating appeal that is answered than it is a structure of mutual answerability: articulations of diaspora in tension and in dissonance, without necessary resolution or synthesis. As Kenneth Warren argues, diasporic thought is marked by ambiguities and contradictions that exceed capture by any one individual or text, but it is "perhaps most of all, a desire to speak these contradictions in a single voice. Yet . . . this voice could not be single but was, and is, poignantly dependent on getting an answer from invisible shores" (Warren 405). In this sense, diaspora can only be conceived as the uneasy and unfinished *practice* of such dialogue—where each text fulfills the demand of the other's call and at the same time exposes its necessary misrecognitions, its particular distortions of the way race travels beyond the borders of nation and language.

What are the effects of this dialogue on the shape of the Renaissance? In fact, there are deep reverberations out from what is at first glance a moment of mishearing and miscommunication. The two men begin an energetic correspondence and exchange of information that would last decades, and Locke starts to have Maran's work translated regularly for publication in *Opportunity*.[28] Through Maran, Locke would meet the younger generation of Francophone students in Paris such as the Nardal sisters, Louis Achille, Léon-Gontran Damas, and Léopold Sédar Senghor.

Moreover, this dialogue had important consequences for the shape of *Opportunity* itself. Critical readers of the journal such as David Levering Lewis, Abby Arthur Johnson, and Ronald Maberry Johnson have noted a shift in the magazine's focus during its second year of existence, a transformation usually linked to the influence of the famous March 1924 Civic Club dinner (in celebration of the publication of Fauset's novel *There is Confusion*) that the journal's editor, Charles S. Johnson, and Locke used to inaugurate the Harlem Renaissance. In Levering Lewis's view, this shift was the result of Johnson's new editorial emphasis on literary material in the journal, moving away from the previously dominant sociological vision of Urban League directors George Edmund Haynes and Eugene Kinckle Jones (Lewis 1989, 95). It is just as important, however, to consider this shift in terms of diasporic issues in the wake of Maran's "Open Letter." Since its first issue in January 1923, *Opportunity* had always evidenced an interest in questions of black internationalism, reporting on a wide variety of diasporic topics: McKay's attendance at the Communist International, the awarding of the Prix Goncourt (France's highest literary honor) to Maran's *Batouala* in 1921, sociological studies and fiction in French on "Negro" topics, the racism of American tourists in France, and the condition of Africa after World War I.[29] This interest was certainly reflected in the May 1924 issue of the journal, which focused on "African art" and included essays by Locke, Albert C. Barnes, and the French art critic and collector Paul Guillaume, as well as a significant essay by Carl Van Doren introducing the "Younger School of Negro Writers." We should not ignore the fact that two of the three poems included as examples of the emergent school (McKay's "Africa" and Lewis Alexander's "Africa") are thematically not "Harlem" poems, but works reflecting the "Africa interest" of the issue.[30]

In other words, it may not be possible to separate the turn to culture in *Opportunity* from the turn to the diasporic. The clearest example is indeed the first time the journal decided to publish creative material, in April 1923. One of the two poems in the issue was Cullen's "The Dance of Love (After Reading René Maran's *Batouala*)." It is one of Cullen's weaker efforts, certainly, apparently inspired by one of the controversial erotic scenes in Maran's novel: "All night we danced upon our windy hill, / Your dress a cloud of tangled midnight hair, / And love was much too much for me to wear / My leaves; the killer roared above his kill, / But we danced on. . . ."[31] But it is also certainly significant that the journal chose this expressly intertextual evocation of a French Caribbean novel about Africa as one of its first forays into publishing creative work.

Even more interestingly, Cullen's exoticist poem goes on to become part of the initial batch of material exchanged between *Opportunity* and *Les Continents* in the wake of Maran's "Open Letter." The letter was published in *Les Continents* in June 1924, and must have been sent to Locke at that time although it did not appear in *Opportunity* until September (presumably Locke composed his response during the summer). But other material was exchanged as well: Houénou's "The Problem of Negroes in French Colonial Africa" appeared in the July 1924 *Opportunity*, preceding his speaking tour in the United States that fall.[32] And the exchange was reciprocal: in the September *Les Continents*, there was a feature on the new generation of U.S. black poets, which reprinted Cullen's "The Dance of Love" as its centerpiece. It seems that Houénou and Maran had asked Locke to provide a brief statement on the "younger" New Negro writers, such as McKay, Hughes, and Cullen. In the Parisian journal, "The Dance of Love" was published in English, but Locke's brief introduction was translated into French under the title "La jeune poésie afro-américaine."

Locke's statement is notable, not only because it is one of the first descriptions of the Harlem Renaissance's younger generation published anywhere, but also for the way the translation introduces yet another racial appellation ("Africo-Americans")—another instance of the awkward ways black modern thought is translated, often in such novel and oddly formulated vocables. Locke prefaces the Cullen poem with these words:

> The youngest generation of Africo-American culture [*la culture Africo-Américaine*] is brilliantly represented by a whole host of young Negro poets [*jeunes poètes noirs*]: Claude McKay, Jean Toomer, Langston Hughes, and Countée Cullen, to whom we owe the poem that follows. In all of them, one easily recognizes great accomplishment and a fulfilled hope, something triply significant, from a point of view at once personal, national and racial. We may insist upon this last characteristic, their importance from a racial point of view, because it seems to have demonstrated that the movement called "the rising tide of the black peril" by reactionary alarmists is destined not to bog down and engulf civilization, but more realistically to render culture deeper and broader. Doesn't the poem about René Maran's "Batouala" itself imply the future enrichment of art by this new movement of the African genius, by this new intellectual commerce between the continents?[33]

Locke introduces a notion of an increasing universalization of culture, which is here understood as inherently cosmopolitan and diverse, rather than as the paradigmatic self-representation of a particular (European) civilization. In fact, Locke returned often to this call for a strategic disjuncture between culture and civilization, which should be understood, in its most robust sense, as an early and salutary attempt to think beyond what Edward Said has more recently helped us comprehend as the "cultures of imperialism." As Locke puts it elsewhere, "Our cultural relations, especially with widely divergent cultures, have thus been in the mood of imperialism, and with the more closely related bodies of art there has been too much of the spirit of exclusive proprietary claims and too little of the feeling of equivalent human expressions."[34]

What is particularly interesting about "La jeune poésie africo-américaine" is that Locke finds evidence of a cultural "enrichment" in Cullen's poem, as an example of black "intellectual commerce between the continents." Left unsaid, but implicit in the positioning of the passage, is that Locke considers his own exchanges with Maran and *Les Continents* to be equally felicitous commerce— a diasporic "movement of the African genius" that deepens and broadens art, even as it explores a "racially" specific literary expression. Moreover, a reading of *Opportunity* demonstrates the degree to which Locke considered translation to be the necessary mode of such exchange. The many translations subsequently published in the journal by some of the major Renaissance intellectuals

(Fauset, Mercer Cook, Rayford Logan, Cullen) may indeed be the major legacy of the Maran-Locke exchange.[35] Diasporic reciprocity, for Locke and Maran, is above all a call to translate.

TRANSLATING THE "COMMON PEOPLE"

The international civil society of the League of Nations was not the only emerging Western discourse of internationalism in the interwar period, of course. Black intellectuals engaged just as productively with the "adversarial internationalizations,"[36] particularly international Communism that attempted to counter the globe-girdling ambitions of institutions such as the League. One such radical engagement, McKay's 1929 novel *Banjo*, is the American book that along with Locke's *The New Negro* had the most profound influence on black intellectuals in Paris in the 1930s.[37] *Banjo* is an extraordinarily rich novel, and there is not space here to take up the multitude of issues it raises about black music in transnational cultural circuits, about literary propaganda, about gender and sex in diaspora, and about a Black Mediterranean space at least as vibrant as any "Black Atlantic." I will concentrate here on the novel's depiction of a particular segment of the black masses—the beachcombers, day laborers, musicians, pimps, and dockers who hang out in Marseilles "as if all the derelicts of all the seas had drifted up here to sprawl out the days in the sun" (C. McKay 1957, 18). To the writer Ray, the novel's protagonist, this itinerant, black, port population is a kind of underground international, ephemeral and multilingual: "In no other port had he ever seen congregated such a picturesque variety of Negroes. Negroes speaking civilized tongues, Negroes speaking all the African dialects, black Negroes, brown Negroes, yellow Negroes. It was as if every country of the world had sent representatives drifting into Marseilles" (68).

One of the most celebrated passages in *Banjo* is Ray's encounter, in Chapter 16, with a Martinican student in Marseilles and their heated argument about racial "renaissance" and the "common people." It was this passage that was reproduced in the 1932 single issue of *Légitime Défense*, the legendary journal influenced both by André Breton's surrealism and by international Communism, put together by a group of Caribbean students in Paris including Etienne Léro and René Ménil. *Légitime Défense* is often considered to mark a first burgeoning of Negritude in the metropolitan context, which would bear fruit later that decade with the publication of the journal *L'Étudiant Noir* in 1935, Léon-Gontran Damas's *Piments* in 1937, and the first version of Aimé Césaire's *Cahier* in 1939. And McKay's novel is often credited with opening the racial consciousness of a generation of black Francophone intellectuals. The chapter opens:

> Ray had met a Negro student from Martinique, to whom the greatest glory of the island was that the Empress Josephine was born there. That event placed Martinique above all the other islands of the Antilles in importance.
>
> "I don't see anything in that for *you* to be so proud about," said Ray. "She was not colored."
>
> "Oh no, but she was a Créole, and in Martinique we are rather Créole than Negro. We are proud of the Empress in Martinique. Down there the best people are very distinguished and speak a pure French, not anything like this vulgar Marseilles French." (199)

Ray spends the next two pages putting the *aliéné* Martinican student in his place, telling him that the only way to foster a "racial renaissance" is to "get down to our racial roots to create it" (200). Excerpted in *Légitime Défense*, then, it seems to serve a clear didactic purpose, preaching respect for black folk culture; advocating the models of the Irish cultural movement, Gandhi, and the Indian revolution; and praising the beauty of "native African dialects" (201).

The journal frames the passage from *Banjo* under the title "L'étudiant antillais vu par un noir américain" [The Caribbean student seen by an American Negro], in a manner that elides the specifics of that "Americanness." For McKay himself, of course, was Jamaican, and his character Ray is—as is often forgotten—Haitian.[38] In *Légitime Défense,* the passage seems to present the "étudiant antillais" learning blackness socratically from the U.S. Negro, in a selection from an exemplary text of the Harlem Renaissance; it is a narrative of African-American vanguardism and "influence" that is often taken for granted. But when one thinks of this encounter as an *intra-Caribbean* dialogue in the metropole, when one considers what a Haitian perspective on Napoleon's Empress might actually entail, this exchange takes on quite different contours.

Banjo was translated by Ida Treat and Paul Vaillant-Couturier, the Communist politician from Paris who edited the French Communist Party newspaper, *L'Humanité,* and maintained close ties to the radical black pressure groups in Paris in the 1920s, such as Lamine Senghor's *Ligue de Défense de la Race Nègre.* As the critic Martin Steins has pointed out, the French version of *Banjo* plays a direct role in a subtle but crucial misrecognition of the Harlem Renaissance in *Légitime Défense.* Take the central passage of Ray's speech:

> We educated Negroes are talking a lot about a racial renaissance. And I wonder how we're going to get it. On one side we're up against the world's arrogance—a mighty cold hard white stone thing. On the other the *great sweating*

army—our race. It's the *common people,* you know, who furnish the bone and sinew and salt of any race or nation. (200; emphasis added for comparison)

The last two sentences are translated into French as

De l'autre, l'immense *armée des travailleurs:* notre race. C'est le *prolétariat* qui fournit, savez-vous, l'os, le muscle et le sel de toute race ou de toute nation (257).

[On the other, the great *army of workers:* our race. It is the *proletariat,* you know, who furnish the bone, muscle and salt of any race or nation.]

Steins enumerates a number of examples of this kind of dogma-adding (mis)translation as contributing directly to the abortive project of the black Martinican surrealist group, which in *Légitime Défense* never comes close to espousing the racial consciousness we associate with later forms of Negritude, and which—buttressed in part by this passage—positions itself in terms of a "black proletariat" that it does not know how to grasp conceptually, much less approach organizationally.[39]

I depart from Steins when he sets up an easy opposition between the Communist-inflected surrealism of the *Légitime Défense* group and the "ethnic renaissance of the race" (Steins 589) that he reads in McKay's novel. For Steins, McKay's ambition in *Banjo* is to bring about neither a class revolution nor a racial nationalism, but instead "to promote in each of the different black populations of the world the consciousness that they formed peoples, ethnicities" (588). One might easily argue instead that McKay's brand of "vagabond internationalism" in *Banjo,* with its dizzying portrayal of the great idiosyncratic variety of ideological and group commitment among shifting black male communities in Marseilles, is shaped by an extreme skepticism about any such promotion of consciousness.

This skepticism is worked out on the grounds of translation, the slippery Babel of tongues and dialects clashing in color on the waterfront. DuBois's review of *Banjo* called it "on the one hand, the description of a series of episodes on the docks of Marseilles, and on the other hand a sort of international philosophy of the Negro race. . . ."[40] But finally the episodes *are* the philosophy, and it is not an internationalism of coordinated social movement, but an internationalism of debate, miscommunication, lighthearted and hot-headed accusation—the Dozens writ large, with Ananse, Frère Lapin, and the Signifying Monkey soused and clamoring for the soapbox. As Michel Fabre has noted, the French language is positioned in *Banjo* as "a barrier, or an open sesame. Language and culture appear as important as color or nationality in creating cleavages in group consciousness."[41] This point is only emphasized all the more when one reads the novel in English next to the French translation read later by the "fathers" of Negritude, Léopold Sédar Senghor and Aimé Césaire. A basic grammar of blackness is often fully dislodged, seemingly lost in translation, as it becomes impossible to trace the putative links between "Negro," "black," "darky," "coon," "man of color," on the one hand, and "noir," "nègre," "bon nèg," "raton," "homme de couleur," on the other. More than any other interwar novel, *Banjo* relentlessly emphasized the inescapable, nearly mundane, gaps in comprehension: the impossibility of translating a diaspora through some foolproof or stable system. We are left with the vertigo of communication, the small and crucial work of carrying words over, one by one, often only to have them thrown back or misconstrued. Indeed, McKay's novel reminds us that "diaspora" *is* first of all a translation: after all, it is the Greek word used to translate *galut* and other Hebrew references to "scattering" and "exile" in Hellenic translations of the Old Testament.[42]

The difficulty of translation in *Banjo* should not be understood to be solely negative, however—language as some sort of impassable wall; the novel also makes it clear that the walls are continually vaulted. The constant arguments in the novel, even when they involve sharp misunderstandings, do not come across as frustrating dead ends, but instead as precisely the most vibrant and creative moments. It is with an awareness of this creativity in a hostile linguistic context, and across difference—with the recognition that the workable translation, the "passable word," is *always* discovered—that Ray admires

> the black boys' unconscious artistic capacity for eliminating the rotten-dead stock words of the proletariat and replacing them with startling new ones. There were no dots or dashes in their conversations—nothing that could not be frankly said and therefore decently—no act or fact of life for which they could not find a simple passable word. He gained from them finer nuances of the necromancy of language and the wisdom that any word may be right and magical in its proper setting. (C. McKay 1957, 321)

We are still left with the consequences of that "crossing over," of course—exemplified most starkly in the ideological mutation from McKay's "common people" to the French *Banjo's* "le prolétariat," misrecognitions that seem unavoidable in any effort to translate among diasporic settings.

In other words, we are still confronted with difference—with those inextricable gaps and discrepancies, stitched up provisionally in the "necromantic" fabric of diasporic exchange. What Warren calls the "ambiguities that inhere in diasporic thought" are the traces of difference—not just linguistic, but more broadly what resists translation or what sometimes cannot help elude translation across boundaries of class, language, gender, sexuality, and the nation-state. On the one hand, the French translation of "common people" as "le prolétariat" is simply incorrect, an imposition of an explicit Marxist vocabulary onto a text that in English is nothing if not reluctant to assent to such institutional forms of radicalism (indeed, the linguistic creativity of the "black boys" starts by "eliminating the rotten-dead stock words of the proletariat"). On the other hand, the translation raises the necessary question of just how one might translate in this period from a phrase like "common people" (or "folk"), which resonates in English with American populist discourse and the history of African-American lives in the rural South, to a French metropolitan context molded by a very different set of forces, including labor migrancy and imperial notions of a "backward" native populace in the overseas colonies. The translation certainly should not be "le prolétariat" (in part because the French Communist Party showed such hostility to the efforts of African radicals like Lamine Senghor and Kouyaté to organize black dock workers in Marseilles), but neither would "le peuple commun" exactly catch the connotation of the phrase in English.

These ambiguities do not resolve. But it is imperative to recognize, as I hope the preceding examples have shown, that one cannot consider ideology or representation in reading the Renaissance without considering at the same time language and language difference. If the movement is notably fascinated with discourses of internationalism, in their many varieties, the ideological multi-accentuality of signs such as the "New Negro," "France," and the "common people" is also multilinguistic, reverberating through the many tongues spoken among peoples of African descent.[43] The point of reading these flash points of translating the Renaissance is not just to remark upon the prevalence of translation work in the 1920s. It is more importantly to note that the discourse of diaspora that emerges in the print culture of the period is practiced through the complex and diverse attempts to understand the race problem as a world problem, to carry blackness over the boundaries that would contain it. In this sense, in the Renaissance, diaspora is translation.

NOTES

1. Alain Locke, "The New Negro," in *The New Negro,* hereafter referred to as NN (1925; reprint, New York: Atheneum, 1968), 13, 14.

2. Nathan Huggins, *Harlem Renaissance* (New York: Oxford University Press, 1971), 41.

3. The piece continues: "Other folks of the world who think, believe and act;— THIRTY-TWO NATIONS, PEOPLES and RACES, have permanent headquarters in Paris. Not simply England, Italy and the Great Powers are there, but all the little nations; not simply little nations, but little groups who want to be nations, like the Letts and Finns, the Armenians and Jugo-Slavs, Irish and Ukrainians. Not only groups, but races have come—Jews, Indians, Arabs and all-Asia. . . . The League of Nations is ab-

solutely necessary to the salvation of the Negro race" (DuBois, "My Mission," *The Crisis* 19 [May 1919]: 9–10).

4. On this document, and on Garvey's many attempts to gain the attention of the League of Nations, see Tony Martin, *Race First: The Ideological and Organizational Struggles of Marcus Garvey and the Universal Negro Improvement Association* (Dover, Massachusetts: The Majority Press, 1976), 42–47; and Theodore Vincent, "A World-wide Movement," *Black Power and the Garvey Movement* (New York: The Ramparts Press, 1971), 165–85.

5. Locke, "The New Negro," 14. One might argue that this imperative actually commences long before the war, with DuBois's famous prediction that "the problem of the twentieth century is the problem of the colour-line" in his closing remarks to the 1900 Pan-African Conference organized in London by Trinidadian lawyer Henry Sylvester Williams. DuBois, "To the Nations of the World," quoted in David Levering Lewis, *W.E.B. DuBois: Biography of a Race, 1868–1919* (New York: Henry Holt, 1993), 251. At the same time, this is not to suggest that black internationalism began only with the twentieth century. African-Americans have long made recourse, of course, to such a two-pronged strategy of national civil rights work and international appeal: one could track this strategy back to abolitionism (the European appeals against slavery in the United States of Frederick Douglass, William Wells Brown, and Mary Prince) and forward to movements such as the "Double V" in World War II (the phrase articulates the war as a struggle for "victory against fascism abroad" and "victory against racism at home"). Here I want to emphasize the persistence of the black international imperative and the impact of black interventions in the interwar period—what is usually recognized to be the high point of Western investment in projects of internationalism. Nikhil Pal Singh has recently termed this persistence "black worldliness," a useful phrase in that it encapsulates both the considered breadth (the move beyond the level of the nation-state) and the explicit political ambition (the universalism) of such a stance. Indeed, Singh argues that this black imperative "is perhaps this country's only consistent universalism." Singh, "Culture/Wars: Recoding Empire in an Age of Democracy," *American Quarterly* 50 (September 1998): 514.

6. Here I take up the complexities of "Harlem" and the "New Negro" as tropes in this period. I am equally uncomfortable with the term "Renaissance," which likewise has often been critiqued as an inappropriate designation. But I have used the term here, in scare quotes, to mark what I consider to be certain consistencies in the transnational literary field of the interwar period. (In general, I am not as concerned as some critics have been to find the "right" name or metaphor to designate this field—I am more interested in the ways any name travels through it, and is contested in a range of ideological "re-accentuations.") George Hutchinson has recently made a convincing argument that "Harlem Renaissance" is in fact an appropriate moniker, at least for *The New Negro*, in his fine reading of the journal culture of the period; see *The Harlem Renaissance in Black and White* (Cambridge, Massachusetts: Harvard University Press, 1995), 424–28.

7. Robert B. Stepto, "Sterling A. Brown: Outsider in the Harlem Renaissance?" *The Harlem Renaissance: Reevaluations*, Amritjit Singh, William S. Shiver, and Stanley Brodwin, eds. (New York: Garland, 1989), 73. See also Melvin Dixon, "Toward a World Black Literature & Community," *Chant of Saints: A Gathering of Afro-American Literature, Art, and Scholarship*, Michael S. Harper and Stepto, eds. (Urbana: University of Illinois Press, 1979), 175–94.

8. Kenneth W. Warren, "Appeals for (Mis)recognition: Theorizing the Diaspora," *Cultures of United States Imperialism,* Amy Kaplan and Donald E. Pease, eds. (Durham: Duke University Press, 1993), 393.

9. See Tyler Stovall, *Paris Noir: African-Americans in the City of Light* (Boston: Houghton Mifflin, 1996); Kenneth R. Janken, "African-American and Francophone Black Intellectuals During the Harlem Renaissance," *The Historian* 60 (1998): 487–505.

10. French policy during the war envisioned Africans mainly as soldiers, not as workers, and the numbers reflect this: in 1918, the projections were for 85,000 soldiers from Africa (70,000 from French West Africa and 15,000 from French Equatorial Africa), but only 10,000 workers; this in comparison to 10,000 soldiers and 15,000 workers from Madagascar and 80,000 soldiers and 100,000 workers from Indochina. See Jean Vidalenc, "La main d'oeuvre étrangère en France et la Première Guerre Mondiale (1901–1926)," *Francia* 2 (1974): 524–50; Tyler Stovall, "Colour-Blind France? Colonial workers during the First World War," *Race and Class* 35 (1993): 35–55; Philippe De Witte, "Le Paris noir de l'entre-deux-guerres," *Le Paris des étrangers: depuis un siècle,* A. Kaspi and A. Marès, eds. (Paris: Imprimerie Nationale, 1989), 157–69. As De Witte points out, it should be noted that French Caribbeans were considered citizens and thus not counted as immigrants.

11. Reid Badger, *A Life in Ragtime: A Biography of James Reese Europe* (New York: Oxford University Press, 1995); Chris Goddard, *Jazz Away From Home* (New York: Paddington Press, 1979); Michael Haggerty, "Transes Atlantiques," *Jazz Magazine* 325 (January 1984): 30–31.

12. *Batouala* was published simultaneously in French and in English by Albin Michel in Paris and by Jonathan Cape in London; in 1922, another, less felicitous translation was published by Selzter in New York. (There have been a number of translations of the novel; the most complete is the one by Barbara Reck and Alexandre Mboukou, published by Black Orpheus Press in 1972.) *Batouala* was widely reviewed in the United States, and, in spite of its faults, the 1922 English edition was extremely influential on Harlem Renaissance literati. (It is not without a certain ironic significance that U.S. black reviewers, seemingly oblivious to the author's background as a French Guyanese from Martinique who had worked in the colonial administration in French Equatorial Africa, often assumed that Maran was a "contemporary African.") For a consideration of the influence of *Batouala* in the Harlem Renaissance, see Michel Fabre's "René Maran, the New Negro and Negritude," *Phylon* 36 (September 1975): 340–51; and Tony Martin's *Literary Garveyism: Garvey, Black Arts, and the Harlem Renaissance* (Dover, Massachusetts: The Majority Press, 1983).

13. For an introduction to the career of Kojo Tovalou Houénou, see in particular J. Ayodele Langley, *Pan-Africanism and Nationalism in West Africa, 1900–1945: A Study in Ideology and Social Classes* (London: Oxford University Press, 1973), 286–325. His speech to the UNIA was printed in *Les Continents* and in the *Negro World.* Houénou, "Discours Prononcé le 19 Août, 1924, au Congrès Annuel de l'Association Universelle pour l'Avancement de la Race Noire," *The Negro World* [French Section] (September 13, 1924): 14. On Houénou's links to the UNIA, see also *The Marcus Garvey and Universal Negro Improvement Association Papers, Vol. 5: September 1922–August 1924,* Robert A. Hill, ed. (Berkeley: University of California Press, 1983), 750, 823.

14. Alan McLeod (Port Washington, New York: Kennikat Press, 1979), 49. Jan-

ken has also discussed the celebration in the U.S. black press of the "apparent absence of racism in Europe" (490–91, 503–504).

15. David Levering Lewis, *When Harlem Was in Vogue* (New York: Oxford University Press, 1981), 157.

16. Nardal, "L'Internationalisme Noir," *La Dépêche Africaine* 1 (February 1928): 1. All translations are my own.

17. Her claim that "To be Afro-American, to be Afro-Latin, means to be an encouragement, a comfort, an example for the blacks of Africa . . ." recalls Locke's comment that the American Negro acts as "the advance-guard of the African peoples in their contact with Twentieth Century civilization" (*The New Negro* 14).

18. Lamine Senghor, "Le réveil des nègres," *Le Paria* 38 (April 1926): 1–2. This article was reprinted as a nearly identical piece in the newspaper of Senghor's *Ligue de Défense de la Race Nègre*, now signed by the Ligue's "Comité": "Le Mot *Nègre*," *La Voix des Nègres* (January 1927): 1. See Christopher Miller, "Involution and Revolution: African Paris in the 1920s," in *Nationalists and Nomads: Essays on Francophone African Literature and Culture* (Chicago: University of Chicago Press, 1998), 30–37; Philippe De Witte, *Les Mouvements Nègres en France, 1919–1935* (Paris: L'Harmattan, 1985), 143–46.

19. Gates, "The Trope of a New Negro and the Reconstruction of the Image of the Black," *Representations* 24 (Fall 1988): 129–57; Levine, "The Concept of the New Negro and the Realities of Black Culture," in *The Unpredictable Past: Explorations in American Cultural History* (New York: Oxford University Press, 1993), 86–106.

20. On internationalism in *The Messenger,* see for example Theodore Kornweibel, Jr., *No Crystal Stair: Black Life and the Messenger, 1917–1928* (Westport, Connecticut: Greenwood Press, 1975), 67–68, 83–84. I take up this issue with regard to *Opportunity* subsequently.

21. Locke, "The Black Watch on the Rhine," *Opportunity* 2 (January 1924): 6–9.

22. Maran, "Lettre Ouverte au professeur Alain-Leroy Locke, de l'Université d'Howard (États-Unis)," *Les Continents* 3 (15 June 1924): 1; Maran and Locke, "French Colonial Policy: Open Letters," *Opportunity* 2 (September 1924): 261–63. *Les Continents* appeared as a bimonthly publication from May to October 1924, when it was forced to cease publication, after being sued for libel by the Senegalese deputy Blaise Diagne. On the journal's brief but important publication history, see Iheanachor Egonu, "*Les Continents* and the Francophone Pan-Negro Movement," *Phylon* 42 (September 1981): 245–54.

23. It is unclear whether Maran is aware of Locke's 1923 article on "The Colonial Literature of France," in which Locke reviews not only Maran's own *Batouala*, but also the Tharauds' *La Randonnée de Samba Diouf,* Gaston Joseph's *Koffi* (1923), Cousturier's *La Forêt du Haut-Niger* (1923), and Llewellyn Powys's *Ebony and Ivory* (1922).

24. The translation is uncredited, but it should be noted that Maran's sarcasm has been somewhat attenuated in the English. Thus, the last two sentences I have quoted are more literally rendered as follows: "C'est ainsi, cher Monsieur Locke, que les représentants de la France officielle *superimposent* la civilisation de la France tout court. Ah! oui, comme elle s'y entend, la France officielle et coloniale, à cette besogne là" [This, my dear Mr. Locke, is how the representatives of official France *superimpose* the civilization of France *tout court.* Ah, yes, official and colonial France understands that task very well] (emphasis in original).

25. Locke, "The Colonial Literature of France," *Opportunity* 1 (November 1923): 331.

26. Locke, "America Must Aid in Affairs of Africa: Philosopher Sees New Era for Continent," *Chicago Defender* (October 22, 1927), II: 1.

27. For Locke's notion of reciprocity, see also his "The Contribution of Race to Culture," *The Student World* 23 (1930): 349–53; collected in *The Philosophy of Alain Locke: Harlem Renaissance and Beyond*, Leonard Harris, ed. (Philadelphia: Temple University Press, 1989), 201–206.

28. See René Maran, "Gandhi," Edna Worthley Underwood, trans., *Opportunity* 3 (February 1925): 40–42; Maran, "The Harriet Beecher Stowe of France" [on Lucie Cousturier], Edna Worthley Underwood, trans., *Opportunity* 3 (August 1925): 229–31; Maran, "Two Book Reviews" [on Albert Londres, *Terre d'Ebene;* Claire Goll, *Le Nègre Jupiter Enlève Europe*], Rayford W. Logan, trans., *Opportunity* 7 (December 1929): 379–80, 394; Maran, "French Colonization—What It Might Have Been," Francis Hammond, trans., *Opportunity* 14 (1936): 57, 63.

29. Here are just a few examples, besides Locke's "The Colonial Literature of France," cited previously: "More About René Maran," *Opportunity* 1 (January 1923): 30 (this article was reprinted in part from *Brentano's Book Chat* [Thanksgiving 1922]); William H. Baldwin, "Africa—A Study in Misunderstanding," *Opportunity* 1 (February 1923): 5–6, 28; "Claude McKay Before the Internationale," *Opportunity* 1 (September 1923): 258–59; "The Color Line in Paris," *Opportunity* 1 (September 1923): 287–88; "Fair France," *Opportunity* 1 (October 1923): 317–18; Alain Locke, "As Others See Us" [on Franck Schoell, *La Question des Noirs aux États-Unis*], *Opportunity* 2 (April 1924): 109–10.

30. "African Art" issue, *Opportunity* 2 (May 1924). The other poem is Langston Hughes's "Our Land"; the three appear on p. 142. The pivotal influence of French and German art criticism on Locke's thinking is described in Matgorzata Irek, "From Berlin to Harlem: Felix von Luschan, Alain Locke, and the New Negro," in *The Black Columbiad: Defining Moments in African-American Literature and Culture*, W. Sollors and M. Diedrich, eds. (Cambridge: Harvard University Press, 1994), 174–84; Mark Helbling, "African Art: Albert C. Barnes and Alain Locke," *Phylon* 43 (March 1982): 57–67; and Locke, "Europe Discovers Negro Art," in *Negro Art: Past and Present* (1936; reprint New York: Arno, 1969), 34–42. One might also note that Locke met both Barnes and Guillaume in Paris.

31. The other poem in this issue is Leslie Pinckney Hill, "Voyaging," *Opportunity* 1 (April 1923): 23.

32. Kojo Tovalou Houénou, "The Problem of Negroes in French Colonial Africa," *Opportunity* 2 (July 1924): 203–207. This lecture was originally delivered in February 1924 at the École Interalliée des Hautes Études Sociales in Paris.

33. Locke, "La jeune poésie africo-américaine," *Les Continents* 8 (September 1, 1924): 2. The translation back into English is my own.

34. Locke, "Internationalism—Friend or Foe of Art?" *The World Tomorrow* (March 1925): 75–76.

35. Maran's work in *Opportunity* is cited previously. For other translations from the French, see for example: Louis Charbonneau, "Fièvres d'Afrique," Edna Worthley Underwood, trans., *Opportunity* 4 (April 1926): 114–15, 138; "Legend of Ngurangurane" [from Blaise Cendrars, *Anthologie Nègre*], Violette de Mazie, trans., *Opportunity* 4

(May 1926): 153–55, 170; Dantès Bellegarde, "Haiti Under the Rule of the United States," Rayford W. Logan, trans., *Opportunity* 5 (Dec. 1927): 354–57; Frederic Marcelin, "Jan-Jan: A Haitian Idyll," Suzanne Sylvain, trans., *Opportunity* 6 (January 1928): 16–18, 27; Jenner Bastien, "Haiti and Haitian Society," Countée Cullen, trans., *Opportunity* 6 (June 1928): 176–77; Dantès Bellegarde, "The American Occupation of Haiti," J.A. Rogers, trans., *Opportunity* 8 (December 1929): 10–12; Fernand Gregh, "Negroisms," Countée Cullen, trans., *Opportunity* 8 (April 1930): 124–25.

I should note that it is equally possible to trace such an interest in the pages of the other major Harlem Renaissance journal, *The Crisis*. This is especially due to the work of Fauset as literary editor in the 1920s. See Yvette Guilbert, "Joseph and Mary Come to Bethlehem," Jessie Fauset, trans., *The Crisis* 21 (Dec. 1920): 72–73; Amédée Brun, "The Pool," Fauset, trans., *The Crisis* 22 (September 1921): 205; Oswald Durand, "To a Foreign Maid," Fauset, trans., *The Crisis* 25 (February 1923): 158; G.D. Perier, "Kirongozi" (from *Curiosités Congolaises*), Fauset, trans., *The Crisis* 27 (March 1924): 208–209; Frank L. Schoell, "La Question des Noirs aux États-Unis" (selections), Fauset, trans., *The Crisis* 28 (June 1924): 83–86; Af Carl Kjersmeier, "Negere Som Digtere" [Negroes as Poets], E. Franklin Frazier, trans., *The Crisis* 30 (August 1925): 186–89.

36. Edward Said, "Third World Intellectuals and Metropolitan Culture," *Raritan* 9 (Winter 1990): 31.

37. Claude McKay, *Banjo, A Story Without a Plot* (1929; reprint New York: Harcourt Brace Jovanovich, 1957). The influential French translation is McKay, *Banjo*, Ida Treat and Paul Vaillant-Couturier, trans. (Paris: Rieder, 1931).

38. "L'étudiant antillais vu par un noir américain," *Légitime Défense* 1 (1932): 13–14. The journal has been reprinted in Paris by the publisher Jean-Michel Place (1979). See McKay's earlier novel, *Home to Harlem*, in which Ray gives Jake a long lesson in Haitian and Ethiopian history. In fact, Ray originally comes to the United States in exile from the U.S. occupation of Haiti, where his father had been jailed and his brother murdered by U.S. Marines. *Home to Harlem* (1928; reprint Boston: Northeastern University Press, 1987), 131–39, 155–56.

39. Martin Steins, *Les antecédents et la genèse de la négritude senghorienne* (Paris: Université Paris III, unpublished Thèse d'État, 1981), 588–89. On the translation of the novel, also see Michel Fabre, "Du Mouvement nouveau noir à la négritude césairienne," in *Soleil éclaté: Mélanges offerts à Aimé Césaire à l'occasion de son soixante-dixième anniversaire par une équipe internationale d'artistes et chercheurs*, J. Leiner, ed. (Tübingen: Gunter Narr Verlag, 1984), 154–56. Fabre has recently published a new translation of *Banjo* that corrects many of these faults: *Banjo*, Fabre, trans. (Paris: André Dimanche, 1999).

40. DuBois, "The Browsing Reader," *The Crisis* 36 (July 1929): 324.

41. Michel Fabre, *From Harlem to Paris: Black American Writers in France, 1840–1980* (Urbana: University of Illinois Press, 1991), 110.

42. Khachig Tölölyan dates the first appearance of *diaspeirein* in a Greek version of the Torah to approximately 250 BCE. See Tölölyan, "Rethinking *Diaspora*(s): Stateless Power in the Transnational Moment," *Diaspora* 5 (1996): 11.

43. V. N. Volosinov, *Marxism and the Philosophy of Language* (1929), L. Matejka and I. R. Titunik, trans. (Cambridge, Massachusetts: Harvard University Press, 1996), 22–23.

17. The Harlem Renaissance Abroad: French Critics and the New Negro Literary Movement (1924–1964)

Michel Fabre

I. BETWEEN WARS: 1924–1939

The first information ever printed in France on the New Negro movement was provided by Alain Locke to Martinique writer René Maran, who published it in *Les Continents* as "La jeune poésie africo-américaine" on September 1, 1924. This brief presentation of young African-American poets stressed their positive offerings as exemplified by Countée Cullen's "The Dance of Love (After reading Maran's *Batouala*)," reprinted in English. *Les Continents,* a newspaper edited by Maran and pro-Garvey Prince Kojo Touvalou Houénou, reached only a limited, mostly black audience. This presentation was followed in December 1925 by Maran's essay on "Le mouvement négro-littéraire aux États-Unis" in the better-known magazine *Vient de paraître.* The Goncourt prize-winner stressed the role of periodicals such as *The Crisis* and *Opportunity,* as well as the work of historian Charles S. Johnson and philosopher Alain Locke in the Negro Renaissance. The authors mentioned were Paul Laurence Dunbar, Countée Cullen, Langston Hughes, James Weldon Johnson, Jessie Fauset, Georgia Douglas Johnson, and journalist Joel A. Rogers. A detailed review of Walter White's *Fire in the Flint* concluded that this "truthful, well-balanced, human, and exceedingly moving" novel deserved to be translated into French.[1]

For a time, this was about all. In March 1926, a brief praise of J.W. Johnson's *The Book of American Spirituals* appeared in *Le Mercure de France,*[2] and Jean Catel's review of "Lettres anglo-américaines" in the December 1, 1927,

Mercure included a brief presentation of *God's Trombones* followed by excerpts from "The Creation." In the December 1928 *Mercure de France*, Catel also mentioned the new publication of Johnson's *Autobiography of an Ex-Coloured Man*, "the best book ever written by a colored American,"[3] and Harold Salemson mentioned it most favorably in *Le Monde*.[4]

That year, 1928, Eugène Jolas edited an *Anthologie de la nouvelle poésie américaine* for Editions Kra, which had already published a translation of Carl Van Vechten's *Nigger Heaven*. Cullen, Hughes, Claude McKay, and Jean Toomer were represented in the anthology, each with one poem. Cullen, who had graduated from New York University and become famous in 1924 with "The Shroud of Color," was introduced as "the son of a Protestant pastor."[5] Cullen's "Simon the Cyrenian" was printed in translation. Langston Hughes's studies and jobs as ticket collector and sailor were mentioned. He was "a Negro poet who makes use of the rhythms of jazz and Negro songs in his poetry."[6] Hughes's "Po' Boy Blues" followed. McKay's Jamaican origin, his diverse jobs, and his work at *The Liberator* in 1920 were listed. "A full-blooded Negro, McKay brought a new violent accent to the poetry of his race."[7] His "Black Spiritual" was selected. Toomer was said to have been born in the South and to be "probably the most gifted poet of his race. The publication of *Cane*, a collection of stories or prose poems reveal[ed] his great originality and imagination. He live[d] in utter solitude away from literary circles."[8] "Harvest Song" was the Toomer poem selected.

In *Le Nègre qui chante*, Jolas's own study of Negro songs, Jolas insisted on the distinction between the pure primitivism of African-Americans living below the Mason-Dixon line and the imitation of it by whites. The blues, spirituals, work songs, and ballads expressed the yearnings of an oppressed people. Their African origins were not to be questioned. The themes and language of these songs were discussed but no allusion was made to the New Negro movement, and the selection was limited to folk songs.[9]

That same year, in "La poésie nègre aux États-Unis," a brief article in *Candide*, novelist André Maurois praised the lyrical achievements of Cullen, Hughes, McKay, and Angelina Grimké and provided quotations from their poems. He devoted more space, however, to DuBose Heyward's *Porgy*, a translation of which was to appear shortly in Paris.[10]

Academics, too, helped discover the New Negro. A Whitman scholar, Léon Bazalgette, was instrumental in getting Claude McKay's fiction published by Editions Rieder. Sorbonne Professor Régis Michaud expressed interesting views in his *Littérature américaine:* America was the home of the blues, jazz, and the spirituals, to be seen as "the revenge of the blacks in poetry and art." At the dawn of the American poetic renaissance, Negro verse brimmed over with rhythm and color: Paul Laurence Dunbar, W. E. B. DuBois, William S. Braithwaite, J. W. Johnson made up the established generation. Cullen, Hughes, the "errant bard" Claude McKay, Jean Toomer, Joseph Cotter, Jessie Fauset, Gwendolyn Bennett, Jeffrey Hays, and Lewis Alexander, among the new generation, expressed "the regrets, rancor, and aspirations of their race." Their worship of the "Black Venus" gave "a strange fragrance of paganism" to their "luxuriant imagery" and "lively rhythms."[11]

Reviewing *Cane* for *Les Nouvelles Littéraires,* Professor Franck Louis Schoell—a Frenchman teaching at Tulane—extolled Toomer's artistry and delicate handling of language by contrasting him with other black writers who were characterized by "primitive impetuosity" and exaggeration. Only in Toomer's case was "the novelist the true essence, and the black man the accident."[12]

In 1929, André Lévinson, also in *Les Nouvelles littéraires,* was inclined to deny that the Negro's intellect equaled his sensitivity; he wrote that "the art of the primitive is intense, colorful, direct; it is also superficial, monotonous and short-winded."[13] Toomer, Cullen, and Eric Walrond were mentioned, but most of the piece was devoted to a biographical sketch of McKay and to disparaging *Home to Harlem,* which insisted on the "debauchery of Harlem life." Jessie Fauset's *There Is Confusion* was noted as dealing with "quasi-whiteness." The following month, Lévinson followed up with "De Harlem à la Canebière," a rather unfavorable review of McKay's *Banjo.* To its mood of rebellious and "primitive racial vainglory," Lévinson opposed Toomer's *Cane* as the literary embodiment of the "victory of spirit over instinct."[14] *Banjo* he found anti-French and "an apology for the abdication of the intellect." Walrond's *Tropic Death* was presented sympathetically.

Louis Piérard, another reviewer for *Les Nouvelles littéraires,* contributed "Poètes de l'Aframérique" in November 1929. This brief retrospect focused on the Negro Renaissance. Translations of poems by Hughes ("Je suis noir" and "Le noir parle des rivières") and by Cullen ("Les presque blancs" and "Les Dieux") were printed. J. W. Johnson's *God's Trombones* was praised.[15]

By that time, Professor Schoell's "La Renaissance nègre aux USA" had already appeared in *La Revue de Paris* in January 1929. This important study examined the situation of African-Americans after World War I: their urbanization and the growth of a black middle class, the development of the black press, and the vogue of *art nègre.* The first section dealt with the fashion of African art and of jazz. The second section focused on literature about and by the Negro. "Our Land" and "I Too" by Hughes, "Tropics in New York" by McKay, and poems by Countée Cullen were quoted. *Cane* by Jean Toomer was praised as "a most curious . . . collection of tales."[16] *Fire in the Flint* by Walter

White, *There Is Confusion* by Jessie Fauset, and *Tropic Death* by Eric Walrond were mentioned, as was "a very fine book by J. W. Johnson, *The Autobiography of an Ex-Coloured Man,* too long out of print." There were few good black dramatists, Schoell claimed, because of their "lack of detachment and objectivity," but excellent black actors abounded, "brimming with vitality." Schoell cited *Shuffle Along,* out of which came "that beautiful jumping animal, Josephine Baker."[17] Poetry, he noted, according to Gobineau, was more attuned to the Negro's sensual gifts: it had blossomed in the twenties, with "a high class poet," Langston Hughes; McKay vibrantly celebrated Harlem, and Cullen sang exquisitely of dancing girls. J. W. Johnson was again mentioned among the poets, and Schoell believed that the African theme probably remained most characteristic in this poetry, which was endowed with fresh sensitivity and originality. Schoell later sent "Un poète nègre: Langston Hughes" to the *Revue politique et littéraire.* In this piece, a (inaccurate) biographical notice preceded six poems in translation: "Cabaret," "Jeune Danseuse," "Lamentation pour les hommes au teint foncé," "La peur," "Moi aussi," and "Une mère à son fils." It was hoped that Hughes would not confine himself to racial themes, "the source of which would soon become dry."[18]

French discovery of the New Negro movement in its wider context was now possible, and, in the early thirties, it proceeded more quickly. Olga and Jean Roux-Delimal published five pages on "Nègres d'Amérique" in *Les Cahiers du Sud* (October 1930). Prior to a panorama of the situation of African-Americans, they introduced J. W. Johnson's *God's Trombones,* insisting on the creativity of black American dialect.[19] This elicited a note from Charles-Henri Hirsch in the December 1930 issue of *Le Mercure de France.* In "Un sermon nègre issu du folklore: la Création du monde," he emphasized the genius of the spirituals in the South and quoted Roux-Delimal's parallel between that genre and the medieval chanson de geste.[20] A two-page translation from "The Creation" sermon followed (but the expected French publication of *God's Trombones* did not materialize). Meanwhile, Langston Hughes was introduced again in *Les Cahiers libres.* A (mostly biographical) notice emphasized his original, powerful talent and his role as a representative of his race. "Spiritual power and the power to dream" were "magnificently imprinted on the face and the poetry of Langston Hughes."[21]

When McKay's *Banjo* was translated by Ida Treat and young Communist leader Paul Vaillant-Couturier, sociologist Georges Friedmann wrote a preface to it. Friedmann found that, in contrast to the Booker T. Washington generation, the New Negro writers dealt with the masses and criticized Western civilization. Such was the case with Jamaica-born McKay, whose career was retraced. Several poems by McKay were quoted, and Friedmann evoked his own friendship with the novelist in Antibes. *Banjo* combined a deep, colorful sensitivity with a meditation on black life in a white racist environment. "It would be a mistake to limit *Banjo* to its descriptive and picturesque value. There are also in this book remarkable reflections on the life of blacks in a white world."[22] The novel was entertaining yet provided a perceptive analysis of racial relations, not only in Marseilles and within the black diaspora, but in a worldwide context of economic exploitation that cut across color lines.

In December 1931, Léone Louis devoted a biographical and critical essay to Langston Hughes, quoting his manifesto, "The Negro Artist and the Racial Mountain," and his desire to express his black self without shame or fear. Hughes dedicated his art to the defense of his race. His major themes were said to be Africa, the hope of obtaining victory, and a great confidence in the beauty of his race. He also pointed to instances of racial discrimination in the United States. *The Weary Blues, Not Without Laughter,* and other works were analyzed and quoted.[23]

That year, *Quartier noir,* a translation of *Home to Harlem,* by the well-known left-wing novelist Louis Guilloux, was published by Editions Rieder. Even more interesting to our present concern, the Communist-sponsored review *Europe* carried a translation, by Louis Guilloux and his wife Renée, of Alain Locke's introduction to the famous 1924 "New Negro" issue of the *Survey Graphic* and included a brief note on Locke.[24] But there was no talk of translating the whole *New Negro* anthology.

To all evidence, Maran and his circle had not been able to sell the book to a French publisher. But, by that time, Martinique student Paulette Nardal and her friends had succeeded in launching the *Revue du Monde noir* (in French and in English), and the initial issue reviewed readings given by Grace Walker in London and Geneva of verse by Cullen, McKay, Hughes, and Toomer, "chosen in such a way as to touch on the highlights of the artistic temperament of these different Negro poets, distinctive in inspiration and style."[25] Indeed, many African-Americans were represented in the *Revue:* Cullen; McKay by an excerpt from *Banjo,* "Spring in New Hampshire," and "To America"; Hughes by "I Too Sing America"; John F. Matheus by "Fog"; Walter White by the lynching scene in *The Fire in the Flint.* Jessie Fauset also contributed.

In the sixth and final issue (1931) of the *Revue,* Nardal's long essay, "Eveil de la conscience de race," retraced the development of African-American literature: slave narratives; the dialect poetry of Dunbar; the influence of W. S. Braithwaite; the "new attitude" in the poetry of McKay and Hughes, who rejected any inferiority complex; the theories of Marcus Garvey; the "revolt of [our] American brothers";[26] and the latest phase in their intellectual evolution. Nardal paralleled the blossoming of black consciousness in the United States and in France. In France, where the atmosphere was more liberal and open, it had taken moderate forms, while black American revolt was more explicit in the New Negro movement:

> Quite different was the situation among the American Negroes. Though they are not of pure African origin either, the deliberate scorn with which they have always been treated by white Americans, incited them to seek for social and cultural pride in their African past.[27]

African-American literature has given up the imitative romanticism of *Les Cenelles* and become the vehicle of debate and protest; the impact of Garveyism, the first Pan-African Conference in Paris, the launching of *Les Continents* by René Maran and of *La Dépêche africaine* by Maurice Satineau were steps toward a new awareness evidenced by the Antillean and African students' desire to complete Sorbonne master of arts degrees on Negro topics. But the *Revue* ceased publication in 1931, at the time of the Exposition Coloniale in Paris, the heyday of the French colonial empire.

The liberating influence of the New Negro movement for French-speaking colonials was further celebrated in the single issue of *Légitime Défense* in 1932. In "Misère d'une poésie," the Martinique iconoclast Etienne Léro claimed

> The wind that blows from black America will soon manage, let us hope, to cleanse our Antilles of the aborted fruit of an obsolete culture. Langston Hughes and Claude McKay, two revolutionary black poets, have brought to us, marinated in red alcohol, the African love of life, the African joy of love, the African dream of death.[28]

An excerpt from *Banjo* is used to criticize assimilated French West Indians: it deals with a Martinique student who refuses to enter a café kept by a Senegalese because he is afraid of demeaning himself by associating with Africans.

In 1932, reviews of the French translations of *Banjo* and *Home to Harlem* began to appear. Gabriel Bertin detailed several aspects of life on the Marseilles waterfront that McKay seemed to know extremely well; Bertin even claimed to have met the person on whom McKay had based his protagonist.[29] Guilloux, in *Europe*, emphasized the "serene humanness of the characters" and declared McKay "a genuine artist . . . without doubt one of the most gifted" Negro writers.[30] Pierre Lorson, the critic for the Jesuit journal *Etudes,* started with a description of *Quartier noir* (the translation of *Home to Harlem)* and concluded, "the composition of the book is so disorderly that, if Mr. McKay is a Negro, he certainly provides M. Lévy-Brühl with arguments for his theory on the pre-logical mind of primitive peoples." In Lorson's eyes, the novel was "weak, foul, and demeaning."[31]

As for colored Georges Joseph-Henri, he greatly loved *Banjo* and said so in *La Revue de la Martinique:* his detailed review focused on McKay's denunciation of so-called "civilization" and the Negro's attempt to whiten himself psychologically and culturally. Black nationalism was extolled, and McKay's declarations in the novel were quoted at length. The myth of black hypersexuality was deflated. Like Aldous Huxley, D. H. Lawrence, and Katherine Mansfield, McKay was intent upon denouncing the deleterious influence of Christianity. The book deserved close reading: "Maybe, some of those who are asleep will awaken and listen to its important message."[32]

Although he devoted little space to African-American writing in his books, Professor Charles Cestre liked *Banana Bottom* in 1934. He emphasized the value of the novel as a social document: the lack of ideological and racial bias, either concerning tyrants or in favor of the victims, made the novel of indisputable interest, "a living book" and "a crucial document on the itinerary of a race."[33] Meanwhile, Catholic Pierre Lorson was discovering more about McKay, including his Jamaican origins. His evaluation of *Banana Bottom* focused on the plot: Bita comes back home to Jamaica after having enjoyed a refined education in Great Britain. She gradually scrubs the white education off her black skin and can only find happiness when marrying a male of her race, one hundred percent black.[34]

Pierre Lorson also wrote a brief review of *Sandy* (the translation by Gabrielle Beauroy of Hughes's *Not without Laughter,* which was published by Rieder in 1934). "Yet another American Negro novel," it was found "less brutal than others [*Banjo* and *Home to Harlem*] in the same series," and "moving because of the depth of feeling expressed." Because of these qualities, it would "bring honor to any white novelist."[35]

In 1933, there was talk of Eric Walrond. Mathilde Camhi was supposed to translate *Tropic Death,* but only Walrond's story "Sur les chantiers de Panama" came out in a Brussels magazine.[36] Its theme was the racial conflict among the canal workers that ensued when a Spanish shopkeeper shot a couple of Negroes as a threatening mob drew near. Walrond's "Harlem," a colorful reportage on how the smart set invaded the Harlem cabarets and how Strivers' Row entrepreneurs such as Jasbo Brown capitalized on that fashion, appeared in the February 4, 1933, issue of *Lectures du Soir* with a brief notice. Jacques Lebar introduced Walrond as "one of the most characteristic and colorful representatives of Negro literature together with Claude McKay."[37]

This was about the extent of the criticism of the Harlem Renaissance production in the French press for two decades. In 1935, Martinique poet Emmanuel Flavia-Léopold reviewed Nancy Cunard's *Negro* for *Europe.* In his essay, he examined the ideological perspectives of the anthology, emphasizing its comprehensiveness, the "indisputable link" between racial and social oppression, and how the former stems from economic exploitation. He denounced disguised job discrimination in France. Rayford Logan, Walter White, Cullen, Locke, Arthur Schomburg, W. E. B. DuBois, and Zora Neale Hurston were mentioned only as contributors to the volume.[38] But as early as 1938, the French version of the Soviet magazine *Littérature internationale* carried a translation of Richard Wright's "Big Boy Leaves Home," prefaced by Isidor Schneider, who celebrated Wright: The title of his *Uncle Tom's Children* was explained in detail; his stories portrayed the rebellious black, and it was significant that he should be a Communist. His poetry reverberated with the spirituals and also with the manly accents of black workers: "The Negroes in America have finally found in him an authentic writer of the people, *their* own writer."[39]

It is difficult to gauge the impact of *Littérature internationale,* but it is a fact, as we shall see, that Léopold Senghor first mentioned Wright as a poet. Meanwhile, the work of the Harlem Renaissance poets was inspiring French-speaking black writers, but it took Senghor to evaluate this influence. Lecturing in Dakar on December 10, 1937, he stated that vernacular languages were as beautiful as recognized literary tongues. He claimed that Dunbar, McKay, Hughes, and Sterling Brown had turned "the Negro American dialect, that poor faltering speech of uprooted slaves, into a marvel—*a thing of beauty.*"[40] In *L'Homme de couleur,* published as early as 1939, Senghor stated that the Negro "negrifies" God and makes man partake of the supernatural. Cullen was quoted as "making black Gods," and the African-American poet was said to prefer to address Christ rather than God the Father. Further, Senghor stated that black workers in the North of the United States looked nostalgically at the southern countryside where their brothers toiled like serfs. He quoted McKay as an instance and remarked that Aimé Césaire was able to write his master of arts thesis on the theme of the South in Afro-American literature. He also quoted Lewis Alexander to claim that "to those who have destroyed their culture, to the slave trader and the lyncher, the African-American poets only reply with words of peace."[41]

In 1945, Léopold Senghor again made a point of translating poems by Cullen, Toomer, and Hughes. In his introduction to this selection, he stressed the energy and sense of rhythm of black poetry. Song and poetry appeared to be one and the same for the black man, rooted as they were in folk expression. Among the New Negro poets, Senghor gave consideration to J. W. Johnson, Hughes, McKay, Cullen, Frank Marshall Davis, and Richard Wright. Characterized by "fecund differences," their poetry was unsophisticated, full of rhythm and images—"the poetry of peasants who have not lost contact with telluric forces . . . , the most human face of America."[42] Senghor used much of his 1945 essay in a 1950 lecture on African-American poetry, examining its socio-cultural roots and political context; he dealt with folk poetry, mostly the spirituals and the blues, then turned to the poetry of the New Negro, which was made fashionable by white interest in jazz and African art; this allowed a Negro Renaissance about whose ideology Hughes ["The Negro Artist and the Racial Mountain"] was quoted.

Senghor's view of the "dialect school" of Dunbar and J. W. Johnson led him to focus on the stylistic "Negro features" of those poets. For him, "the essential quality of Negro poetic style lies in rhythm."[43] Nothing was codified or rigid in the verse of Joseph Cotter, Dunbar, Hughes, Sterling Brown, and others. Religion and humor often went hand in hand. Further, McKay, Cullen, and Toomer were the best representatives of "learned poetry." The poems in which *négritude* is proclaimed were not necessarily the "blackest" ones, since "*négritude* resides in style and emotion."[44] Finally, Senghor quoted from "I Have Seen Black Hands" to comment on Wright's proletarian poetry. "The poem is beautiful and its inspiration epic. . . . Yet proletarian poetry is not the most beautiful one. Maybe because we feel that proletarian solidarity is postulated rather than lived,"[45] Senghor ranked Hughes and McKay among leading poets who transcended racial themes.

II. AFTER WORLD WAR II: 1940–1959

During the war, only a handful of French publications dealt with African-American authors. From Martinique, Aimé Césaire provided a major essay in the July 1941 issue of *Tropiques,* which was printed in Fort-de-France. For Césaire, African-American poetry spoke in the name of millions of the "most pitiful humanity," which explained its closeness to original man and its ability to sympathize. It boasted no beautiful images but deep, self-conscious drives toward art: frenzy, ancestral paganism reached for a form of mysticism but also for "poetry as the escape of people who have been wounded for centuries." Yet "black lyricism remains short of grandeur." It "flows tempestuously like a torrent and remains devoid of artifice; its greatness lies in its ability to remain alive, to open onto the whole of man."[46] Translations of poems by Jean Toomer and J. W. Johnson followed this appraisal. The 1943 issue of the French underground review *L'Arbalète* printed translations of Wright's "Big Boy Leaves Home" and an excerpt from Hurston's *Jonah's Gourd Vine.* And the issue of revue *Fontaine* (based in Algiers) devoted to American literature in 1945 included poems by Hughes.

In 1946, Pierre Guerre gathered an extensive section of Negro poetry, "Le Sang noir," for *Les Cahiers du Sud.* In his introduction to poems of the Americas, he focused on the "American" part of "the black body" through which the blood of the black diaspora flows.[47] Translations of Negro spirituals, songs, an extract from Hurston's *Jonah's Gourd Vine*, blues by Josh White, poems by Dunbar, Hughes, Waring Cuney, Frank Marshall Davis, and Sterling Brown followed.

In a contemporary essay in *Jazz Hot*, Langston Hughes was said to be the greatest poet, while McKay and Wright vied for first rank as novelists. Alfredo Papo claimed that white writers misunderstood the Negro, that even Carl Van Vechten and Sherwood Anderson were afraid to reach the core of "black laughter." McKay's best books were *Home to Harlem* and *Gingertown*. The former showed little sympathy for the black man who wants to escape ghetto life. The short stories in the latter painted the South under the shadow of white oppression, while the difficulties arising from mixed ancestry are evoked in "Near White" or "Brownskin Blues." Such writing was "not philosophical but simple, fresh, unpretentious and full of life," claimed Papo. It should be known that "jazz and poetry properly constitute the message of the American Negro."[48]

Langston Hughes benefited from a special treatment in France as an embattled progressive rather than as a Harlem Renaissance figure. The reviews of his autobiography, *Les Grandes Profondeurs* (*The Big Sea*), stressed its value as a document on the depth of Negro life and the stereotypes about it. One review was written after the fashion of Jacques Prévert's poem "Inventory," contrasting discordant aspects of American society from ghetto to jazz, from brass spittoons to lynchings, in order to celebrate the scope of black resilience.[49] In *Présence Africaine*, Pierre Minne claimed that "*The Big Sea* retraces, after Claude McKay and before Richard Wright, a quest for freedom which is being pursued from country to country, from continent to continent. . . ."[50] Hughes's writings were seen as the expression of conflicts and problems that would only be solved when social justice was established. Meanwhile, Hughes was routinely lauded in the Communist press. A 1949 issue of *Europe* provided a brief introduction to "the greatest black American poet," followed by "La charrue de la liberté" ("Freedom's Plow").[51] The following year, E. Cary, in "Trois cent trente ans d'esclavage," provided a historical and sociological introduction to Hughes's poetry, considered largely from an ideological perspective.[52] But less politically inclined reviewers continued to consider Hughes in the context of the Harlem Renaissance. For instance, Paul Trédant's essay in *Les Nouvelles littéraires* included long references to Lorca's "Poeta en Nueva York" and to the verse and personalities of Hughes and Cullen as related to the Harlem setting.[53]

But the Harlem Renaissance was over, and the "protest school" of Wright and Chester Himes now occupied the foreground. It took an old-timer like

René Maran, who first met Locke in 1924, to write an homage to "one of the highest and noblest illustrations of black American university life" for *Présence Africaine*. The general scope of Locke's work and his promotion of the "New Negro" were emphasized, as were his frequent trips to Europe.[54]

Academic critics, insofar as they paid any interest to African-American literature, insisted on the impact of the New Negro poets. In his conclusion to *Les Poètes américains*, Professor Charles Cestre granted black authors a single sentence: "One would have to stop at the work of Negro poets, Paul Dunbar, James Weldon Fenton [sic] Johnson, Langston Hughes, Countée Cullen, Jean Toomer and Miss Weeden."[55] But Professor Maurice Le Breton's remarks in the introduction to his *Anthologie de la poésie américaine contemporaine* were more extensive: according to him, among the "jazz age" poets, African-Americans adapted to the contemporary scene the poetry to be found in black folklore anthologies dealing with the South. Langston Hughes was seen as the greatest American Negro poet because his directness rendered the language and particular sensibilities of his race adequately. Cullen was too imbued with white culture to be able to go back to the naivete and spontaneity of Hughes, even in his self-conscious search for African ancestry. Cullen's "Heritage" and Hughes's "Brass Spittoons" and "Homesick Blues" were the only poems by African-Americans included in the anthology.[56]

Professor Cyrille Arnavon devoted two of the 462 pages of his *Histoire littéraire des États-Unis* to Negro poetry. He stated that the spirituals resulted from a fusion between atavistic African chants and the Protestant hymnal: "These child-like, wounded souls" have thus come to represent oppression all over the world. Dunbar was mentioned with Countée Cullen, J. W. Johnson, and Langston Hughes. Not without paternalism, Arnavon concluded, "Poetry written by people of color has not produced any masterpieces yet."[57] In Professor John Brown's *Panorama de la littérature contemporaine aux États-Unis*, four pages are devoted to Richard Wright and a few contemporary black authors. Hurston, Arna Bontemps, Cullen, McKay, Rudolph Fisher, George Lee, and W. E. Turpin are merely mentioned.[58]

François Dodat, the enthusiastic translator and editor of a bilingual edition of 36 poems by Hughes, saw things differently from the academics. In his introduction to *Poèmes*, he compared Hughes's poetry to that of Carl Sandburg, but also recalled Hughes's debt to Wordsworth and Shakespeare. According to Dodat, Hughes's race accounted for his themes and militancy; the black poet laureate had introduced the blues and spirituals into American poetry yet his work was not more "folkloristic" than Chopin's music.[59] Alain Bosquet's *Anthologie de la poésie américaine des origines à nos jours* seemed to follow suit: although no African-American poet appeared except Hughes, Cullen, and Dunbar, black folk poetry was well represented in this anthology. For Bosquet, Paul Laurence Dunbar was "with J. W. Johnson the first important Negro poet, but his work will last longer" than Johnson's.[60] Hughes had "done more than anyone to bring jazz and poetry, folklore and language closer together," and Cullen was an "admirable craftsman in verse," influenced by Baudelaire, and "a most accomplished black poet, greatly underrated."[61]

Présence africaine also gave Langston Hughes enviable exposure. Haitian poet René Depestre wrote a review of Dodat's bilingual volume of Hughes's poetry and stated that the "excellent translation of some thirty poems reveals the realism in Hughes' gifts," although Depestre believed more space should have been devoted to Hughes's revolutionary poetry and to the celebration of Africa and Harlem. According to Depestre, "Unity is basic to Hughes's inspiration . . . the authenticity of his lyricism, the emotional efficacy of his song" characterized his verse, whether it made use of the blues, the spirituals or the Whitman-like stanza.[62] R. Fernandot, who reviewed the book for the conservative *Figaro littéraire*, showed much appreciation for *The Weary Blues* and called Hughes "the most authentic black American poet, an author of well-appreciated blues and spirituals."[63]

Yet ideology was not necessarily a reason for preference or exclusion. Renaud de Jouvenel, speaking of the difficulties of selecting authors for *Europe*'s special 1959 issue on American literature, justified his decision not to include Sterling Brown by labeling him a poet who could not be translated properly because he wrote "in a sort of black dialect."[64] De Jouvenel's selections of Hughes's poetry resulted from an ideological choice, however. The translator's introduction to "Le poète au bigot," "La charrue de la liberté," and an extract from *Simple Takes a Wife* described Hughes as "the most important black writer because he is the most authentic, the firmest supporter of the black cause and the most unwavering in his attitude, as well as one of the most representative American writers."[65]

W. E. B. DuBois, the father of the Harlem Renaissance, was practically unknown in France as opposed to W. E. B. DuBois, the Communist supporter of the peace movement. Thanks to the efforts of Jean-Jacques Recht and Présence africaine publishers, a translation of *The Souls of Black Folk* finally appeared in 1959. And there was nothing strange in Catholic André Rétif's excitement about it. His review in the Jesuit journal *Etudes* stressed the historical importance of the volume but ended on its literary qualities: "It retains such freshness and poetry, such love for the black race that reading it remains an enchantment and a benefit. It belongs to the heritage of mankind."[66]

III. IN THE SIXTIES: 1960–1966

In 1963, Editions Présence africaine also published a large *Anthologie de la littérature négro-africaine,* prepared by West Indian Léonard Sainville. He aimed at comprehensiveness; his scholarship was far from impeccable, yet he had an interesting notice for each author selected.

Among New Negro luminaries published in the anthology, Bontemps was described as an elder, prolific writer who deserved better recognition in Europe. Sainville stressed McKay's Jamaican birth and placed him at the top of the monument of Negro-African literature: *Banjo* elicited more enthusiasm than any other novel among young French-speaking blacks of Sainville's generation. Sainville declared that, before the war, Hughes was the best-known African-American writer in Europe; he no longer appeared to be one of the greatest poets in the world, but his varied and immense work was important. He was a precursor, a master, who wrote in order to become a spokesman of all black people in the world in a perspective of human brotherhood. In that same group, W. E. B. DuBois needed no introduction as an intellectual and political leader of immense culture and efficiency. But although he was a universal thinker, he was not a novelist.

It took Jean Wagner, then assistant professor at the University of Strasbourg, to introduce Hughes to a wider readership in 1961 via the American Cultural Center (USIS) publication *Informations et Documents.*[67] In 1964, Wagner published a landmark 637-page dissertation: *Les Poètes nègres des États-Unis: Le sentiment racial et religieux dans la poésie de P. L. Dunbar á L. Hughes (1890–1940).* This study of African-American poetry included long accounts of the oral tradition, the blackface minstrels, Dunbar and his contemporaries, the Harlem Renaissance ideologies, and the roles of DuBois and Garvey. Wagner provided detailed analyses of the themes and artistry of Hughes, McKay, Toomer, Cullen, J. W. Johnson, and Sterling Brown, as well as biographical sketches of these authors. Unpublished poems by McKay, Hughes, Cullen, Brown, and Fenton Johnson appeared in the appendix.[68]

One of the first French-speaking scholars to assess the impact of the Harlem Renaissance on *négritude* was Belgian Lilyan Kesteloot. In her dissertation, *Les Écrivains noirs de langue française: naissance d'une littérature,* she documented the debt of the founders of *négritude* to McKay, Hughes, Cullen, and Toomer. Some works by those writers were analyzed, and their possible influence on Damas, Senghor, and Césaire was briefly explored.[69] Only Langston Hughes had the distinction, with Walt Whitman and Emily Dickinson, of being American authors selected for the "Poètes d'aujourd'hui" series by Seghers. The monograph by François Dodat appeared in 1964. In a 70-page introduction to a selection of Hughes's poems, Dodat sketched "the Birth of the Poet" and considered "the Enraptured Traveler" and "the Writer" before analyzing the themes and forms of Hughes's verse.[70]

Likewise, René Depestre's article, "Langston Hughes, ou la main sur la charrue de la poésie," abundantly illustrated with quotations from Hughes's poetry and Dodat's opinion of it, emphasized the universality of Hughes's art. According to Depestre, Hughes's poetry, inspired by Whitman and the British Romantics, was rooted in folklore without being regional. Although it expressed rebellion, it was essentially lyrical, and Hughes's point of view remained broadly humanistic.[71]

In the spring of 1966, the USIS organized a weekend seminar in France on African-American writing, and Langston Hughes participated with two younger novelists.[72] That same year, Hughes was among the stars of the Dakar Black Arts Festival.

When Hughes died, *Présence africaine* devoted an issue to him. Lamine Diakhaté's homage places Hughes's poetry within the context of the *négritude* movement. Diakhaté recalled that Hughes not only went back in search of his cultural roots but also "attempted to impose Africa on white America and on the black bourgeoisie whose major preoccupation was to pass." According to Diakhaté, Hughes restored the rhythms of Africa, which jazz had preserved. "He [Hughes] has now gone to join Garvey and McKay, DuBois and Dunbar."[73] François Dodat honored Hughes as the "citizen of Harlem" who had chosen to remain in the United States without forsaking any of the genius of his race. He stressed Hughes's quest for equality along the lines of the National Association for the Advancement of Colored People (NAACP) and his attempt to promote racial reconciliation. Dodat saw that an examination of Hughes's poetry also revealed a strong influence of black music and jazz rhythms.[74] In the same issue, Nicolas Guillen evoked his encounters with Hughes in Cuba in 1930, in Spain in 1937, and in New York. According to Guillen, from *The Weary Blues* to his last poems, Hughes's writings expressed his struggle for equality and black liberation. Guillen noted that most of Hughes's short, moving pieces in which laughter serves to hide tears were formally structured after the blues: "His drive, sincerity and endurance in furthering the cause of his people deserve the deepest reverence."[75] In June 1967, Marc Saporta wrote Hughes's obituary for *Informations et Documents*. His homage only mentioned *Fine Clothes to the Jew* and the *Simple* stories. Hughes, commented Saporta, "whose mixed racial origins are probably the cause for his openness of mind . . . is black and a Harlemite. . . . No one else has managed such a close synthesis of Anglo-Saxon poetry and jazz."[76]

In 1960, J. W. Johnson's *God's Trombones: Sermons noirs en vers* was published by Editions de l'Epi. But only when "Trumpets of the Lord," based on *God's Trombones* and staged by Donald McKayle, was performed by the Circle in the Square troupe in May 1967 did Johnson finally enjoy a critical comeback.

By that time, the New Negro movement had found its place in the literary history of the black diaspora. Published in *Présence africaine* in December 1965, Léon-Gontran Damas's "Nouvelle somme de poésie; présentation afro-américaine" was a panorama of *négritude* which emphasized the pioneering role of Hughes's essay "The Negro Artist and the Racial Mountain" and its impact upon Nicolas Guillen and Jacques Roumain. The role of Claude McKay as a literary ancestor was also emphasized. The Cuban poems included in this selection were "a result of a common situation" within the worldwide black diaspora.[77] A few years later, the Haitian poet René Depestre, considering the changes in the forms of *négritude* in America, proposed a scheme for the exploration of the origins and evolution of the African Renaissance movement. After Haitian "*indigenism,*" its second stage was represented by the New Negro movement in the United States. The roles of DuBois and Garvey were emphasized by Depestre as were the contributions of Hughes, McKay, and Cullen.[78] With the Black Power era and Stokely Carmichael, Malcolm X, Martin Luther King, and Eldridge Cleaver making the headlines, critics paid more attention to political than to literary developments. Yet the political climate prompted USIS to publish a translation of *The Harlem Renaissance Remembered,* edited by Arna Bontemps that—together with Wagner's dissertation—remained until the 1990s the major source of information in French on the New Negro movement.

NOTES

Unless otherwise indicated, translation from French quotations are mine. Capitals are used in French titles according to French usage.

1. *Vient de paraître,* No. 49 (December 1925), 645–46. White's novel appeared as *L'Etincelle* in the 1930s.

2. No. 666 (March 15, 1926), 733.

3. "Bilan de l'année littéraire," *Mercure de France,* No. 731 (December 1, 1928), 474.

4. "Quelques livres sur la question nègre aux États-Unis," *Le Monde,* October [?], 1927.

5. He was the "youngest of Black American poets" (Jolas, *Anthologie de la nouvelle poésie américaine,* 48) (hereafter referred to as *Anthologie*).

6. Jolas, *Anthologie,* 108.

7. Jolas, *Anthologie,* 155.

8. Jolas, *Anthologie,* 332.

9. Jolas, *Le Nègre qui chant,* 9–28 (hereafter referred to as *Le Nègre*).

10. André Maurois, "La poésie nègre aux États-Unis," *Candide,* No. 203 (March 15, 1928), 3.

11. Jolas, *Anthologie* 206–208.

12. "Un romancier noir américain: Jean Toomer," *Les Nouvelles littéraires,* No. 290 (May 5, 1928), 6.

13. "Aframérique," *Les Nouvelles littéraires,* 7 (August 31, 1929), 6.

14. "Aframérique," *Les Nouvelles littéraire,* 7 (September 14, 1929), 7. These two articles were incorporated in André Lévinson's *Figures américaines: dix-huit études sur des écrivains de ce temps* published in Paris by Victor Attinger the same year.

15. "Poètes de l'Aframérique," *Les Nouvelles littéraires,* No. 372 (November 30, 1929), 9.

16. No. 1 (January 1, 1929), 124–65.

17. No. 1 (January 1, 1929), 161. In the following section, "The Negro horizon broadens—preoccupations with Africa," of Schoell's collection of essays *U.S.A.: Du côté des blancs et du côté des noirs* (Paris: Honoré Champion, 1929), W.E.B. DuBois and Garvey are mentioned alongside the travels in Africa of black writers such as McKay and Hughes. An attempt is made to relate African-Americans to their African origins and to examine the future of the New Negro movement.

18. No. 14 (June 20, 1929), 436–38.

19. No. 14 (June 20, 1929), 561–66.

20. No. 779 (December 1, 1930), 420–22.

21. Nouvelle Série, Vol. 1, No. 6 (October 15, 1930), 353–54.

22. Preface to *Banjo* (Paris: Rieder, 1930), 17.

23. "Langston Hughes," *Nouvel Age,* No. 12 (December 1931), 1060–61.

24. *Europe,* No. 102 (June 15, 1931), 288–300.

25. *La Revue du monde noir,* No. 1 (1930), 36–37

26. *La Revue du monde noir,* No. 6 [1931], 30.

27. *La Revue du monde noir,* No. 6 [1931], 30.

28. *Légitime Défense,* 1 [June 1932], 12

29. "Claude MacKay: *Banjo,*" *Les Cahiers du Sud,* No. 141 (June 1932), 397.

30. "Banjo," *Europe,* No. 110 (February 15, 1932), 270.

31. "*Quartier noir,*" *Etudes,* No. 215 (April 5, 1933), 118.

32. "*Banjo* par Claude MacKay," *Revue de la Martinique,* 2, No. 20 (July 1934), 59.

33. "*Banana Bottom,* roman de Claude MacKay," *Revue anglo-américaine,* No. 5 (June 1934), 471–72.

34. "*Banana Bottom,*" *Etudes,* No. 220 (August 20, 1934), 511–12.

35. "*Sandy,*" *Etudes,* No. 221 (November 5, 1934), 416.

36. It came out in the January 7, 1933, issue of *Lectures du Soir.* See Mathilde Camhi's note on Eric Walrond, *Lectures du Soir* (February 4, 1933). A similar piece, "Harlem, la perle noire de New York," appeared in *Voilà* on May 27, 1933.

37. According to the article, Walrond, having read *Madame Bovary* repeatedly, considered Flaubert a major novelist. He liked Cendrars best among French contemporary writers for his "unique understanding of the world, the psychology and the art of the Negro." He utterly dismissed Paul Morand's depictions of the Negro in *Black Magic* and contrasted the black Frenchman's and the black American's psychological choices.

The United States was a paradoxical country, and blacks were a creative race drawn to mysticism, the arts, and music. "Avec Eric Walrond," Brussels *Lectures du Soir* (January 14, 1933), 4.

38. "*Negro*, Anthologie préparée par Nancy Cunard," *Europe*, No. 140 (February 15, 1935), 301–304.

39. "Un livre sur la nouvelle génération nègre," *Littérature internationale*, 10 (1938), 101.

40. Léopold Sédar Senghor, "Le problème culturel en A.O.F." in his *Liberté I: Négritude et Humanisme* (Paris: Editions du Seuil, 1964) (hereafter referred to as *Liberté*), 19.

41. In his *L'Homme de Couleur* (Paris: Librairie Plon, 1939).

42. Léopold Sédar Senghor, introduction to "Trois poètes négro-américains: Countée Cullen, Jean Toomer, Langston Hughes," *Poésie 45*, No. 23 (February 1945), 33.

43. See P-L. F., "Aux midis de la poésie: Léopold Sédar Senghor parle de la poésie négro-américaine," Brussels *Le Journal des poètes*, No. 26 (January 1956), 1. Also Léopold Sédar Senghor, "La poésie négro-américaine," *Liberté I: Négritude et Humanisme* (Paris: Editions du Seuil, 1964), 104–21.

44. *Liberté*, 119

45. *Liberté* 120. In 1956, Senghor lectured again on African-American poetry. He began with P.L. Dunbar and Langston Hughes, the latter being regarded as the embodiment of the Harlem Renaissance. This movement comprised two trends: the dialect poets, including J.W. Johnson, represented the epic and mystical current, and Sterling Brown and Hughes represented the elegiac and secular perspective; both trends were close to the blues and spirituals. McKay, Arna Bontemps, and Countée Cullen all celebrated their blackness with pride, but Jean Toomer foregrounded the South and the land as well as a return to the African sources. According to Senghor, it was anti-racist racism that sustained African-American poetry.

46. "Introduction à la poésie nègre américaine," *Tropiques*, No. 2 (July 1941), 37–42. In addition, Haitian René Piquion published *Un Chant nouveau* in Port-au-Prince in 1941. In this first book-length perspective on Langston Hughes, an unevenly documented biographical sketch preceded a thematic study of Hughes's poetry, privileging his commitment to the social and racial struggle.

47. No. 279 (2nd semester 1946), 182.

48. Alfredo Papo, "Jazz et littérature," *Jazz hot*, 12, 4 (April 1946), 9.

49. S. R., "Quelques livres: *Les Grandes Profondeurs; Histoires de blancs*," *Poésie 46*, No. 39 (December 1946), 142–44.

50. Pierre Minne, "Langston Hughes ou 'Le train de la liberté'," *Présence africaine*, No. 2 (January 1948), 341.

51. Anon. Notice on Langston Hughes, *Europe*, No. 38 (February 1949), 7. The same year, Renaud de Jouvenel, writing on American literature, lambasted Wright while high praise went to Hughes in "D'une bibliothéque américaine," *Europe*, No. 39 (March 1949), 108–15.

52. E. Cary, "Trois cent trente ans d'esclavage," *Europe*, No. 50 (February 1950), 6–7.

53. "De Brooklyn à Harlem—Lettre de New York," *Les Nouvelles littéraires*, No. 1072 (March 18, 1948), 1–2.

54. "Le Professeur Alain Leroy Locke," *Présence africaine*, No. 6 (1st trimester

1949), 135–38. Alain Locke's *Negro in American Culture,* edited by Margaret Just Butcher, came out in French only in 1958.

55. Charles Cestre, *Les Poètes américains* (Paris: Presses Universitaires de France, 1948), 223.

56. Maurice Le Breton, *Anthologie de la poésie américaine contemporaine* (Paris: Denoël, 1948), 55–57.

57. Cyrille Arnavon, *Histoire littéraire des États-Unis* (Paris: Hachette, 1953), 16–17.

58. John Brown, *Panorama de la littérature contemporaine des États-Unis* (Paris: Gallimard, 1954), 174–78.

59. "La poésie de Langston Hughes," Introduction to *Poèmes/Poems* by Langston Hughes (Paris: Seghers, 1955).

60. Alain Bosquet, *Anthologie de la poésie américaine des origines à nos jours* (Paris: Stock, 1956), 288. See also Alain Bosquet, "Jeune poésie américaine," *Les Cahiers du Sud,* No. 336 (August 1956), 163–67. The latter includes a brief evaluation of the poetry of Cullen and Hughes and alludes to the music of Louis Armstrong.

61. Paris: Stock, 1956, p. 302.

62. "Deux poètes d'aujourd'hui," *Présence africaine,* N.S. No. 6 (February–March 1956), 166.

63. R. Fernandot, "Langston Hughes," *Le Figaro littéraire,* No. 547 (October 13, 1956), 10.

64. *Europe,* Nos. 358–59 (February–March 1959), 23.

65. *Europe,* Nos. 358–59 (February–March 1959), 144–52.

66. "*Ames noires* par W.E.B. DuBois," *Etudes,* No. 303 (October 1959), 123.

67. "Langston Hughes," *Informations et Documents,* No. 135 (January 15, 1961), 30–35. A detailed, accurate retrospective of Hughes's career provided information on the poet's evolution and major themes. The poems "Negro," "My Lord," "Pride," and "Trumpet Player" were included in bilingual inserts.

68. This was published by Librairie Istra and later came out in the United States as *Black Poets of the United States* (University of Illinois Press, 1973).

69. Brussels: Université Libre, 1963, pp. 53–63.

70. *Langston Hughes* (Paris: Seghers, 1964), 190.

71. René Depestre, "Langston Hughes, ou la main sur la charrue de la poésie," *Présence africaine,* No. 58 (2nd trimester 1966), 189–93.

72. Hughes had already prepared *La Poésie négro-américaine,* which was published by Seghers that year. His introduction provided a brief panorama of Negro poetry in the United States: "Not love, nor moonlight, nor even despair and death characterize this verse but race and color and the plight of black people." The selection ranges from the Afro-Creole poets of *Les Cenelles* (1845) to contemporaries such as James Emanuel and Jay Wright. See *La Poésie négro-américaine,* Edition bilingue, anthologie réunie et préfacée par Langston Hughes (Paris: Seghers, 1966).

73. Lamine Diakhaté, "Langston Hughes, conquérant de l'espoir," *Présence africaine,* No. 64 (4th trimester 1967), 46.

74. François Dodat, "Situation de Langston Hughes," *Présence africaine,* No. 64 (4th trimester 1967), 47–50.

75. Nicolas Guillen, "Le souvenir de Langston Hughes," *Présence africaine,* No. 64 (4th trimester 1967), 36.

76. Marc Saporta, "Un poète est mort," *Informations et Documents* (June 15, 1967), 24. Hughes's death coincided with the French publication of *The Best of Simple*. The book got a score of laudatory reviews, which often broached other aspects of Hughes's career as well. See Serge Gilles's "*L'Ingénu de Harlem,* de Langston Hughes," *France nouvelle,* No. 1129 (June 7, 1967), 21.

77. Léon-Gontran Damas, "Nouvelle somme de poésie; présentation afro-américaine," *Présence africaine,* No. 57 (December 15, 1965), 353–56.

78. René Depestre, "Les métamorphoses de la négritude en Amérique," *Présence africaine,* No. 75 (3rd trimester 1970), 19–33.

Year	Literature	Visual and Plastic Arts, Film	The Performing Arts	Society	The International Scene
1892	Anna Julia Cooper's *A Voice from the South by a Black Woman of the South*				
1893				World Columbian Exposition held in Chicago	
1895				Booker T. Washington delivers Atlanta Exposition speech Victoria E. Matthews addresses the First Congress of Colored Women of the United States on "The Value of a Race Literature"	
1896				Supreme Court *Plessy vs. Ferguson* decision	
1899	W.E.B. DuBois's *The Philadelphia Negro*				
1900	Booker T. Washington, Fannie Barrier Williams, and N.B. Woods's *A New Negro for a New Century*				

Year	Literature	Visual and Plastic Arts, Film	The Performing Arts	Society	The International Scene
1902					Special issue of *Paris qui chante* describes ragtime
1906					Exposition Coloniale in Marseilles
1909				National Association for the Advancement of Colored People (NAACP) founded	
1910				NAACP magazine *The Crisis* debuts under W.E.B. Du-Bois's editorship	Raymond Roussel's *Impression d'Afrique*
1912	James Weldon Johnson's *The Autobiography of an Ex-Coloured Man*				
1913		New York Armory Show gives post-impressionism its American debut	*Darktown Follies* at the Lafayette Theater, Harlem		
1915		Release of D.W. Griffith's *The Birth of a Nation*; ensuing protests against the film's racist images lead to creation of the Association for the Study of Negro Life and History and to efforts to create independent black motion picture industry			
1916			Angelina Weld Grimké's *Rachel* performed in Washington, D.C. (first full-length play written and produced by African-Americans in 20th century)	Journal *Challenge* debuts under the William Bridges's editorship	

Year	Literature	Visual and Plastic Arts, Film	The Performing Arts	Society	The International Scene
1917			*Three Plays for a Negro Theatre* by white playwright opens on Broadway	*The Messenger* ("The Only Radical Negro Magazine in America") debuts under A. Philip Randolph and Chandler Owen's editorship East St. Louis riots: in response, Silent Protest Parade held in New York, with W.E.B. DuBois and James W. Johnson at forefront	Louis Mitchell goes to Paris and forms the *Jazz Kings*; they perform at the *Casino de Paris* in 1920s Paul Guillaume publishes his first volume on sculptures *nègres*; preface by G. Apollinaire Igor Stravinsky's "Ragtime"
1918	Georgia D. Johnson's *The Heart of a Woman* Natalie Curtis's *Negro Folksongs*		Will Marion Cook founds *Southern Syncopated Orchestra*		W. M. Cook and the *Southern Syncopated Orchestra* go to London in 1919; perform in Paris in 1920s; inspire Philippe Soupault's *Le Nègre* in 1927 James Reese Europe conducts members of *The Hellfighters* (the 369th Regiment) in Paris, outside a hospital

Year	Literature	Visual and Plastic Arts, Film	The Performing Arts	Society	The International Scene
1919	Claude McKay's *If We Must Die*			Wave of nationwide, anti-black violence and lynching known as the "Red Summer"	Black U.S. 369th Regiment of Harlem awarded French *croix de guerre*
					Sculptor Augusta Savage leaves Jamaica for London; attends art schools
				All-black 369th Regiment marches up New York's Fifth Avenue	Du Bois organizes first Pan-African Congress in Paris
				NAACP conference on lynchings; publishes *Thirty Years of Lynchings in the United States 1889–1919*	Dada movement in Paris, activities highlighting explosive sounds of jazz
					Igor Stravinsky's *Le Sacre du Printemps*
					Ernest Ansermet conducts the Ballets Russes "Sur un Orchèstre Nègre"
1920		Palmer C. Hayden enrolls at Columbia University	Eugene O'Neill's *The Dreamy Kid*	Marcus Garvey founds *Negro World*, an arts and literature journal backed by United Negro Improvement Association (UNIA)	Albert Alexander Smith, graphic artist (student at National Academy of Design in New York) and jazz musician, moves to Europe
				Marcus Garvey's First International Convention of the Negro Peoples of the World: Madison Square Garden, New York	

Year	Literature	Visual and Plastic Arts, Film	The Performing Arts	Society	The International Scene
		Meta Vaux Warrick Fuller's sculpture at Pennsylvania Academy of the Fine Arts	The Theatrical Owners and Bookers Association (TOBA), for performers on the black circuit, is founded		André Salmon's "Negro Art" in *Burlington Magazine*
1921		August Savage leaves Florida; attends Cooper Union, New York	Musical revue *Shuffle Along* starring Florence Mills, with Josephine Baker, opens at David Belasco Theater		René Maran wins France's Prix Goncourt for *Batouala*
		James V. Herring establishes the Department of Art at Howard University in Washington, D.C.	Noble Sissle and Eubie Blake, "I'm Just Wild about Harry"		
		Exhibit of works by Negro artists at 135th Street Branch, New York Public Library	Paul Robeson's debut in Mary Hoyt Wilborg's *Taboo*		
		The Museum of Fine Arts, Boston, exhibition on ancient Nubian and Axum art			
		William H. Johnson enters the National Academy of Design			
		Oscar Micheaux's *The Gunsaulus Mystery* and *Deceit*			
1922	Claude McKay's *Harlem Shadows*				Blaise Cendrar's *Anthologie Nègre*
					Edmund Wilson writes "Influence of Jazz in Paris" and "Americanization of French Literature and Art" in *Vanity Fair*

Year	Literature	Visual and Plastic Arts, Film	The Performing Arts	Society	The International Scene
	James Weldon Johnson's *The Book of American Negro Poetry*	Albert Alexander Smith's portrait of Martinican novelist René Maran on cover of *The Crisis* Tanner Art League Exhibition of Negro artists at Dunbar High School, Washington, D.C. August Savage creates a bust of Marcus Garvey Meta Vaux Warrick Fuller's *The Awakening of Ethiopia* exhibited in Making of America exposition in New York	Eugene O'Neill's *The Emperor Jones* with Charles Gilpin Roland Hayes's "Go Down, Moses" King Oliver's *Creole Jazz Band* in Chicago, joined by Louis Armstrong Howard Players perform *Genefrede*, a play about Toussaint L'Ouverture, in Washington, D.C.	Marcus Garvey in UNIA parade in New York	Edna Manley, sculptor, goes to Kingston, Jamaica Nancy E. Prophet attends *École des Beaux Arts* in Paris; exhibits sculpture in *Salons d'automne*
1923	Jean Toomer's *Cane* Rudolph Fisher's *The Conjure-Man Dies*	Artist Miguel Covarrubias arrives in New York from Mexico City	Willis Richardson's one-act *The Chip Woman's Fortune* on Broadway Bessie Smith makes her first recordings: "Downhearted Blues" and "Gulf Coast Blues" Cotton Club opens in Harlem	Urban League journal *Opportunity* debuts under Charles S. Johnson's editorship Student rebellions at Howard and southern black colleges	Henry O. Tanner awarded French Legion of Honor Augusta Savage denied acceptance at Fontainebleau School of Fine Arts because of her race Ballets Suédois production of *La Création du Monde*, with Milhaud, Cocteau and Léger collaborating
1924	Jessie Fauset's *There is Confusion*	Sculptor Richmond Barthé moves from Mississippi to Chicago; attends School of Art Institute	Ida Cox records "Wild Women Don't Have the Blues"	Marcus Garvey addresses First Annual Convention of the UNIA	Eugene O'Neill's *All God's Chillun Got Wings*

Year	Literature	Visual and Plastic Arts, Film	The Performing Arts	Society	The International Scene
	Walter White's *Fire in the Flint*	The Barnes Foundation opens in Merion, Pennsylvania		Alfred A. Knopf introduces Carl Van Vechten to Walter White, Asst. Secretary for the NAACP	Laura Wheeler Waring returns to Paris to study at the Académie de la Grande Chaumière
	Opportunity gives a "coming-out" party at the Civic Club for black writers; event considered the formal launching of the New Negro movement	Gilbert Seldes's *Seven Lively Arts* examines popular culture and ragtime			
	Alain Locke's "A Note on African Art" in *Opportunity*				
1925	Alain Locke edits a special issue of *Survey Graphic* (Harlem: Mecca of the New Negro), with illustrations by Winold Reiss; this publication will later serve as basis for *The New Negro*	Winold Reiss's one-man exhibition *Representative Negroes* opens at the 135th Street Branch, New York Public Library	Garland Anderson's *Appearances* is first full-length black Broadway production	Marcus Garvey imprisoned	Musical production *La Revue Negre* opens six-week run at the Théatre des Champs-Elysées in Paris and introduces Josephine Baker; Sydney Bechet also performs; Covarrubias is set designer of musical production *La Revue Negre*
	Countée Cullen's *Color*	Archibald J. Motley, Jr., exhibits *Syncopation* in the Art Institute of Chicago's annual exhibition and receives award		Alain Locke's sympathy for student movement leads to his dismissal from Howard University until 1927; heads up the Negro Art movement in New York	
	Alain Locke publishes anthology *The New Negro: An Interpretation*; Winold Reiss's and Aaron Douglas's works featured in the volume				
	DuBose Heyward's novel *Porgy* appears (later adapted into Gershwin's *Porgy and Bess*)	Covarrubias illustrates Langston Hughes's *The Weary Blues*	Bessie Smith records "St. Louis Blues"	A. Philip Randolph founds The Brotherhood of Sleeping Car Porters in Harlem	

Year	Literature	Visual and Plastic Arts, Film	The Performing Arts	Society	The International Scene
	Zora Neale Hurston editor of *The Spokesman*	Aaron Douglas arrives in New York and designs covers of *Opportunity* and *The Crisis*			Josephine Baker performs at the Folies Bergère in Paris; portrayed throughout France by Paul Colin, Alexander Calder, Tsuguharo Foujita, Henri Laurens, Kees van Dongen, Georges Rouault and Marie Laurencin
1926	W.E.B. DuBois's editorial "The Negro in Art: How Shall He Be Portrayed?" in *The Crisis*	Aaron Douglas commissioned by *Theatre Arts Monthly* to illustrate O'Neill's *The Emperor Jones*	Performance of Louis Gruenberg's symphonic rendition of James W. Johnson's sermon *The Creation*, with black baritone Jules Bledsoe	The Savoy Ballroom opens in Harlem with Fletcher Henderson and his orchestra	
	Langston Hughes's essay "The Negro Artist and the Racial Mountain" in June 23 issue of *The Nation*	*New Masses* showcases artists such as Miguel Covarrubias and James Lesesne Wells		Carter G. Woodson founds Negro History Week	Miguel Covarrubias travels to Havana, Cuba and later travels to Paris; illustrates composer W. C. Handy's *Blues*
	Langston Hughes's collection of poems *The Weary Blues*				Thomas Munro and Paul Guillaume publish study *Primitive Negro Sculpture*
	Walter White's *Flight*				Palmer Hayden, winner of Harmon Foundation's gold award leaves New York for Paris, where he will remain until 1932
	Carl Van Vechten's *Nigger Heaven*; Aaron Douglas designs advertisements for novel				André Coeuroy and André Schaeffner's *Le Jazz*

Year	Literature	Visual and Plastic Arts, Film	The Performing Arts	Society	The International Scene
	Gwendolyn Bennett introduces "Ebony Flute," a regular literary column in *Opportunity*				Léon Poirier's documentary film *La Croisière noire*
	Opportunity magazine publishes portfolio with drawings by Aaron Douglas and poems by Langston Hughes				
	Fire!! arts and literary journal illustrated by Aaron Douglas and Richard Bruce Nugent				
	Harmon Foundation's first annual art exhibition, with works by African-Americans				
1927	James Weldon Johnson's *God's Trombones*, illustrated by Aaron Douglas	Aaron Douglas illustrations of Countée Cullen's *Caroling Dusk*, Langston Hughes's *Fine Clothes to the Jew*, Charles S. Johnson's *Ebony and Topaz*, James Weldon Johnson's *God's Trombones*, and Alain Locke and Gregory Montgomery's *Plays of Negro Life*	Louis Armstrong records "Hotter Than That"	Charlotte Osgood Mason sponsors works of Douglas, Covarrubias, Locke, Hughes, and Hurston; Florence Mills dies; large funeral procession attended by many well-known artists and Harlem elite	Palmer C. Hayden exhibits at Galerie Bernheim-Jeune in Paris
		The Blondiau Theatre Arts Collection of African Arts is at the New Art Circle Gallery in New York	Marita Bonner's play *The Pot Maker*	Marcus Garvey deported	William H. Johnson exhibits at the Student and Artist Club in Paris

Year	Literature	Visual and Plastic Arts, Film	The Performing Arts	Society	The International Scene
		Harmon Foundation gold award to Laura Wheeler Waring	Carnegie Hall premiere of James P. Johnson's *Yamekraw*, in collaboration with W.C. Handy, William Grant Still, Fats Waller, and the Harlem Symphony Orchestra	A'Lelia Walker opens "The Dark Tower" salon, attracting talented circle of Harlemites	Winold Reiss visits St. Helena Island and makes portraits of its inhabitants
		Miguel Covarrubias's book *Negro Drawings* Sculptor Jacob Epstein in New York, where he meets Carl Van Vechten, Albert Barnes, Frank Crowninshield, and Paul Robeson (who sits for bust portrait) Aaron Douglas's murals *Jungle and Jazz* for the Club Ebony in Harlem Chicago Women's Club sponsors The Negro in Art Week exhibition Archibald J. Motley, Jr.'s, *Mending Socks* at Newark Museum's exhibition Paintings and Watercolors by Living American Artists Henry O. Tanner elected member of the National Academy of Design	Duke Ellington at the Cotton Club		Painter Hale Woodruff leaves Indiana to settle in Paris *Le Tumulte Noir* appears; Paul Colin's portfolio of lithographs tracing Josephine Baker and the jazz movement in Paris

Year	Literature	Visual and Plastic Arts, Film	The Performing Arts	Society	The International Scene
1928	Nella Larsen's *Quicksand*	Archibald J. Motley, Jr., exhibits at New Galleries in New York	Marita Bonner's play *The Purple Flower*	Oscar dePriest is elected as first black in new century to sit in Congress	Afro-Cuban sculptor Teodoro Ramos-Blanco studies at the Academy of San Alejandro in Rome (1928–30); his work *The Slave* wins award at exhibition in Seville, Spain
	Claude McKay's *Home to Harlem*	Miguel Covarrubias at the Valentine Gallery in New York	Ethels Waters records "West End Blues"	Charles S. Johnson resigns from the Urban League; becomes head of Department of Social Sciences at Fisk University in Tennessee	Haitian Jean Price-Mars publishes *Ainsi Parla l'Oncle*
	Rudolph Fisher's *The Walls of Jericho*	Aaron Douglas receives fellowship from Barnes Foundation			*Show Boat* in London with Paul Robeson and Alberta Hunter
	Wallace Thurman publishes *Harlem: A Forum of Negro Life*, the successor to *Fire!!*	Loïs Mailou Jones head of the art department at the Palmer Memorial Institute in Sedalia, North Carolina			
		Miguel Covarrubias illustrates Taylor Gordon's *Born to Be*			
		Archibald J. Motley, Jr., wins gold award from the Harmon Foundation			
		Sargent Claude Johnson wins the Otto H. Kahn Prize for sculpture from the Harmon Foundation			Paul Morand's *Magie Noire*

Year	Literature	Visual and Plastic Arts, Film	The Performing Arts	Society	The International Scene
1929	Claude McKay's *Banjo*	Aaron Douglas illustrates Paul Morand's *Black Magic* (*Magic Noire*)	Marita Bonner's play *Exit: An Illusion*	Stock market crashes	Augusta Savage is awarded fellowships by the Julius Rosenwald Foundation and the Carnegie Foundation; studies at l'Académie de la Grande Chaumière, Paris
	Wallace Thurman's *The Blacker the Berry* (jacket cover by Aaron Douglas)	William H. Johnson returns to New York; within months, wins the Harmon Foundation's gold award	Fats Waller records "Ain't Misbehavin'"		Archibald J. Motley, Jr., wins a Guggenheim Fellowship to study in Paris
	Singer Taylor Gordon's autobiographical *Born to Be*	Sargent Claude Johnson wins bronze award for sculpture from Harmon Foundation	The Negro Experimental Theater founded		Le Corbusier's scenario *Ballet nègre* for Josephine Baker
		Doris Ulmann exhibits photographs of black workers from South Carolina in New York			
		Richmond Barthé receives a Julius Rosenwald fellowship; leaves Chicago and attends the Art Students' League in New York			
		Duke Ellington and his orchestra in musical short *Black and Tan*			
		Bessie Smith in film *St. Louis Blues*			
	Melvin Gray Johnson wins Otto H. Kahn Prize from the Harmon Foundation				

Year	Literature	Visual and Plastic Arts, Film	The Performing Arts	Society	The International Scene
1930	Nella Larsen's *Passing*	Aaron Douglas commissioned by Fisk University to create a series of murals and by the Sherman Hotel in Chicago to paint a mural, *Dance Magic* James VanDerZee's photographic works in a showroom on Seventh Avenue in Harlem Clive Bell's article "Negro Sculpture" in *Arts and Decoration* Nancy Elizabeth Prophet wins the Otto H. Kahn Prize from the Harmon Foundation James V. Herring creates the Howard University Gallery of Art, the first African-American-run art gallery in the United States	Marc Connelly's *The Green Pastures* opens on Broadway		During a tour of Havana, Langston Hughes meets black sculptor Teodor Ramos-Blanco Augusta Savage meets Paulette Nardal, editor of Paris-based journal *La Revue du Monde Noir* Philippe Soupault discusses the influence of jazz on the surrealist movement in *The American Influence in France*
1931	George Schuyler's *Black No More* Jean Toomer's *Essentials: Definitions and Aphorisms*	Aaron Douglas is commissioned to paint his *Harriet Tubman* mural for Bennett College Hale Woodruff returns to the United States to teach at Atlanta University	Duke Ellington records "Mood Indigo"	Rape charges against Scottsboro Boys spark nationwide protest	Aaron Douglas's *Forge Foundry* in *La Revue du Monde Noir* Aaron Douglas enrolls for a year at *L'Académie Scandinave* in Paris *Exposition Coloniale Internationale* opens in Paris

Year	Literature	Visual and Plastic Arts, Film	The Performing Arts	Society	The International Scene
	Alain Locke's "The American Negro as Artist" in the *American Magazine of Art* / *The Negro Mother* by Langston Hughes and Carl Van Vechten, with illustrations by Prentiss Taylor	Augusta Savage opens Augusta Savage School of Arts and Crafts in Harlem / Richmond Barthé's first solo exhibition at the Caz-Delbos Gallery in New York			
		James Lesesne Wells is awarded the gold medal from the Harmon Foundation			
	James Weldon Johnson's *Black Manhattan* / Marcel Savage's *Voyages et Aventure de Josephine Baker*				After a stay in Tunisia, William H. Johnson returns to Denmark, where he exhibits his African-themed works
1932	Wallace Thurman's *Infants of the Spring*	James Lesesne Wells exhibits at the Delphic Studios in New York			At Paris auction, Jacob Epstein acquires a Fang art piece *Great Bieri* from Paul Guillaume collection
	Sterling A. Brown's *Southern Road*	Carl Van Vechten photographs prominent African-Americans			Twenty-two African-Americans set sail for the Soviet Union to participate in film on racial segregation, *Black and White*
		Prentiss Taylor illustrates Langston Hughes's *Scottsboro Limited*			
		Jacob Lawrence trains at the Harlem Workshop under Charles Alston			

Year	Literature	Visual and Plastic Arts, Film	The Performing Arts	Society	The International Scene
	Nancy Elizabeth Prophet returns to United States and teaches at Atlantic University				Single issue of *Légitime Défense*
1933	Carter G. Woodson's essay *Miseducation of the Negro*	Aaron Douglas's mural for the Harlem YMCA		President Roosevelt's "New Deal"; The Public Works of Arts Projects and the WPA's Federal Arts Projects begin	Walker Evans in Havana, Cuba, on photographic assignment
	Doris Ulmann's *Roll, Jordan, Roll*, in collaboration with writer Julia Peterkin, on black folk life	Aaron Douglas exhibits works at the Caz-Delbos Gallery, New York			Bernard Champigneulle assesses importance of "Jazz in the After-War Years" in *La Revue Française*
		Archibald Motley, Jr., in the Art Institute exhibition *A Century of Progress International Exhibition*			
		James Lesesne Wells named director of the Harlem Art Workshop and Studio			
		Palmer C. Hayden wins Harmon Foundation's painting prize for *Fétiche et Fleurs*			
		The Field Museum of Natural History's Hall of Man opens in Chicago (with bronzes by sculptor Malvina Hoffman)			

Year	Literature	Visual and Plastic Arts, Film	The Performing Arts	Society	The International Scene
1934	Zora Neale Hurston's *Jonah's Gourd Vine* Nancy Cunard compiles and edits the *Negro Anthology*		*Four Saints in Three Acts* by Gertrude Stein and Virgil Thomson on Broadway		Following President Franklin D. Roosevelt's visit to Haiti to end U.S. occupation of Haiti, Charles Dawson publishes linocut portraits, *ABC's Great Negroes*
1935		In an article in *Opportunity*, Harlem painter Romare Bearden criticizes the Harmon Foundation's philanthropy and art patronage Miguel Covarrubias illustratres Zora Neale Hurston's *Mules and Men* *African Negro Art* exhibition at New York Museum of Modern Art Carl Van Vechten's photograph exhibition in *The Leica Exhibition* at Bergdorf Goodman, New York	Willis Richardson and May Miller collaborate to write *Negro History in Thirteen Plays* William Grant Still publishes orchestral score for *Afro-American Symphony* George Gershwin's *Porgy and Bess* opens at the Alvin Theatre in New York	National Council of Negro Women founded Riot in Harlem erupts after protest against job discrimination by white-owned stores in Harlem Aaron Douglas elected president of the Harlem Artists' Guild	Jamaican sculptor Ronald C. Moody exhibits at Adams Gallery, London
1936		Jacob Lawrence receives scholarship to the American Artists' School in New York	*Haitian Macbeth*, directed by Orson Welles, opens at the Lafayette Theatre in Harlem		Jessie Owen wins four gold medals at the Berlin Olympics

Year	Literature	Visual and Plastic Arts, Film	The Performing Arts	Society	The International Scene
		Aaron Douglas's murals for the Hall of Negro Life at the Texas Centennial Exposition in Dallas, Texas; and *Exhibition of Fine Art Productions by American Negroes*			Miguel Covarrubias goes back to Mexico City
1937	Zora Neale Hurston's *Their Eyes Were Watching God* Aaron Douglas joins faculty at Fisk University				Hale Woodruff studies mural painting with Diego Rivera in Mexico City Loïs Mailou Jones studies at L'Académie Julian, Paris *Tropiques* exhibition (with Matisse, André Lhote, Raoul Dufy, and others) at Galerie Billiet in Paris; Ronald C. Moody included Henry Ossawa Tanner dies in Paris Léon Damas's *Piment*
1938	Zora Neale Hurston's *Tell My Horse*, on Jamaican and Haitian culture Jacob Lawrence completes *Toussaint L'Ouverture* series at Harlem YMCA	Richmond Barthé's *Dance* reliefs for the Harlem River Houses in New York Goldwater's *Primitivism in Modern Painting*		James Weldon Johnson dies in automobile accident	
1939					First edition of *Cahier d'un Rétour au Pays Natal* by Aimé Césaire, a source of the "*négritude*" movement

Selected Bibliography

Aaron, Daniel. *Writers on the Left*. Oxford: Oxford University Press, 1977.

Abatino, Pepito. *Joséphine Baker vue par la presse française*. Paris, 1931.

Abramson, Doris E. *Negro Playwrights in the American Theater, 1925–1959*. New York: Columbia University Press, 1969.

———. "Angelina Weld Grimke, Mary T. Burrill, Georgia Douglas Johnson, and Marita O. Bonner: An Analysis of their Plays." *SAGE* 2:1 (Spring 1985): 9–13.

Albertson, Chris. *Bessie: Empress of the Blues*. London: Abacus, 1975.

Allen, James S. *The Negro Question in the United States*. London: Lawrence & Wishart, 1936.

Anderson, Jervis. *Harlem: The Great Black Way, 1900–1950*. London: Orbis, 1982.

———. *This Was Harlem: A Cultural Portrait, 1900–1950*. New York: Farrar, Straus, and Giroux, 1982.

Anderson, Marian. *My Lord, What a Morning: An Autobiography*. Wisconsin; London: University of Wisconsin Press, 1992.

Anderson, Sherwood. *Dark Laughter*. New York: Boni & Liveright, 1925.

Andrews, William L., ed. *Classic Fiction of the Harlem Renaissance*. New York: Oxford University Press, 1994.

Appel, Alfred, Jr. *The Art of Celebration: Twentieth-Century Painting, Literature, Sculpture, Photography, and Jazz*. New York: Knopf, 1992.

Aptheker, Herbert, ed. *A Documentary History of the Negro People in the United States*. New York: Citadel Press, 1951.

———. *Annotated Bibliography of the Published Writings of W.E.B. DuBois*. Millwood, New York: Kraus-Thomson Organization, 1973.

———, ed. *The Correspondence of W.E.B. DuBois. Vol. I: Selections, 1877–1934*. Amherst: University of Massachusetts Press, 1973.

———, ed. *Book Reviews by W.E.B. DuBois*. Millwood, New York: Kraus-Thompson, 1977.

———, ed. *Writings by W.E.B. DuBois in Periodicals*. Millwood, New York: Kraus-Thomson, 1982.

———, ed. *Selections from The Crisis*. Vol. 1, 1911–1925. Millwood, New York: Kraus-Thomson, 1983.

———, ed. *Creative Writings by W.E.B. DuBois: A Pageant, Poems, Short Stories and Playlets*. White Plains, New York: Kraus-Thomson, 1985.

———, ed. *Pamphlets and Leaflets by W.E.B. DuBois*. White Plains, New York: Kraus-Thomson, 1986.

Arata, Esther S., ed. *More Black American Playwrights: A Bibliography*. London; Metuchen, New Jersey: Scarecrow Press, 1978.

Arata, Esther S., and Nicholas John Roboli, eds. *Black American Playwrights, 1800 to the Present: A Bibliography*. Metuchen, New Jersey: Scarecrow Press, 1976.

Armstrong, John. "The Real Negro." *New York Tribune*, 14 October 1923: 26.

Armstrong, Louis. *Swing that Music*. London: Longmans, Green & Co., 1937.

———. *Satchmo: My Life in New Orleans*. New York: Prentice-Hall, 1954.

Badger, Reid. *A Life in Ragtime: A Biography of James Reese Europe*. New York: Oxford University Press, 1995.

Baker, Houston A. *A Many-Colored Coat of Dreams: The Poetry of Countée Cullen*. Detroit: Broadside Press, 1974.

———. *The Journey Back: Issues in Black Literature and Criticism*. Chicago: University of Chicago Press, 1980.

———. *Modernism and the Harlem Renaissance*. Chicago: University of Chicago Press, 1987.

———. *Afro-American Poetics: Revisions of Harlem and the Black Aesthetic*. Madison: University of Wisconsin Press, 1988.

———. *Workings of the Spirit: The Poetics of Afro-American Women's Writing*. Chicago: University of Chicago Press, 1991.

Bakish, David, and Edward Margolies. *Afro-American Fiction, 1853–1976*. Detroit: Gale Research Co., 1979.

Baldwin, Brooke. "The Cakewalk: A Study in Stereotype and Reality." *Journal of Social History* 15 (Winter 1981): 205–18.

Barbeau Arthur E., and Henri Florette. *The Unknown Soldiers: African-American Troops in World War I*. Philadelphia: Temple University Press, 1974.

Barkan, Elazar, and Ronald Bush, eds. *Prehistories of the Future: The Primitivist Project and the Culture of Modernism*. Stanford, California: Stanford University Press, 1995: 357–72.

Berlin, Edward A. *Ragtime: A Musical and Cultural History*. Berkeley and Los Angeles: University of California Press, 1980.

Berry, Faith. *Langston Hughes: Before and Beyond Harlem*. Westport, Connecticut: L. Hill, 1983.

Berry, Jay R. "Eric Walrond (1898–1966)." *Dictionary of Literary Biography*. Detroit: Gale Research Group, 1998: 51.

Berry, Linda S. "Georgia Douglas Johnson." In Mainiero and Faust, *American Women Writers*, vol. 2. New York: Ungar, 1980.

Berzson, Judith R. *Neither Black nor White: The Mulatto Character in American Fiction*. New York: New York University Press, 1978.

Bigsby, C.W.E., ed. *Superculture: American Popular Culture and Europe*. Bowling Green, Ohio: Popular Press, 1975.

Birbalsingh, Franck, ed. *Frontiers of Caribbean Literature in English*. New York: St. Martin's Press, 1996.

Blake, Jody. *Le Tumulte noir: Modernists Art and Popular Entertainment in Jazz-Age Paris, 1900–1930*. University Park: Pennsylvania State University Press, 1999.

Blanche, Jacques-Emile. *Propos de peintre: De Gauguin à la Revue Nègre*. 4th ed. Paris: Emile-Paul Frères, 1928.

Blesh, Rudolph, and Harriet Grossman Janis. *They All Played Ragtime*. London: Sidgwick & Jackson, 1958.

Blight, David W. "W.E.B. DuBois and the Struggle for American Historical Memory." In *History and Memory in African-American Culture*. Geneviève Fabre and Robert O'Meally, eds. New York: Oxford University Press, 1994.

Bloom, Harold, ed. *Modern Critical Views on Langston Hughes*. New York: Chelsea House, 1989.

Boas, Franz. *The Mind of Primitive Man*. New York: Macmillan, 1911.

Bogle, Donald. *Toms, Coons, Mulattoes, Mammies and Bucks: An Interpretive History of Blacks in American Films*. New York: Continuum, 1989.

Bonds, Margaret. "A Reminiscence." In *International Library of Negro Life and History: The Negro in Music and Art*. Compiled by Lindsay Patterson. New York: Publishers Co., 1969: 191–93.

Bone, Robert. *The Negro Novel in America*. New Haven: Yale University Press, (1958) 1969.

———. *Down Home: A History of Afro-American Short Fiction from Its Beginnings to the End of the Harlem Renaissance*. New York: Putnam's Sons, 1975.

Bontemps, Arna W. "The Negro Renaissance: Jean Toomer and the Harlem Writers of the 1920s." In *Anger and Beyond: The Negro Writer in the United States*. Herbert Hill, ed. New York: Harper & Row, 1968: 24.

———, ed. *The Harlem Renaissance Remembered: Essays*. New York: Dodd, Mead & Co., 1972.

———, and Langston Hughes, eds. *The Poetry of the Negro, 1746–1949*. Garden City, New York: Doubleday & Co., 1951.

———. *The Book of Negro Folklore*. New York: Dodd, Mead & Co., 1959.

Borders, Florence E. *Guide to the Microfilm Edition of the Countée Cullen Papers, 1921–1969*. New Orleans: Amistad Research Center, 1975.

Braithwaite, William S. "The Negro in American Literature." *The Crisis* 28 (September 1924): 204–10.

Brantlinger, Patrick. *Bread and Circuses: Theories of Mass Culture as Social Decay*. Ithaca: Cornell University Press, 1983.

Brawley, Benjamin G. *A Short History of the American Negro*. New York: Macmillan Co., 1913.

———. *Africa and the War*. New York: Duffield & Co., 1918.

———. *The Negro in Literature and Art in the United States*. New York: Duffield & Co., 1918.

———. *Your Negro Neighbor*. New York: Macmillan, 1918.

———. *Women of Achievement*. Chicago: Woman's American Baptist Home Mission Society, 1919.

———. *A Social History of the American Negro, Being a History of the Negro Problem in the United States. Including a History and Study of the Republic of Liberia*. New York: Macmillan Co., 1921.

———. "The Negro Literary Renaissance." *The Southern Workman* (April, 1927): 182.

———. *Negro Builders and Heroes*. Chapel Hill: University of North Carolina Press, 1937.

————. *The Negro Genius: A New Appraisal of the Achievement of the American Negro in Literature and the Fine Arts.* New York: Dodd, Mead & Co., 1937.

Breamer, Sidney. "Home in Harlem, New York: Lessons from the Harlem Renaissance Writers." *PMLA* 105:1 (January 1990): 47–56.

Brion-Guerry, Liliane, ed. *L'Année 1913: Les Formes esthétiques de l'œuvre d'art à la veille de la Première Guerre Mondiale.* 2 vols. Paris: Klincksieck, 1971.

Brisbane, Robert. *The Black Vanguard: Origins of the New Social Revolution.* Valley Forge, Pennsylvania: Judson Press, 1970.

Broer, Lawrence R., ed. *Dancing Fools and Weary Blues: The Great Escape of the Twenties.* Bowling Green, Ohio: Popular Press, 1989.

Bronz, Stephen H. *Roots of Negro Racial Consciousness, the 1920s: Three Harlem Renaissance Authors.* [Johnson, Cullen, and McKay] New York: Libra Publishers, 1964.

Brotz, Howard M. *The Black Jews of Harlem: Negro Nationalism and the Dilemmas of Negro Leadership.* New York: Free Press of Glencoe, 1964.

Brown, Evelyn S. "The Harmon Awards." *Opportunity* (March 1933): 78.

Brown, Hallie Q., ed. *Homespun Heroines and Other Women of Distinction.* New York: Oxford University Press, 1988.

Brown, Lloyd W. "The African Heritage and the Harlem Renaissance: A Re-evaluation." *African Literature Today,* 9 (1978): 1–9.

Brown, Rae L. "William Grant Still, Florence Price, and William Dawson: Echoes of the Harlem Renaissance." In *Black Music in the Harlem Renaissance: A Collection of Essays.* Samuel A. Floyd, Jr., ed. Westport, Connecticut: Greenwood Press, 1990.

————. *The Heart of a Woman: The Life and Music of Florence B. Price.* Urbana: The University of Illinois Press. Forthcoming.

Brown, Sterling A. *The New Negro Thirty Years Afterward.* Washington, D.C.: Howard University Press, 1955.

————. *The Negro in American Fiction.* Port Washington, New York: Kennikat Press, 1968.

————. *Negro Poetry and Drama.* New York: Arno, (1937) 1969 (with *The Negro in American Fiction*).

————, Arthur P. Davis, and Ulysses Lee, eds. *The Negro Caravan: Writings by American Negroes.* New York: Dryden Press, 1941. Reprint, New York: Arno Press, 1970.

Brown-Guillory, Elizabeth. *Their Place on the Stage: Black Women Playwrights in America.* New York: Praeger, (1988) 1990.

————, ed. *Wines in the Wilderness: Plays by African-American Women from the Harlem Renaissance to the Present.* New York; London: Greenwood Press, 1990.

Buni, Andrew. *Robert L. Vann of the* Pittsburgh Courier: *Politics and Black Journalism.* Pittsburgh: University of Pittsburgh Press, 1974.

Bushell, Garvin. *Jazz from the Beginning.* Oxford: Bayou Press, 1984.

Byrd, Rudolph P. *Jean Toomer's Years with Gurdjieff: Portrait of an Artist, 1923–1936.* Athens; London: University of Georgia Press, 1990.

————. *Generations in Black and White.* Photographs by Carl Van Vechten from the James Weldon Johnson Memorial Collection. Athens: University of Georgia Press, 1993.

Calloway, Cab. *Of Minnie the Moocher & Me.* New York: Crowell, 1976.

Carmichael, Waverly T. *From the Heart of a Folk: A Book of Songs.* Boston: Cornhill, 1918.

Case, Brian, and Stan Britt. *The Illustrated Encyclopedia of Jazz.* London: Salamander Books, 1978.

Castle, Irene, and Vernon Castle. *Modern Dancing.* New York: World Syndicate, 1914.

Cendrars, Blaise. *Complete Postcards from the Americas: Poems of Road and Sea.* Monique Chefdor, trans. Berkeley and Los Angeles: University of California Press, 1976.

Chapman, Abraham. "The Harlem Renaissance in Literary History." *CLA Journal* 11 (September 1967): 44–45.

Charters, Samuel B., and Leonard Kunstadt. *Jazz: A History of the New York Scene.* Garden City, New York: Doubleday, 1962.

Chase, Gilbert. *America's Music: From the Pilgrims to the Present.* New York: McGraw-Hill Book Co., 1955.

Chesnutt, Charles W. *The Marrow of Tradition.* Ann Arbor, University of Michigan Press, (1901) 1969.

———. *Collected Stories of Charles W. Chesnutt.* William L. Andrews, ed. New York: Mentor, 1992.

Chisholm, Anne. *Nancy Cunard: A Biography.* New York: Knopf, 1979.

Christian, Barbara. *Black Women Novelists: The Development of a Tradition, 1892–1976.* Westport, Connecticut; London: Greenwood Press, 1980.

Clark, William B. "The Letters of Nella Larsen to Carl Van Vechten: A Survey." *Resources for American Literary Study* 8 (Fall 1978): 193–99.

Clarke, Donald. *Wishing on the Moon: The Life and Times of Billie Holiday.* New York: Viking, 1994.

———. *The Rise and Fall of Popular Music.* London: Penguin Books, 1995.

Clarke, John H. *Harlem: Voices from the Soul of Black America.* New York: New American Library, 1970.

Clifford, James. *The Predicament of Culture: Twentieth-Century Ethnography, Literature, and Art.* Cambridge, Massachusetts: Harvard University Press, 1988.

Cohen, William B. *The French Encounter with Africans: White Response to Blacks, 1530–1880.* Bloomington: Indiana University Press, 1980.

Coleman, Leon. *Carl Van Vechten and the Harlem Renaissance: A Critical Assessment.* New York: Garland Publishing, 1998.

Colin, Paul. *Le Tumulte noir.* Paris, 1929.

Connelly, Frances S. *The Sleep of Reason: Primitivism in Modern European Art and Aesthetics, 1725–1907.* University Park: Pennsylvania University Press, 1995.

Conte, Gérard. "Jim Europe et les Hellfighters." *Jazz Hot* 34 (October 1968): 8–9.

———. "Les Mitchell's Jazz Kings." *Jazz Hot* 34 (November 1968): 34–36.

Cooper, Wayne F., ed. *The Passion of Claude McKay: Selected Prose and Poetry, 1912–1948.* New York: Schocken Books, 1973.

———. *Claude McKay, Rebel Sojourner in the Harlem Renaissance: A Biography.* Baton Rouge: Louisiana State University Press, 1987. Reprint, New York: Schocken Books, 1990.

Cotter, Joseph S. *Caleb, the Degenerate: A Play in Four Acts.* Louisville: Bradley & Gilbert, 1903.

———. *Negro Tales.* New York: Cosmopolitan Press, 1912.

Covarrubias, Miguel. *Negro Drawings.* New York; London: Alfred A. Knopf, 1927.

Crane, Clare B. *Alain Locke and the Negro Renaissance.* San Diego: University of California Press, 1971.

Cripps, Thomas. *Black Film as a Genre*. Bloomington; London: Indiana University Press, 1978.

Cronon, Edmund D. *Black Moses: The Story of Marcus Garvey and the Universal Negro Improvement Association*. Madison: University of Wisconsin Press, 1955.

Crowther, Bruce, and Mike Pinfold. *The Jazz Singers*. Poole, United Kingdom: Blanford Press, 1986.

Cruse, Harold. *The Crisis of the Negro Intellectual: A History Analysis of the Failure of Black Leadership*. New York: William Morrow, 1967: 22–32. Reprint, New York: Quill, 1984.

Cullen, Countée P. "The Dance of Love (After Reading René Maran's *Batouala*)." *Opportunity* 1 (April 1923): 30. Reprinted in *Les Continents* 8 (September 1, 1924): 2.

———. *Color*. New York; London: Harper & Bros., 1925.

———. *The Ballad of the Brown Girls*. New York; London: Harper & Bros., 1927.

———, ed. *Caroling Dusk: An Anthology of Verse by Negro Poets*. London; New York: Harper & Bros., 1927.

———. *The Copper Sun*. New York; London: Harper & Bros., 1927.

———. "The Dark Tower." *Opportunity* (March 1928): 90.

———. *The Black Christ, and Other Poems*. New York; London: G.P. Putnam's Sons, 1929.

Cunard, Nancy. *Negro: Anthology Made by N. Cunard, 1931–1933*. London: Nancy Cunard, 1934.

Cuney-Hare, Maud. *Norris Wright Cuney: A Tribune of the Black People*. New York: The Crisis Publishing Co., 1913.

———. *The Message of the Trees: An Anthology of Leaves and Branches*. Boston: The Cornhill Co., 1918.

———. *Negro Musicians and Their Music*. Washington: Associated Publishers, 1936.

Curtis Burlin, Natalie. *Negro Folk Songs*. New York, 1918.

Davis, Angela. "Back to the Roots." *Time* (June 8, 1998).

———. *Blues Legacies and Black Feminism*. New York: Vintage Books, (1998) 1999.

Davis, Arthur P. *From the Dark Tower: Afro-American Writers, 1900–1960*. Washington, D.C.: Howard University Press, 1974.

Davis, Thadious M. *Nella Larsen, Novelist of the Harlem Renaissance: A Woman's Life Unveiled*. Baton Rouge; London: Louisiana State University Press, 1994.

De Jongh, James. *Vicious Modernism: Black Harlem and the Literary Imagination*. New York: Cambridge University Press, 1990.

Dean, Sharon, and Erlene Stetson. "Flower-Dust and Springtime: Harlem Renaissance Women." *Radical Teacher* 18 (1980): 1–8.

Delany, Samuel R. "Atlantis: Model 1924." In *Atlantis: Three Tales*. Hanover, London: Wesleyan University Press, 1995.

Dennison, Sam. *Scandalize My Name: Black Imagery in American Popular Music*. New York: Garland Publishing, 1982.

De Witte, Philippe. *Les Mouvements Nègres en France, 1919–1939*. Paris: L'Harmattan, 1985.

———. "Le Paris noir de l'entre-deux-guerres." In *Le Paris des étrangers: depuis un siècle*. A. Kaspi and A. Mariès, eds. Paris: Imprimerie Nationale, 1989: 157–69.

Dickinson, Donald C. *A Bio-bibliography of Langston Hughes, 1902–1967*. Hamden, Connecticut: Archon Books, 1972.

Dillard, Mabel. "Jean Toomer: Herald of the Negro Renaissance." *DA* 28 (1967). Ohio University: 3178A-79A.

Dixon, Melvin. "Toward a World Black Literature & Community." In *Chant of Saints: A Gathering of Afro-American Literature, Art, and Scholarship.* Michael S. Harper and Robert B. Stepto, eds. Urbana: University of Illinois Press, 1979: 175–94.

———. *Ride Out the Wilderness: Geography and Identity in Afro-American Literature.* Urbana and Chicago: University of Illinois Press, 1987.

Dixon, Robert M.W., and William John Goodrich. *Blues and Gospel Records, 1902–1942.* Harrow, England: Oxford University Press, 1964.

Dixon, Thomas, Jr. *The Clansman.* New York: Doubleday, 1905.

Douglas, Ann. *Terrible Honesty: Mongrel Manhattan in the 1920s.* New York: Farrar, Straus and Giroux, 1995.

Draper, Muriel. *Music at Midnight.* New York; London: Harper & Bros., 1929.

Duberman, Martin B. *Paul Robeson.* New York: Knopf, 1988.

DuBois, W.E.B. "Star of Ethiopia." *The Crisis* 11 (December 1915).

———. "My Mission." *The Crisis* 18 (May 1919): 9–10.

———. *Darkwater: Voices from Within the Veil.* London: Constable & Co., 1920.

———. *The Gift of Black Folk: The Negroes in the Making of America.* Boston: Stratford Co., 1924.

———. *Amenia Conference: An Historic Negro Gathering.* Amenia, New York: Troutbeck Press, 1925.

———. *Black Reconstruction: An Essay Toward a History of the Part which Black Folk Played in the Attempt to Reconstruct Democracy in America, 1860–1880.* New York: Harcourt, Brace & Co., 1935.

———. *The Autobiography of W.E.B. DuBois: A Soliloquy on Viewing My Life from the Last Decade of Its First Century.* New York: International Publishers, 1968.

———. *Black North in 1901: A Social Study. A Series of Articles Originally Appearing in the New York Times, November–December 1901.* (Reprint edition.) New York: Arno Press & *The New York Times,* 1969.

———. *The Negro.* New York: Oxford University Press, (1915) 1970.

———. *Dark Princess: A Romance.* Millwood, New York: Kraus-Thompson Organization, (1928) 1974.

———. *Dusk of Dawn: An Essay Toward an Autobiography of a Race Concept.* Millwood, New York: Kraus-Thomson, (1940) 1975.

———. "Larsen, Nella. *Quicksand.* McKay, Claude. *Home to Harlem.* Herskovits, Melville J. *The American Negro.*" *The Crisis* (June). Reprinted in Aptheker, ed. (1928) 1977: 113–15.

———. "Locke, Alain, ed. *The New Negro.*" *The Crisis* (January). Reprinted in Aptheker, ed., (1926) 1977: 78–79.

———. "The Talented Tenth: Memorial Address." In *The Negro Problem.* New York: James Port & Co., 1903. Reprinted in Aptheker, ed., 1982: 78–83.

———. *Writings by W.E.B. DuBois in Non-Periodical Literature.* Millwood, New York: Kraus-Thomson, 1982.

———. *Writings by W.E.B. DuBois in Periodicals Edited by Others.* Millwood, New York: Kraus-Thomson, 1982.

———. *Against Racism: Unpublished Essays, Papers, Addresses, 1887–1961.* Herbert Aptheker, ed. Amherst: University of Massachusetts Press, 1985: 78.

———. "'To The World', Manifesto of the Second Pan-African Congress." *The Crisis* (November). Reprinted in Aptheker, ed. (1921) 1986: 192–99.

———. *Writings.* New York: The Library Press of America, 1986.

———. *The Souls of Black Folk.* New York: The Library of America, (1903) 1992.

———. "Criteria of Negro Art." *The Crisis* (October 1926). Reprinted in Lewis, ed., 1994: 100–105.

———. *Dark Princess: A Romance.* Jackson, Mississippi: Banner Books, 1995.

Dunbar, Paul L. "The Poet." *The Complete Poems of Paul Laurence Dunbar.* New York: Dodd, Mead & Co., 1913: 191.

Dunham, Katherine. *The Dances of Haiti.* Rev. ed. Los Angeles: University of California Press, 1983.

Early, Gerald. "Three Notes Towards Cultural Definition of the Harlem Renaissance." *Callaloo* 14:1 (Winter 1991): 136–49.

———, ed. *My Soul's High Song: The Collected Writings of Countée Cullen, Voice of the Harlem Renaissance.* New York: Doubleday, 1991.

Edmonds, Randolph. *Shades and Shadows.* Boston: Meador, 1930.

———. *Six Plays for a Negro Theatre.* Boston: Walter H. Baker Co., 1934.

Egan, Bill. "Florence Mills: Remembering the Little Blackbird." *Brolga: An Australian Journal about Dance,* Part I, no. 5 (December 1996): 45–58; Part II, no. 6 (June 1997).

Egonu, Iheanachor. "*Les Continents* and the Francophone Pan-Negro Movement." *Phylon* 42 (September 1981): 245–54.

Ellington, Duke. *Music is my Mistress.* London: Quartet Books, 1977.

Ellis, Chris. "Ethel Waters—Jazz Singer." *Storyville* 22 (May 1969): 128–30.

Ellis, Ethel M., comp. *Opportunity; A Journal of Negro Life: Cumulative Index, Volumes 1–17, 1923–1949.* New York: Kraus Reprint Co., 1971.

Ellison, Ralph. "Hidden Name and Complex Fate." In *Shadow and Act.* New York: Random House, 1964.

Emanuel, James A. *Langston Hughes.* New York: Twayne Publishers, 1967.

———. "Renaissance Sonneteers." [McKay, Hughes, and Cullen] *Black World* (September 1975): 32–45, 92–97.

Emery, Lynne F. *Black Dance in the United States from 1619 to 1970.* Palo Alto, California: National Press Books, 1972.

———. *Black Dance: From 1619 to Today.* London: Dance, 1988.

Erenberg, Lewis A. *Steppin' Out: New York Nightlife and the Transformation of American Culture, 1890–1930.* Westport, Connecticut: Greenwood Press, 1981.

Fabre, Geneviève, and Robert O'Meally, eds. *History and Memory in African-American Culture.* New York: Oxford University Press, 1994.

Fabre, Michel. "René Maran, the New Negro and Negritude." *Phylon* 36 (September 1975): 340–51.

———. *From Harlem to Paris: Black American Writers in France, 1840–1980.* Urbana: University of Illinois Press, 1991.

Fauset, Arthur H. *Black Gods of the Metropolis: Negro Religious Cults of the Urban North.* Philadelphia: University of Pennsylvania Press, 1944.

Fauset, Jessie R. *There is Confusion.* New York: Boni & Liveright, 1924.

———. *Plum Bun: A Novel Without a Moral.* London: E. Mathews & Marrot, 1929.

Favor, Jean Martin. *Authentic Blackness: The Folk in the New Negro Renaissance.* Durham, North Carolina: Duke University Press, 1999.

Feather, Leonard G. *The Encyclopedia of Jazz.* London: Arthur Barker, 1956.

Ferguson, Blanche E. *Countée Cullen and the Negro Renaissance.* New York: Dodd, Mead & Co. 1966.

Finch, Minnie. *The NAACP: Its Fight for Justice.* London; Metuchen, New Jersey: Scarecrow Press, 1981.

FIRE!! Devoted to Younger Negro Artists. Vol. 1. No. 1. Westport, Connecticut: Negro Universities Press, 1970.

Fisher, Rudolph. *The Walls of Jericho.* London: Alfred A. Knopf, 1928.

———. "Blades of Steel." *The City of Refuge.* John McCluskey, ed. Columbia: University of Missouri Press, 1987: 132–44.

Fleming, Robert E. *James Weldon Johnson and Arna Wendell Bontemps: A Reference Guide.* Boston: G.K. Hall, 1978.

Floyd, Samuel A., ed. *Black Music in the Harlem Renaissance: A Collection of Essays.* Knoxville: University of Tennessee Press, (1990) 1993.

———. *The Power of Black Music: Interpreting Its History from Africa to the United States.* New York: Oxford University Press, 1995.

Foner, Philip S. *W.E.B. DuBois Speaks: Speeches and Addresses, 1920–1963.* New York; London: Pathfinder, 1970.

Frazier, E. Franklin. *Race and Culture Contacts in the Modern World.* New York: Alfred A. Knopf, 1957.

———. *Black Bourgeoisie: The Rise of a New Middle Class in the United States.* New York: Collier, (1957) 1962.

———. *The Negro Family in the United States.* London: University of Chicago Press, (1939) 1966.

Fredrickson, George M. *The Black Image in the White Mind: The Debate on Afro-American Character and Destiny.* New York: Harper & Row, 1971.

Fullinwider, S.P. "Jean Toomer: Lost Generation or Negro Renaissance?" *Phylon* 27.4 (Winter 1966): 396–403.

———. *The Mind and Mood of Black America: Twentieth Century Thought.* Homewood, Illinois: Dorsey Press, 1969.

Gabbard, Krin, ed. *Representing Jazz.* Durham: University of North Carolina Press, 1995.

Gaines, Jane. "Fire and Desire: Race, Melodrama and Oscar Micheaux." In *Black American Cinema.* Diawara Manthia, ed. London: Routledge, 1993.

———. "'The Birth of a Nation' and 'Within Our Gates': Two Tales of the American South." In *Dixie Debates: Perspectives on Southern Culture.* Richard H. King, ed. London: Pluto Press, 1996.

Gallagher, Brian. "Explorations of Black Identity from *The New Negro* to *Invisible Man.*" *Perspectives on Contemporary Literature* 8 (1982): 1–9.

Garvey, Marcus M. *Selections from the Poetic Meditations of Marcus Garvey.* New York: A.J. Garvey, 1927.

———. *The Tragedy of White Injustice.* New York: A.J. Garvey, 1927.

———. *Speech Delivered by Marcus Garvey at Royal Albert Hall, London, England, on Wednesday Evening, June 6th, 1928 "The Case of the Negro for International Racial Adjustment," etc.* London: African Publication Society, 1968.

———. *Philosophy and Opinions of Marcus Garvey.* New York: Atheneum, 1969.

———. "Declaration of the Rights of the Negro Peoples of the World." *The Marcus*

Garvey and U.N.I.A. Papers Vol. 2. Hill, ed. Berkeley: University of California Press, 1983: 571–80.

Gates, Henry L., Jr., ed. *Black Literature and Literary Theory.* New York: Methuen, 1984.

———. *Figures in Black: Words, Signs and the "Racial" Self.* New York: Oxford University Press, 1987.

———. *The Signifying Monkey: A Theory of African-American Literary Criticism.* New York; London: Oxford University Press, 1988.

———. "The Trope of a New Negro and the Reconstruction of the Image of the Black." *Representations* (Fall 1988): 129–55.

———, and K.A. Appiah, eds. *Zora Neale Hurston: Critical Perspectives Past and Present.* New York: Amistad, 1993.

———, and Nellie McKay, eds. *The Norton Anthology of African-American Literature.* New York: Norton, 1997.

Gayle, Addison, Jr. *The Black Aesthetic.* New York: Doubleday, 1971.

Gibson, Donald B., ed. *Modern Black Poets: A Collection of Critical Essays.* Englewood Cliffs, New Jersey: Prentice-Hall, 1973.

———. "The Harlem Renaissance City: Its Multi-Illusionary Dimension." In *The City in African-American Literature.* Hakutani Yoshinobu, ed. Madison, New Jersey: Farleigh Dickenson, 1995.

Gibson, Lovie H. "W.E.B. DuBois as a Propaganda Novelist." *Negro American Literature Forum* 10 (1976): 75–77, 79–82.

Giddens, Gary. *Riding on a Blue Note.* New York: Oxford University Press, 1981.

Gilbert, Sandra, and Susan M. Gubar. *The Norton Anthology of Literature by Women.* New York; London: W.W. Norton & Co., 1985.

Gilpin, Patrick J. "Charles S. Johnson: Entrepreneur of the Harlem Renaissance." *The Harlem Renaissance Remembered.* Arna Bontemps, ed. New Haven: Yale University Press, 1972.

Gilroy, Paul. *The Black Atlantic: Modernity and Double Consciousness.* Cambridge, Massachusetts: Harvard University Press, 1993; London: Verso, 1993.

Glassberg, David. *American Historical Pageantry: The Uses of Tradition in the Early Twentieth Century.* Chapel Hill: University of North Carolina Press, 1990.

Gobineau, Arthur de. *Essai sur l'inégalité des races humaines.* 2 vols. 1st ed. Paris, 1835, 1855.

Goffin, Robert. *Aux frontières du jazz.* 4th ed. Paris, 1932.

Goldwater, Robert. *Primitivism in Modern Painting.* New York, 1938. Revised as *Primitivism in Modern Art.* New York, 1967; enlarged as *Primitivism in Modern Art.* Cambridge, Massachusetts: Harvard University Press, 1986.

Gossett, Thomas. *Race: The History of an Idea in America.* Dallas: Southern Methodist University Press, 1963.

Gray, John, ed. *Blacks in Classical Music: A Bibliographical Guide to Composers, Performers, and Ensembles.* New York; London: Greenwood Press, 1988.

Green, Paul. *Lonesome Road: Six Plays for the Negro Theatre.* New York: Robert M. McBride & Co., 1926.

———. *In Abraham's Bosom.* London: G. Allen & Unwin, 1929.

Greenfeld, Howard. *The Devil and Dr. Barnes: Portrait of an American Art Collector.* New York: Viking, 1987.

Grimké, Angelina. *Rachel: A Play in Three Acts.* Boston: The Cornhill Co., 1920.

A Guide to Papers of the NAACP. Frederick, Maryland: University Publications of America, 1982.

Guillaume, Paul. "The Discovery and Appreciation of Primitive Negro Sculpture." *Les Arts à Paris.* 12 (May 1926): 12–14.

———, and Guillaume Apollinaire. *Sculptures nègres.* Paris, 1917. Reprint, New York: Hacker Art Books, 1972.

Gysin, Fritz. *The Grotesque in American Negro Fiction: Jean Toomer, Richard Wright, and Ralph Ellison.* Bern: Francke Verlag, 1975.

Hadler, Mona. "Jazz and the Visual Arts." *Arts Magazine* 57 (June 1983): 91–101.

Hammond, Bryan, comp. *Josephine Baker.* Boston: Little, Brown, 1988.

Handy, William C. *Father of the Blues: An Autobiography.* Arna Bontemps, ed. New York: Macmillan Co., 1944. Reprint, New York: Da Capo, 1991.

———. *Blues: An Anthology: Complete Words and Music of 53 Great Songs.* With pictures by Miguel Covarrubias. New York: Da Capo Press, 1990.

Harding, James. *The Ox on the Roof: Scenes from Musical Life in Paris in the Twenties.* New York: St. Martin's Press, 1972.

Harris, Leonard, ed. *The Philosophy of Alain Locke: Harlem Renaissance and Beyond.* Philadelphia: Temple University Press, 1989.

———. *The Critical Pragmatism of Alain Locke: A Reader.* New York: Rowman and Littlefield, 1999.

Harris, Trudier, ed. *Afro-American Writers Before the Harlem Renaissance.* Detroit: Gale Research, 1986.

———. *Afro-American Writers from the Harlem Renaissance to 1940.* Detroit: Gale Research, 1987.

Harrison, Daphne D. *Black Pearls.* New Brunswick, New Jersey: Rutgers University Press, 1990.

Hart, James D. *The Oxford Companion to American Literature.* London: Oxford University Press, 1941.

Hart, Robert C. "Black-White Literary Relations in the Harlem Renaissance." *American Literature* 44 (1973): 612–28.

Haskins, Jim. *The Cotton Club.* London: Robson, 1977.

Haynes, Robert V. *A Night of Violence: The Houston Riot of 1917.* Baton Rouge: Louisiana State University Press, 1976.

Hazzard-Gordon, Katrina. *Jookin': The Rise of Social Dance Formations in African-American Culture.* Philadelphia: Temple University Press, 1990.

Helbling, Mark. "Carl Van Vechten and the Harlem Renaissance." *Negro American Literature Forum* 10 (1976): 39–47.

———. "African Art: Albert C. Barnes and Alain Locke." *Phylon* 43 (March 1982): 57–67.

Hemenway, Robert E. *Zora Neale Hurston: A Literary Biography.* London: Camden Press, (1977) 1986.

Henderson, Mae G. "Speaking in Tongues: Dialogics, Dialectics and the Black Woman Writer's Literary Tradition." In *Changing our Own Words.* Cheryl Wall, ed. New Brunswick, New Jersey: Rutgers University Press, 1991: 16–37.

Henri, Florette. *Black Migration: Movement North, 1900–1920.* Garden City, New York: Anchor Press, 1975.

Herskovits, Melville. *The Myth of the Negro Past.* Boston: Beacon Press, (1941) 1958.

Hill, Anthony D. *Pages from the Harlem Renaissance: A Chronicle of Performance.* New York: Peter Lang, 1996.

Hill, Errol, ed. *The Theater of Black Americans: A Collection of Critical Essays.* London; Englewood Cliffs: Prentice-Hall, 1980.

Hill, Lynda M. *Social Rituals and the Verbal Art of Zora Neale Hurston.* Washington, D.C.: Howard University Press, 1996.

Hill, Patricia Liggins, Bernard W. Bell, Trudier Harris, William J. Harris, R. Baxter Miller, Sondra J. O'Neale, and Horace Porter, eds. *Call & Response: The Riverside Anthology of the African-American Literary Tradition.* Boston: Houghton Mifflin, 1998.

Hill, Robert A. "General Introduction." *The Marcus Garvey and Universal Negro Improvement Association Papers, Vol. 1: 1826–August 1919.* R. Hill, ed. Berkeley: University of California Press, 1983: xxxv–xc.

————, ed. *The Marcus Garvey and Universal Negro Improvement Association Papers, Vol. 2:27 August 1919–31 August 1920.* Berkeley: University of California Press, 1983.

Hiller, Susan, ed. *The Myth of Primitivism: Perspectives on Art.* London: Routledge, 1991.

Hodeir, Catherine, and Michel Pierre. *L'Exposition Coloniale.* Brussels: Ed. Complese, 1991.

Hoffman, Frederick J. *The Twenties: American Writing in the Postwar Decade.* New York: The Free Press, 1965.

Holloway, Karla F.C. *The Character of the Word: The Texts of Zora Neale Hurston.* Washington, D.C.: Howard University Press, 1987.

Holmes, Dwight O.W. *The Evolution of the Negro College.* New York: Teachers College, Columbia University, 1934.

Honour, Hugh. *The Image of the Black in Western Art.* Vol. 2, *From the American Revolution to World War I.* Fribourg: Office du livre, 1989.

Hoshor, John. *God in a Rolls Royce: The Rise of Father Divine, Madman, Menace, or Messiah.* New York: Hillman-Curl, 1936.

Hostetler, Ann E. "The Aesthetics of Race and Gender in Nella Larsen's *Quicksand.*" *PMLA* 105 (1990): 35–46.

Houénou, Kojo T. "The Problem of Negroes in French Colonial Africa." *Opportunity* 2 (July 1924): 203–207.

————. "Discours Prononcé le 19 Août, 1925, au Congrès Annuel de l'Association Universelle pour l'Avancement de la Race Noire, par S.A. le Prince Kojo Tovalou Houénou, Président de la Ligue Universelle pour la défense de la Race Noire, Directeur Fondateur du Journal 'Les Continents.'" *The Negro World* [French Section]. (September 13, 1924): 14.

Huggins, Nathan I. *Harlem Renaissance.* New York: Oxford University Press, 1971.

————, ed. *Voices from the Harlem Renaissance.* New York: Oxford University Press, (1976) 1995.

Hughes, Langston. "The Negro Artist and the Racial Mountain." *The Nation* 16 (June 1926).

————, ed. *The Weary Blues.* New York: Alfred A. Knopf, 1929.

————, ed. *Not Without Laughter.* New York; London: Alfred A. Knopf, 1930.

————, ed. *Scottsboro Limited: Four Poems and a Play in Verse.* New York: Golden Stair Press, 1932.

———, ed. *The Big Sea: An Autobiography.* New York; London: Alfred A. Knopf, 1940.

———. "Gurdjieff in Harlem." In *The Big Sea.* New York: Alfred A. Knopf, 1940: 241–43.

———, ed. *Poetry of the Negro, 1746–1949.* Garden City, New York: Doubleday & Co., 1951.

———, ed. *Langston Hughes Reader.* New York: George Braziller, 1958.

———, ed. *I Wonder as I Wander: An Autobiographical Journey.* New York: Hill & Wang, (1956) 1964.

———. *The Collected Poems of Langston Hughes.* Arnold Rampersad, ed. New York: Vintage, 1995.

———, and Arna W. Bontemps, eds. *Book of Negro Folklore.* (Second printing) New York: Dodd, Mead & Co., 1959.

———, and Zora Neale Hurston, eds. *Mule Bone: A Comedy of Negro Life.* With introductions by George Houston Bass and Henry Louis Gates, Jr., and the complete story of the Mule Bone controversy. New York: Harper Perennial, 1991.

Hugnet, Georges. *L'Aventure dada, 1916–1922.* Exhibition catalog. Galerie de l'Institut, Paris, 1957.

Hull, Gloria T. *Color, Sex and Poetry: Three Women Writers of the Harlem Renaissance.* Bloomington: Indiana University Press, 1987.

Hulten, Karl G.P., ed. *Futurism and Futurisms.* Exhibition catalog. Palazzo Grassi, Venice, 1986.

Humes, Dollena J. *Oswald Garrison Villard: Liberal of the 1920s.* Syracuse, New York: Syracuse University Press, 1960.

Hurston, Zora N. *Jonah's Gourd Vine.* Philadelphia: J.B. Lippincott Co., 1934.

———. *Mules and Men.* Illustrations by Miguel Covarrubias. Philadelphia, London: J.B. Lippincott Co., 1935.

———. *Tell My Horse.* Philadelphia: J.B. Lippincott Co., 1938.

———. *Dust Tracks on a Road: An Autobiography.* Philadelphia: J.B. Lippincott Co., 1942.

———. *Their Eyes Were Watching God.* Philadelphia: J.B. Lippincott Company, 1937. Reprint, New York: Perennial, 1990.

———, and Langston Hughes. *Mule Bone: A Comedy of Negro Life.* New York: Harper Perennial, 1991.

Hutchinson, George. *The Harlem Renaissance in Black and White.* Cambridge: Harvard University Press, 1995.

Ikonné, Chidi. *From DuBois to Van Vechten: The Early New Negro Literature, 1903–1926.* Westport, Connecticut; London: Greenwood Press, 1981.

Inge, M. Thomas, Maurice Duke, and Jackson R. Bryer. *Black American Writers: Bibliographical Essays.* Vol. 1 *The Beginnings, Through the Harlem Renaissance and Langston Hughes.* London: Macmillan, 1978.

Institute of International Visual Arts, Hayward Gallery. *Rhapsodies in Black Art of the Harlem Renaissance.* Berkeley: University of California Press, 1997.

Irek, Matgorzata. "From Berlin to Harlem: Felix Von Luschan, Alain Locke, and the New Negro." In *The Black Columbiad: Defining Moments in African-American Literature and Culture.* W. Sollors and M. Diedrich, eds. Cambridge: Harvard University Press, 1994: 174–84.

Isaacs, Edith J.R. *The Negro in the American Theatre.* College Park, Maryland: McGrath Publishing Co., (1947) 1968.

Jablonski, Edward, and Lawrence Delbert Stewart. *The Gershwin Years.* New York: Doubleday & Co., 1958.

Jackson, Blyden. "The Harlem Renaissance." In *The Comic Imagination in American Literature.* Louis D. Rubin, Jr., ed. New Brunswick, New Jersey: Rutgers University Press, 1973: 295–303.

———. "Renaissance in the Twenties." In *The Twenties: Fiction, Poetry, Drama.* Warren French, ed. Deland, Florida: Everett, 1975.

Jackson, Walter. "Melville Herskovits and the Search For Afro-American Culture." In George W. Stocking, Jr., *Malinowski, Rivers, Benedict and Others.* Madison: University of Wisconsin Press, 1986: 95–126.

James, Winston. *Holding Aloft the Banner of Ethiopia: Caribbean Radicalism in Early Twentieth Century America.* London; New York: Verso, 1998.

Janken, Kenneth R. "African-American and Francophone Black Intellectuals During the Harlem Renaissance." *The Historian* 60 (1998): 487–505.

Johnson, Abby A., and Ronald Maberry Johnson. *Propaganda and Aesthetics: The Literary Politics of Afro-American Magazines in the Twentieth Century.* Amherst: University of Massachusetts Press, 1979.

———. "Civil Rights and Socializing in the Harlem Renaissance: Walter White and the Fictionalization of the New Negro in Georgia." *Georgia Historical Quarterly* 80:4 (Winter 1996).

Johnson, Barbara E. "Metaphor, Metonymy, and Voice in *Their Eyes Were Watching God.*" In *Black Literature and Critical Theory.* Henry Louis Gates, Jr., ed. London; New York: Methuen, 1984: 205–19.

———. "The Quicksands of the Self: Nella Larsen and Heinz Kohut." In *Telling Facts: History and Narration in Psychoanalysis.* Joseph H. Smith and Humphrey Morris, eds. Baltimore: Johns Hopkins University Press, 1992.

Johnson, Charles S. *Ebony and Topaz: A Collectanea.* New York: Opportunity, 1927.

———. *Growing Up in the Black Belt: Negro Youth in the Rural South.* Washington, D.C.: Howard University Press, 1941.

———. *Bitter Canaan: The Story of the Negro Republic.* New Brunswick, New Jersey; London: Transaction Books, 1987.

Johnson, Eloise E. *Rediscovering the Harlem Renaissance: The Politics of Exclusion.* New York: Garland Publishing, 1997.

Johnson, Georgia D. *Plumes: A Play in One Act.* New York; London: Samuel French, 1927.

———. *An Autumn Love Cycle.* New York: H. Vinal, 1928.

———. *Bronze: A Book of Verse.* With an introduction by W.E.B. DuBois. New York: AMS Press, 1975.

Johnson, J. Weldon, ed. *The Book of American Negro Poetry.* New York: Harcourt, Brace & Co., 1922.

———. *The Race Problem and Peace. Presented to the VI International Summer School of the Women's International League for Peace and Freedom, Chicago, May 1924.* New York: National Association for the Advancement of Colored People, 1924.

———, ed. *The Book of American Negro Spirituals.* London; Binghamton: Chapman & Hall, 1926.

———, ed. *The Second Book of Negro Spirituals.* Musical arrangements by J. Rosamond Johnson. New York: Viking Press, 1926.

———. *God's Trombones: Some Negro Sermons in Verse.* Drawings by Aaron Douglas. Lettering by C.B. Falls. New York: Viking Press, 1927.

———. *Along This Way: The Autobiography of James Weldon Johnson.* New York: Viking Press, 1934.

———. *The Autobiography of an Ex-Coloured Man.* New York: Hill and Wang, (1912) 1960.

———. *Black Manhattan: An Account of the Development of Harlem.* New York: Da Capo, (1930) 1991.

Jolas, Eugène. *Anthologie de la nouvelle poésie américaine.* Paris: Editions Kra, 1928.

———. *Le Nègre qui chante.* Paris: Edition des Cahiers Libres, 1928.

Jones, Kirkland C. *Renaissance Man from Louisiana: A Biography of Arna Wendell Bontemps.* Westport, Connecticut: Greenwood Press, 1992.

———. "Bontemps and the Old South." *African-American Review* 27:2 (Summer 1993): 179–85.

Jones, Robert B. *Jean Toomer and the Prison-House of Thought: A Phenomenology of the Spirit.* Amherst: University of Massachusetts Press, 1993.

———, and Margaret Toomer Latimer, eds. *The Collected Poems of Jean Toomer.* Chapel Hill: University of North Carolina Press, 1988.

Kahnweiler, Daniel-Henry. "Negro Art and Cubism." *Horizon* 18 (December 1948): 412–20.

Keller, Frances R. "The Harlem Literary Renaissance." *The North American Review* 5 (May 1968): 29–34.

Kellner, Bruce. *Carl Van Vechten and the Irreverent Decades.* Norman: Oklahoma University Press, 1968.

———, ed. *The Harlem Renaissance: A Historical Dictionary for the Era.* Westport, Connecticut: Greenwood Press, 1984.

———. *The Letters of Carl Van Vechten.* New Haven: Yale University Press, 1987.

Kenneth, R. "African-American and Francophone Black Intellectuals during the Harlem Renaissance." *The Historiam* 60 (1998): 487–505.

Kennington, Don. *The Literature of Jazz: A Critical Guide.* London: Library Association, 1980.

Kerlin, Robert T. *Negro Poets and Their Poems.* Washington, D.C.: Associated Publishers, 1923.

———. "Singers of New Songs." *Opportunity* (May 1926): 162.

Kerman, Cynthia E., and Richard Eldridge. *The Lives of Jean Toomer: A Hunger for Wholeness.* Baton Rouge: London: Louisiana State University Press, 1987.

Kesteloot, Lilyan. *Black Writers in French: A Literary History of Négritude.* Philadelphia: Temple University Press, 1974.

Kirkeby, W.T., ed. *Ain't Misbehavin: The Story of Fats Waller.* London: P. Davies, 1966.

Kirschke, Amy H. *Aaron Douglas: Art, Race, and the Harlem Renaissance.* Jackson: University of Mississippi Press, 1995.

———. "The Depression Murals of Aaron Douglas: Radical Politics and African-American Art." *International Review of African-American Art* 12:4 (1995): 18–29.

Kishimoto, Hisao. *Carl Van Vechten: The Man and His Role in the Harlem Renaissance.* Tokyo: Seibido, 1983.

Kornweibel, Theodore. *No Crystal Stair: Black Life and* The Messenger, *1917–1928.* Westport, Connecticut: Greenwood Press, 1975.

Kramer, Victor A., ed. *The Harlem Renaissance Re-examined.* New York: AMS Press, 1987.

Krehbiel, Henry E. *Afro-American Folksongs: A Study in Racial and National Music.* New York; London: G. Schirmer, 1913.

"Krigwa Players Little Negro Theatre: The Story of a Little Theatre Movement." *The Crisis* (July 1926): 134.

Kuss, Robert A. "The Harlem Renaissance: A Selected Bibliography." In *The Harlem Renaissance Re-examined.* Victor A. Kramer, ed. New York: AMS Press, 1987.

Langley, J. Ayodele. *Pan-Africanism and Nationalism in West Africa, 1900–1945: A Study in Ideology and Social Classes.* London: Oxford University Press, 1973.

Larsen, Nella. *Quicksand.* New York; London: Alfred A. Knopf, 1928.

———. *Passing.* New York; London: Alfred A. Knopf, 1929.

Larson, Charles R. "Three Harlem Novels of the Jazz Age." [McKay, Cullen, and Van Vechten] *Critique* 11:3 (1969): 66–78.

———. *Invisible Darkness: Jean Toomer and Nella Larsen.* Iowa City: Iowa University Press, 1993.

Lawrence, Jacob. *The Migration Series.* Washington, D.C.: The Phillips Collection and the Rappanhannock Press, 1993.

Leab, Daniel J. *From Sambo to Superspade: The Black Experience in Motion Pictures.* London: Secker and Warburg, 1975.

Leib, Sandra. *Mother of the Blues: A Study of Ma Rainey.* Boston: University of Massachusetts Press, 1981.

Leininger, Theresa. "The Transatlantic Tradition: African-American Artists in Paris, 1830–1940." In *Paris Connections: African-American Artists in Paris.* Exhibition catalog. Bomani Gallery, San Francisco, 1992: 9–23.

Lemke, Sieglinde. *Primitivist Modernism.* New York: Oxford University Press, 1998.

Lenz, Günter H. "Symbolic Space, Communal Rituals, and the Sureality of the Urban Ghetto: Harlem in Black Literature From the 1920s to the 1960s." *Callaloo* 11 (Spring, 1988): 309–45.

Levine, Lawrence W. *Black Culture and Black Consciousness.* New York: Oxford University Press, 1977.

Levinson, André. *La Danse d'aujourd'hui.* Paris: Duchâtre et Van Buggenhoudt, 1929.

Levy, Eugene. *James Weldon Johnson: Black Leader, Black Voice.* Chicago: University of Chicago Press, 1973.

Lewis, David L. *When Harlem Was in Vogue.* New York: Knopf, (1979) 1981. Reprint, Oxford: Oxford University Press, 1989.

———. *W.E.B. DuBois: Biography of a Race, 1868–1919.* New York: Henry Holt and Company, 1993.

———, ed. *The Portable Harlem Renaissance Reader.* New York: Penguin Books, 1994.

Lewis, Rupert, and Maureen Warner-Lewis, eds. *Garvey: Africa, Europe, the Americas.* Trenton, New Jersey: Africa World Press, 1994.

Lionnet, Françoise. *Autobiographical Voices: Race, Gender and Self-Portraiture.* Ithaca, New York: Cornell University Press, 1989.

Little, Arthur. *From Harlem to the Rhine: The Story of New York's Colored Volunteers.* New York: Covici Friede, 1936.

Locke, Alain. "The Black Watch on the Rhine." *Opportunity* 2 (January 1924): 6–9.

———. "Apropos of Africa." *Opportunity* 2 (February 1924): 37–40, 58.

———. "La jeune poésie africo-américaine." *Les Continents* 8 (September 1, 1924): 2.

———. "Internationalism—Friend or Foe of Art?" *The World Tomorrow* (March 1925): 75–76.

———. "Le Nègre Nouveau." Louis and Renée Guilloux, trans. *Europe* 26 (15 June 1931): 289–300.

———. *Negro Art: Past and Present.* Washington, D.C.: Associates in Negro Folk Education, 1936.

———, ed. *The Negro in Art: A Pictorial Record of the Negro Artist and of the Negro Theme in Art.* Washington, D.C.: Associates in Negro Folk Education, 1940.

———. "From Native Son to Invisible Man: A Review of the Literature for 1952." *Phylon* 14:1 (1953): 34–44.

———. "Europe Discovers Negro Art." *Negro Art: Past and Present.* New York: Arno, (1936) 1969: 34–42.

———. *The Negro and His Music.* Reprint, New York: Arno Press and *The New York Times,* (1936) 1969.

———. "The New Negro." *The New Negro.* New York: Atheneum, 1986.

———. *Race Contacts and Interracial Relations: Lectures on the Theory and Practice of Race.* Jeffrey C. Stewart, ed. Washington, D.C.: Howard University Press, 1992.

———, ed. *The New Negro: An Interpretation.* Book decoration and portraits by Winold Reiss. New York: A. & C. Boni, 1925. Reprinted as *The New Negro: Voices of the Harlem Renaissance,* with an introduction by Arnold Rampersad. New York: Atheneum, 1992.

———, and Bernard J. Stern, eds. *When Peoples Meet: A Study in Race and Culture Contacts.* New York: Hinds, Hayden, and Eldredge, 1942.

———, and Montgomery Gregory, eds. *Plays of Negro Life: A Source-Book of Native American Drama.* Decorations and illustrations by Aaron Douglas. Westport, Connecticut: Negro Universities Press, 1970.

Logan, Rayford W., and Michael R. Winston, eds. *Dictionary of American Negro Biography.* New York: Norton, 1982.

Loggins, Vernon. *The Negro Author: His Development in America to 1900.* New York: Columbia University Press, 1931.

———. *I Hear America: Literature in the United States Since 1900.* New York: T.Y. Crowell Co., 1937.

Long, Richard. *Grown Deep: Essays on the Harlem Renaissance.* Winter Park, Florida: Four G. Publishers, 1998.

Lorini, Alessandra. *Rituals of Race: American Public Culture and the Search for Racial Democracy.* Charlottesville: University Press of Virginia, 1999.

Lovell, John. *Black Song: The Forge and the Flame: The Story of How the Afro-American Spiritual Was Hammered Out.* New York: Macmillan, 1972.

Lowe, John. *Jump at the Sun: Zora Neale Hurston's Cosmic Comedy.* Champaign, Urbana: University of Illinois Press, 1994.

Malone, Jacqui. *Stepping on the Blues: The Visible Rhythm of African-American Dance.* Urbana: University of Illinois Press, 1996.

Mantle, Burns, ed. *The Best Plays of 1919–20, etc., and the Year Book of the Drama in America.* Boston, 1920.

Mapp, Edward. *Directory of Blacks in the Performing Arts.* Metuchen, New Jersey; London: Scarecrow Press, 1978.

Maran, René. *Batouala: véritable roman nègre.* Paris: Albin Michel, 1921.

———. "Lettre Ouverte au professeur Alain-LeRoy Locke, de l'Université d'Howard (États-Unis)." *Les Continents* 3 (15 June 1924): 1.

———. *Batouala.* Illustrated by Miguel Covarrubias. New York: Limited Editions Club, 1932.

———, and Alain Locke. "French Colonial Policy: Open Letters." *Opportunity* 2 (September 1924): 261–63.

Martin, Marianne W. "Modern Art and Dance: An Introduction." In *Art and Dance: Images of the Modern Dialogue, 1890–1980.* Exhibition catalog. Institute of Contemporary Art, Boston, 1982: 12–55.

Martin, Tony. *Race First: The Ideological and Organizational Struggles of Marcus Garvey and the Universal Negro Improvement Association.* Dover, Massachusetts: The Majority Press, 1976.

———. *Literary Garveyism: Garvey, Black Arts and the Harlem Renaissance.* Dover, Massachusetts: The Majority Press, 1983.

———, ed. *African Fundamentalism: A Literary and Cultural Anthology of Garvey's Harlem Renaissance.* Dover, Massachusetts: The Majority Press, (1983) 1991.

Mathews, Marcia M. *Henry Ossawa Tanner: American Artist.* Chicago; London: University of Chicago Press, 1994.

Matthews, Geraldine O. *Black American Writers, 1773–1949: A Bibliography and Union List.* Boston: G.K. Hall & Co., 1975.

Mays, Benjamin E., and Joseph William Nicholson. *The Negro's Church.* New York: Russell & Russell, 1969.

McCaskill, Barbara. "The Folklore of the Coasts in Black Women's Fiction of the Harlem Renaissance." *CLA Journal* 39:3 (March 1996): 273–301.

McCorkle, Susannah. "The Mother of Us All." *American Heritage* 45 (February/March 1994): 60–73.

McDowell, Deborah E., ed. *Quicksand and Passing.* London: Serpent's Tail, 1989.

McKay, Claude. *Constab Ballads.* London: Watts & Co., 1912.

———. *Songs of Jamaica.* Kingston, Jamaica: Aston W. Gardner & Co., 1912.

———. *Spring in New Hampshire and Other Poems.* London: Grant Richards, 1920.

———. *Harlem Shadows.* New York: Harcourt, Brace, Jovanovich, 1922.

———. *Home to Harlem.* New York; London: Harper & Bros., 1928.

———. *Gingertown.* New York; London: Harper & Bros., 1932.

———. *Banana Bottom.* New York; London: Harper & Bros., 1933.

———. *Harlem: Negro Metropolis.* New York: E.P. Dutton & Co., 1940.

———. *Banjo, a Story Without a Plot.* New York: Harcourt, Brace, Jovanovich, (1929) 1957.

———. *A Long Way From Home.* New York: Harcourt Brace Jovanovich, (1937) 1970.

———. *Trial by Lynching: Stories About Negro Life in North America.* Translated from the Russian by Robert Winter. Mysore, India: University of Mysore, Centre for Commonwealth Literature and Research, 1977.

———. *The Negro in America.* Translated from the Russian by Robert Winter. Alan McLeod, ed. Port Washington, New York: Kennikat Press, 1979.

McKay, Nellie Y. *Jean Toomer, Artist: A Study of His Literary Life and Work, 1894–1936.* Chapel Hill; London: University of North Carolina Press, 1984.

McLaren, Joseph. *Langston Hughes: Folk Dramatist in the Protest Tradition 1921–1945.* Westport, Connecticut: Greenwood Press, 1997.

McLendon, Jacqueline Y. "Self-Representation and Art in the Novels of Nella Larsen." In *Redefining Autobiography in Twentieth Century Women's Fiction: An Essays Collection*. Janice Morgan and Colette T. Hall, eds. New York: Garland Publishing, 1991.

————. *The Politics of Color in the Fiction of Jessie Fauset and Nella Larsen*. Charlottesville: University Press of Virginia, 1995.

McLeod, A.L. "Claude McKay, Alain Locke and the Harlem Renaissance." *Literary Half Yearly* 27:2 (July 1986): 65–75.

McPherson, James M. *The Abolitionist Legacy: From Reconstruction to the NAACP*. Princeton; Guildford: Princeton University Press, 1976.

Micheaux, Oscar. *The Conquest: The Story of a Negro Pioneer*. Miami, Florida: Mnemosyne Publishing, 1969.

Michlin, Monica. *Jean Toomer's* Cane. Paris: CNED—Didier Concours, 1997.

Miller, Christopher. "Involution and Revolution: African Paris in the 1920s." In *Nationalists and Nomads: Essays on Francophone African Literature and Culture*. Chicago: University of Chicago Press, 1998: 30–37.

Miller, Jeanne Marie A. "Georgia Douglas Johnson and May Miller: Forgotten Playwrights of the New Negro Renaissance." *CLA Journal* 33:4 (June 1990): 349–66.

Mitchell, Angelyn, ed. *Within the Circle: An Anthology of African-American Literary Criticism from the Harlem Renaissance to the Present*. Durham, University of North Carolina Press; London: Duke University Press, 1994.

Moni, Ovadia. *Perché no? L'ebreo corrosivo*. Milano: Bompiani, 1996.

Moore, Jesse T. *A Search for Equality: The National Urban League, 1910–1961*. University Park: Pennsylvania State University Press, 1981.

Morand, Paul. *Black Magic*. Illustrations by Aaron Douglas. London: William Heinemann, 1929.

Morrison Toni. "Memory, Creation and Writing." *Thought* 59 (1984): 385–90.

————. "Unspeakable Things Unspoken: The Afro-American Presence in American Literature." *Michigan Quarterly Review* 28:1 (Winter 1989): 1–35.

————. *Jazz*. London: Picador, 1992.

Moses, Wilson J. *The Golden Age of Black Nationalism*. New York: Oxford University Press, 1978.

————. "More Stately Mansions: New Negro Movements and Langston Hughes's Literary Theory." *The Langston Hughes Review* 4:1 (Spring 1985): 40–46.

Nardal, Jane. "L'Internationalisme Noir." *La Dépêche Africaine* 1 (February 1928): 1.

Nassira, Chohra. *Volevo diventare bianca*. Rome: Edizioni E/O, 1994.

Naumann, Francis M. *New York Dada, 1915–1923*. New York: Abrams, 1994.

Nederveen Pieterse, Jan. *White on Black: Images of Africa and Blacks in Western Popular Culture*. New Haven: Yale University Press, 1992.

The Negro Almanac: *A Reference Work on the Afro-American*. New York: Chichester Wiley, 1983.

Nesteby, James R. *Black Images in American Films, 1896–1954*. Washington, D.C.: University Press of America, 1982.

Nichols, Charles H., ed. *Arna Bontemps & Langston Hughes Letters, 1925–1967*. New York: Dodd, Mead & Co., 1980.

Nora, Pierre. "Between Memory and History: Les Lieux de Mémoire." In *History and Memory in African-American Culture*, Geneviève Fabre and Robert O'Meally, eds. New York and Oxford: Oxford University Press, 1994: 284–300.

North, Michael. *Dialect of Modernism: Race, Language, and Twentieth-Century Literature*. New York and Oxford: Oxford University Press, 1994.

Notten, Eleonore V. *Wallace Thurman's Harlem Renaissance*. Amsterdam: Rodopi, 1994.

Oakley, Giles. *The Devil's Music: A History of the Blues*. London: British Broadcasting Corporation, 1976.

Odum, Howard W., and Guy Benton Johnson. *The Negro and His Songs: A Study of Typical Negro Songs in the South*. Hatboro, Pennsylvania: Folklore Associates, (1925) 1964.

Ogren, Kathy J. *The Jazz Revolution: Twenties America and the Meaning of Jazz*. New York: Oxford University Press, 1989.

Oliver, Paul H. *The Meaning of the Blues*. New York: Collier, 1963.

———. *Screening the Blues: Aspects of the Blues Tradition*. London: Cassell, 1968.

———. *Blues Fell This Morning: Meaning in the Blues*. Cambridge: Cambridge University Press, (1960) 1990.

Olsson, Martin. *A Selected Bibliography of Black Literature: The Harlem Renaissance*. Exeter: Exeter University Press, 1973.

O'Meally, Robert G. "An Annotated Bibliography of the Works of Sterling A. Brown." *Callaloo*, 5:1–2 [14–15] (1982): 90–105.

O'Neill, Eugene G. *All God's Chillun Got Wings* and *Welded*. New York: Boni & Liveright, 1924.

Opportunity: A Journal of Negro Life. Vol. 1. No. 1–Vol. 27. No. 1. January 1923–Winter 1949. (New York: Department of Research and Investigations, National Urban League, etc., 1969.)

Osofsky, Gilbert. *Harlem: The Making of a Ghetto. Negro New York, 1890–1930*. New York: Harper & Row, 1968.

Ottley, Roi, and William J. Weatherby, eds. *The Negro in New York: An Informal Social History*. Dobbs Ferry, New York: Oceana Publications, 1967.

Ovington, Mary W. *Half a Man: The Status of the Negro in New York*. With a Foreword by Dr. Franz Boas. New York: Longmans & Co., 1911.

———. *The Walls Came Tumbling Down: A History of the National Association for the Advancement of Colored People*. New York: Harcourt, Brace & Co., 1947.

Owens, Irma W. *Blood Relations: Caribbean Immigrants and the Harlem Community, 1900–1930*. Bloomington: Indiana University Press, 1996.

Parascandola, Louis, ed. *"Winds Can Wake Up the Dead": An Eric Walrond Reader*. Detroit: Wayne University Press, 1998.

Peplow, Michael W., and Arthur P. Davis, eds. *The New Negro Renaissance: An Anthology*. New York; London: Holt, Rinehart and Winston, 1975.

Perrett, Geoffrey. *America in the Twenties: A History*. New York: Simon and Schuster, 1982.

Perry, Margaret. *A Bio-bibliography of Countée P. Cullen, 1903–1946*. Westport, Connecticut: Greenwood Press, 1971.

———. *Silence to the Drums: A Survey of the Literature of the Harlem Renaissance*. Westport, Connecticut: Greenwood Press, 1976.

———. *The Harlem Renaissance: An Annotated Bibliography and Commentary*. New York: Garland Publishing, 1982.

Peterkin, Julia. *Black April*. Indianapolis: Bobbs-Merrill Co., 1927.

———. *Bright Skin*. Indianapolis: Bobbs-Merrill Co., 1932.

Pickens, William. *The New Negro: His Political, Civil and Mental Status, and Related Essays.* New York: Neale Publishing Co., 1916.

———. *Bursting Bonds.* [Enlarged edition] Boston: Jordan & More Press, 1923.

———. *American Aesop: Negro and Other Humor.* Boston: Jordan & More Press, 1926.

———. *The Vengeance of the Gods, and Three Other Stories of Real American Color Line Life.* New York: AMS Press, 1975.

Pisiak, Roxanna. "Irony and Subversion in James Weldon Johnson's *The Autobiography of an Ex-Coloured Man.*" *Studies in American Fiction* 21:1 (Spring 1993): 83–96.

Placksin, Sally. *Jazzwomen, 1900 to the Present: Their Words, Lives and Music.* London: Pluto, 1985.

Pleasants, Henry. *The Great American Popular Singers.* New York: Simon & Schuster, 1974.

Pobi-Asamani, Kwadwo O. *W.E.B. DuBois: His Contribution to Pan-Africanism.* San Bernardino, California: Borgo Press, 1994.

Podesta, Guido. "An Ethnographic Reproach to the Theory of the Avant-Garde: Modernity and Modernism in Latin America and the Harlem Renaissance." *MLN* 106:2 (March 1991): 395–422.

Portelli, Alessandro. "*The Autobiography of an Ex-Coloured Man* di James Weldon Johnson." *Studi Americani* 18 (1972): 241–67.

———. *Bianchi e neri nella letteratura americana. La dialettica dell'identità.* Bari: De Donato, 1977.

Porter, James A. *Modern Negro Art.* [With 85 halftone plates.] New York: Dryden Press, 1943.

Posnock, Ross. *Color and Culture: Black Writers and the Making of the Modern Intellectual.* Cambridge: Harvard University Press, 1998.

Powell, Richard J. *The Blues Aesthetic: Black Culture and Modernism.* Washington, D.C.: Washington Project for the Arts, 1989.

———. *Black Art and Culture in the 20th Century.* London: Thames and Hudson, 1997.

Powers, Anne, ed. *Blacks in American Movies: A Selected Bibliography.* Metuchen, New Jersey: Scarecrow Press, 1974.

Prevots, Naima. *American Pageantry: A Movement for Art and Democracy.* Ann Arbor: University of Michigan Press, 1990.

Ramchand, Kenneth. "The Writer Who Ran Away: Eric Walrond and *Tropic Death.*" *Savacou,* I:2 (September 1970).

———. *The West Indian Novel and its Background.* London: Heinemann, (1970) 1983.

Rampersad, Arnold. *The Art and Imagination of W.E.B. DuBois.* Cambridge: Harvard University Press, 1976.

———. "W.E.B. DuBois as a Man of Literature." *American Literature* 51 (1979): 50–68.

———. *The Life of Langston Hughes. Vol. 1: 1902–1941, I Too, Sing America.* New York; Oxford: Oxford University Press, 1986.

———. *The Life of Langston Hughes. Vol. 2: 1941–1967, I Dream a World.* New York; Oxford: Oxford University Press, 1988.

———. "The Poetry of the Harlem Renaissance." In *The Columbia History of American Poetry.* Jay Parini, ed. New York: Columbia University Press, 1993.

———, and David Roessel, eds. *The Collected Poems of Langston Hughes.* New York: Alfred A. Knopf, 1994.

Ramsey, Frederic, and Charles Edward Smith, eds. *Jazzmen*. New York: Harcourt, Brace & Co., 1940.

Raynaud, Claudine. *Rites of Coherence: Autobiographical Writings by Hurston, Brooks, Angelou and Lorde*. Ph.D. Dissertation, The University of Michigan, Ann Arbor, 1991.

———. "Rubbing a Paragraph with a Soft Cloth? Muted Voices and Editorial Constraints in *Dust Tracks on a Road*." In *De/Colonizing the Subject: Women's Autobiographical Writings*. Sidonie Smith and Julia Watson, eds. Minneapolis: University of Minnesota Press, 1992: 34–64.

———. "'Words Walking without Masters': *Their Eyes Were Watching God* de Zora Neale Hurston." In *Jean Toomer's Cane and The Harlem Renaissance*. Françoise Clary and Claude Julien eds. Paris: Ellipses, 1997: 95–109.

Reboux, Paul. *Blancs et noirs, carnet de voyage: Haïti, Cuba, Jamaïque, États-Unis*. Paris: Flammarion, 1915.

Redding, J. Saunders. *To Make A Poet Black*. College Park, Maryland: McGrath, (1939) 1968.

Reed, Ishmael. *Mumbo Jumbo*. London: Allyson & Busby, (1972) 1988.

Reid, Margaret A. *The Harlem Renaissance and Sixties in Retrospect*. New York: Peter Lang, 1998.

Ribemont-Dessaignes, Georges. "Hallelujah: Film de King Vidor." *Documents* 2:4 (1930): 237–38.

Richardson, Willis, and May Miller, eds. *Negro History in Thirteen Plays*. Washington, D.C.: Associated Publishers, 1935.

———, ed. *Plays and Pageants from the Life of the Negro*. Jackson: University of Mississippi Press, (1930) 1993.

Riddel, Joseph N. *The Turning Word: American Literary Modernism and Continental Theory*. Philadelphia: University of Pennsylvania Press, 1996.

Riis, Thomas L. "The Experience and Impact of Black Entertainers in England, 1895–1920." *American Music* 4 (Spring 1986): 50–58.

———. *Just Before Jazz: Black Musical Theater in New York, 1890–1915*. Washington, D.C.: Smithsonian Institution Press, 1989.

Le Rire, n.s., no. 6 (14 March 1903). Special issue on the cakewalk.

Roach, Hildred. *Black American Music: Past and Present*. Vol. 1. Malabar: Robert E. Krieger, 1984.

Robeson, Susan. *The Whole World in His Hands: A Pictorial Biography of Paul Robeson*. Secaucus, New Jersey: Citadel, 1981.

Romains, Jules. *La Vie unanime: Poèmes 1904–1907*. 6th ed. Paris: Mercure de France, (1908) 1926.

Rose Bibliography Project. *Analytical Guide and Indexes to "The Crisis," 1910–1960*. Westport, Connecticut: Greenwood Press, 1975.

Rose, Phyllis. *Jazz Cleopatra: Josephine Baker in Her Time*. London: Chatto & Windus, 1989.

Roses, Lorraine E., and Ruth Elizabeth Randolph. *Harlem Renaissance and Beyond: Literary Biographies of 100 Black Women Writers 1900–1945*. Cambridge: Harvard University Press, 1990.

———. *Harlem Glory: Black Women Writing, 1900–1950*. Cambridge: Harvard University Press, 1996.

Rubin, William. *Dada and Surrealist Art*. New York: Abrams, 1968.

Runcie, John. "Marcus Garvey and the Harlem Renaissance." *Afro-Americans in New York Life and History* 10 (July 1986): 19–20.

Rusch, Frederik L., ed. *A Jean Toomer Reader.* New York; Oxford: Oxford University Press, 1993.

Salmon, André. *The Black Venus.* Slater Brown, trans. New York: The Macauley Company, 1929.

Sampson, Henry T. *Blacks in Black and White: A Source Book on Black Films.* Metuchen, New Jersey: Scarecrow Press, 1980.

———. *Blacks in Blackface: A Source Book on Early Black Musical Shows.* Metuchen, New Jersey; London: Scarecrow Press, 1980.

———. *The Ghost Walks: A Chronological History of Blacks in Show Business, 1865–1910.* Metuchen, New Jersey: Scarecrow Press, 1988.

Sanconie, Maïca. "Symbolisme du regard." In *Jean Toomer's* Cane *and the Harlem Renaissance.* Françoise Clary and Claude Julien, eds. Paris: Ellipses, 1997: 120–35.

Sato, Hirako. "Under the Harlem Shadow: A Study of Jessie Fauset and Nella Larsen." In *The Harlem Renaissance Remembered.* Arna Bontemps, ed. New York: Dodd, Mead & Co., 1972: 63–89.

Scheiner, Seth M. *Negro Mecca: A History of the Negro in New York City, 1865–1920.* New York: New York University Press, 1965.

Schiffman, Jack. *Uptown: The Story of Harlem's Apollo Theatre.* New York: Cowles Book Co., 1971.

Schoener, Allon, ed. *Harlem on My Mind: Cultural Capital of Black America, 1900–1968.* New York: Random House, 1968.

Schuyler, George S. "The Negro-Art Hokum." *The Nation* (23 June 1926): 662–63.

Schwartz, Daniel R. *Reconfiguring Modernism: Explorations in the Relationships between Modern Art and Modern Literature.* New York: St. Martin's Press, 1997.

Scott, Bonnie K. *Refiguring Modernism.* Bloomington: Indiana University Press, 1995.

Scott, Emmett. *Negro Migration During the War.* New York: Oxford University Press, 1920.

Scott, Frieda. "Black Drama and the Harlem Renaissance." *Theater Journal* 37:4 (December 1985): 426–39.

Scruggs, Charles. "'All Dressed Up But No Place to Go': The Black Writer and His Audience During the Harlem Renaissance." *American Literature* 48 (1977): 543–63.

———. *The Sage in Harlem: H.L. Mencken and the Black Writers of the 1920s.* Baltimore: Johns Hopkins University Press, 1984.

Selzer, Jack. *Kenneth Burke in Greenwich Village: Conversing with the Moderns, 1915–1931.* Madison: University of Wisconsin Press, 1996.

Senghor, Léopold Sédar. *L'Homme de couleur.* Paris: Librairie Plon, 1939.

——— *Liberté I: Négritude et Humanisme.* Paris: Editions du Seuil, 1964.

Sergeant, Elizabeth S. "The New Negro." *New Republic* 44 (1926): 371–72.

Severini, Gino. "Symbolisme plastique et symbolisme littéraire." *Mercure de France* (1 February 1916): 466–76.

Sheffey, Ruthe T., ed. *A Rainbow Round Her Shoulder: The Zora Neale Hurston Symposium Papers.* Baltimore: Morgan State University Press, 1982.

Shipton, Alyn. *Fats Waller: His Life & Times.* London: Omnibus, 1988.

Shockley, Ann A. *Afro-American Women Writers, 1746–1933: An Anthology and Critical Guide.* Boston: G.K. Hall, 1988.

Sieglinde, Lemke. *Primitivist Modernism: Black Culture and the Origins of Transatlantic Modernism.* Oxford and New York: Oxford University Press, 1998.

Singer, Barry. *Black and Blue: The Life and Lyrics of Andy Razaf.* New York: Schirmer Books, 1995.

Singh, Amritjit, ed. *The Novels of the Harlem Renaissance: Twelve Black Writers, 1923–1933.* University Park; London: Pennsylvania State University Press, 1976.

———, William S. Shiver, and Stanley Brodwin, eds. *The Harlem Renaissance: Revaluations.* New York: Garland Publishing, 1989.

Singleton, Gregory H. "Birth, Rebirth, and the 'New Negro' of the 1920s." *Phylon* 43 (1982): 29–45.

Smith, William G. "Ethel Waters." In *Speech & Power.* Gerald Early, ed. Hopewell, New Jersey: Ecco Press, 1992: 291–97.

Sollors, Werner. *Neither Black Nor White Yet Both.* New York; Oxford: Oxford University Press, 1997.

Soupault, Philippe. *The American Influence in France.* Seattle: University of Washington Press, 1930.

———. *Le Nègre.* Paris: Sehers, (1927) 1975.

Southern, Eileen. *Biographical Dictionary of Afro-American and African Musicians.* Westport, Connecticut; London: Greenwood Press, 1982.

———, ed. *Readings in Black American Music.* 2nd ed. New York: Norton, 1983.

———. *The Music of Black Americans: A History.* New York; London: Norton, 1983.

Spear, Allan H. *Black Chicago: The Making of a Negro Ghetto, 1890–1920.* Chicago; London: University of Chicago Press, 1967.

Spencer, Jon M. *Blues and Evil.* Knoxville: University of Tennessee Press, 1993.

Spero, Sterling D., and Abram Lincoln Harris. *The Black Worker: The Negro and the Labor Movement [in the United States of America].* New York: Columbia University Press, 1931.

Spillers, Hortense. "Notes on an Alternative Model: Neither/Nor." In *The Difference Within.* Elizabeth Meese and Alice Parker, eds. Amsterdam and Philadelphia: John Benjamins Publishing, 1989.

Spingarn, Arthur. *Collecting a Library of Negro Literature.* Washington, D.C., 1938.

Stearns, Marshall W. *The Story of Jazz.* New York: Oxford University Press, 1956.

Stein, Judith. *The World of Marcus Garvey: Race and Class in Modern Society.* Baton Rouge: Louisiana State University Press, 1986.

Stepto, Robert B. "Sterling A. Brown: Outsider in the Harlem Renaissance." In *The Harlem Renaissance: Revaluations.* Amritjit Singh, William S. Shiver, and Stanley Brodwin, eds. New York: Garland Publishing, 1989: 73–81.

Stewart, Jeffrey C., ed. *The Critical Temper of Alain Locke: A Selection of His Essays on Art and Culture.* New York; London: Garland Publishing, 1983.

———. *To Color America.* [Portraits by Winold Reiss]. Washington, D.C.: Smithsonian Institution Press, 1989.

———, ed. *Race Contacts and Interracial Relations: Lectures on the Theory and Practice of Race: Alain LeRoy Locke.* Washington, D.C.: Howard University Press, 1992.

———. "Black Modernism and White Patronage." *International Review of African-American Art* 11:3 (1994): 43–55.

Stewart, Rex W. *Jazz Masters of the Thirties.* New York: Macmillan Co.; London: Collier-Macmillan, 1972.

Stoff, Michael B. "Claude McKay and the Cult of Primitivism." In *The Harlem Renaissance Remembered.* Arna Bontemps, ed. New Haven: Yale University Press, 1972: 126–146.

Story, Ralph D. "Patronage and the Harlem Renaissance: You Get What You Pay for." *CLA Journal* 32:3 (March 1989): 284–95.

Stovall, Tyler. "Colour-Blind France? Colonial Workers during the First World War." *Race and Class* 35 (1993): 35–55.

———. *Paris Noir: African-Americans in the City of Light.* Boston: Houghton Mifflin, 1996.

Stribling, Thomas S. *Birthright.* New York: Century Co., 1922.

Survey Graphic. "Harlem: Mecca of the New Negro." New York, March 1925.

Tate, Claudia. "Nella Larsen's *Passing:* A Problem of Interpretation." *Black American Literature Forum* 14 (Winter 1980): 142–46.

Taylor, Clyde. "Garvey's Ghost: Revamping the Twenties." *Black World* (February 1976): 54–67.

———. "The Human Image in Sterling Brown's Poetry." *Black Scholar* (February–March 1982): 13–20.

Taylor, Frank C., with Gerald Cook. *Alberta Hunter: A Celebration in Blues.* New York: McGraw-Hill, 1987.

Taylor, Prentiss. *The Lithographs of Prentiss Taylor: A Catalogue Raisonné.* Bronx, New York: Fordham University Press, 1996.

Thompson, Robert F. *African Art in Motion: Icon and Art.* Exhibition catalog. National Gallery of Art, Washington, D.C., 1974.

Thorpe, Edward. *Black Dance.* Woodstock, New York: Overlook Press, 1989.

Thurman, Wallace. *Infants of the Spring.* Carbondale: Southern Illinois University Press; London: Feffer and Simons, (1932) 1979.

———. *The Blacker the Berry.* London: The X Press, 1994.

Thygesen, Helge, Mark Berresford, and Russ Shor. *Black Swan: The Record Label of the Harlem Renaissance.* Nottingham, Great Britain: Vintage Jazz Mart Publications, 1996.

Tidwell, John E. "Alain Locke: A Comprehensive Bibliography of His Published Writings." *Callaloo: A Journal of African-American Arts & Letters* 4:1–3 (February–October): 11–13.

Titon, Jeff T. *Early Downhome Blues.* Chapel Hill: University of North Carolina Press, 1994.

Toomer, Jean. *Cane.* Introduction by Arna Bontemps. New York: Harper & Row, 1969.

Torgovnick, Marianna. *Gone Primitive: Savage Intellects, Modern Lives.* Chicago: University of Chicago Press, 1990.

Torrence, Ridgely. *"Grammy Maumee," "The Rider of Dreams," "Simon the Cyrenian":
Plays for a Negro Theater.* New York: Macmillan, 1917.

Tracy, Stephen. "Langston Hughes: Poetry, Blues, and Gospel: Somewhere to Stand." In *Langston Hughes: The Man, His Art, & His Continuing Influence.* James C. Trotman, ed. New York: Garland Publishing, 1995: 51–61.

Trautmann, René. *Au pays de "Batouala": Noirs et blancs en Afrique.* Paris: Payot, 1922.

Trotman, C. James, ed. *Langston Hughes: The Man, His Art, & His Continuing Influence.* New York: Garland Publishing, 1995.

Tucker, Mark, ed. *Ellington: The Early Years.* Oxford: Bayou, 1991.

———. *The Duke Ellington Reader.* Oxford: Oxford University Press, 1993.

Turner, Darwin T. "And Another Passing." *Negro American Literature Forum* 1.1 (Fall 1967): 3–4.

———. *In a Minor Chord: Three Afro-American Writers and Their Search for Identity.* [Toomer, Cullen, and Hurston] Carbondale: Southern Illinois University Press, 1971.

———, ed. *The Wayward and the Seeking: A Collection of Writings by Jean Toomer.* Washington, D.C.: Howard University Press, 1980.

Turner, W.B., and Joyce Moore Turner. *P.B. Moore: Caribbean Militant in Harlem.* Bloomington: Indiana University Press, 1988.

Turpin, Waters E. "Four Short Fiction Writers of the Harlem Renaissance—Their Legacy of Achievement." [Toomer, Fisher, Hughes, and McKay] *CLA Journal* 11.1 (September 1967): 59–72.

University Art Museum, Minneapolis, Minnesota. *A Stronger Soul within a Finer Frame Portraying African-Americans in the Black Renaissance.* With an introduction by Tracy E. Smith. 1990.

U.S. Department of Commerce, Bureau of the Census. *Negroes in the United States, 1920–1932.* Washington, D.C.: Government Printing Office, 1935.

Van Der Zee, James, Owen Dodson, and Camille Bishops. *The Harlem Book of the Dead.* Dobbs Ferry, New York: Morgan & Morgan, 1978.

Van Vechten, Carl. *Nigger Heaven.* London: Alfred A. Knopf, 1926.

———. *Parties: Scenes from Contemporary New York Life.* New York: Alfred A. Knopf, 1930.

———. *"Keep a-Inchin' Along": Selected Writings of Carl Van Vechten About Black Art and Letters.* Bruce Kellner, ed. Westport, Connecticut: Greenwood Press, 1979.

———. *Letters of Carl Van Vechten.* Bruce Kellner, ed. New Haven; London: Yale University Press, 1987.

Vincent, Ted. *Keep Cool: The Black Activists Who Built the Jazz Age.* London: Pluto Press, 1995.

Vincent, Theodore G. *Black Power and the Garvey Movement.* New York: The Ramparts Press, 1971.

———, ed. *Voices of a Black Nation: Political Journalism in the Harlem Renaissance.* San Francisco: The Ramparts Press, 1973.

Wagner, Jean. *Black Poets of the United States: From Paul Laurence Dunbar to Langston Hughes.* Urbana: University of Illinois Press, 1973.

Waldron, Edward E. *Walter White and the Harlem Renaissance.* Port Washington, New York; London: Kennikat Press, 1978.

Walker, Edward S. "The Southern Syncopated Orchestra." *Storyville* 42 (August–September 1972): 204–206.

Wall, Cheryl A. "Poets and Versifiers, Signers and Signifiers: Women of the Harlem Renaissance." In *Women, the Arts and the 1920s in Paris and New York.* Kenneth W. Wheeler, ed. New Brunswick, New Jersey: Transaction Books, 1982.

———, ed. *Zora Neale Hurston: Folklore, Memoirs, and Other Writings,* 2 vols. New York: Literary Classics of the United States, The Library of America, 1995.

———, ed. *Women of the Harlem Renaissance.* Bloomington: Indiana University Press, 1995.

Walrond, Eric. *Tropic Death.* New York: Collier Books, (1926) 1972.

Warner-Lewis, Rupert, and Maureen Warner-Lewis, eds. *Garvey: Africa, Europe, the Americas.* Trenton, New Jersey: Africa World Press, 1994.

Warren, Kenneth W. "Appeals for (Mis)recognition: Theorizing the Diaspora." In *Cultures of United States Imperialism.* Amy Kaplan and Donald E. Pease, eds. Durham, North Carolina: Duke University Press, 1993: 392–406.

Washington, Johnny. *A Journey into the Philosophy of Alain Locke.* Westport, Connecticut: Greenwood Press, 1994.

Washington, Mary H. "Zora Neale Hurston: A Woman Half in Shadow." In Alice Walker. *I Love Myself When I Am Laughing. . . .* Old Westbury, New York: The Feminist Press, 1979: 7–25.

Waters, Ethel. *His Eye is on the Sparrow.* London: W.H. Allen, 1951.

———, with Charles Samuels. *His Eye is on the Sparrow.* New York: Da Capo, 1992.

Watkin-Owens, Irma. *Blood Relations: Caribbean Immigrants and the Harlem Community 1900–1930.* Bloomington: Indiana University Press, 1996.

Watson, Steven. *The Harlem Renaissance: Hub of African-American Culture 1920–30.* New York: Pantheon, 1995.

Watts, Jill. *God, Harlem U.S.A.: The Father Divine Story.* Berkeley; Oxford: University of California Press, 1992.

Weiss, Nancy J. *The National Urban League, 1910–1940.* New York: Oxford University Press, 1974.

West, Cornel. "Black Strivings in a Twilight Civilization." In Henry Louis Gates, Jr., and Cornel West. *The Future of the Race.* New York: Knopf, 1996: 53–112.

West, Dorothy. *The Living Is Easy.* London: Virago, 1987.

White, Walter. *A Man Called White: The Autobiography of Walter White.* London: Victor Gollancz, 1949.

Williams, Eric. *British Historians and the West Indies.* New York: Scribners, 1966.

———. *The Negro in the Caribbean.* Brooklyn, N&B Books, (1942) 1994.

Williams, Raymond A., ed. *The Politics of Modernism: Against the New Conformists.* London: Verso, 1989.

Wintz, Cary D., ed. *Black Culture and the Harlem Renaissance.* Houston, Texas: Rice University Press, 1988.

———, ed. *Black Writers Interpret the Harlem Renaissance.* New York; London: Garland Publishing, 1996.

———, ed. *Remembering the Harlem Renaissance.* New York; London: Garland Publishing, 1996.

———, ed. *The Critics and the Harlem Renaissance.* New York; London: Garland Publishing, 1996.

———, ed. *The Emergence of the Harlem Renaissance.* New York; London: Garland Publishing, 1996.

———, ed. *The Politics and Aesthetics of the "New Negro."* New York; London: Garland Publishing, 1996.

Woll, Allen. *Black Musical Theatre.* New York: Da Capo, 1989.

Wolseley, Roland E. *The Black Press, U.S.A.* Ames: Iowa State University Press, 1972.

Wolters, Raymond. *The New Negro on Campus: Black College Rebellions of the 1920s.* Princeton; London: Princeton University Press, 1975.

Woodson, Carter G. "Negro Life and History in Our Schools." *Journal of Negro History* (July 1919): 274–75.

————. *History of the Negro Church.* Washington, D.C.: Associated Publishers, 1921.

————. *Negro in Our History.* Second edition. Washington, D.C.: Associated Publishers, 1922.

————. *Negro Orators and Their Orations.* Washington, D.C.: Associated Publishers, 1925.

————. *Ten Years of Collecting and Publishing the Records of the Negro.* (Reprinted from the *Journal of Negro History.*) Washington, D.C.: Associated Publishers, 1925.

————. *The Story of the Negro.* Washington, D.C.: Associated Publishers, 1942.

Woofter, Thomas J. *Negro Migration: Changes in Rural Organization and Population of the Cotton Belt.* New York: Negro Universities Press, 1920.

Work, Monroe N. *Negro Year Book . . . 1918–1919.* [etc.] Tuskegee, Alabama: Negro Yearbook Publishing Co., 1919.

————, ed. *A Bibliography of the Negro in Africa and America.* New York: H.W. Wilson Co., 1928.

Worth, Robert F. "Nigger Heaven and the Harlem Renaissance." *African-American Review* 29:3 (Fall 1995): 461–73.

Wright, John S. "'A Scintillating Send Off for Falling Stars': The Black Renaissance Reconsidered." In *A Stronger Soul.* Minneapolis: University Art Museum, 1990: 13–46.

Wright, Richard. *Black Boy.* New York: Harper, 1945.

————. "Blueprint for Negro Writing." In *Richard Wright Reader.* Ellen Wright and Michel Fabre, eds. New York: Harper and Row, (1937) 1978: 36–50.

Young, Joseph A. *Black Novelist as White Racist: The Myth of Black Inferiority in the Novels of Oscar Micheaux.* New York; London: Greenwood Press, 1989.

Zangrando, Robert L. *The NAACP Crusade Against Lynching, 1909–1950.* Philadelphia: Temple University Press, 1980.

Contributors

William Boelhower directs the American Studies Program at the University of Padua. He has translated the cultural writings of Antonio Gramsci, the work of Lucien Goldmann, and the immigrant autobiography of Carmine Biagio Iannace, *The Discovery of America*. Boelhower's essays have appeared in *Early American Literature, American Literary History, Journal of American Studies, MELUS, American Studies/Amerika Studien,* and *Contemporary Literature*. His books include *Immigrant Autobiography in the United States; Through a Glass Darkly: Ethnic Semiosis in American Literature;* and *Autobiographical Transactions in Modernist America*. He recently co-edited the volume *Adjusting Sites: New Essays in Italian American Studies* and a bilingual edition of Frederick Douglass's *The Heroic Slave*.

Rae Linda Brown is associate professor of music and the Robert and Marjorie Rawlins Chair of the Music Department at the University of California, Irvine. She holds a Ph.D. in musicology from Yale University. She has completed a biography of composer Florence B. Price (forthcoming) and has been involved in editing many of Price's scores for performance. Ensembles that have recently performed Brown's editions of Price's music include the American Symphony Orchestra, the Bay Area Women's Philharmonic (Berkeley, California), the Chicago String Ensemble, the Orchestra of the Plymouth Music Series (Minneapolis), the Savannah Symphony, the Albany (Georgia) Symphony, the Springfield (Missouri) Symphony, and the Camellia Symphony (Sacramento). Brown's editions of Price's music have been recorded on the Cambria and Koch labels. Her publications of Price's music include Sonata in E Minor for Piano (1997). Price's Symphony in E Minor and the Symphony No. 3 in C Minor will be published in *Music in the United States of America,* and they will be recorded by the Ukrainian State Symphony Orchestra (Nanox Records, forthcoming). Brown's articles have appeared in *American Music; Black Music Research Journal; Black Music in the Harlem Renaissance: A Collection of Essays* (1990); and the *New Grove Dictionary of Music*. Brown was music editor of the five-volume *Encyclopedia of American History and Culture* (1996).

Françoise Charras has taught American literature as associate professor at the University of Paris 7 for a number of years. She was also at the Université Paul Valéry, Montpellier 3, specifically in African-American and Caribbean studies. Charras has co-edited *Romantisme Noir* (Cahier de l'Herne) and has published several articles and translations in the field of American Gothic fiction as well as articles on F. Douglass, D. Bradley, R. Hayden, P. Marshall, T. Morrison, K. Brathwaite, G. Lamming, and C. Phillips.

Randall Cherry, a freelance translator, is an instructor at the American University of Paris. He attended New York and Columbia Universities and is currently a doctoral student at the University of Paris–Denis Diderot, where he is completing his dissertation on Ethel Waters.

Brent Hayes Edwards teaches in the English Department at Rutgers University. His recent publications include essays in *Transition, The Jazz Cadence of American Culture,* and *Callaloo.* He is currently completing a book titled *The Practice of Diaspora.*

Geneviève Fabre is professor at the University Paris 7 where she is director of the Center of African-American Research. The author of books on James Agee and on African-American Theatre, she has contributed to several collective volumes and encyclopedias. Co-author of books on F. S. Fitzgerald and on American minorities, Fabre has edited or co-edited several volumes: on Hispanic literatures, on Barrio culture in the United States, on ethnicity, two volumes on "Feasts and Celebrations among Ethnic Communities," two volumes on Toni Morrison, and a book on history and memory in African-American culture. A fellow at the W.E.B. DuBois Institute, Harvard University, The National Humanities Center, and the American Antiquarian Society, Fabre is currently working on African-American celebrative culture (1730–1880).

Michel Fabre is professor emeritus at the Université de la Sorbonne Nouvelle (Paris III) and president of the Cercle d'Études Africaines-Américaines. His recent books include *From Harlem to Paris: Black American Writers in France, 1840–1980* (1991); *The French Critical Reception of African-American Literature: An Annotated Bibliography* (1993); and *The Several Lives of Chester Himes,* in collaboration with Edward Margolies (1997).

Michel Feith is assistant professor at the University of Nantes, France. He has spent several years abroad; his experience living in Australia, Japan, and the United States has sensitized him to issues of multiculturalism. He wrote a doctoral thesis titled "Myth and History in Chinese-American and Chicano Literature" (1995), and his publications include articles on Maxine Hong Kingston, John Edgar Wideman, and the Harlem Renaissance.

George Hutchinson holds the Tarkington Chair of Literary Studies at Indiana University in Bloomington. His most recent work is *The Harlem Renaissance in Black and White*, and he is currently writing a cultural biography of Nella Larsen.

Amy H. Kirschke is assistant professor in the Department of Fine Arts and African American Studies at Vanderbilt University. She is the author of *Aaron Douglas: Art, Race, and the Harlem Renaissance* (1995) and is currently completing a book titled *Art in Crisis: The Art of* The Crisis *Magazine*.

Dorothea Löbbermann teaches American literature at Technische Universität and Humboldt Universität, Berlin. She is currently working on a literary (re)construction of Harlem in the 1920s, a subject about which she has given various papers in Berlin, Leipzig, Cardiff, Paris, and Birmingham. Her publication "Looking for Harlem: Queering, Passing and the Harlem Renaissance" (*Amerikastudien/American Studies*) was published in 2000.

Alessandra Lorini (Ph.D., Columbia University) has published many articles and essays on the history of North American culture, and is the author of *Rituals of Race: American Public Culture and the Search for Racial Democracy* (1999). She is currently working on issues of gender in the history of American anthropology and on ethnological exhibits at international expositions. She teaches North American history at the University of Florence.

Monica Michlin is maitresse de conferences in American civilization at Paris-IV (Sorbonne). She wrote her doctoral thesis on Toni Morrison ("Toni Morrison and the Forbidden Voices"). She followed it with a study of Jean Toomer's *Cane* (*Jean Toomer: Cane*) in 1997, the year Toomer was on the aggregation program. Michlin is currently working on the literary voices of abused children (in African-American literature but also in contemporary American literature in general) and on committed contemporary American literature.

Carl Pedersen is associate professor of American Studies at the University of Southern Denmark. He is an executive board member of the Collegium for African-American Research in Europe. His latest publication, co-edited with Maria Diedrich and Henry Louis Gates, Jr., is *Black Imagination and the Middle Passage* (1999).

Alessandro Portelli teaches American literature at the University of Rome "La Sapienza" and is secretary of the Collegium for African-American Research. He is the author of *The Text and the Voice: Speaking, Writing, and Democracy in American Literature* (1994); *The Battle of Valle Giulia: Oral History and the Art* *of Dialogue* (1997); and *The Death of Luigi Trastulli and Other Stories: Form and Meaning in Oral History* (1991).

Arnold Rampersad is the author of *The Art and Imagination of W.E.B. DuBois* (1976) and of the two-volume *Life of Langston Hughes* (1986, 1988). He is also editor of *The Collected Poems of Langston Hughes* (1994).

Claudine Raynaud, educated in the United States (University of Michigan) and in France (Montpellier), is professor of English and American literature at the University of Tours, France. She is vice president of the Center for African-American Studies and currently heads the doctoral program and the research group GRAAT in Tours. She has published a large number of articles on African-American autobiography (Hurston, Lorde, Brooks, Wideman) in American anthologies and journals (*Life/Lines, DeColonizing the Subject, Callaloo*) and French publications. The author of a monograph on Toni Morrison (Belin, 1997) and the co-author with Geneviève Fabre of an anthology of articles on Morrison's *Beloved,* Raynaud is also completing a book on the Harlem Renaissance, which gathers articles from the 1998 Tours conference, and a manuscript on Hurston's autobiographical selves.

Clyde Taylor is professor in the Africana Studies Program and the Gallatin School, New York University. He is the author of *The Mask of Art: Breaking the Aesthetic Contract.* Taylor has published widely on African-American independent cinema. He also wrote the script for *Midnight Ramble: The Life and Legacy of Oscar Micheaux,* a Public Broadcasting System documentary.

Index

Page references to illustrations are in italics.

Achille, Louis, 290–91
Aesthetic co-optation, 11, 48, 60
Aesthetic vision, 61–69, 236, 239
Africa: artistic influences of, 14–16, 73–83, 165–68, 173, 302; historical sources on, 170; nationalism and, 264–65; representations of, 53–61; travel to, 60, 82
African diaspora, 259–68, 271, 288–313; DuBois on, 169–74; Harlem as antidote to, 3, 210
Aida (Verdi), 168
Albertson, Chris, 107
Alexander, Lewis, 302, 316, 321
Anderson, Jervis, 285n16
Anderson, Madeline, 133
Anderson, Sherwood, 11, 323
Antheil, George, 11, 47
Ariadne myth, 179–80, 187
Armstrong, Louis, 19, 25, 105, 107, 114; discography, 123
Arnavon, Cyrille, 324
Arnould, Marthe, 227
Assoun, Paul-Laurent, 224

Back to Africa movement, 37–38, 81, 257, 282. *See also* Garvey, Marcus
Bailey, Mildred, 104, 124
Baker, Houston, 117, 191n5, 206, 279
Baker, Josephine, 19, 21, 106, 293, 317; discography, 123
Ballads, 64, 315
Baraka, Imamu Amiri, 133
Barnes, Albert C., 302
Barnes, Alfred, 48

Barthé, Richmond, 58
Barthes, Roland, 227, 231
Bayes, Nora, 111–12
Bazalgette, Léon, 315
Be-bop music, 245
Bearden, Romare, 62
Bennett, Gwendolyn, 56, 59, 290, 293, 316
Berry, Jay R., 280–81
Bertin, Gabriel, 319
Bethune, Mary McLeod, 133
Birbalsingh, Frank, 283
Birth of a Nation, 13, 21, 35, 162
Black dialect, 238–40, 251, 321
Black nationalism, 263–65, 271
Black Swan (recording firm), 101, 107, 121n20
Black Swan Troubadours, 102
Blake, Jody, 48
Blight, David, 160–61
Blues, the, 17; cabaret role in, 215; critiques of, 112, 132; in Hughes, 236–53; origin of, 100, 315; singers of, 99–124, 241–42; subjects of, 155
Boas, Franz, 37, 173–74
Bolshevism, 265
Bonds, Margaret, 19, 89
Bontemps, Arna, 324, 326, 328
Bosquet, Alain, 324–25
Bowser, Pearl, 131
Braithwaite, Edward Kamau, 262
Braithwaite, William S., 316, 318
Braque, Georges, 66
Briggs, Cyril, 8, 264, 271, 284n4
Brooks, Van Wyck, 52

Johnson, J. Rosamond, 18, 20, 90, 168

Johnson, J. W., 314

Johnson, James P., 19

Johnson, James Weldon: Caribbean roots of, 272; class in, 149–50, 154–55; French assessment of, 314–32; McKay and, 8; music and folk culture in, 18, 20, 90, 153–56; publishers of, 127; as "renaissance man," 14; travel of, 290, 292; Waters and, 109; *The Autobiography of an Ex-Coloured Man*, 143–58, 293, 315, 317; *God's Trombones*, 64, 315–17, 327–28; "Harlem: The Culture Capital," 278

Johnson, Malvin Gray, 61–62, *63*

Johnson, Ronald Maberry, 301

Johnson, Sargent Claude, 58

Johnson, William H., 48, 251

Jolas, Eugène, 315

Jolson, Al, 101, 119n5, 123

Jones, Leroi, 151

Jones, Lois Mailou, 55–56

Jones, Peter, 126

Joseph-Henri, Georges, 319–20

Josey, Charles Conant, 37

Jouvenel, Renaud de, 325

Kellog, Paul U., 274

Kesteloot, Lilyan, 266, 326

Kincaid, Jamaica, 267

King, Martin Luther, Jr., 23

Kouyaté, Tiemoko Garan, 291

Krigwa workshops, 162–63

Ku Klux Klan, 13, 35

Kubitschek, Missy, 191nn8,10

Lacan, Jacques, 223–24

Langford, Sam, 129

Larsen, Nella: cabaret in, 215–16; Caribbean and, 261, 272; class in, 185; DuBois and, 160; Harlem as memory space in, 212; Harlem entrance topos in, 186, 195; travel of, 290; *Passing*, 131, 141; *Quicksand*, 131, 140–41, 160, 177–92, 206, 293

Laude, Jean, 71n9

Lawrence, Jacob, 251

Le Breton, Maurice, 324

League of Nations, 288, 304

Lebar, Jacques, 320

Lee, George, 324

Légitime Défense, 304

Leib, Sandra, 117–18

Lejeune, Philippe, 146

Lenin, V. I., 172–73

Lenz, Günter, 215

Léro, Etienne, 319

Lévi-Strauss, Claude, 22

Levine, Lawrence, 296

Lévinson, André, 316

Lewis, David Levering, 60, 161, 260, 292, 301

Lewis, Robert Benjamin, 170

Locke, Alain: aesthetic co-optation and, 48; art and, 15, 53–54, 61, 73–74, 140; biopolitical language of, 194–95, 197–98; civil rights and, 300–301; on cultural ambivalence, 5, 9–10; cultural nationalism and, 277; cultural pluralism and, 53; diaspora concept in, 289; DuBois and, 160; French assessment of, 314, 318; on Garveyism, 278; gift imagery in, 276–77; on Harlem as cultural capital, 2–3, 207, 216–17; on internationalism, 288, 299–300; Maran and, 298–304, 324; music and, 15, 18, 53, 94–97, 129; on race and culture, 6–7; as "renaissance man," 14; on southern stereotypes, 280; travel of, 290; on vanguardism, 295, 299–300; on younger generation of writers, 302–303, 314; West Indies and, 268; women, attitude toward, 97; "Apropos of Africa," 10, 299; "The Black Watch on the Rhine," 296–97; "The Colonial Literature of France," 311n23; "The Concept of Race as Applied to Social Culture," 6; "The Negro and his Music," 18; *The New Negro*, 24, 70, 79, 160, 270–87, 296, 318

Logan, Rayford, 321

Long, Richard, 20–21

Lorson, Pierre, 319–20

Louis, Joe, 133

Louis, Léone, 318

Low versus high art, 18–19, 23–24, 47

Lowell Lectures, 36

MacDougall, William, 36

Malliett, W., 282

Malmin, Judge, 282

Marable, Manning, 5–6

Maran, René: Locke and, 298–304, 324; translation of, 301; travel of, 290; *Batouala*, 261, 302, 310n12, 314

Marcus, George, 26